CISCO

Course Booklet

IT Essentials

Version 7

Cisco Press

IT Essentials Course Booklet, Version 7

1 2019

Library of Congress Control Number: 2019950242

ISBN-13: 978-0-13-561216-3

ISBN-10: 0-13-561216-0

Warning and Disclaimer

Editor-in-Chief
Mark Taub

Alliances Manager,
Cisco Press
Arezou Gol

Product Line Manager
Brett Bartow

Senior Editor
James Manly

Managing Editor
Sandra Schroeder

Senior Project Editor
Tonya Simpson

Editorial Assistant
Cindy Teeters

Cover Designer
Chuti Prasertsith

Composition
codeMantra

Indexer
Cheryl Lenser

CISCO.

Trademark Acknowledgments

All terms mentioned in this book that are known to be trademarks or service marks have been appropriately capitalized. Cisco Press or Cisco Systems, Inc., cannot attest to the accuracy of this information. Use of a term in this book should not be regarded as affecting the validity of any trademark or service mark.

Special Sales

For information about buying this title in bulk quantities, or for special sales opportunities (which may include electronic versions; custom cover designs; and content particular to your business, training goals, marketing focus, or branding interests), please contact our corporate sales department at corpsales@pearsoned.com or (800) 382-3419.

For government sales inquiries, please contact governmentsales@pearsoned.com.

For questions about sales outside the U.S., please contact intlcs@pearson.com.

Feedback Information

At Cisco Press, our goal is to create in-depth technical books of the highest quality and value. Each book is crafted with care and precision, undergoing rigorous development that involves the unique expertise of members from the professional technical community.

Readers' feedback is a natural continuation of this process. If you have any comments regarding how we could improve the quality of this book, or otherwise alter it to better suit your needs, you can contact us through email at feedback@ciscopress.com. Please make sure to include the book title and ISBN in your message.

We greatly appreciate your assistance.

CISCO.

Americas Headquarters	Asia Pacific Headquarters	Europe Headquarters
Cisco Systems, Inc.	Cisco Systems (USA) Pte. Ltd.	Cisco Systems International BV Amsterdam,
San Jose, CA	Singapore	The Netherlands

Cisco has more than 200 offices worldwide. Addresses, phone numbers, and fax numbers are listed on the Cisco Website at **www.cisco.com/go/offices.**

Cisco and the Cisco logo are trademarks or registered trademarks of Cisco and/or its affiliates in the U.S. and other countries. To view a list of Cisco trademarks, go to this URL: www.cisco.com/go/trademarks. Third party trademarks mentioned are the property of their respective owners. The use of the word partner does not imply a partnership relationship between Cisco and any other company. (1110R)

Contents at a Glance

Chapter 1   Introduction to Personal Computer Hardware   1

Chapter 2   PC Assembly   17

Chapter 3   Advanced Computer Hardware   31

Chapter 4   Preventive Maintenance and Troubleshooting   51

Chapter 5   Networking Concepts   63

Chapter 6   Applied Networking   85

Chapter 7   Laptops and Other Mobile Devices   103

Chapter 8   Printers   133

Chapter 9   Virtualization and Cloud Computing   151

Chapter 10   Windows Installation   159

Chapter 11   Windows Configuration   173

Chapter 12   Mobile, Linux, and macOS Operating Systems   223

Chapter 13   Security   241

Chapter 14   The IT Professional   273

               Index   295

Contents

Chapter 1   **Introduction to Personal Computer Hardware**   1

1.0   **Introduction to Personal Computers**   1

1.1   **Personal Computers**   1

1.1.1   What is in a Computer?   1

    1.1.1.1   Video Explanation - What's in a Computer?   *1*

1.1.2   Electrical and ESD Safety   1

    1.1.2.1   Electrical Safety   *1*

    1.1.2.2   ESD   *2*

    1.1.2.3   Check Your Understanding - ESD Characteristics   *2*

1.2   **PC Components**   2

1.2.1   Case and power supplies   2

    1.2.1.1   Cases   *2*

    1.2.1.2   Power Supplies   *3*

    1.2.1.3   Connectors   *3*

    1.2.1.4   Power Supply Voltage   *4*

    1.2.1.5   Check Your Understanding - Cases and Power Supplies   *4*

1.2.2   Motherboards   4

    1.2.2.1   Motherboards   *4*

    1.2.2.2   Motherboard Components   *4*

    1.2.2.3   Motherboard Chipset   *5*

    1.2.2.4   Motherboard Form Factors   *5*

    1.2.2.5   Check Your Understanding - Motherboards   *5*

1.2.3   CPUs and Cooling Systems   6

    1.2.3.1   What is a CPU?   *6*

    1.2.3.2   Cooling Systems   *6*

    1.2.3.3   Check Your Understanding - CPUs and Cooling Systems   *6*

1.2.4   Memory   6

    1.2.4.1   Types of Memory   *6*

    1.2.4.2   Types of ROM   *7*

    1.2.4.3   Types of RAM   *7*

    1.2.4.4   Memory Modules   *7*

    1.2.4.5   Check Your Understanding - Memory   *8*

1.2.5   Adapter Cards and Expansion Slots   8

    1.2.5.1   Adapter Cards   *8*

    1.2.5.2   Check Your Understanding - Adapter Cards and Expansion Slots   *8*

1.2.6   Hard disk drives and SSDs   9

    1.2.6.1   Types of Storage Devices   *9*

    1.2.6.2   Storage Device Interfaces   *9*

    1.2.6.3   Magnetic Media Storage   *9*

    1.2.6.4   Semiconductor Storage   *10*

    1.2.6.5   Check Your Understanding - Data Storage Devices   *10*

1.2.7   Optical Storage Devices   11

    1.2.7.1   Types of Optical Storage Devices   *11*

    1.2.7.2   Check Your Understanding - Types of Optical Media   *11*

1.2.8   Ports, Cables, and Adaptors   11

    1.2.8.1   Video Ports and Cables   *11*

    1.2.8.2   Other Ports and Cables   *11*

1.2.8.3   *Adapters and Converters   11*
1.2.8.4   *Check Your Understanding - Cables and Connectors   12*
1.2.9   Input Devices   12
1.2.9.1   *The Original Input Devices   12*
1.2.9.2   *New Input Devices   12*
1.2.9.3   *More New Input Devices   12*
1.2.9.4   *Most Recent Input Devices   12*
1.2.9.5   *Check Your Understanding - Input Devices   12*
1.2.10   Output Devices   12
1.2.10.1   *What are Output Devices?   12*
1.2.10.2   *Monitors and Projectors   12*
1.2.10.3   *VR and AR Headsets   12*
1.2.10.4   *Printers   13*
1.2.10.5   *Speakers and Headphones   13*
1.2.10.6   *Check Your Understanding - Visual and Auditory Output Device Characteristics   13*

1.3   Computer Disassembly   13
1.3.1   The Technician's Toolkit   13
1.3.1.1   *Video Explanation - Technician's Toolkit   13*
1.3.1.2   *Check Your Understanding - Technician's Toolkit   13*
1.3.2   Computer Disassembly   13
1.3.2.1   *Video Demonstration - Computer Disassembly   13*
1.3.2.2   *Lab - Disassemble a Computer   14*

1.4   Summary   14

Chapter 1 Quiz   15

Chapter 1 Exam   15

Your Chapter Notes   15

Chapter 2   PC Assembly   17

2.0   Introduction to PC Assembly   17

2.1   Assemble the Computer   17
2.1.1   General and Fire Safety   17
2.1.1.1   *Video Explanation - General and Fire Safety   17*
2.1.2   Open the Case and Connect the Power Supply   17
2.1.2.1   *Video Demonstration - Install the Power Supply   17*
2.1.2.2   *Check Your Understanding - Install the Power Supply   18*
2.1.2.3   *Select the Case and Fans   18*
2.1.2.4   *Select a Power Supply   18*
2.1.2.5   *Lab - Install the Power Supply   19*
2.1.3   Install the Motherboard Components   19
2.1.3.1   *Video Demonstration - Install the CPU   19*
2.1.3.2   *Check Your Understanding - Install the CPU   19*
2.1.3.3   *Video Demonstration - Install the RAM   19*
2.1.3.4   *Check Your Understanding - Install the RAM   19*
2.1.3.5   *Video Demonstration - Install the Motherboard   19*
2.1.3.6   *Check Your Understanding - Install the Motherboard   19*
2.1.3.7   *Select the Motherboard   19*
2.1.3.8   *Select the CPU and CPU Cooling   20*
2.1.3.9   *Select the RAM   20*
2.1.3.10   *Lab - Install the Motherboard in a Computer   21*

2.1.4   Install Internal Drives   21

    2.1.4.1   Video Demonstration - Install the Drives   21

    2.1.4.2   Select Hard Drives   21

    2.1.4.3   Select Optical Drives   21

    2.1.4.4   Install the Hard Drive   22

    2.1.4.5   Install the Optical Drive   22

    2.1.4.6   Check Your Understanding - Installing Drives   22

    2.1.4.7   Lab - Install the Drives   22

2.1.5   Install the Adapter Cards   23

    2.1.5.1   Video Demonstration - Install the Adapter Cards   23

    2.1.5.2   Select Adapter Cards   23

    2.1.5.3   Other Factors for Adapter Card Selection   24

    2.1.5.4   Install the Adapter Cards   24

    2.1.5.5   Check Your Understanding - Installing Adapter Cards   25

    2.1.5.6   Lab - Install Adapter Card   25

2.1.6   Select Additional Storage   25

    2.1.6.1   Select a Media Reader   25

    2.1.6.2   Select External Storage   26

    2.1.6.3   Check Your Understanding - Media Cards   26

2.1.7   Install the Cables   26

    2.1.7.1   Video Demonstration - Connect the Internal Power Cables   26

    2.1.7.2   Check Your Understanding - Identify the Power Connectors   26

    2.1.7.3   Video Demonstration - Connect the Internal Data Cables   26

    2.1.7.4   Lab - Install Internal Cables   26

    2.1.7.5   Video Demonstration - Install the Front Panel Cables   26

    2.1.7.6   Install the Front Panel Cables   26

    2.1.7.7   Checking Your Understanding - Identify the Front Panel Cables   28

    2.1.7.8   Lab - Install the Front Panel Cables   28

    2.1.7.9   Video Demonstration - Complete the Computer Assembly   28

    2.1.7.10   Check Your Understanding - Identify the External Connectors   28

    2.1.7.11   Lab - Complete the Computer Assembly   28

2.2   Summary   28

Chapter 2 Quiz   30

Chapter 2 Exam   30

Your Chapter Notes   30

Chapter 3   Advanced Computer Hardware   31

3.0   Introduction to Advanced Computer Hardware   31

3.1   Boot the Computer   31

3.1.1   POST, BIOS, CMOS and UEFI   31

    3.1.1.1   Video Demonstration - BIOS - UEFI Menus   31

    3.1.1.2   POST   31

    3.1.1.3   BIOS and CMOS   32

    3.1.1.4   UEFI   32

    3.1.1.5   Check Your Understanding - BIOS and UEFI Terminology   33

    3.1.1.6   Lab - Investigate BIOS or UEFI Settings   33

3.1.2   BIOS/UEFI Configuration   33

    3.1.2.1   Video Demonstration - Configure BIOS - UEFI Settings   33

    3.1.2.2   BIOS and UEFI Security   33

    3.1.2.3   Update the Firmware   34

3.1.2.4   *Check Your Understanding - BIOS and UEFI Configuration Terminology*   35

3.1.2.5   *Lab - Search for BIOS or UEFI Firmware Updates*   35

3.1.2.6   *Lab - Install Windows*   35

3.1.2.7   *Lab - Install Third-Party Software in Windows*   35

3.2   Electrical Power   35

3.2.1   Wattage and Voltage   35

3.2.1.1   *Wattage and Voltage*   35

3.2.1.2   *Power Supply Voltage Setting*   35

3.2.1.3   *Lab - Ohm's Law*   36

3.2.2   Power Fluctuation and Protection   36

3.2.2.1   *Power Fluctuation Types*   36

3.2.2.2   *Power Protection Devices*   36

3.2.2.3   *Check Your Understanding - Power Fluctuation Terms*   37

3.3   Advanced Computer Functionality   37

3.3.1   CPU Architectures and Operation   37

3.3.1.1   *CPU Architectures*   37

3.3.1.2   *Enhancing CPU Operation*   37

3.3.1.3   *Multicore Processors*   38

3.3.1.4   *CPU Cooling Mechanisms*   39

3.3.1.5   *Check Your Understanding - CPU Architectures and Operation*   39

3.3.2   RAID   39

3.3.2.1   *What Do You Already Know? - RAID*   39

3.3.2.2   *RAID Concepts*   39

3.3.2.3   *RAID Levels*   39

3.3.2.4   *Check Your Understanding - RAID Levels*   39

3.3.3   Ports, Connectors, and Cables   40

3.3.3.1   *Legacy Ports*   40

3.3.3.2   *Video and Graphic Ports*   40

3.3.3.3   *USB Cables and Connectors*   40

3.3.3.4   *SATA Cables and Connectors*   40

3.3.3.5   *Twisted Pair Cables and Connectors*   40

3.3.3.6   *Coax Cables and Connectors*   40

3.3.3.7   *SCSI and IDE Cables and Connectors*   41

3.3.3.8   *Check Your Understanding - Identify the External Connectors*   41

3.3.4   Monitors   41

3.3.4.1   *Monitor Characteristics*   41

3.3.4.2   *Monitor Terms*   42

3.3.4.3   *Display Standards*   42

3.3.4.4   *Using Multiple Monitors*   42

3.3.4.5   *Check Your Understanding - Monitor Terminology*   42

3.4   Computer Configuration   42

3.4.1   Upgrade Computer Hardware   42

3.4.1.1   *Motherboard Upgrade*   42

3.4.1.2   *Steps to Upgrade a Motherboard*   43

3.4.1.3   *CPU Upgrade*   44

3.4.1.4   *Storage Device Upgrade*   44

3.4.1.5   *Peripheral Upgrades*   45

3.4.1.6   *Power Supply Upgrade*   45

3.4.1.7   *Lab - Research a Hardware Upgrade*   45

3.4.2   Configurations for Specialized Computers   45

3.4.2.1   *What Do You Already Know? - Configure a CAx Workstation*   45

        3.4.2.2   What Do You Already Know? - Configure an Audio Video Editing Workstation 45

        3.4.2.3   What Do You Already Know? - Configure a Virtualization Workstation 45

        3.4.2.4   What Do You Already Know? - Configure a Gaming PC 46

        3.4.2.5   Check Your Understanding - Specialized Computer Component Types 46

        3.4.2.6   Thick and Thin Clients 46

        3.4.2.7   NAS 46

3.5   Protecting the Environment 47

    3.5.1   Safe Disposal of Equipment and Supplies 47

        3.5.1.1   Safe Disposal Methods 47

        3.5.1.2   Safety Data Sheets 48

        3.5.1.3   Check Your Understanding - Safe Disposal 48

3.6   Summary 48

Chapter 3 Quiz 50

Chapter 3 Exam 50

Your Chapter Notes 50

Chapter 4   Preventive Maintenance and Troubleshooting 51

4.0   Introduction 51

4.1   Preventive Maintenance 51

    4.1.1   PC Preventive Maintenance Overview 51

        4.1.1.1   Benefits to Preventive Maintenance 51

        4.1.1.2   Preventive Maintenance - Dust 52

        4.1.1.3   Preventive Maintenance - Internal Components 52

        4.1.1.4   Preventive Maintenance - Environmental Concerns 53

        4.1.1.5   Preventive Maintenance - Software 53

        4.1.1.6   Check Your Understanding - Preventive Maintenance 53

4.2   Troubleshooting Process 53

    4.2.1   Troubleshooting Process Steps 53

        4.2.1.1   Introduction to Troubleshooting 53

        4.2.1.2   Troubleshooting Process Steps 54

        4.2.1.3   Identify the Problem 54

        4.2.1.4   Check Your Understanding - Identify the Problem 56

        4.2.1.5   Establish a Theory of Probable Cause 56

        4.2.1.6   Test the Theory to Determine the Cause 56

        4.2.1.7   Establish a Plan of Action to Resolve the Problem and Implement the Solution 57

        4.2.1.8   Verify Full Functionality and, If Applicable, Implement Preventive Measures 57

        4.2.1.9   Document Findings, Actions, and Outcomes 57

        4.2.1.10 Check Your Understanding - Number the Steps 57

    4.2.2   Common Problems and Solutions for PCs 58

        4.2.2.1   PC Common Problems and Solutions 58

        4.2.2.2   Common Problems and Solutions for Storage Devices 58

        4.2.2.3   Common Problems and Solutions for Motherboards and Internal Components 58

        4.2.2.4   Common Problems and Solutions for Power Supplies 58

        4.2.2.5   Common Problems and Solutions for CPUs and Memory 58

        4.2.2.6   Common Problems and Solutions for Displays 58

4.2.3   Apply Troubleshooting Process to Computer Components and
            Peripherals   58
    4.2.3.1   *Personal Reference Tools   58*
    4.2.3.2   *Internet Reference Tools   59*
    4.2.3.3   *Check Your Understanding - Reference Tools   59*
    4.2.3.4   *Advanced Problems and Solutions for Hardware   59*
    4.2.3.5   *Lab - Use a Multimeter and a Power Supply Tester   59*
    4.2.3.6   *Lab - Troubleshoot Hardware Problems   59*

4.3   **Summary   60**

Chapter 4 Quiz   61

Chapter 4 Exam   61

Your Chapter Notes   61

Chapter 5   **Networking Concepts   63**

5.0   **Introduction   63**

5.1   **Network Components and Types   63**
    5.1.1   Types of Networks   63
        5.1.1.1   *Network Icons   63*
        5.1.1.2   *Network Topologies and Description   64*
        5.1.1.3   *Check Your Understanding - Types of Networks   64*
    5.1.2   Internet Connection Types   64
        5.1.2.1   *Brief History of Connection Technologies   64*
        5.1.2.2   *DSL, Cable, and Fiber   65*
        5.1.2.3   *Line of Sight Wireless Internet Service   66*
        5.1.2.4   *Satellite   66*
        5.1.2.5   *Cellular   66*
        5.1.2.6   *Mobile Hotspot and Tethering   66*
        5.1.2.7   *Check Your Understanding - Internet Connection Types   66*

5.2   **Networking Protocols, Standards, and Services   67**
    5.2.1   Transport Layer Protocols   67
        5.2.1.1   *Video Explanation - Transport Layer Protocols   67*
        5.2.1.2   *Activity - Transport Layer Protocols   67*
        5.2.1.3   *The TCP/IP Model   67*
        5.2.1.4   *TCP   67*
        5.2.1.5   *UDP   67*
        5.2.1.6   *Check Your Understanding - Transport Layer Protocols   68*
    5.2.2   Application Port Numbers   68
        5.2.2.1   *Video Explanation - Application Port Numbers   68*
        5.2.2.2   *Classify Application Port Numbers   68*
        5.2.2.3   *Check Your Understanding - Application Port Numbers   68*
    5.2.3   Wireless Protocols   69
        5.2.3.1   *WLAN Protocols   69*
        5.2.3.2   *Bluetooth, NFC, and RFID   69*
        5.2.3.3   *Zigbee and Z-Wave   69*
        5.2.3.4   *Cellular Generations   70*
        5.2.3.5   *Check Your Understanding - Wireless Protocols   70*
    5.2.4   Network Services   70
        5.2.4.1   *Video Explanation - Network Services   70*
        5.2.4.2   *Client - Server Roles   70*
        5.2.4.3   *DHCP Server   71*
        5.2.4.4   *DNS Server   71*
        5.2.4.5   *Print Server   71*

          5.2.4.6 File Server 71

          5.2.4.7 Web Server 72

          5.2.4.8 Mail Server 72

          5.2.4.9 Proxy Server 73

          5.2.4.10 Authentication Server 73

          5.2.4.11 Syslog Server 73

          5.2.4.12 Check Your Understanding - Network Services 73

5.3   Network Devices 73

     5.3.1   Basic Network Devices 73

          5.3.1.1 Video Explanation - Basic Network Devices 73

          5.3.1.2 Network Interface Card 74

          5.3.1.3 Repeaters, Bridges, and Hubs 74

          5.3.1.4 Switches 74

          5.3.1.5 Wireless Access Points 75

          5.3.1.6 Routers 75

          5.3.1.7 Check Your Understanding - Basic Network Devices 75

     5.3.2   Security Devices 76

          5.3.2.1 Video Explanation - Security Devices 76

          5.3.2.2 Firewalls 76

          5.3.2.3 IDS and IPS 76

          5.3.2.4 UTMs 76

          5.3.2.5 Endpoint Management Server 77

          5.3.2.6 Check Your Understanding - Security Devices 77

     5.3.3   Other Network Devices 77

          5.3.3.1 Legacy and Embedded Systems 77

          5.3.3.2 Patch Panel 78

          5.3.3.3 Power over Ethernet and Ethernet over Power 78

          5.3.3.4 Cloud-based Network Controller 78

          5.3.3.5 Check Your Understanding - Other Network Devices 78

5.4   Network Cables 79

     5.4.1   Network Tools 79

          5.4.1.1 Video Explanation - Network Cable Tools 79

          5.4.1.2 Network Tools and Descriptions 79

          5.4.1.3 Check Your Understanding - Network Tools 79

     5.4.2   Copper Cables and Connectors 79

          5.4.2.1 Cable Types 79

          5.4.2.2 Coaxial Cables 79

          5.4.2.3 Twisted-Pair Cables 79

          5.4.2.4 Twisted-Pair Category Ratings 80

          5.4.2.5 Twisted-Pair Wire Schemes 80

          5.4.2.6 Activity - Cable Pinouts 80

          5.4.2.7 Video Demonstration - Build and Test a Network Cable 80

          5.4.2.8 Lab - Build and Test a Network Cable 80

     5.4.3   Fiber Cables and Connectors 80

          5.4.3.1 Fiber-Optic Cables 80

          5.4.3.2 Types of Fiber Media 81

          5.4.3.3 Fiber-Optic Connectors 81

          5.4.3.4 Check Your Understanding - Fiber Cables and Connectors 81

5.5   Summary 81

Chapter 5 Quiz 83

Chapter 5 Exam 83

Your Chapter Notes 83

Chapter 6   Applied Networking   85

6.0   Introduction   85

6.1   **Device to Network Connection   85**

    6.1.1   Network Addressing   85

        6.1.1.1   *Video Explanation - MAC Addressing   85*

        6.1.1.2   *Video Explanation - IPv4 Addressing   85*

        6.1.1.3   *Video Explanation - IPv6 Addressing   85*

        6.1.1.4   *Two Network Addresses   86*

        6.1.1.5   *Displaying the Addresses   86*

        6.1.1.6   *IPv4 Address Format   86*

        6.1.1.7   *IPv6 Address Formats   87*

        6.1.1.8   *Static Addressing   88*

        6.1.1.9   *Dynamic Addressing   88*

        6.1.1.10   *Link-local IPv4 and IPv6 Addresses   89*

        6.1.1.11   *Check Your Understanding - Network Addressing   89*

    6.1.2   Configure a NIC   89

        6.1.2.1   *Packet Tracer - Add Computers to an Existing Network   89*

        6.1.2.2   *Network Design   89*

        6.1.2.3   *Selecting a NIC   90*

        6.1.2.4   *Installing and Updating a NIC   90*

        6.1.2.5   *Configure a NIC   91*

        6.1.2.6   *ICMP   91*

        6.1.2.7   *Lab - Configure a NIC to Use DHCP in Windows   91*

    6.1.3   Configure a Wired and Wireless Network   92

        6.1.3.1   *Video Explanation - Configure a Wired and Wireless Network   92*

        6.1.3.2   *Connecting Wired Devices to the Internet   92*

        6.1.3.3   *Logging in to the Router   93*

        6.1.3.4   *Basic Network Setup   93*

        6.1.3.5   *Basic Wireless Settings   93*

        6.1.3.6   *Configure a Wireless Mesh Network   93*

        6.1.3.7   *NAT for IPv4   93*

        6.1.3.8   *Quality of Service   94*

        6.1.3.9   *Packet Tracer - Connect to a Wireless Network   94*

        6.1.3.10   *Lab - Configure a Wireless Network   94*

    6.1.4   Firewall Settings   94

        6.1.4.1   *Video Explanation - Firewall Settings   94*

        6.1.4.2   *UPnP   95*

        6.1.4.3   *DMZ   95*

        6.1.4.4   *Port Forwarding   95*

        6.1.4.5   *MAC Address Filtering   96*

        6.1.4.6   *Whitelisting and Blacklisting   96*

        6.1.4.7   *Packet Tracer - Configure Firewall Settings   97*

        6.1.4.8   *Lab - Configure Firewall Settings   97*

    6.1.5   IoT Device Configuration   97

        6.1.5.1   *Internet of Things   97*

        6.1.5.2   *IoT Devices in Packet Tracer   97*

        6.1.5.3   *Packet Tracer - Control IoT Devices   97*

6.2   **Basic Troubleshooting Process for Networks   98**

    6.2.1   Applying the Troubleshooting Process to   98

        6.2.1.1   *The Six Steps of the Troubleshooting Process   98*

        6.2.1.2   *Identify the Problem   98*

        6.2.1.3   *Establish a Theory of Probable Cause   98*

        6.2.1.4   *Test the Theory to Determine the Cause   98*

6.2.1.5 *Establish a Plan of Action to Resolve the Problem and Implement the Solution 98*

6.2.1.6 *Verify Full Functionality and, If Applicable, Implement Preventive Measures 98*

6.2.1.7 *Document Findings, Actions, and Outcomes 99*

6.2.1.8 *Check Your Understanding - Network Troubleshooting Process 99*

6.2.2 Network Problems and Solutions 99

6.2.2.1 *Common Problems and Solutions for Networking 99*

6.2.2.2 *Advanced Problems and Solutions for Network Connections 99*

6.2.2.3 *Advanced Problems and Solutions for FTP and Secure Internet Connections 99*

6.2.2.4 *Advanced Problems and Solutions Using Network Tools 99*

6.2.2.5 *Lab - Troubleshoot Network Problems 99*

6.3 Summary 99

Chapter 6 Quiz 101

Chapter 6 Exam 101

Your Chapter Notes 101

Chapter 7   Laptops and Other Mobile Devices 103

7.0 Introduction 103

7.1 Characteristics of laptops and other mobile devices 103

7.1.1 Mobile Device Overview 103

7.1.1.1 *What Do You Already Know? - Mobile Devices 103*

7.1.1.2 *Mobility 103*

7.1.1.3 *Laptops 104*

7.1.1.4 *Smartphone Characteristics 104*

7.1.1.5 *Smartphone Features 104*

7.1.1.6 *Tablets and E-Readers 105*

7.1.1.7 *Wearables: Smartwatches and Fitness Trackers 105*

7.1.1.8 *Wearables: Augmented and Virtual Realities 106*

7.1.1.9 *Check Your Understanding - Laptops and Other Mobile Devices 106*

7.1.1.10 *Lab - Mobile Device Information 106*

7.1.2 Laptop Components 106

7.1.2.1 *Video Explanation - External Features Unique to Laptops 106*

7.1.2.2 *Video Explanation - Common Input Devices and LEDs in Laptops 106*

7.1.2.3 *Motherboards 106*

7.1.2.4 *Internal Components 107*

7.1.2.5 *Check Your Understanding - External Laptop components 107*

7.1.2.6 *Special function keys 107*

7.1.2.7 *Video Explanation - Docking Station Versus Port Replicator 108*

7.1.2.8 *Lab - Research Docking Stations and Port Replicators 108*

7.1.3 Laptop Display Components 108

7.1.3.1 *LCD, LED, and OLED Displays 108*

7.1.3.2 *Laptop Display Features 108*

7.1.3.3 *Backlights and Inverters 108*

7.1.3.4 *Check Your Understanding - Laptop Display Components 108*

7.1.3.5 *Wi-Fi Antenna Connectors 109*

7.1.3.6 *Webcam and Microphone 109*

7.2   **Laptop Configuration   109**

   7.2.1   Power Settings Configuration   109

      7.2.1.1   Power Management   109

      7.2.1.2   Managing ACPI Settings in the BIOS   109

      7.2.1.3   Check Your Understanding - Match ACPI Standards   110

      7.2.1.4   Video Demonstration - Managing Laptop Power Options   110

   7.2.2   Wireless Configuration   110

      7.2.2.1   Bluetooth   110

      7.2.2.2   Bluetooth Laptop Connections   110

      7.2.2.3   Video Demonstration - Bluetooth Configuration   111

      7.2.2.4   Cellular WAN   111

      7.2.2.5   Wi-Fi   111

      7.2.2.6   Video Demonstration - Wi-Fi Configuration   111

      7.2.2.7   Check Your Understanding - Wireless Configuration   111

7.3   **Laptop Hardware and Component Installation and Configuration   112**

   7.3.1   Expansion Slots   112

      7.3.1.1   Expansion Cards   112

      7.3.1.2   Flash Memory   112

      7.3.1.3   Smart Card Reader   113

      7.3.1.4   SODIMM Memory   113

      7.3.1.5   Video Demonstration - Install SODIMM   114

      7.3.1.6   Check Your Understanding - Expansion Modules   114

   7.3.2   Replacing Laptop Components   114

      7.3.2.1   Overview of Hardware Replacement   114

      7.3.2.2   Video Demonstration - Keyboard Replacement   115

      7.3.2.3   Video Demonstration - Screen Replacement   115

      7.3.2.4   Lab - Research Laptop Screens   115

      7.3.2.5   Power   115

      7.3.2.6   Video Demonstration - DC Jack Replacement   116

      7.3.2.7   Lab - Research Laptop Batteries   116

      7.3.2.8   Internal Storage and Optical Drive   116

      7.3.2.9   Video Demonstration - Internal Storage and Optical Drive Replacement   116

      7.3.2.10   Lab - Research Laptop Drives   116

      7.3.2.11   Video Demonstration - Wireless Card Replacement   116

      7.3.2.12   Video Demonstration - Speakers Replacement   117

      7.3.2.13   Video Demonstration - CPU Replacement   117

      7.3.2.14   Video Demonstration - Motherboard Replacement   117

      7.3.2.15   Video Demonstration - Plastic Frames   117

      7.3.2.16   Check Your Understanding - Replacing Laptop Components   117

7.4   **Other Mobile Device Hardware Overview   117**

   7.4.1   Other Mobile Device Hardware   117

      7.4.1.1   Cell Phone Parts   117

      7.4.1.2   Wired connectivity   118

      7.4.1.3   Wireless Connections and Shared Internet Connections   118

      7.4.1.4   Check Your Understanding - Identify Connection Types   118

   7.4.2   Specialty Mobile Devices   118

      7.4.2.1   Wearable Devices   118

      7.4.2.2   Specialty Devices   118

7.5 Network Connectivity and Email 119

    7.5.1 Wireless and Cellular Data Networks 119

        7.5.1.1 Wireless Data Networks 119

        7.5.1.2 Lab - Mobile Wi-Fi 120

        7.5.1.3 Cellular Communication Standards 120

        7.5.1.4 Airplane Mode 120

        7.5.1.5 Hotspot 121

        7.5.1.6 Check Your Understanding - Wireless Technology 121

    7.5.2 Bluetooth 121

        7.5.2.1 Bluetooth for Mobile Devices 121

        7.5.2.2 Bluetooth Pairing 121

    7.5.3 Configuring Email 122

        7.5.3.1 Introduction to Email 122

        7.5.3.2 Activity - Matching Email Protocols 122

        7.5.3.3 Android Email Configuration 122

        7.5.3.4 iOS Email Configuration 123

        7.5.3.5 Internet Email 123

    7.5.4 Mobile Device Synchronization 124

        7.5.4.1 Types of Data to Synchronize 124

        7.5.4.2 Enabling Synchronization 124

        7.5.4.3 Synchronization Connection Types 125

7.6 Preventive Maintenance for Laptops and other Mobile Devices 126

    7.6.1 Scheduled Maintenance for Laptops and other Mobile Devices 126

        7.6.1.1 What Do You Already Know? - Preventive Maintenance 126

        7.6.1.2 The Reason for Maintenance 126

        7.6.1.3 Laptop Preventive Maintenance Program 126

        7.6.1.4 Mobile Device Preventive Maintenance Program 127

7.7 Basic Troubleshooting Process for Laptops and other Mobile Devices 127

    7.7.1 Applying the Troubleshooting Process to Laptops and other Mobile Devices 127

        7.7.1.1 The Troubleshooting Process 127

        7.7.1.2 Identify the problem 127

        7.7.1.3 Establish a theory of probable cause 128

        7.7.1.4 Test the Theory to Determine Cause 128

        7.7.1.5 Establish a Plan of Action to Resolve the Problem and Implement the Solution 128

        7.7.1.6 Verify Full System Functionality and if Applicable, Implement Preventative Measures 128

        7.7.1.7 Document Findings, Actions, and Outcomes 128

    7.7.2 Common Problems and Solutions for Laptops and Other Mobile Devices 128

        7.7.2.1 Identify Common Problems and Solutions 128

        7.7.2.2 Common Problems and Solutions for Laptops 128

        7.7.2.3 Common Problems and Solutions for Other Mobile Devices 128

        7.7.2.4 Lab - Research Laptop Specifications 129

        7.7.2.5 Lab - Gather Information from the Customer 129

        7.7.2.6 Lab - Investigate Support Websites 129

7.8 Summary 129

Chapter 7 Quiz 131

Chapter 7 Exam 131

Your Chapter Notes 131

Chapter 8   Printers   133

8.0   Introduction   133

8.1   Common Printer Features   133

    8.1.1   Characteristics and Capabilities   133

        8.1.1.1   Characteristics of Printers   133

        8.1.1.2   Printer Speed, Quality, and Color   133

        8.1.1.3   Reliability and Total Cost of Ownership   134

        8.1.1.4   Automatic Document Feeder   134

        8.1.1.5   Check Your Understanding - Printer Capabilities and Characteristics   134

    8.1.2   Printer Connections   135

        8.1.2.1   Printer Connection Types   135

        8.1.2.2   Check Your Understanding - Printer Connections   135

8.2   Printer Type Comparison   135

    8.2.1   Inkjet Printers   135

        8.2.1.1   Inkjet Printer Characteristics   135

        8.2.1.2   Inkjet Printer Parts   135

        8.2.1.3   Check Your Understanding - Inkjet Printers   135

    8.2.2   Laser Printers   135

        8.2.2.1   Laser Printer Characteristics   135

        8.2.2.2   Laser Printer Parts   136

        8.2.2.3   Check Your Understanding - Laser Printers   136

    8.2.3   Laser Printing Process   136

        8.2.3.1   How Laser Printing Works   136

        8.2.3.2   Check Your Understanding - The Laser Printing Process   136

    8.2.4   Thermal Printers and Impact Printers   136

        8.2.4.1   Thermal Printer Characteristics   136

        8.2.4.2   Impact Printer Characteristics   136

        8.2.4.3   Check Your Understanding - Thermal Printers and Impact Printers   137

    8.2.5   Virtual Printers   137

        8.2.5.1   Virtual Printer Characteristics   137

        8.2.5.2   Cloud Printing   137

        8.2.5.3   Check Your Understanding - Virtual Printers   137

    8.2.6   3D Printers   137

        8.2.6.1   3D Printer Characteristics   137

        8.2.6.2   3D Printer Parts   138

        8.2.6.3   Check Your Understanding - 3D Printers   138

8.3   Installing and Configuring Printers   138

    8.3.1   Installing and Updating a Printer   138

        8.3.1.1   Installing a Printer   138

        8.3.1.2   Test Printer Functions   138

        8.3.1.3   Lab - Install a Printer in Windows   139

    8.3.2   Configuring Options and Default Settings   139

        8.3.2.1   Common Configuration Settings   139

        8.3.2.2   Check Your Understanding - Configuration Options   139

    8.3.3   Optimizing Printer Performance   139

        8.3.3.1   Software Optimization   139

        8.3.3.2   Hardware Optimization   140

        8.3.3.3   Check Your Understanding - Printer Optimization   140

8.4 **Sharing Printers 140**

    8.4.1   Operating System Settings for Sharing Printers   140

        8.4.1.1   Configuring Printer Sharing   140

        8.4.1.2   Wireless Printer Connections   141

        8.4.1.3   Lab - Share a Printer in Windows   141

    8.4.2   Print Servers   141

        8.4.2.1   Purposes of Print Servers   141

        8.4.2.2   Software Print Servers   142

        8.4.2.3   Hardware Print Servers   142

        8.4.2.4   Dedicated Print Servers   142

        8.4.2.5   Check Your Understanding - Print Servers   142

8.5 **Maintaining and Troubleshooting Printers 143**

    8.5.1   Printer Preventive Maintenance   143

        8.5.1.1   Vendor Guidelines   143

        8.5.1.2   What Do You Already Know? Printer Operating Environment   143

    8.5.2   Inkjet Printer Preventive Maintenance   143

        8.5.2.1   Video Demonstration - Inkjet Printer Preventive Maintenance   143

        8.5.2.2   Lab - Perform Preventive Maintenance on an Inkjet Printer   144

    8.5.3   Laser Printer Preventive Maintenance   144

        8.5.3.1   Video Demonstration - Laser Printer Preventive Maintenance   144

        8.5.3.2   Lab - Perform Preventive Maintenance on a Laser Printer   144

    8.5.4   Thermal Printer Preventive Maintenance   145

        8.5.4.1   Preventive Maintenance on a Thermal Printer   145

        8.5.4.2   Check Your Understanding - Thermal Printer Preventive Maintenance   145

    8.5.5   Impact Printer Preventive Maintenance   145

        8.5.5.1   Preventive Maintenance of an Impact Printer   145

        8.5.5.2   Check Your Understanding - Impact Printer Preventive Maintenance   145

    8.5.6   3D Printer Preventive Maintenance   145

        8.5.6.1   Video Demonstration - 3D Printer Preventive Maintenance   145

        8.5.6.2   Video Demonstration - 3D Printer Printing a Component   145

    8.5.7   Applying the Troubleshooting Process to Printers   146

        8.5.7.1   The Six Steps of the Troubleshooting Process   146

        8.5.7.2   Identify the Problem   146

        8.5.7.3   Establish a Theory of Probable Cause   146

        8.5.7.4   Test the Theory to Determine Cause   146

        8.5.7.5   Establish a Plan of Action to Resolve the Problem and Implement the Solution   146

        8.5.7.6   Verify Full System Functionality and, if Applicable, Implement Preventive Measures   146

        8.5.7.7   Document Findings, Actions, and Outcomes.   146

    8.5.8   Problems and Solutions   147

        8.5.8.1   Identify Printer Problems and Solutions   147

        8.5.8.2   Common Problems and Solutions for Printers   147

        8.5.8.3   Advanced Problems and Solutions for Printers   147

8.6 **Summary 147**

Chapter 8 Quiz 149

Chapter 8 Exam 149

Your Chapter Notes 149

Chapter 9   Virtualization and Cloud Computing   151

    9.0   Introduction   151

    9.1   Virtualization   151

        9.1.1   Virtualization   151

            9.1.1.1   Video Explanation - What is the Cloud?   151

            9.1.1.2   Cloud Computing and Virtualization   151

            9.1.1.3   Traditional Server Deployment   152

            9.1.1.4   Server Virtualization   152

            9.1.1.5   Advantages of Server Virtualization   153

            9.1.1.6   Check Your Understanding - Match the Advantages of Virtualization   153

        9.1.2   Client-Side Virtualization   153

            9.1.2.1   Client-Side Virtualization   153

            9.1.2.2   Type 1 and Type 2 Hypervisors   153

            9.1.2.3   Virtual Machine Requirements   154

            9.1.2.4   Check Your Understanding - Virtualization Terminology   155

            9.1.2.5   Lab - Install Linux in a Virtual Machine and Explore the GUI   155

    9.2   Cloud Computing   155

        9.2.1   Cloud Computing Applications   155

            9.2.1.1   How We Use the Cloud   155

        9.2.2   Cloud Services   155

            9.2.2.1   Cloud Services   155

            9.2.2.2   What Do You Already Know? - Cloud Models   156

            9.2.2.3   Check Your Understanding - Cloud Service and Cloud Model Terminology   156

            9.2.2.4   Cloud Computing Characteristics   156

            9.2.2.5   Check Your Understanding - Match the Cloud Characteristics   156

    9.3   Summary   156

    Chapter 9 Quiz   158

    Chapter 9 Exam   158

    Your Chapter Notes   158

Chapter 10   Windows Installation   159

    10.0   Introduction   159

    10.1   Modern Operating Systems   159

        10.1.1   Operating System Features   159

            10.1.1.1   Terms   159

            10.1.1.2   Basic Functions of an Operating System   160

            10.1.1.3   Windows Operating Systems   160

            10.1.1.4   Check Your Understanding - Windows Terminology   160

        10.1.2   Customer Requirements for an Operating System   160

            10.1.2.1   Compatible System Software and Hardware Requirements   160

            10.1.2.2   Minimum Hardware Requirements and Compatibility with OS   161

            10.1.2.3   32-bit vs. 64-bit Processor Architecture   161

            10.1.2.4   What Do You Already Know? Choosing a Windows Edition   161

            10.1.2.5   Check Your Understanding - Choosing an Operating System   161

10.1.3   Operating System Upgrades   162
   10.1.3.1   *Checking OS Compatibility   162*
   10.1.3.2   *Windows OS Upgrades   162*
   10.1.3.3   *Data Migration   162*
   10.1.3.4   *Check Your Understanding - OS Upgrades   162*

10.2   **Disk Management   163**

10.2.1   Disk Management   163
   10.2.1.1   *Storage Device Types   163*
   10.2.1.2   *Hard Drive Partitioning   163*
   10.2.1.3   *Partitions and Logical Drives   164*
   10.2.1.4   *Check Your Understanding - Disk Terminology   164*
   10.2.1.5   *File Systems   164*
   10.2.1.6   *Video Demonstration - Disk Management Utility and Disk Partitioning   165*
   10.2.1.7   *Video Demonstration - Multiboot Procedures   165*
   10.2.1.8   *Lab - Create a Partition in Windows   165*

10.3   **Installation and Boot Sequence   166**

10.3.1   Basic Windows Installation   166
   10.3.1.1   *Lab - Windows Installation   166*
   10.3.1.2   *Account Creation   166*
   10.3.1.3   *Finalize the Installation   166*
   10.3.1.4   *Lab - Finalize the Windows Installation   166*

10.3.2   Custom Installation Options   167
   10.3.2.1   *Disk Cloning   167*
   10.3.2.2   *Other Installation Methods   167*
   10.3.2.3   *Remote Network Installation   168*
   10.3.2.4   *Unattended Network Installation   168*
   10.3.2.5   *Video Demonstration - Windows Restore and Recovery   169*
   10.3.2.6   *Recovery Partition   169*
   10.3.2.7   *Upgrade Methods   169*
   10.3.2.8   *Check your Understanding– Identify OS Installation Terminology   170*

10.3.3   Windows Boot Sequence   170
   10.3.3.1   *Windows Boot Sequence   170*
   10.3.3.2   *Windows 7 Startup Modes   170*
   10.3.3.3   *Windows 8 and10 Startup Modes   171*
   10.3.3.4   *Check Your Understanding - Windows Boot Sequence   171*

10.4   **Summary   171**

Chapter 10 Quiz   172

Chapter 10 Exam   172

Your Chapter Notes   172

Chapter 11   Windows Configuration   173

11.0   **Introduction   173**

11.1   **Windows Desktop and File Explorer   173**

11.1.1   Comparing Windows Versions   173
   11.1.1.1   *Windows Versions   173*
   11.1.1.2   *Windows 7   174*
   11.1.1.3   *Windows 8   174*
   11.1.1.4   *Windows 8.1   175*

11.1.1.5   *Windows 10   175*

11.1.1.6   *Check Your Understanding - Windows Versions   175*

11.1.2   The Windows Desktop   175

11.1.2.1   *The Windows 7 Desktop   175*

11.1.2.2   *The Windows 8 Desktop   176*

11.1.2.3   *The Windows 8.1 Desktop   176*

11.1.2.4   *Personalizing the Windows Desktop   176*

11.1.2.5   *Video Demonstration - The Windows 10 Desktop   177*

11.1.2.6   *The Windows 10 Start Menu   177*

11.1.2.7   *The Windows 8.1 and 8.0 Start Menu   177*

11.1.2.8   *The Windows 7 Start Menu   178*

11.1.2.9   *The Taskbar   178*

11.1.2.10   *Lab - Explore the Windows Desktop   178*

11.1.2.11   *Check Your Understanding - Identify Elements of the Windows Desktop   178*

11.1.3   Windows Task Manager   178

11.1.3.1   *Video Demonstration - Working With Task Manager   178*

11.1.3.2   *Windows 10 Task Manager Functions   179*

11.1.3.3   *Task Manager in Windows 7   179*

11.1.3.4   *Lab - Work with Task Manager   179*

11.1.3.5   *Check Your Understanding - Compare Task Manager in Windows 7 and 10   179*

11.1.4   Windows File Explorer   180

11.1.4.1   *File Explorer   180*

11.1.4.2   *Video Demonstration - Working with File Explorer   180*

11.1.4.3   *This PC   180*

11.1.4.4   *Run as Administrator   180*

11.1.4.5   *Windows Libraries   181*

11.1.4.6   *Directory Structures   181*

11.1.4.7   *User and System File Locations   181*

11.1.4.8   *File Extensions   181*

11.1.4.9   *File Attributes   182*

11.1.4.10   *Video Demonstration - File and Folder Properties   182*

11.1.4.11   *Lab - Working with File Explorer   182*

11.1.4.12   *Check Your Understanding - File Explorer   182*

11.2   Configure Windows with Control Panels   183

11.2.1   Control Panel Utilities   183

11.2.1.1   *Windows 10: Settings and Control Panels   183*

11.2.1.2   *Introduction to Control Panel   183*

11.2.1.3   *Control Panel Views   183*

11.2.1.4   *Define Control Panel Categories   184*

11.2.1.5   *Lab - Explore Control Panel Categories   184*

11.2.1.6   *Check Your Understanding - Control Panel Categories   184*

11.2.2   User and Account Control Panel Items   184

11.2.2.1   *User Accounts   184*

11.2.2.2   *User Account Control Settings   184*

11.2.2.3   *Lab - User Accounts   184*

11.2.2.4   *Credential Manager   185*

11.2.2.5   *Sync Center   185*

11.2.2.6   *Check Your Understanding - User and Account Control Panels   185*

11.2.3   Network and Internet Control Panels 185

    11.2.3.1   Network Settings 185
    11.2.3.2   Internet Options 186
    11.2.3.3   Network and Sharing Center 186
    11.2.3.4   HomeGroup 186
    11.2.3.5   Lab - Configure Browser Settings 187
    11.2.3.6   Check Your Understanding - Network and Internet Control
           Panel 187

11.2.4   Display Settings and Control Panel 187

    11.2.4.1   Display Settings and Configuration 187
    11.2.4.2   Display Features 187
    11.2.4.3   Check Your Understanding - Display Features 188

11.2.5   Power and System Control Panels 188

    11.2.5.1   Power Options 188
    11.2.5.2   Power Options Settings 188
    11.2.5.3   Power Options Actions 188
    11.2.5.4   Check Your Understanding - Power Options 189
    11.2.5.5   System Control Panel Item 189
    11.2.5.6   System Properties 189
    11.2.5.7   Increasing Performance 189
    11.2.5.8   Lab - Manage Virtual Memory 190
    11.2.5.9   Check Your Understanding - Power Options and System
           Properties 190

11.2.6   Hardware and Sound Control Panels 190

    11.2.6.1   Device Manager 190
    11.2.6.2   Lab - Use Device Manager 190
    11.2.6.3   Devices and Printers 190
    11.2.6.4   Sound 191
    11.2.6.5   Check Your Understanding - Device Manager Alerts 191

11.2.7   Clock, Region, and Language 191

    11.2.7.1   Clock 191
    11.2.7.2   Region 191
    11.2.7.3   Language 192
    11.2.7.4   Lab - Region and Language Options 192
    11.2.7.5   Check Your Understanding - Clock, Region, and Language 192

11.2.8   Programs and Features Control Panels 192

    11.2.8.1   Programs 192
    11.2.8.2   Windows Features and Updates 192
    11.2.8.3   Default Programs 192
    11.2.8.4   Check Your Understanding - Programs and Features 193

11.2.9   Other Control Panels 193

    11.2.9.1   Troubleshooting 193
    11.2.9.2   BitLocker Drive Encryption 193
    11.2.9.3   File Explorer and Folder Options 193
    11.2.9.4   Check Your Understanding - Other Control Panels 194

11.3   System Administration 194

11.3.1   Administrative Tools 194

    11.3.1.1   Administrative Tools Control Panel Item 194
    11.3.1.2   Computer Management 194
    11.3.1.3   Event Viewer 195
    11.3.1.4   Local Users and Groups 195
    11.3.1.5   Performance Monitor 196
    11.3.1.6   Component Services and Data Sources 196

11.3.1.7   Services   196

11.3.1.8   Data Sources   196

11.3.1.9   Print Management   197

11.3.1.10   Windows Memory Diagnostics   197

11.3.1.11   Lab - Monitor and Manage System Resources   197

11.3.1.12   Check Your Understanding - Administrative Tools   197

11.3.2   System Utilities   197

11.3.2.1   System Information   197

11.3.2.2   System Configuration   197

11.3.2.3   The Registry   198

11.3.2.4   Regedit   198

11.3.2.5   Microsoft Management Console   198

11.3.2.6   DxDiag   199

11.3.2.7   Lab - System Utilities   199

11.3.2.8   Lab - Manage System Files   199

11.3.2.9   Check Your Understanding - System Utilities   199

11.3.3   Disk Management   199

11.3.3.1   What Do You Already Know? - Disk Operations   199

11.3.3.2   Disk Management Utility   199

11.3.3.3   Drive Status   199

11.3.3.4   Mounting a Drive   200

11.3.3.5   Adding Arrays   200

11.3.3.6   Disk Optimization   200

11.3.3.7   Disk Error - Checking   201

11.3.3.8   Lab - Hard Drive Maintenance   201

11.3.3.9   Check Your Understanding - Disk Management   201

11.3.4   Application Installation and Configuration   202

11.3.4.1   System Requirements   202

11.3.4.2   Installation Methods   202

11.3.4.3   Installing an Application   202

11.3.4.4   Compatibility Mode   203

11.3.4.5   Uninstalling or Changing a Program   203

11.3.4.6   Lab - Install Third-Party Software   203

11.3.4.7   Security Considerations   203

11.3.4.8   Check Your Understanding - Application Installation and Configuration   203

11.4   Command-Line Tools   204

11.4.1   Using Windows CLI   204

11.4.1.1   PowerShell   204

11.4.1.2   The Command Shell   204

11.4.1.3   Basic Commands   204

11.4.1.4   Video Demonstration - Managing CLI Sessions   204

11.4.1.5   Lab - Work in the Windows Command Shell   205

11.4.1.6   Check Your Understanding - Basic Command Line Commands   205

11.4.2   File System CLI Commands   205

11.4.2.1   Command Syntax Conventions   205

11.4.2.2   File System Navigation   205

11.4.2.3   File System Navigation - Commands   206

11.4.2.4   Video Demonstration - Working with Files and Folders   206

11.4.2.5   Manipulating Folders - Commands   206

11.4.2.6   Manipulating Files - Commands   206

11.4.2.7   Lab - File System Commands   206

11.4.2.8   Check Your Understanding - File System CLI Commands   206

11.4.3   Disk CLI Commands   206
    11.4.3.1   Disk Operations - Commands   206
    11.4.3.2   Lab - Disk CLI Commands   207
    11.4.3.3   Check Your Understanding - Disk Operations Commands   207
11.4.4   Task and System CLI Commands   207
    11.4.4.1   System CLI Commands   207
    11.4.4.2   Lab - Task and System CLI Commands   207
    11.4.4.3   Check Your Understanding - Task and System Commands   207
11.4.5   Other Useful CLI Commands   207
    11.4.5.1   Other Useful Commands   207
    11.4.5.2   Running System Utilities   207
    11.4.5.3   Lab - Other Useful Commands   208
    11.4.5.4   Check Your Understanding - Other Useful CLI Commands   208

11.5   Windows Networking   208

11.5.1   Network Sharing and Mapping Drives   208
    11.5.1.1   Domain and Workgroup   208
    11.5.1.2   Homegroup   208
    11.5.1.3   Video Demonstration - Connecting to a Workgroup or Domain   209
    11.5.1.4   Network Shares and Mapping Drives   209
    11.5.1.5   Administrative Shares   209
11.5.2   Sharing Local Resources with Others   210
    11.5.2.1   Sharing Local Resources   210
    11.5.2.2   Printer Sharing vs. Network Printer Mapping   210
    11.5.2.3   Video Demonstration - Sharing Files and Folders on a Local Network   210
    11.5.2.4   Lab - Share Resources   210
11.5.3   Configure a Wired Network Connection   211
    11.5.3.1   Configuring Wired Network Interfaces in Windows 10   211
    11.5.3.2   Configuring a Wired NIC   211
    11.5.3.3   Setting a Network Profile   211
    11.5.3.4   Verify Connectivity with the Windows GUI   212
    11.5.3.5   ipconfig Command   212
    11.5.3.6   Network CLI Commands   212
    11.5.3.7   Video Demonstration - Network Testing and Verification with CLI Commands   212
11.5.4   Configure a Wireless Network Interfaces in Windows   213
    11.5.4.1   Wireless Settings   213
    11.5.4.2   Lab - Connect and Test the Wireless Connection   213
11.5.5   Remote Access Protocols   213
    11.5.5.1   VPN Access in Windows   213
    11.5.5.2   Telnet and SSH   214
    11.5.5.3   Packet Tracer - Use Telnet and SSH   214
11.5.6   Remote Desktop and Assistance   214
    11.5.6.1   Video Demonstration - Remote Desktop and Remote Assistance   214
    11.5.6.2   Lab - Windows Remote Desktop and Assistance   215
    11.5.6.3   Check Your Understanding - Remote Desktop and Assistance   215

11.6   Common Preventive Maintenance Techniques for Operating Systems   215

11.6.1   OS Preventive Maintenance Plan   215
    11.6.1.1   Preventive Maintenance Plan Contents   215
    11.6.1.2   Lab - Manage the Startup Folder   216

　　　　11.6.1.3　*Windows Updates   216*
　　　　11.6.1.4　*Video Demonstration - Scheduling Tasks   217*
　　　　11.6.1.5　*Lab - Schedule a Task using the GUI and the Command Line   217*
　　11.6.2　Backup and Restore   217
　　　　11.6.2.1　*Restore Points   217*
　　　　11.6.2.2　*Hard Drive Backup   217*
　　　　11.6.2.3　*Video Demonstration - Back up and Restore   218*
　　　　11.6.2.4　*Lab - System Restore and Hard Drive Backup   218*

11.7　Basic Troubleshooting Process for Windows Operating Systems   218

　　11.7.1　Applying Troubleshooting Process to Windows Operating Systems   218
　　　　11.7.1.1　*The Six Steps of the Troubleshooting Process   218*
　　　　11.7.1.2　*Identify the Problem   218*
　　　　11.7.1.3　*Establish a Theory of Probable Cause   218*
　　　　11.7.1.4　*Test the Theory to Determine the Cause   218*
　　　　11.7.1.5　*Establish a Plan of Action to Resolve the Problem and Implement the Solution   219*
　　　　11.7.1.6　*Verify Full System Functionality and if Applicable Implement Preventive Measures   219*
　　　　11.7.1.7　*Document Findings, Actions, and Outcomes   219*
　　11.7.2　Common Problems and Solutions for Windows Operating Systems   219
　　　　11.7.2.1　*Common Problems and Solutions for Windows Operating Systems   219*
　　11.7.3　Advanced Troubleshooting for Windows Operating Systems   219
　　　　11.7.3.1　*Advanced Problems and Solutions for Windows Operating Systems   219*
　　　　11.7.3.2　*Lab - Troubleshoot Operating System Problems   219*

11.8　Summary   219

Chapter 11 Quiz   221

Chapter 11 Exam   221

Your Chapter Notes   221

Chapter 12　Mobile, Linux, and macOS Operating Systems   223

12.0　Introduction   223

12.1　Mobile Operating Systems   223

　　12.1.1　Android vs. iOS   223
　　　　12.1.1.1　*Open Source vs. Closed Source   223*
　　　　12.1.1.2　*Applications and Content Sources   224*
　　　　12.1.1.3　*Check Your Understanding - Compare Android and iOS   224*
　　12.1.2　Android Touch Interface   224
　　　　12.1.2.1　*Home Screen Items   224*
　　　　12.1.2.2　*Lab - Working with Android   224*
　　12.1.3　iOS Touch Interface   224
　　　　12.1.3.1　*Home Screen Items   224*
　　　　12.1.3.2　*Lab - Working with iOS   225*
　　12.1.4　Common Mobile Device Features   225
　　　　12.1.4.1　*Screen Orientation   225*
　　　　12.1.4.2　*Screen Calibration   225*
　　　　12.1.4.3　*GPS   225*
　　　　12.1.4.4　*Lab - Mobile Device Features   225*
　　　　12.1.4.5　*Wi-Fi Calling   226*
　　　　12.1.4.6　*NFC Payment   226*

12.1.4.7 Virtual Private Network 226
12.1.4.8 Virtual Assistants 226

12.2 Methods for Securing Mobile Devices 227

12.2.1 Screen Locks and Biometric Authentication 227

12.2.1.1 What Do You Already Know? - Locks 227
12.2.1.2 Lab - Passcode Locks 227
12.2.1.3 Restrictions on Failed Login Attempts 227
12.2.1.4 Check your Understanding - Screen Locks and Biometric Authentication 227

12.2.2 Cloud-Enabled Services for Mobile Devices 227

12.2.2.1 Remote Backup 227
12.2.2.2 Locator Applications 228
12.2.2.3 Remote Lock and Remote Wipe 228
12.2.2.4 Check Your Understanding - Cloud-Enabled Services for Mobile Devices 228

12.2.3 Software Security 228

12.2.3.1 Antivirus 228
12.2.3.2 Rooting and Jailbreaking 229
12.2.3.3 Patching and Updating Operating Systems 230
12.2.3.4 Check Your Understanding - Mobile Security Features 230

12.3 Linux and macOS Operating Systems 230

12.3.1 Linux and macOS tools and features 230

12.3.1.1 Introduction to Linux and macOS Operating Systems 230
12.3.1.2 Overview of Linux GUI 231
12.3.1.3 Overview macOS GUI 231
12.3.1.4 Overview of Linux and macOS CLI 232
12.3.1.5 Linux Backup and Recovery 232
12.3.1.6 macOS Backup and Recovery 232
12.3.1.7 Overview of Disk Utilities 233
12.3.1.8 Check your understanding - Linux and macOS Operating Systems 233

12.3.2 Linux and macOS Best Practices 233

12.3.2.1 Scheduled Tasks 233
12.3.2.2 Operating System Updates 234
12.3.2.3 Security 234
12.3.2.4 Check Your Understanding - Linux and macOS Best Practices 234

12.3.3 Basic CLI Commands 234

12.3.3.1 Syntax Checker - File and Directory Commands 234
12.3.3.2 Check Your Understanding - File and Directory commands 234
12.3.3.3 The ls -l command output 234
12.3.3.4 Basic Unix File and Directory Permissions 234
12.3.3.5 Syntax Checker: File and Directory Permissions 235
12.3.3.6 Check Your Understanding - File and Directory Permission 235
12.3.3.7 Linux Administrative Commands 235
12.3.3.8 Linux Administrative Commands Requiring Root Access 235
12.3.3.9 Check Your Understanding: - Administrative Commands 235
12.3.3.10 Syntax Checker - File Ownership and Permission 235

12.4 Basic Troubleshooting Process for Mobile, Linux, and macOS Operating Systems 236

12.4.1 Applying the Troubleshooting Process to Mobile, Linux, and macOS Operating Systems 236

12.4.1.1 The Six Steps of the Troubleshooting Process 236

        12.4.1.2 Identify the Problem 236

        12.4.1.3 Establish a theory of Probable Cause 236

        12.4.1.4 Test the Theory to Determine the Cause 236

        12.4.1.5 Establish a Plan of Action to Resolve the Problem and Implement the Solution 236

        12.4.1.6 Verify Full System Functionality and if Applicable, Implement Preventive Measures 237

        12.4.1.7 Document Findings, Actions, and Outcomes. 237

    12.4.2 Common Problems and Solutions for Other Operating Systems 237

        12.4.2.1 Common Problems and Solutions for Mobile Operating Systems 237

        12.4.2.2 Common Problems and Solutions for Mobile OS Security 237

        12.4.2.3 Common Problems and Solutions for Linux and macOS Operating Systems 237

        12.4.2.4 Lab - Troubleshoot Mobile Devices 237

12.5 Summary 237

Chapter 12 Quiz 239

Chapter 12 Exam 239

Your Chapter Notes 239

Chapter 13   Security 241

13.0 Introduction 241

13.1 Security Threats 241

    13.1.1 Malware 241

        13.1.1.1 Malware 241

        13.1.1.2 What Do You Already Know? - Malware 242

        13.1.1.3 Viruses and Trojan Horses 242

        13.1.1.4 Types of Malware 243

        13.1.1.5 Check Your Understanding - Malware 243

    13.1.2 Preventing Malware 243

        13.1.2.1 Anti-Malware Programs 243

        13.1.2.2 Signature File Updates 244

        13.1.2.3 Video Explanation - Protecting Against Malware 245

        13.1.2.4 Remediating Infected Systems 245

        13.1.2.5 Video Explanation - Remediating an Infected System 245

        13.1.2.6 Check Your Understanding - Preventing Malware 245

    13.1.3 Network Attacks 246

        13.1.3.1 Networks Are Targets 246

        13.1.3.2 Types of TCP/IP Attacks 246

        13.1.3.3 Check Your Understanding - Identify the TCP/IP Attack 246

        13.1.3.4 Zero-Day 246

        13.1.3.5 Protecting Against Network Attacks 247

    13.1.4 Social Engineering Attacks 247

        13.1.4.1 Social Engineering 247

        13.1.4.2 What Do You Already Know? - Social Engineering Techniques 247

        13.1.4.3 Social Engineering Techniques 247

        13.1.4.4 Protecting Against Social Engineering 248

        13.1.4.5 Check Your Understanding - Personal and Corporate Social Engineering Techniques 248

13.2 Security Procedures 248

13.2.1 Security Policy 248
13.2.1.1 What is a Security Policy 248
13.2.1.2 Security Policy Category 248
13.2.1.3 Securing Devices and Data 248

13.2.2 Protecting Physical Equipment 249
13.2.2.1 Physical Security 249
13.2.2.2 Types of Secure Locks 249
13.2.2.3 Mantraps 249
13.2.2.4 Securing Computers and Network Hardware 249
13.2.2.5 Check Your Understanding - Locking Mechanisms 250

13.2.3 Protecting Data 250
13.2.3.1 Data - Your Greatest Asset 250
13.2.3.2 Data Backups 251
13.2.3.3 File and Folder Permissions 251
13.2.3.4 File and Folder Encryption 252
13.2.3.5 Windows BitLocker and BitLocker To Go 252
13.2.3.6 Video Demonstration - Bitlocker and Bitlocker To Go 253
13.2.3.7 Lab - Bitlocker and Bitlocker To Go 253

13.2.4 Data Destruction 253
13.2.4.1 Data Wiping Magnetic Media 253
13.2.4.2 Data Wiping Other Media 253
13.2.4.3 Hard Drive Recycling and Destruction 254
13.2.4.4 Check Your Understanding - Data Protection 254

13.3 Securing Windows Workstations 254

13.3.1 Securing a Workstation 254
13.3.1.1 Securing a Computer 254
13.3.1.2 Securing BIOS 255
13.3.1.3 Securing Windows Login 255
13.3.1.4 Local Password Management 256
13.3.1.5 Usernames and Passwords 256
13.3.1.6 Check your Understanding - Secure a Workstation 256

13.3.2 Windows Local Security Policy 256
13.3.2.1 The Windows Local Security Policy 256
13.3.2.2 Account Policies Security Settings 257
13.3.2.3 Local Policies Security Settings 257
13.3.2.4 Exporting the Local Security Policy 257
13.3.2.5 Lab - Configure Windows Local Security Policy 258
13.3.2.6 Check Your Understanding- Local Security Policy 258

13.3.3 Managing Users and Groups 258
13.3.3.1 Maintaining Accounts 258
13.3.3.2 Managing Users Account Tools and User Account Tasks 258
13.3.3.3 Local Users and Groups Manager 258
13.3.3.4 Managing Groups 259
13.3.3.5 Active Directory Users and Computers 259
13.3.3.6 Lab - Configure Users and Groups in Windows 260
13.3.3.7 Check your Understanding - User Account Tools and User Account Tasks 260

13.3.4 Windows Firewall 260
13.3.4.1 Firewalls 260
13.3.4.2 Software Firewalls 261
13.3.4.3 Windows Firewall 261
13.3.4.4 Configuring Exceptions in Windows Firewall 261
13.3.4.5 Windows Firewall with Advanced Security 262

          13.3.4.6   Lab - Configure Windows Firewall   262

          13.3.4.7   Check your Understanding - Windows Firewall   262

      13.3.5   Web Security   262

          13.3.5.1   Web Security   262

          13.3.5.2   InPrivate Browsing   263

          13.3.5.3   Pop-up Blocker   263

          13.3.5.4   SmartScreen Filter   264

          13.3.5.5   ActiveX Filtering   264

          13.3.5.6   Check Your Understanding - Web Security   264

      13.3.6   Security Maintenance   264

          13.3.6.1   Restrictive Settings   264

          13.3.6.2   Disable Auto-Play   265

          13.3.6.3   Operating System Service Packs and Security Patches   265

          13.3.6.4   Check your Understanding - Security Maintenance   265

  13.4   Wireless Security   265

      13.4.1   Configure Wireless Security   265

          13.4.1.1   What Do You Already Know? - Wireless Security   265

          13.4.1.2   Common Communication Encryption Types   266

          13.4.1.3   Wi-Fi Configuration Best Practices   266

          13.4.1.4   Authentication Methods   267

          13.4.1.5   Wireless Security Modes   267

          13.4.1.6   Firmware Updates   267

          13.4.1.7   Firewalls   267

          13.4.1.8   Port Forwarding and Port Triggering   267

          13.4.1.9   Universal Plug and Play   268

          13.4.1.10   Packet Tracer - Configure Wireless Security   268

  13.5   Basic Troubleshooting Process for Security   268

      13.5.1   Applying the Troubleshooting Process to Security   268

          13.5.1.1   The Six Steps of the Troubleshooting Process   268

          13.5.1.2   Identify the Problem   268

          13.5.1.3   Establish a Theory of Probable Cause   268

          13.5.1.4   Test the Theory to Determine Cause   268

          13.5.1.5   Establish a Plan of Action to Resolve the Problem and Implement the Solution   269

          13.5.1.6   Verify Full System Functionality and, If Applicable Implement Preventive Measures   269

          13.5.1.7   Document Findings, Actions, and Outcomes   269

      13.5.2   Common Problems and Solutions for Security   269

          13.5.2.1   Common Problems and Solutions for Security   269

          13.5.2.2   Lab - Document Customer Information in a Work Order   269

  13.6   Summary   269

  Chapter 13 Quiz   271

  Chapter 13 Exam   271

  Your Chapter Notes   271

Chapter 14   The IT Professional   273

  14.0   Introduction   273

  14.1   Communication Skills and the IT Professional   273

      14.1.1   Communication Skills, Troubleshooting, and Professional Behavior   273

          14.1.1.1   Relationship Between Communication Skills and Troubleshooting   273

14.1.1.2 *Lab - Technician Resources 274*

14.1.1.3 *Relationship Between Communication Skills and Professional Behavior 274*

14.1.2 Working with a Customer 275

14.1.2.1 *Know, Relate, and Understand 275*

14.1.2.2 *Active Listening 275*

14.1.2.3 *Check Your Understanding - Closed-Ended and Open-Ended Questions 275*

14.1.2.4 *Video Demonstration - Active Listening and Summarizing 275*

14.1.3 Professional Behavior 276

14.1.3.1 *Using Professional Behavior with the Customer 276*

14.1.3.2 *Tips for Hold and Transfer 277*

14.1.3.3 *Video Demonstration - Hold and Transfer 277*

14.1.3.4 *What Do You Already Know? - Netiquette 277*

14.1.4 The Customer Call 277

14.1.4.1 *Keeping the Customer Call Focused 277*

14.1.4.2 *Video Demonstration - The Talkative Customer 277*

14.1.4.3 *Video Demonstration - The Rude Customer 278*

14.1.4.4 *Video Demonstration - The Knowledgeable Customer 278*

14.1.4.5 *Video Demonstration - The Angry Customer 279*

14.1.4.6 *Video Demonstration - The Inexperienced Customer 279*

14.2 Operational Procedures 280

14.2.1 Documentation 280

14.2.1.1 *Documentation Overview 280*

14.2.1.2 *IT Department Documentation 280*

14.2.1.3 *Regulatory Compliance Requirements 280*

14.2.1.4 *Check Your Understanding - Documentation 280*

14.2.2 Change Management 281

14.2.2.1 *Change Control Process 281*

14.2.3 Disaster Prevention and Recovery 281

14.2.3.1 *Disaster Recovery Overview 281*

14.2.3.2 *Preventing Downtime and Data Loss 282*

14.2.3.3 *Elements of a Disaster Recovery Plan 283*

14.2.3.4 *Check Your Understanding - Disaster Recovery 283*

14.3 Ethical and Legal Considerations 284

14.3.1 Ethical and Legal Considerations in the IT Profession 284

14.3.1.1 *Ethical and Legal Considerations in IT 284*

14.3.1.2 *Personal Identifiable Information (PII) 284*

14.3.1.3 *Payment Card Industry (PCI) 285*

14.3.1.4 *Protected Health Information (PHI) 285*

14.3.1.5 *Lab - Investigate Breaches of PII, PHI, PCI 285*

14.3.1.6 *Legal Considerations in IT 286*

14.3.1.7 *Licensing 286*

14.3.1.8 *Check Your Understanding - Licensing 286*

14.3.2 Legal Procedures Overview 287

14.3.2.1 *Computer Forensics 287*

14.3.2.2 *Data Collected in Computer Forensics 287*

14.3.2.3 *Cyber Law 287*

14.3.2.4 *First Response 288*

14.3.2.5 *Documentation 288*

14.3.2.6 *Chain of Custody 289*

14.3.2.7 *Check Your Understanding - Legal Procedures Overview 289*

14.4   Call Center Technicians   289

   14.4.1   Call Centers, Level One and Level Two Technicians   289

      14.4.1.1   Call Centers   289

      14.4.1.2   Level One Technician Responsibilities   289

      14.4.1.3   Level Two Technician Responsibilities   290

      14.4.1.4   Lab - Remote Technician - Fix a Hardware Problem   290

      14.4.1.5   Lab - Remote Technician - Fix an Operating System Problem   290

      14.4.1.6   Lab - Remote Technician - Fix a Network Problem   290

      14.4.1.7   Lab - Remote Technician - Fix a Security Problem   290

   14.4.2   Basic Scripting and the IT Professional   291

      14.4.2.1   Script Examples   291

      14.4.2.2   Scripting Languages   291

      14.4.2.3   Basic Script Commands   291

      14.4.2.4   Variables / Environmental Variables   291

      14.4.2.5   Conditional Statements   292

      14.4.2.6   Loops   292

      14.4.2.7   Lab - Write Basic Scripts in Windows and Linux   292

14.5   Summary   292

Chapter 14 Quiz   294

Chapter 14 Exam   294

Your Chapter Notes   294

Index   295

Command Syntax Conventions

The conventions used to present command syntax in this book are the same conventions used in the IOS Command Reference. The Command Reference describes these conventions as follows:

- **Boldface** indicates commands and keywords that are entered literally as shown. In actual configuration examples and output (not general command syntax), boldface indicates commands that are manually input by the user (such as a **show** command).

- *Italic* indicates arguments for which you supply actual values.

- Vertical bars (|) separate alternative, mutually exclusive elements.

- Square brackets ([ ]) indicate an optional element.

- Braces ({ }) indicate a required choice.

- Braces within brackets ([{ }]) indicate a required choice within an optional element.

About This Course Booklet

Your Cisco Networking Academy Course Booklet is designed as a study resource you can easily read, highlight, and review on the go, wherever the Internet is not available or practical:

- The text is extracted directly, word-for-word, from the online course so you can highlight important points and take notes in the "Your Chapter Notes" section.

- Headings with the exact page correlations provide a quick reference to the online course for your classroom discussions and exam preparation.

- An icon system directs you to the online curriculum to take full advantage of the images embedded within the Networking Academy online course interface and reminds you to do the labs, interactive activities, packet tracer activities, watch videos, and take the chapter quizzes.

The Course Booklet is a basic, economical paper-based resource to help you succeed with the Cisco Networking Academy online course.

Introduction to Personal Computer Hardware

1.0 Introduction to Personal Computers

Refer to
Online Course
for Illustration

People prepare for work in the information technology fields by earning certifications, seeking formal education, and by experience through internships and jobs. In this chapter, you will learn about all the components that make up a PC starting with the case that houses all of the internal components. Computers, computer components, and computer peripherals all contain hazards that can cause severe injury. Therefore, this chapter begins with safety guidelines that you should follow to prevent electrical fires, injuries, and fatalities while working inside a computer. You will also learn about Electrostatic Discharge (ESD) and how it can damage computer equipment if it is not discharged properly.

This chapter will introduce you to all of the components that go inside of a computer case starting with the motherboard. You will learn about all the internal components that are connected to the motherboard, including the power supply, the central processing unit (CPU), random access memory (RAM), expansion cards, and storage drives. You will also learn about the connectors, ports, and cables that physically connect the devices to the motherboard.

It is important to not only learn about computer components but also build hands-on skills. In this chapter you will have a in which you will disassemble a computer so that you can become more familiar with all of the components and how they are connected.

1.1 Personal Computers

1.1.1 What is in a Computer?

Refer to **Video**
in online course

1.1.1.1 Video Explanation - What's in a Computer?

Click Play in the figure to see an explanation of what is in a computer.

Click here to read the transcript of this video.

1.1.2 Electrical and ESD Safety

Refer to
Online Course
for Illustration

1.1.2.1 Electrical Safety

Follow electrical safety guidelines to prevent electrical fires, injuries, and fatalities.

Some printer parts, such as power supplies, contain high voltage. Check the printer manual for the location of high-voltage components. Some components retain a high voltage even after the printer is turned off.

Electrical devices have certain power requirements. For example, AC adapters are manufactured for specific laptops. Exchanging AC adapters with a different type of laptop or device may cause damage to both the AC adapter and the laptop.

Electric equipment must be grounded. If a fault causes metal parts of the equipment to become live with electrical current, the ground will provide a path of least resistance for the current to flow harmlessly away. Typically computer product connect to ground via the power plug. Large equipment such as server racks that house network devices must also be grounded.

Refer to **Online Course** for Illustration

1.1.2.2 ESD

Electrostatic discharge (ESD) can occur when there is a buildup of an electric charge (static electricity) that exists on a surface which comes into contact with another, differently charged surface. ESD can cause damage to computer equipment if not discharged properly. Follow proper handling guidelines, be aware of environmental issues, and use equipment that stabilizes power to prevent equipment damage and data loss.

At least 3,000 volts of static electricity must build up before a person can feel ESD. For example, static electricity can build up on you as you walk across a carpeted floor. When you touch another person, you both receive a shock. If the discharge causes pain or makes a noise, the charge was probably above 10,000 volts. By comparison, less than 30 volts of static electricity can damage a computer component. Static buildup can be discharged by touching a grounded object prior to touching any electronic equipment. This is known as self-grounding.

ESD can cause permanent damage to electrical components. Follow these recommendations to help prevent ESD damage:

- Keep all components in antistatic bags until you are ready to install them.
- Use grounded mats on workbenches.
- Use grounded floor mats in work areas.
- Use antistatic wrist straps when working inside computers.

Refer to **Interactive Graphic** in online course

1.1.2.3   Check Your Understanding - ESD Characteristics

1.2   PC Components

1.2.1   Case and power supplies

Refer to **Interactive Graphic** in online course

1.2.1.1   Cases

The case of a desktop computer houses the internal components such as the power supply, motherboard, central processing unit (CPU), memory, disk drives, and assorted adapter cards.

Cases are typically made of plastic, steel, or aluminum and provide the framework to support, protect, and cool the internal components.

A device form factor refers to its physical design and look. Desktop computers are available in a variety of form factors including:

- Horizontal case

- Full-Size Tower

- Compact Tower

- All-in-one.

This list is not exhaustive, as many case manufacturers have their own naming conventions. These may include super tower, full tower, mid tower, mini tower, cube case, and more.

Computer components tend to generate a lot of heat; therefore, computer cases contain fans that move air through the case. As the air passes warm components, it absorbs heat and then exits the case. This process keeps the computer components from overheating. Cases are also designed to protect against static electricity damage. The computer's internal components are grounded via attachment to the case.

Note   Computer cases are also referred to as the computer chassis, cabinet, tower, housing, or simply box.

Refer to
Online Course
for Illustration

1.2.1.2   Power Supplies

Electricity from wall outlets is provided in alternating current (AC). However, all components inside a computer require direct current (DC) power. To obtain DC power, computers use a power supply, as shown here, to convert AC power into a lower voltage DC power.

The following describes the various computer desktop power supply form factors that have evolved over time:

- **Advanced Technology (AT)** - This is the original power supply for legacy computer systems now considered obsolete.

- **AT Extended (ATX)** - This is the updated version of the AT but still considered to be obsolete.

- **ATX12V** - This is the most common power supply on the market today. It includes a second motherboard connector to provide dedicated power to the CPU. There are several versions of ATX12V available.

- **EPS12V** - This was originally designed for network servers but is now commonly used in high-end desktop models.

Refer to
Interactive Graphic
in online course

1.2.1.3   Connectors

A power supply includes several different connectors, as shown in here. These connectors are used to power various internal components such as the motherboard and disk drives. The connectors are "keyed" which means that they are designed to be inserted in only one orientation.

Refer to
Online Course
for Illustration

1.2.1.4   Power Supply Voltage

The different connectors also provide different voltages. The most common voltages supplied are 3.3 volts, 5 volts, and 12 volts. The 3.3 volt and 5 volt supplies are typically used by digital circuits, while the 12 volt supply is used to run motors in disk drives and fans.

Power supplies can also be single rail, dual rail, or multi rail. A rail is the printed circuit board (PCB) inside the power supply to which the external cables are connected. A single rail has all of the connectors connected to the same PCB while a multi rail PCB has separate PCBs for each connector.

A computer can tolerate slight fluctuations in power, but a significant deviation can cause the power supply to fail.

Refer to
Interactive Graphic
in online course

1.2.1.5   Check Your Understanding - Cases and Power Supplies

1.2.2   Motherboards

Refer to
Online Course
for Illustration

1.2.2.1   Motherboards

The motherboard, also known as the system board or the main board, is the backbone of the computer. As shown in the figure, a motherboard is a printed circuit board (PCB) that contains buses, or electrical pathways, that interconnect electronic components. These components may be soldered directly to the motherboard, or added using sockets, expansion slots, and ports.

Refer to
Online Course
for Illustration

1.2.2.2   Motherboard Components

These are some connections on the motherboard where computer components can be added, as shown in the Figure 1:

- **Central Processing Unit (CPU)** - This is considered the brain of the computer.

- **Random Access Memory (RAM)** - This is a temporary location to store data and applications.

- **Expansion slots** - These provide locations to connect additional components.

- **Chipset** - This consists of the integrated circuits on the motherboard that control how system hardware interacts with the CPU and motherboard. It also establishes how much memory can be added to a motherboard and the type of connectors on the motherboard.

- **Basic input/output system (BIOS) chip and Unified Extensible Firmware Interface (UEFI) chip** - BIOS is used to help boot the computer and manage the flow of data between the hard drive, video card, keyboard, mouse, and more. Recently the BIOS has been enhanced by UEFI. UEFI specifies a different software interface for boot and runtime services but still relies on the traditional BIOS for system configuration, power-on self -test (POST), and setup.

Some additional important connectors are shown in Figure 2.

Refer to
Online Course
for Illustration

1.2.2.3   Motherboard Chipset

The figure illustrates how a motherboard connects various components.

Most chipsets consist of the following two types:

- **Northbridge** - Controls high speed access to the RAM and video card. It also controls the speed at which the CPU communicates with all of the other components in the computer. Video capability is sometimes integrated into the Northbridge.

- **Southbridge** - Allows the CPU to communicate with slower speed devices including hard drives, Universal Serial Bus (USB) ports, and expansion slots

Refer to
Online Course
for Illustration

1.2.2.4   Motherboard Form Factors

The form factor of motherboards pertains to the size and shape of the board. It also describes the physical layout of the different components and devices on the motherboard.

There have been many variations of motherboards developed over the years. There are three common motherboard form factors:

- **Advanced Technology eXtended (ATX)** - This is the most common motherboard form factor. The ATX case accommodates the integrated I/O ports on the standard ATX motherboard. The ATX power supply connects to the motherboard via a single 20-pin connector.

- **Micro-ATX** - This is a smaller form factor that is designed to be backward-compatible with ATX. Micro-ATX boards often use the same Northbridge and Southbridge chipsets and power connectors as full-size ATX boards and therefore can use many of the same components. Generally, Micro-ATX boards can fit in standard ATX cases. However, Micro-ATX motherboards are much smaller than ATX motherboards and have fewer expansion slots.

- **ITX** - The ITX form factor has gained in popularity because of its very small size. There are many types of ITX motherboards; however, Mini-ITX is one of the most popular. The Mini-ITX form factor uses very little power, so fans are not needed to keep it cool. A Mini-ITX motherboard has only one PCI slot for expansion cards. A computer based on a Mini-ITX form factor can be used in places where it is inconvenient to have a large or noisy computer.

The table in the figure highlights these and other form factor variations.

Note   It is important to distinguish between form factors. The choice of motherboard form factor determines how individual components attach to it, the type of power supply required, and the shape of the computer case. Some manufacturers also have proprietary form factors based on the ATX design. This causes some motherboards, power supplies, and other components to be incompatible with standard ATX cases.

Refer to
Interactive Graphic
in online course

1.2.2.5   Check Your Understanding - Motherboards

1.2.3   CPUs and Cooling Systems

Refer to
Online Course
for Illustration

1.2.3.1   What is a CPU?

The central processing unit (CPU) is responsible for interpreting and executing commands. It handles instructions from the computer's other hardware, such as a keyboard, and software. The CPU interprets the instructions and outputs the information to the monitor or performs the requested tasks.

The CPU is a small microchip that resides within a CPU package. The CPU package is often referred to as the CPU. CPU packages come in different form factors, each style requiring a particular socket on the motherboard. Common CPU manufacturers include Intel and AMD.

The CPU socket is the connection between the motherboard and the processor. Modern CPU sockets and processor packages are built around the following architectures:

- **Pin Grid Array (PGA)** - (Figure 1) In PGA architecture, the pins are on the underside of the processor package and is inserted into the motherboard CPU socket using zero insertion force (ZIF). ZIF refers to the amount of force needed to install a CPU into the motherboard socket or slot.

- **Land Grid Array (LGA)** - (Figure 2) In an LGA architecture, the pins are in the socket instead of on the processor.

Refer to
Online Course
for Illustration

1.2.3.2   Cooling Systems

The flow of current between electronic components generates heat. Computer components perform better when kept cool. If the heat is not removed, the computer may run more slowly. If too much heat builds up, the computer could crash, or components can be damaged. Therefore, it is imperative that computers be kept cool.

Computers are kept cool using active and passive cooling solutions. Active solutions require power while passive solutions do not. Passive solutions for cooling usually involve reducing the speed at which a component is operating or adding heat sinks to computer chips. A case fan is considered as active cooling. The figure shows examples of passive and active cooling solutions.

Refer to
Interactive Graphic
in online course

1.2.3.3   Check Your Understanding - CPUs and Cooling Systems

1.2.4   Memory

Refer to
Online Course
for Illustration

1.2.4.1   Types of Memory

A computer might use different types of memory chips, as shown in the figure. However, all memory chips store data in the form of bytes. A byte is a grouping of digital information and represents information such as letters, numbers, and symbols. Specifically, a byte is a block of eight bits stored as either 0 or 1 in the memory chip.

Read-Only Memory

An essential computer chip is the read-only memory (ROM) chip. ROM chips are located on the motherboard and other circuit boards and contain instructions that can be directly accessed by a CPU. The instructions stored in ROM include basic operation instructions such as booting the computer and loading the operating system.

ROM is nonvolatile which means that the contents are not erased when the computer is powered off.

Random Access Memory

RAM is the temporary working storage for data and programs that are being accessed by the CPU. Unlike ROM, RAM is volatile memory, which means that the contents are erased every time the computer is powered off.

Adding more RAM in a computer enhances the system performance. For instance, more RAM increases the memory capacity of the computer to hold and process programs and files. With less RAM, a computer must swap data between RAM and the much slower hard drive. The maximum amount of RAM that can be installed is limited by the motherboard.

> Refer to
> **Interactive Graphic**
> in online course

1.2.4.2   Types of ROM

> Refer to
> **Interactive Graphic**
> in online course

1.2.4.3   Types of RAM

> Refer to
> **Interactive Graphic**
> in online course

1.2.4.4   Memory Modules

Early computers had RAM installed on the motherboard as individual chips. The individual memory chips, called dual inline package (DIP) chips, were difficult to install and often became loose. To solve this problem, designers soldered the memory chips to a circuit board to create a memory module which would then be placed into a memory slot on the motherboard.

The different types of memory modules are described in Figure 1.

Note   Memory modules can be single-sided or double-sided. Single-sided memory modules contain RAM on only one side of the module. Double-sided memory modules contain RAM on both sides.

The speed of memory has a direct impact on how much data a processor can process in a given period of time. As processor speed increases, memory speed must also increase. Memory throughput has also been increased through multichannel technology. Standard RAM is single channel, meaning that all of the RAM slots are addressed at the same time. Dual channel RAM adds a second channel to be able to access a second module at the same time. Triple channel technology provides another channel so that three modules can be accessed at the same time.

The fastest memory is typically static RAM (SRAM) which is cache memory for storing the most recently used data and instructions by the CPU. SRAM provides the processor with faster access to the data than retrieving it from the slower dynamic RAM (DRAM), or main memory.

The three most common types of cache memory are described in Figure 2.

Memory errors occur when the data is not stored correctly in the chips. The computer uses different methods to detect and correct data errors in memory.

Different types of error checking methods are described in Figure 3.

Refer to
Interactive Graphic
in online course

1.2.4.5   Check Your Understanding - Memory

Refer to
Online Course
for Illustration

1.2.5   Adapter Cards and Expansion Slots

1.2.5.1   Adapter Cards

Adapter cards increase the functionality of a computer by adding controllers for specific devices or by replacing malfunctioning ports.

There are a variety of adapter cards available that are used to expand and customize the capability of a computer:

- **Sound adapter** - Sound adapters provide audio capability.

- **Network Interface Card (NIC)** - A NIC connects a computer to a network using a network cable.

- **Wireless NIC** - A wireless NIC connects a computer to a network using radio frequencies.

- **Video adapter** - Video adapters provide video capability.

- **Capture card** - Capture cards send a video signal to a computer so that the signal can be recorded to a storage drive with video capture software.

- **TV tuner card** - These provide the ability to watch and record television signals on a PC by connecting a cable television, satellite, or antenna to the installed tuner card.

- **Universal Serial Bus (USB) controller card** - Provides additional USB ports to connect the computer to peripheral devices.

- **eSATA card** - Adds additional internal and external SATA ports to a computer through a single PCI Express slot.

Figure 1 shows some of these adapter cards. It should be noted that some of these adapter cards can be integrated on the motherboard.

Note   Older computers may also have a modem adapter, Accelerated Graphics Port (AGP), a Small Computer System Interface (SCSI) adapter, and more.

Computers have expansion slots on the motherboard to install adapter cards. The type of adapter card connector must match the expansion slot. Refer to Figure 2 to learn about expansion slots.

Refer to
Interactive Graphic
in online course

1.2.5.2   Check Your Understanding - Adapter Cards and Expansion Slots

Refer to
Online Course
for Illustration

1.2.6 Hard disk drives and SSDs

1.2.6.1 Types of Storage Devices

A number of different types of devices are available for data storage on a PC, as shown in the figure. Data drives provide non-volatile storage of data, meaning that when the drive loses power, the data is retained and available the next time the drive is powered on. Some drives have fixed media, and other drives have removable media. Some offer the ability to read and write data, while others only allow data to be accessed, but not written. Data storage devices can be classified according to the media on which the data is stored; magnetic like HDD and tape drives, solid state, or optical.

Refer to
Online Course
for Illustration

1.2.6.2 Storage Device Interfaces

Internal storage devices often connect to the motherboard using Serial AT Attachment (SATA) connections. The SATA standards define the way that data is transferred, the transfer rates, and physical characteristics of the cables and connectors.

There are three main versions of the SATA standard: SATA 1, SATA 2, and SATA 3, as shown in the figure. The cables and connectors are the same, but the data transfer speeds are different. SATA 1 allows for a maximum data transfer rate of 1.5 Gb/s while SATA 2 can reach up to 3 Gb/s. SATA 3 is the fastest with speeds up to 6 Gb/s.

Note   Legacy internal drive connection methods include the Parallel ATA standards known as Integrated Drive Electronics (IDE) and Enhanced Integrated Drive Electronics (EIDE).

Small Computer System Interface (SCSI) is another interface between motherboards and data storage devices. It is an older standard that originally used parallel, rather than serial, data transfers. A new version of SCSI known as Serially Attached SCSI (SAS) has been developed. SAS is a popular interface used for server storage.

Refer to
Online Course
for Illustration

1.2.6.3 Magnetic Media Storage

One type of storage represents binary values as magnetized or non-magnetized physical areas of magnetic media. Mechanical systems are used to position and read the media. The following are common types of magnetic media storage drives:

- **Hard Disk Drive (HDD)** - HDDs are the traditional magnetic disk devices that have been used for years. Their storage capacity ranges from gigabytes (GBs) to terabytes (TBs). Their speed is measured in revolutions per minute (RPM). This indicates how fast the spindle turns the platters that hold the data. The faster the spindle speed, the faster a hard drive can find data on the platters. This can correspond to faster transfer speeds. Common hard drive spindle speeds include 5400, 7200, 10,000, and 15,000 RPM. HDDs come in 1.8, 2.5 and 3.5 inch form factors, as shown in Figure 1. The 3.5 inch form factor is standard for personal computers. 2.5 inch HDDs are typically used in mobile devices. 1.8 inch HDDs were used in portable media players and other mobile applications, but are seldom used in new devices.

- **Tape Drive** - Magnetic tapes are most often used for archiving data. At one time they were useful for backing up PCs, however as HDDs became cheaper, external HDD drives are now frequently used for this purpose. However, tape backups are still used in enterprise networks. Tape drives use a magnetic read/write head and removable tape cartridge, as shown in Figure 2. Although data retrieval using a tape drive can be fast, locating specific data is slow because the tape must be wound on a reel until the data is found. Common tape storage capacities vary between a few GBs to many TBs.

Note   Older computers may still incorporate legacy storage devices including floppy disk drives.

Refer to
Online Course
for Illustration

1.2.6.4   Semiconductor Storage

Solid-state drives (SSD) store data as electrical charges in semiconductor flash memory. This makes SSDs much faster than magnetic HDDs. SSD storage capacity ranges from around 120 GBs to many TBs. SSDs have no moving parts, make no noise, are more energy efficient, and produce less heat than HDDs. Because SSDs have no moving parts to fail, they are considered to be more reliable than HDDs.

SSDs come in three form factors:

- **Disc drive form factor** - These are similar to an HDD in which the semiconductor memory is in a closed package that can be mounted in computer cases like an HDD. They can be 2.5, 3.5, and 1.8 inches, although those are rare.

- **Expansion cards** - This plugs directly into the motherboard and mounts in the computer case like other expansion cards.

- **mSata or M.2 modules** - These packages may use a special socket. M.2 is a standard for computer expansion cards. It is a family of standards that specify physical aspects of expansion cards such as connectors and dimension.

These form factors are shown in Figure 1. Figure 2 shows the 2.5 inch and M.2 form factors in comparison to a 3.5 inch magnetic HDD.

The Non-Volatile Memory Express (NVMe) specification was developed specifically to allow computers to take greater advantage of the features of SSDs by providing a standard interface between SSDs, the PCIe bus, and operating systems. NVMe allows compliant SSD drives to attach to the PCIe bus without requiring special drivers, in much the same way that USB flash drives can be used in multiple computers without requiring installation on each.

Finally, Solid State Hybrid Drives (SSHDs) are a compromise between a magnetic HDD and an SSD. They are faster than an HDD but less expensive than an SSD. They combine a magnetic HDD with onboard flash memory serving as a non-volatile cache. The SSHD drive automatically caches data that is frequently accessed, which can speed up certain operations such as operating system start up.

Refer to
Interactive Graphic
in online course

1.2.6.5   Check Your Understanding - Data Storage Devices

1.2.7 Optical Storage Devices

Refer to
Online Course
for Illustration

1.2.7.1 Types of Optical Storage Devices

Optical drives are a type of removable media storage device that use lasers to read and write data on optical media. They were developed to overcome the storage capacity limitations of removable magnetic media such as floppy discs and magnetic storage cartridges. Figure 1 shows an internal optical drive. There are three types of optical drives:

■ **Compact Disc (CD)** - audio and data

■ Digital Versatile Disc (DVD) - digital video and data

■ **Blu-ray Disc (BD)** - HD digital video and data

CD, DVD, and BD media can be pre-recorded (read only), recordable (write once), or re-recordable (read and write multiple times). DVD and BD media can also be single layer (SL) or dual layer (DL). Dual layer media roughly doubles the capacity of a single disc.

Figure 2 describes the various types of optical media and their approximate storage capacities.

Refer to
Interactive Graphic
in online course

1.2.7.2 Check Your Understanding - Types of Optical Media

1.2.8 Ports, Cables, and Adaptors

Refer to
Interactive Graphic
in online course

1.2.8.1 Video Ports and Cables

A video port connects a monitor cable to a computer. Video ports and monitor cables transfer analog signals, digital signals, or both. Computers are digital devices that create digital signals. The digital signals are sent to the graphics card where they are transmitted through a cable to a display.

Refer to
Interactive Graphic
in online course

1.2.8.2 Other Ports and Cables

Input/output (I/O) ports on a computer connect peripheral devices such as printers, scanners, and portable drives. In addition to the ports and interfaces previously discussed, a computer may also have other ports.

Refer to
Interactive Graphic
in online course

1.2.8.3 Adapters and Converters

There are many connection standards in use today. Many are interoperable but require specialized components. These components are called adapters and converters:

■ **Adapter** - This is a component that physically connects one technology to another. For example, a DVI to HDMI adapter. The adapter could be one component or a cable with different ends.

■ **Converter** - This performs the same function as an adapter but also translates the signals from one technology to the other. For example, a USB 3.0 to SATA converter enables a hard disk drive to be used as a flash drive.

Refer to **Interactive Graphic** in online course

1.2.8.4   Check Your Understanding - Cables and Connectors

1.2.9   Input Devices

Refer to **Interactive Graphic** in online course

1.2.9.1   The Original Input Devices

Input devices allow the user to communicate with a computer. The images below are some of the first input devices.

Refer to **Interactive Graphic** in online course

1.2.9.2   New Input Devices

Some new input devices include touch screen, a stylus, a magnetic strip reader and a barcode scanner.

Refer to **Interactive Graphic** in online course

1.2.9.3   More New Input Devices

Refer to **Interactive Graphic** in online course

1.2.9.4   Most Recent Input Devices

The newest input devices include NFC devices and terminals, facial recognition scanners, fingerprint scanners, voice recognition scanners, and virtual reality headsets.

Refer to **Interactive Graphic** in online course

1.2.9.5   Check Your Understanding - Input Devices

1.2.10   Output Devices

Refer to **Online Course** for Illustration

1.2.10.1   What are Output Devices?

An output device takes binary information (ones and zeroes) from the computer and converts it into a form that is easily understood by the user.

Monitors and projectors are output devices that create visual and audio signals for the user (Figure 1). Virtual Reality (VR) headsets are another type of output device. Televisions may also be output devices. Printers are visual output devices that create hard copies of computer files.

Speakers and headphones are output devices that produce only audio signals (Figure 2). Output devices make it possible for users to interact with computers.

Refer to **Online Course** for Illustration

1.2.10.2   Monitors and Projectors

Refer to **Online Course** for Illustration

1.2.10.3   VR and AR Headsets

Virtual Reality (VR) uses computer technology to create a simulated, three-dimensional environment. The user feels immersed in this 'virtual world' and manipulates it. A VR headset completely encases the upper portion of users' faces, not allowing in any ambient light from their surroundings. Most VR experiences have three-dimensional images that seem life-sized to the user. VR experiences also track a user's motions, and adjust the images on the user's display accordingly.

Augmented Reality (AR) uses similar technology but superimposes images and audio over the real world in real time. AR can provide users with immediate access to information about their real surroundings. An AR headset usually does not close off ambient light to users, allowing them to see their real life surroundings. Not all AR requires a headset. Some AR can simply be downloaded onto a smart phone. Pokemon GO is an early version of an AR game that uses a player's smart phone to 'see and capture' virtual objects in the real world. Other AR devices are smart glasses. They weigh much less than the headsets and are often designed for a specific audience, such as cyclists.

Refer to
Online Course
for Illustration

1.2.10.4   Printers

Printers are output devices that create hard copies of files. A hard copy might be a on a sheet of paper. It could also be a plastic form created from a 3D printer.

The figure shows a variety of printer types. Today's printers may be wired, wireless, or both. They use different technology to create the image you see. All printers require printing material (such as ink, toner, liquid plastic, etc.) and a method to place it accurately on the paper or extrude it into the desired shape. All printers have hardware that must be maintained. Most printers also have software, in the form of drivers that must be kept up to date.

Refer to
Online Course
for Illustration

1.2.10.5   Speakers and Headphones

Refer to
Interactive Graphic
in online course

1.2.10.6   Check Your Understanding - Visual and Auditory Output Device Characteristics

1.3   Computer Disassembly

1.3.1   The Technician's Toolkit

Refer to **Video**
in online course

1.3.1.1   Video Explanation - Technician's Toolkit

Click Play in the figure to view an explanation of the items in a technician's toolkit.

Click here to read the transcript of this video.

Refer to
Interactive Graphic
in online course

1.3.1.2   Check Your Understanding - Technician's Toolkit

1.3.2   Computer Disassembly

Refer to **Video**
in online course

1.3.2.1   Video Demonstration - Computer Disassembly

Click Play in the figure to view a demonstration of the disassembly of a computer.

Click here to read the transcript of this video.

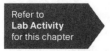
Refer to
Lab Activity
for this chapter

1.3.2.2 Lab - Disassemble a Computer

In this lab, you will disassemble a computer.

Lab - Disassemble a Computer

1.4 Summary

Refer to
Online Course
for Illustration

In the beginning of this chapter, you were introduced to the contents of a computer and the safety guidelines that can prevent electrical fires and injuries while working inside a computer. You also learned about ESD and how it can damage the computer equipment if not discharged properly.

Next, you learned about all the components that make up a PC starting with the case that houses all of the internal components. You learned about the various form factors of case and power supplies and how they have evolved over time. Next, the various types of connectors that are used to power various internal components such as the motherboard and storage drives, such as Serial AT Attachment (SATA), Molex, and PCIe were discussed as were the voltages provided by the connectors.

You also learned about motherboards, which is the backbone of the computer that contains buses, or electrical pathways, that connect electronic components. These components include the CPU, RAM, expansion slots, chipset, the BIOS and the UEFI chips.

Different types of storage devices such as hard disk drives, optical drives, and solid-state drives were also discussed along with the different versions of PATA and SATA interfaces that connect them to the motherboard.

The commonly used tools were explained, and the computer disassembly process was demonstrated. At the end of the chapter, you disassembled a computer as part of a hands-on lab.

Go to the online course to take the quiz and exam.

Chapter 1 Quiz

This quiz is designed to provide an additional opportunity to practice the skills and knowledge presented in the chapter and to prepare for the chapter exam. You will be allowed multiple attempts and the grade does not appear in the gradebook.

Chapter 1 Exam

The chapter exam assesses your knowledge of the chapter content.

Your Chapter Notes

PC Assembly

Refer to **Online Course** for Illustration

2.0 Introduction to PC Assembly

Assembling computers is often a large part of an IT technician's job. You must work in a logical, methodical manner when working with computer components. At times, you might have to determine whether a component for a customer's computer needs to be upgraded or replaced. It is important that you develop skills in installation procedures, troubleshooting techniques, and diagnostic methods. This chapter discusses the importance of component compatibility. It also covers the need for adequate system resources to efficiently run the customer's hardware and software. Computers, computer components, and computer peripherals all contain hazards that can cause severe injury. Therefore, this chapter begins with general and fire safety guidelines to follow when working with computer components.

In this chapter, you will learn about PC power supplies and the voltages they provide to other computer components. You will learn about the components that are installed on the motherboard; the CPU, RAM, and various adapter cards. You will learn about different CPU architectures and how to select RAM that is compatible with the motherboard and the chipset. You will also learn about various types of storage drives and the factors to consider when selecting the appropriate drive.

It is important to not only learn about assembling computer components but also to build hands-on skills. In this chapter there are several labs where you will assemble a computer. Each of the labs have you progressively install components such as the power supply, CPU, RAM, drives, adapter cards, and cables until computer assembly is complete.

2.1 Assemble the Computer

2.1.1 General and Fire Safety

Refer to **Video** in online course

2.1.1.1 Video Explanation - General and Fire Safety

Click Play in the figure to view a demonstration of general and fire safety.

Click here to read the transcript of this video.

2.1.2 Open the Case and Connect the Power Supply

Refer to **Video** in online course

2.1.2.1 Video Demonstration - Install the Power Supply

Click Play in the figure to view a demonstration of how to install the power supply.

Click here to read the transcript of this video.

Refer to
Interactive Graphic
in online course

Refer to
Interactive Graphic
in online course

2.1.2.2   Check Your Understanding - Install the Power Supply

2.1.2.3   Select the Case and Fans

The choice of motherboard and external components influences the selection of the case and power supply. The motherboard form factor must be matched with the correct type of computer case and power supply. For example, an ATX motherboard requires both an ATX-compatible case and power supply.

You can select a larger computer case to accommodate additional components that may be required in the future. Or you might select a smaller case that requires minimal space. In general, the computer case should be durable, easy to service, and have enough room for expansion.

Various factors affecting the choice of a computer case are described in Figure 1.

Cases often come with a power supply preinstalled. In this situation, you still need to verify that the power supply provides enough power to operate all the components that will be installed in the case.

A computer has many internal components that generate heat while the computer is running. Case fans should be installed to move cooler air into the computer case while moving heat out of the case. When choosing case fans, there are several factors to consider as described in Figure 2.

Note   The direction of air flow created by all the fans in the case must work together to inject cooler air and expel hotter air. Installing a fan backwards or using fans with the incorrect size or speed for the case can cause the air flows to work against each other.

Refer to
Online Course
for Illustration

2.1.2.4   Select a Power Supply

Power supplies convert AC input to DC output voltages. Power supplies typically provide voltages of 3.3V, 5V, and 12V, and are measured in wattage. The power supply must provide enough power for the installed components and allow for other components that may be added at a later time. If you choose a power supply that powers only the current components, you might need to replace the power supply when other components are upgraded.

The table in the figure describes various factors to consider when selecting a power supply.

Be careful when connecting the power supply cables to other components. If you have a difficult time inserting a connector, try repositioning it, or check to make sure that there are no bent pins or foreign objects in the way. If it is difficult to plug in a cable or other part, something is wrong. Cables, connectors, and components are designed to fit together snugly. Never force a connector or component. If a connector is plugged in incorrectly, it can damage the plug and the connector. Take your time and make sure that you are connecting the hardware correctly.

Note   Make sure to select a power supply with the proper connectors for the types of devices to be powered.

Refer to
Lab Activity
for this chapter

2.1.2.5   Lab - Install the Power Supply

In this lab, you will install a power supply in a computer case.

Lab - Install the Power Supply

2.1.3   Install the Motherboard Components

Refer to **Video**
in online course

2.1.3.1   Video Demonstration - Install the CPU

Click Play in the figure to view a demonstration of how to install the CPU.

Click here to read the transcript of this video.

Refer to
Interactive Graphic
in online course

2.1.3.2   Check Your Understanding - Install the CPU

Refer to **Video**
in online course

2.1.3.3   Video Demonstration - Install the RAM

Click Play in the figure to view a demonstration of how to install the RAM.

Click here to read the transcript of this video.

Refer to
Interactive Graphic
in online course

2.1.3.4   Check Your Understanding - Install the RAM

Refer to **Video**
in online course

2.1.3.5   Video Demonstration - Install the Motherboard

Click Play in the figure to view a demonstration of how to install the motherboard.

Click here to read the transcript of this video.

Refer to
Interactive Graphic
in online course

2.1.3.6   Check Your Understanding - Install the Motherboard

Refer to
Online Course
for Illustration

2.1.3.7   Select the Motherboard

New motherboards often have new features or standards that may be incompatible with older components. When you select a replacement motherboard, make sure that it supports the CPU, RAM, video adapter, and other adapter cards. The socket and chipset on the motherboard must be compatible with the CPU. The motherboard must also accommodate the existing heat sink and fan assembly when reusing the CPU. Pay particular attention to the number and type of expansion slots. Make sure that they match the existing adapter cards and allow for new cards that will be used. The existing power supply must have connections that fit the new motherboard. Finally, the new motherboard must physically fit into the current computer case.

When building a computer, choose a chipset that provides the capabilities that you need. For example, you can purchase a motherboard with a chipset that enables multiple USB ports, eSATA connections, surround sound, and video.

The CPU package must match the CPU socket type. A CPU package contains the CPU, connection points, and materials that surround the CPU and dissipate heat.

Data travels from one part of a computer to another through a collection of wires known as the bus. The bus has two parts. The data portion of the bus, known as the data bus, carries data between the computer components. The address portion, known as the address bus, carries the memory addresses of the locations where data is read or written by the CPU.

The bus size determines how much data can be transmitted at one time. A 32-bit bus transmits 32 bits of data at one time from the processor to RAM, or to other motherboard components, while a 64-bit bus transmits 64 bits of data at one time. The speed at which data travels through the bus is determined by the clock speed, measured in MHz or GHz.

PCI expansion slots connect to a parallel bus, which sends multiple bits over multiple wires simultaneously. PCI expansion slots are being replaced with PCIe expansion slots that connect to a serial bus, which sends one bit at a time at a much faster rate.

When building a computer, choose a motherboard that has slots to meet your current and future needs.

<table>
<tr><td>Refer to
Online Course
for Illustration</td></tr>
</table>

2.1.3.8   Select the CPU and CPU Cooling

Before you buy a CPU, make sure that it is compatible with the existing motherboard. Manufacturers' websites are a good resource to investigate the compatibility between CPUs and other devices. The table in Figure 1 lists the various sockets available and their supported processors. The speed of a modern processor is measured in GHz. A maximum speed rating refers to the maximum speed at which a processor can function without errors. Two primary factors can limit the speed of a processor:

The processor chip is a collection of transistors interconnected by wires. Transmitting data through the transistors and wires creates delays.

As the transistors change state from on to off or off to on, a small amount of heat is generated. The amount of heat generated increases as the speed of the processor increases. When the processor becomes too hot, it begins to produce errors.

The front-side bus (FSB) is the path between the CPU and the Northbridge. It is used to connect various components, such as the chipset, expansion cards, and RAM. Data can travel in both directions across the FSB. The frequency of the bus is measured in MHz. The frequency at which a CPU operates is determined by applying a clock multiplier to the FSB speed. For example, a processor running at 3200 MHz might be using a 400 MHz FSB. 3200 MHz divided by 400 MHz is 8, so the CPU is eight times faster than the FSB.

Processors are further classified as 32-bit and 64-bit. The primary difference is the number of instructions that can be handled by the processor at one time. A 64-bit processor processes more instructions per clock cycle than a 32-bit processor. A 64-bit processor can also support more memory. To utilize the 64-bit processor capabilities, ensure that the operating system and applications installed support a 64-bit processor.

The CPU is one of the most expensive and sensitive components in the computer case. The CPU can become very hot; therefore most CPUs require an air-cooled or liquid cooled heat sink, combined with a fan for cooling.

Figure 2 list several factors to consider when choosing a CPU cooling system.

<table>
<tr><td>Refer to
Online Course
for Illustration</td></tr>
</table>

2.1.3.9   Select the RAM

New RAM may be needed when an application locks up or the computer displays frequent error messages. When selecting new RAM, you must ensure that it is compatible with the current motherboard. Memory modules are commonly purchased in matched capacity pairs to support dual channel RAM that can be accessed at the same time. Also, the speed of the new RAM must be supported by the chipset. It may be helpful to take written notes about the original memory module when you shop for the replacement RAM.

Memory may also be categorized as unbuffered or buffered:

- **Unbuffered memory** - This is regular memory for computers. The computer reads data directly from the memory banks making it faster than buffered memory. However, there is a limit on the amount of RAM that can be installed.

- **Buffered memory** - This is specialized memory for servers and high-end workstations that use a large amount of RAM. These memory chips have a control chip built into the module. The control chip assists the memory controller in managing large quantities of RAM. Avoid buffered RAM for a gaming computer and the average workstation because the extra controller chip reduces RAM speed.

Refer to Lab Activity for this chapter

2.1.3.10   Lab - Install the Motherboard in a Computer

In this lab, you will install a CPU, a heat sink/fan assembly, and RAM module(s) on the motherboard. You will then install the motherboard in the computer case.

Lab - Install the Motherboard in a Computer

2.1.4   Install Internal Drives

Refer to Video in online course

2.1.4.1   Video Demonstration - Install the Drives

Click Play in the figure to view a demonstration of how to install the drives.

Click here to read the transcript of this video.

Refer to Online Course for Illustration

2.1.4.2   Select Hard Drives

You may need to replace an internal storage device when it no longer meets your customer's needs, or it fails. Signs that an internal storage device is failing might be unusual noises, unusual vibrations, error messages, or even corrupt data or applications that do not load.

Factors to consider when purchasing a new hard disk drive are listed in the figure.

Internal drives usually connect to the motherboard with SATA while external drives connect with USB, eSATA, or Thunderbolt. Legacy motherboards may only offer the IDE or EIDE interface. When selecting a HDD, it is important to choose one that is compatible with the interfaces offered by the motherboard.

Most internal HDDs are available in the 3.5 inch (8.9 cm) form factor, however 2.5 inch (6.4 cm) drives are becoming popular. SSDs are generally available in the 2.5 inch (6.4 cm) form factor.

Note   SATA and eSATA cables are similar but they are not interchangeable.

Refer to Online Course for Illustration

2.1.4.3   Select Optical Drives

Factors to consider when purchasing an optical drive are listed in Figure 1.

The table in Figure 2 summarizes optical drive capabilities.

DVDs hold significantly more data than CDs and Blu-ray discs (BD) store significantly more data than DVDs. DVDs and BDs can also have dual layers for recording data, essentially doubling the amount of data that can be recorded on the media.

Refer to
Online Course
for Illustration

2.1.4.4   Install the Hard Drive

A computer case holds drives in drive bays. The table in Figure 1 describes the three most common types of drive bays.

To install an HDD, find an empty hard drive bay in the case that will accommodate the width of the drive. Smaller drives can often be installed in wider drive bays using special trays or adapters.

When installing multiple drives in a case, it is recommended to maintain some space between the drives to help airflow and enhance cooling. Also, mount the drive with the metal side face up. This metal face helps to dissipate heat from the hard drive.

Installation Tip   Slightly hand-tighten all the screws before tightening any of them with a screw driver. This will make it easier to tighten the last two screws.

Refer to
Online Course
for Illustration

2.1.4.5   Install the Optical Drive

Optical drives are installed in 5.25 inch (13.34 cm.) drive bays that are accessed from the front of the case. The bays allow access to the media without opening the case. In new installations, the bays are covered with a plastic insert that keeps dust from entering the case. Remove the plastic cover prior to mounting the drive.

To install an optical drive, follow these steps:

Step 1.   From the front of the case, choose the drive bay that you want to hold the drive. Remove the faceplate from that bay if necessary.

Step 2.   Position the optical drive so that it aligns with the 5.25 inch (13.34 cm.) drive bay opening at the front of the case, as shown in the figure.

Step 3.   Insert the optical drive into the drive bay so that the optical drive screw holes align with the screw holes in the case.

Step 4.   Secure the optical drive to the case using the proper screws.

Installation Tip   Slightly hand-tighten all the screws before tightening any of them with a screw driver. This will make it easier to tighten the last two screws.

Refer to
Interactive Graphic
in online course

2.1.4.6   Check Your Understanding - Installing Drives

Refer to
Lab Activity
for this chapter

2.1.4.7   Lab - Install the Drives

In this lab, you will install hard drive and an optical drive in a computer case.

Lab - Install the Drives

2.1.5   Install the Adapter Cards

Refer to **Video**
in online course

2.1.5.1   Video Demonstration - Install the Adapter Cards

Click Play in the figure to view a demonstration of how to install adapter cards.

Click here to read the transcript of this video.

Refer to
Online Course
for Illustration

2.1.5.2   Select Adapter Cards

Many of the functions of the hardware of a computer are found onboard the motherboard, such as audio, USB, or network connection. Adapter cards, also called expansion cards or add-on cards, are designed for a specific task and add extra functionality to a computer. They can also be installed when an onboard function has failed. There are a variety of adapter cards available that are used to expand and customize the capability of a computer.

The following list provides an overview of expansion cards that may be upgraded:

- **Graphics card** - The type of graphics card installed affects the overall performance of a computer. For example, a graphics card that needs to support intensive graphics could be RAM intensive, CPU intensive, or both. The computer must have the slots, RAM, and CPU to support the full functionality of an upgraded graphics card. Choose the graphics card based on current and future needs. For example, to play 3D games, the graphics card must meet or exceed the minimum requirements. Some GPUs are integrated into the CPU. When the GPU is integrated into the CPU, there is no need to purchase a graphics card unless advanced video features, such as 3D graphics, or very high resolution are required.

- **Sound card** - The type of sound card installed determines the sound quality of your computer. A computer system must have quality speakers and a subwoofer to support the full functionality of an upgraded sound card. Choose the correct sound card based on your customer's current and future needs. For example, if a customer wants to hear a specific type of surround sound, the sound card must have the correct hardware decoder to reproduce it. In addition, the customer can get improved sound accuracy with a sound card that has a higher sample rate.

- **Storage controller** - Storage controllers can be integrated or added as an expansion card. They allow for the expansion of internal and external drives for a computer system. Storage controllers, such as RAID controllers, can also provide fault tolerance or increased speed. The amount of data and the level of data protection needed for the customer influences the type of storage controller required. Choose the correct storage controller based on your customer's current and future needs. For example, if a customer wants to implement RAID 5, a RAID storage controller with at least three drives is needed.

- **I/O card** - Installing an I/O card in a computer is a fast and easy way to add I/O ports. USB are some of the most common ports to install on a computer. Choose the correct I/O card based on your customer's current and future needs. For example, if a customer wants to add an internal card reader, and the motherboard has no internal USB connection, a USB I/O card with an internal USB connection is needed.

- **NIC** - Customers often upgrade a network interface card (NIC) to get wireless connectivity or to increase bandwidth.

■ **Capture card** - A capture card imports video into a computer and records it on a hard drive. The addition of a capture card with a television tuner allows you to view and record television programming. The computer system must have enough CPU power, adequate RAM, and a high-speed storage system to support the capture, recording, and editing demands of the customer. Choose the correct capture card based on your customer's current and future needs. For example, if a customer wants to record one program while watching another, either multiple capture cards or a capture card with multiple TV tuners must be installed.

Adapter cards are inserted into two types of expansion slots on a motherboard:

■ **Peripheral Component Interconnect (PCI)** - PCI is commonly available to support older expansion cards.

■ **PCI Express (PCIe)** - PCIe has four types of slots; x1, x4, x8, and x16. These PCIe slots vary in length from shortest (X1) to longest (x16) respectively.

The figure displays the different types of expansion slots.

Note If the motherboard does not have a compatible expansion slot, an external device may be an option.

Refer to
Interactive Graphic
in online course

2.1.5.3 Other Factors for Adapter Card Selection

Before purchasing an adapter card, consider the following questions:

■ What are the user's current and future needs?

■ Is there an open and compatible expansion slot available?

■ What are the possible configuration options?

Refer to
Online Course
for Illustration

2.1.5.4 Install the Adapter Cards

Expansion cards are installed into an empty but appropriate slot on a computer motherboard.

For example, a wireless NIC enables a computer to connect to a wireless (Wi-Fi) network. Wireless NICs can be integrated into the motherboard, connected using a USB connector, or installed using a PCI or PCIe expansion slots on the motherboard.

Many video adapter cards require separate power from the power supply using a 6-pin or 8-pin power connector. Some cards may need two of these connectors. If possible, provide some space between the video adapter and other expansion cards. Video adapters create excessive heat, which is often moved away from the card with a fan.

Installation Tip Research the length of the video card (and other adapter cards) before purchase. Longer cards may not be compatible with certain motherboards. Chips and other electronics may stand in the way of the adapter card when trying to seat them in the expansion slot. Some cases might also limit the size of adapter cards that can be installed. Some adapter cards may come with mounting brackets of different heights to accommodate these cases.

Installation Tip   Some cases have small slots at the bottom of the hole where the cover was removed. Slide the bottom of the mounting bracket into this slot before seating the card.

Refer to
Interactive Graphic
in online course

2.1.5.5   Check Your Understanding - Installing Adapter Cards

Refer to
Lab Activity
for this chapter

2.1.5.6   Lab - Install Adapter Card

In this lab, you will install a NIC, a wireless NIC, and a video adapter card.

Lab - Install Adapter Card

2.1.6   Select Additional Storage

Refer to
Online Course
for Illustration

2.1.6.1   Select a Media Reader

Many digital devices such as cameras, smart phones, and tablets use media cards to store information, music, pictures, videos, data, and more.

Several media card formats have been developed over the years including:

- **Secure digital (SD)** - SD cards were designed for use in portable devices such as cameras, MP3 players, and laptops. SD cards can hold as much as 2 TB of data.

- **MicroSD** - This is a much smaller version of SD, commonly used in smartphones and tablets.

- **MiniSD** - A version of SD between the size of an SD card and a microSD card. The format was developed for mobile phones.

- **CompactFlash** - CompactFlash is an older format, but still in wide use because of its high speed and high capacity (up to 128 GB is common). CompactFlash is often used as storage for video cameras.

- **Memory Stick** - Created by Sony Corporation, Memory Stick is a proprietary flash memory used in cameras, MP3 players, hand-held video game systems, mobile phones, cameras, and other portable electronics.

- **xD** - Also known as Picture Card, it was used in some digital cameras.

Figure 1 displays some of these media cards.

It is useful to have an internal or external device that can be used to read or write to media cards. When purchasing or replacing a media reader, ensure that it supports the types of media cards that will be used.

Figure 2 displays an external media card reader and lists factors to consider when purchasing a media reader.

Choose the correct media reader based on your customer's current and future needs. For example, if a customer needs to use multiple types of media cards, a multiple format media reader is needed.

Refer to
Online Course
for Illustration

2.1.6.2   Select External Storage

External storage offers portability and convenience when working with multiple computers. External USB flash drives, sometimes called thumb drives, are commonly used as removable external storage. External storage devices connect to an external port using USB, eSATA, or Thunderbolt ports.

The figure displays an external flash drive and lists factors to consider when purchasing an external storage solution.

Choose the correct type of external storage for your customer's needs. For example, if your customer needs to transfer a small amount of data, such as a single presentation, an external flash drive is a good choice. If your customer needs to back up or transfer large amounts of data, choose an external hard drive.

Refer to
Interactive Graphic
in online course

2.1.6.3   Check Your Understanding - Media Cards

2.1.7   Install the Cables

Refer to **Video**
in online course

2.1.7.1   Video Demonstration - Connect the Internal Power Cables

Click Play in the figure to view a demonstration of how to connect internal power cables.

Click here to read the transcript of this video.

Refer to
Interactive Graphic
in online course

2.1.7.2   Check Your Understanding - Identify the Power Connectors

Refer to **Video**
in online course

2.1.7.3   Video Demonstration - Connect the Internal Data Cables

Click Play in the figure to view a demonstration of how to connect internal data cables.

Click here to read the transcript of this video.

Refer to
Lab Activity
for this chapter

2.1.7.4   Lab - Install Internal Cables

In this lab, install the internal power and data cables in the computer.

Lab - Install Internal Cables

Refer to **Video**
in online course

2.1.7.5   Video Demonstration - Install the Front Panel Cables

Click Play in the figure to view a demonstration of how to connect the front panel cables.

Click here to read the transcript of this video.

Refer to
Online Course
for Illustration

2.1.7.6   Install the Front Panel Cables

A computer case typically has a power button and visible activity lights on the front of the case. The case will include front panel cables that must be connected to a common system panel connector on a motherboard as shown in Figure 1. Writing on the motherboard near the system panel connector shows where each cable is connected.

System panel connectors include:

- **Power Button** - The power button turns the computer on or off. If the power button fails to turn off the computer, hold down the power button for several (i.e., 5 or more) seconds.

■ **Reset Button** - The reset button (if available) restarts the computer without turning it off.

■ **Power LED** - The power LED remains lit when the computer is on, and often blinks when the computer is in sleep mode.

■ **Drive Activity LEDs** - The drive activity LED remains lit or blinks when the system is reading or writing to hard drives.

■ **System Speaker** - The motherboard uses a case speaker (if available) to indicate the computer's status. For example, one beep indicates that the computer started without problems. If there is a hardware problem, a series of diagnostic beeps is issued to indicate the type of problem. It is important to note that the system speaker is not the same as the speakers the computer uses to play music and other audio. The system speaker cable typically uses four pins on the system panel connector.

■ **Audio** - Some cases have audio ports and jacks on the outside to connect microphones, external audio equipment such as signal processors, mixing boards, and instruments. Special audio panels can also be purchased and connected directly to the motherboard. These panels can install into one or more external drive bays, or be standalone panels.

System panel connectors are not keyed. However, each front panel cable usually has a small arrow indicating pin 1, and each pair of LED pins on the motherboard system panel connector has pin 1 marked with a plus sign (+), as shown in Figure 2.

Note   The markings on your front panel cables and system panel connectors may be different than what is shown as no standards for labeling the case cables or the system panel connectors are defined. Always consult the motherboard manual for diagrams and additional information about connecting front panel cables.

New cases and motherboards have USB 3.0 or may even have USB 3.1 capabilities. The USB 3.0 and 3.1 motherboard connector is similar in design to a USB connector, but has additional pins. USB connector cables are often 9 or 10 pins arranged in two rows. These cables connect to USB motherboard connectors as shown in Figure 3. This arrangement allows for two USB connections, so USB connectors are often in pairs. Sometimes the two connectors are together in one piece, as shown in the figure, and can be connected to the entire USB motherboard connector. USB connectors can also have four or five pins or individual groups of four or five pins. Most USB devices only require the connection of four pins. The fifth pin is used to ground the shielding of some USB cables.

Caution   Make sure that the motherboard connector is marked USB. FireWire connectors are very similar. Connecting a USB cable to a FireWire connector will cause damage.

The table in Figure 4 provides connecting notes on various front panel connections.

Generally, if a button or LED does not function, the connector is incorrectly oriented. To correct this, shut down the computer and unplug it, open the case, and turn the connector around for the button or LED that does not function. To avoid wiring incorrectly, some manufacturers include a keyed pin extender that combines multiple front-panel cables (i.e., power and reset LEDs) connectors into one connector.

Installation Tip   The panel connector and case cable ends are very small. Take pictures of them to locate pin 1. Because space in the case can be limited at the end of assembly, a part retriever can be used to plug the cables into the connectors.

Refer to **Interactive Graphic** in online course

2.1.7.7   Checking Your Understanding - Identify the Front Panel Cables

Refer to **Lab Activity** for this chapter

2.1.7.8   Lab - Install the Front Panel Cables

In this lab, you will install the front panel cables in the computer.

Lab - Install the Front Panel Cables

Refer to **Video** in online course

2.1.7.9   Video Demonstration - Complete the Computer Assembly

Click Play in the figure to view a demonstration of how to reassemble the case and install the external cables.

Click here to read the transcript of this video.

Refer to **Interactive Graphic** in online course

2.1.7.10   Check Your Understanding - Identify the External Connectors

Refer to **Lab Activity** for this chapter

2.1.7.11   Lab - Complete the Computer Assembly

In this lab, you will install the side panels and the external cables on the computer.

Lab - Complete the Computer Assembly

2.2   Summary

In this chapter you learned that assembling computers is often a large part of a technician's job and that as a technician, you must work in a logical, methodical manner when working with computer components. For example, the choice of motherboard and external components influences the selection of the case and power supply and the motherboard form factor must be matched with the correct type of computer case and power supply.

You learned that PC power supplies convert AC input to DC output voltages. Power supplies typically provide voltages of 3.3V, 5V, and 12V to power the various internal components of the computer and that the power supply must have the proper connectors for the motherboard and the various types of devices to be powered.

After learning about power supplies, you installed a power supply as well as other internal components including a CPU and RAM. You learned that when you select a motherboard it must support the CPU, RAM, video adapter, and other adapter cards and that the socket and chipset on the motherboard must be compatible with the CPU. The motherboard sockets may be designed to support Intel CPUs, which support an LGA architecture, or AMD CPUs which support a PGA architecture.

In addition to learning about CPU architectures, you also learned that when selecting new RAM, it must be compatible with the motherboard and that the speed of the RAM must be supported by the chipset. You then performed labs where you installed a CPU, a heat sink/fan assembly, and RAM modules on the motherboard. You also installed the motherboard assembly into the computer case.

Next, you learned about the various types of storage drives, such as internal drives, external drives, hard-disk drives, solid-state drives, and optical drives and the factors to consider when selecting the appropriate drive. You then installed drives in the computer case.

Finally, you learned about adapter cards, which are also called expansion cards, or add-on cards. There are many types of adapter cards and each is designed for a specific task and to add extra functionality to a computer. The chapter covered graphics cards, sound cards, storage controllers, I/O cards, and NICs. These adapter cards are inserted into two types of expansion slots on a motherboard: PCI and PCIe. At the end of the chapter, there were labs where you installed an adapter card, connected the appropriate internal power cables, front panel connectors, and performed final computer assembly.

Go to the online course to take the quiz and exam.

Chapter 2 Quiz

This quiz is designed to provide an additional opportunity to practice the skills and knowledge presented in the chapter and to prepare for the chapter exam. You will be allowed multiple attempts and the grade does not appear in the gradebook.

Chapter 2 Exam

The chapter exam assesses your knowledge of the chapter content.

Your Chapter Notes

Advanced Computer Hardware

Refer to
Online Course
for Illustration

3.0 Introduction to Advanced Computer Hardware

A Technician's knowledge must extend beyond knowing how to assemble a computer. You need to have in-depth knowledge of computer system architecture and how each component operates and interacts with other components. This depth of knowledge is necessary when you have to upgrade a computer with new components that must be compatible with existing components and also when you build computers for very specialized applications. This chapter covers the computer boot process, protecting the computer from power fluctuations, multicore processors, redundancy through multiple storage drives, and protecting the environment from hazardous materials found inside of computer components.

You will learn about the computer boot process including the power on self-test (POST) conducted by the BIOS. Explore various BIOS and UEFI settings and how they impact this process. You will explore basic electrical theory and Ohm's law and calculate voltage, current, resistance, and power. Power fluctuations can damage computer components so you will learn how to mitigate the risk of power fluctuations with surge protectors, uninterruptible power supplies (UPSs), and standby power supplies (SPSs). You will learn how to provide storage redundancy and load balancing using redundant arrays of independent disks (RAID). You will also learn how to upgrade computer components and configure specialized computers. Finally, after upgrading a computer, technicians must dispose of the old parts properly. Many computer components contain hazardous materials, such as mercury and rare earth metals in batteries and deadly voltage levels in power supplies. You will learn the risks posed by these components and how to dispose of them properly.

In this chapter, there is a lab where you research hardware upgrades to a computer system. You will use several sources to gather information about the computer hardware components and make recommendations for upgraded components. You will also discuss your recommended upgrade choices

3.1 Boot the Computer

3.1.1 POST, BIOS, CMOS and UEFI

Refer to **Video**
in online course

3.1.1.1 Video Demonstration - BIOS - UEFI Menus

Click Play in the figure to view a demonstration of a BIOS/UEFI program.

Click here to read the transcript of this video.

Refer to
Online Course
for Illustration

3.1.1.2 POST

When a computer is booted, the basic input/output system (BIOS) performs a hardware check on the main components of the computer. This check is called a power-on self-test (POST).

For instance, Figure 1 displays a screen capture of a sample POST being performed. Notice how the computer checks whether the computer hardware is operating correctly.

If a device is malfunctioning, an error or a beep code alerts the technician of the problem. If there is a hardware problem, a blank screen might appear at bootup, and the computer will emit a series of beeps.

BIOS manufacturers use different codes to indicate hardware problems. Figure 2 shows a chart of common beep codes. However, motherboard manufacturers may use different beep codes. Always consult the motherboard documentation to get the beep codes for your computer.

Installation Tip   To determine if POST is working properly, remove all of the RAM modules from the computer and power it on. The computer should emit the beep code for a computer with no RAM installed. This will not harm the computer.

Refer to **Online Course** for Illustration

3.1.1.3   BIOS and CMOS

All motherboards need BIOS to operate. BIOS is a ROM chip on the motherboard that contains a small program. This program controls the communication between the operating system and the hardware.

Along with the POST, BIOS also identifies:

- Which drives are available
- Which drives are bootable
- How the memory is configured and when it can be used
- How PCIe and PCI expansion slots are configured
- How SATA and USB ports are configured
- Motherboard power management features

The motherboard manufacturer saves the motherboard BIOS settings in a Complementary Metal Oxide Semiconductor (CMOS) memory chip such as the one shown in Figure 1.

When a computer boots, the BIOS software reads the configured settings stored in CMOS to determine how to configure the hardware.

The BIOS settings are retained by CMOS using a battery, such as the one shown in Figure 2. However, if the battery fails, important settings can be lost. Therefore, it is recommended that BIOS settings always be documented.

Note   An easy way to document these settings is to take pictures of the various BIOS settings.

Installation Tip   If the computer's time and date are incorrect, it could indicate that the CMOS battery is bad or is getting very low.

Refer to **Online Course** for Illustration

3.1.1.4   UEFI

Most computers today run Unified Extensible Firmware Interface (UEFI). All new computers come with UEFI, which provides additional features and addresses security issues with legacy BIOS. You may see "BIOS/UEFI" when booting into your BIOS settings. This is because Intel chips currently support backwards compatibility with legacy BIOS systems. However, by 2020, Intel will end support for legacy BIOS. For more information, do an internet search for "Intel to remove legacy BIOS".

Note   This section uses BIOS, UEFI, and BIOS/UEFI interchangeably. In addition, manufacturers may continue to label their UEFI programs with "BIOS" so that users know it supports the same functions.

UEFI configures the same settings as traditional BIOS but also provides additional options. For example, UEFI can provide a mouse-enabled software interface instead of the traditional BIOS screens. However, most systems have a text-based interface, similar to legacy BIOS systems.

UEFI can run on 32-bit and 64-bit systems, supports larger boot drives and includes additional features such as secure boot. Secure boot ensures your computer boots to your specified operating system. This helps prevent rootkits from taking over the system. For more information, do an internet search for "Secure boot and rootkits".

Note   The UEFI setup screens in this section are for reference only and most likely will not look the same as yours. Please consider them as a guide and refer to your motherboard manufacturer documents.

Refer to
Interactive Graphic
in online course

3.1.1.5   Check Your Understanding - BIOS and UEFI Terminology

Refer to
Lab Activity
for this chapter

3.1.1.6   Lab - Investigate BIOS or UEFI Settings

In this lab, you will boot the computer, explore the firmware setup utility program, and change the boot order sequence.

Lab - Investigate BIOS or UEFI Settings

3.1.2   BIOS/UEFI Configuration

Refer to **Video**
in online course

3.1.2.1   Video Demonstration - Configure BIOS - UEFI Settings

Click Play in the figure to view a demonstration of how to configure a BIOS program.

Click here to read the transcript of this video.

Refer to
Online Course
for Illustration

3.1.2.2   BIOS and UEFI Security

The legacy BIOS supports some security features to protect the BIOS setting. UEFI adds additional security features. These are some common security features found in the BIOS/UEFI systems:

- **Passwords** - Passwords allow for different levels of access to the BIOS settings. Usually, there are two password settings that can be altered; the Supervisor Password and the User Password. The Supervisor Password can access all user-access passwords and all BIOS screens and settings. The User Password gives access to the BIOS based on a defined level. The table in Figure 1 displays common levels of user access to BIOS. The Supervisor Password must be set before the User Password can be configured.

- **Drive encryption** - A hard drive can be encrypted to prevent data theft. Encryption changes the data on the drive into code. Without the correct password, the computer cannot boot and data read from the hard drive cannot be understood. Even if the hard drive is placed in another computer, the data remains encrypted.

- **LoJack** - This is a security feature that consists of two programs; the Persistence Module and the Application Agent. The Persistence Module is embedded in the BIOS while the Application Agent is installed by the user. When installed, the Persistence Module in the BIOS is activated and cannot be turned off. The Application Agent routinely contacts a monitoring center over the internet to report device information and location. The owner can perform the functions described in Figure 2.

- **Trusted Platform Module (TPM)** - This is a chip designed to secure hardware by storing encryption keys, digital certificates, passwords, and data. TPM is used by Windows to support BitLocker full-disk encryption.

- **Secure boot** - Secure Boot is a UEFI security standard that ensures that a computer only boots an OS that is trusted by the motherboard manufacturer. Secure boot prevents an "unauthorized" OS from loading during startup.

3.1.2.3   Update the Firmware

Refer to Online Course for Illustration

Motherboard manufacturers may publish updated BIOS versions to provide enhancements to system stability, compatibility, and performance. However, updating the firmware is risky. The release notes, such as those shown in the figure, describe the upgrade to the product, compatibility improvements, and the known bugs that have been addressed. Some newer devices operate properly only with an updated BIOS installed. You can usually find the current version on the main screen of the BIOS/UEFI interface.

Before updating motherboard firmware, record the manufacturer of the BIOS and the motherboard model. Use this information to identify the exact files to download from the motherboard manufacturer's site. Only update the firmware if there are problems with the system hardware or to add functionality to the system.

Early computer BIOS information was contained in ROM chips. To upgrade the BIOS information, the ROM chip had to be physically replaced, which was not always possible. Modern BIOS chips are Electronically Erasable Programmable Read Only Memory (EEPROM) which can be upgraded by the user without opening the computer case. This process is called flashing the BIOS.

To download a new BIOS, consult the manufacturer's website and follow the recommended installation procedures. Installing BIOS software online may involve downloading a new BIOS file, copying or extracting files to removable media, and then booting from the removable media. An installation program prompts the user for information to complete the process.

Many motherboard manufacturers now provide software to flash the BIOS from within an operating system. For example, the ASUS EZ Update utility automatically updates a motherboard's software, drivers, and the BIOS version. It also enables a user to manually update a saved BIOS and select a boot logo when the system goes into POST. The utility is included with the motherboard, or it can be downloaded from the ASUS website.

Caution An improperly installed or aborted BIOS update can cause the computer to become unusable.

Refer to
Interactive Graphic
in online course

3.1.2.4 Check Your Understanding - BIOS and UEFI Configuration Terminology

Refer to
Lab Activity
for this chapter

3.1.2.5 Lab - Search for BIOS or UEFI Firmware Updates

In this lab, you will identify the current BIOS or UEFI version and then search for BIOS or UEFI update files.

Lab - Search for BIOS or UEFI Firmware Updates

Refer to
Lab Activity
for this chapter

3.1.2.6 Lab - Install Windows

In this lab, you will perform a basic installation of Windows.

Lab - Install Windows

Refer to
Lab Activity
for this chapter

3.1.2.7 Lab - Install Third-Party Software in Windows

In this lab, you will install third-party software.

Lab - Install Third-Party Software in Windows

3.2 Electrical Power

3.2.1 Wattage and Voltage

Refer to
Online Course
for Illustration

3.2.1.1 Wattage and Voltage

Power supply specifications are typically expressed in watts (W). To understand what a watt is, refer to the interactive image which describes the four basic units of electricity that a computer technician must know.

A basic equation, known as Ohm's Law, expresses how voltage is equal to the current multiplied by the resistance: $V = IR$. In an electrical system, power is equal to the voltage multiplied by the current: $P = VI$.

Refer to
Online Course
for Illustration

3.2.1.2 Power Supply Voltage Setting

On the back of some power supplies is a small switch called the voltage selector switch, as shown in the image. This switch sets the input voltage to the power supply to either 110V / 115V or 220V / 230V. A power supply with this switch is called a dual voltage power supply. The correct voltage setting is determined by the country where the power supply is used. Setting the voltage switch to the incorrect input voltage could damage the power supply and other parts of your computer. If a power supply does not have this switch, it automatically detects and sets the correct voltage.

Caution Do not open a power supply. Electronic capacitors located inside of a power supply can hold a charge for extended periods of time.

For more information about power supplies, click here.

Refer to
Lab Activity
for this chapter

3.2.1.3   Lab - Ohm's Law

In this lab, you will answer questions based on electricity and Ohm's Law.

Lab - Ohm's Law

3.2.2   Power Fluctuation and Protection

Refer to
Online Course
for Illustration

3.2.2.1   Power Fluctuation Types

Voltage is a measure of energy required to move a charge from one location to another. The movement of electrons is called current. Computer circuits need voltage and current to operate electronic components. When the voltage in a computer is not accurate or steady, computer components might not operate correctly. Unsteady voltages are called power fluctuations.

The following types of AC power fluctuations can cause data loss or hardware failure:

- **Blackout** - Complete loss of AC power. A blown fuse, damaged transformer, or downed power line can cause a blackout.

- **Brownout** - Reduced voltage level of AC power that lasts for a period of time. Brownouts occur when the power line voltage drops below 80 percent of the normal voltage level and when electrical circuits are overloaded.

- **Noise** - Interference from generators and lightning. Noise results in poor quality power, which can cause errors in a computer system.

- **Spike** - Sudden increase in voltage that lasts for a short period and exceeds 100 percent of the normal voltage on a line. Spikes can be caused by lightning strikes, but can also occur when the electrical system comes back on after a blackout.

- **Power surge** - Dramatic increase in voltage above the normal flow of electrical current. A power surge lasts for a few nanoseconds, or one-billionth of a second.

Refer to
Online Course
for Illustration

3.2.2.2   Power Protection Devices

To help shield against power fluctuation problems, use devices to protect the data and computer equipment:

- **Surge protector** - Helps protect against damage from surges and spikes. A surge suppressor diverts extra electrical voltage that is on the line to the ground. The amount of protection offered by a surge protector is measured in joules. The higher the joule rating, the more energy over time the surge protector can absorb. Once the number of joules is reached, the surge protector no longer provides protection and will need to be replaced.

- **Uninterruptible power supply (UPS)** - Helps protect against potential electrical power problems by supplying a consistent level of electrical power to a computer or other device. The battery is constantly recharging while the UPS is in use. The UPS provides a consistent quality of power when brownouts and blackouts occur. Many UPS devices can communicate directly with the computer operating system. This communication allows the UPS to safely shut down the computer and save data prior to the UPS losing all battery power.

- **Standby power supply (SPS)** - Helps protect against potential electrical power problems by providing a backup battery to supply power when the incoming voltage drops below the normal level. The battery is on standby during normal operation. When the voltage decreases, the battery provides DC power to a power inverter, which converts it to AC power for the computer. This device is not as reliable as a UPS because of the time it takes to switch over to the battery. If the switching device fails, the battery cannot supply power to the computer.

Caution   UPS manufacturers suggest never plugging a laser printer into a UPS because the printer could overload the UPS.

Refer to
Interactive Graphic
in online course

3.2.2.3   Check Your Understanding - Power Fluctuation Terms

3.3   Advanced Computer Functionality

3.3.1   CPU Architectures and Operation

Refer to
Online Course
for Illustration

3.3.1.1   CPU Architectures

A program is a sequence of stored instructions. A CPU executes these instructions by following a specific instruction set.

There are two distinct types of instruction sets that CPUs may use:

- **Reduced Instruction Set Computer (RISC)** - This architecture uses a relatively small set of instructions. RISC chips are designed to execute these instructions very rapidly. Some well-known CPUs using RISC are PowerPC and ARM.

- **Complex Instruction Set Computer (CISC)** - This architecture uses a broad set of instructions, resulting in fewer steps per operation. Intel x86 and Motorola 68k are some well-known CPUs using CISC.

While the CPU is executing one step of the program, the remaining instructions and the data are stored nearby in a special, high-speed memory, called cache.

Refer to
Online Course
for Illustration

3.3.1.2   Enhancing CPU Operation

Various CPU manufacturers complement their CPU with performance-enhancing features. For instance, Intel incorporates Hyper-Threading to enhance the performance of some of their CPUs. With Hyper-Threading, multiple pieces of code (threads) are executed simultaneously in the CPU. To an operating system, a single CPU with Hyper-Threading performs as though there are two CPUs when multiple threads are being processed. AMD processors use HyperTransport to enhance CPU performance. HyperTransport is a high-speed connection between the CPU and the Northbridge chip.

The power of a CPU is measured by the speed and the amount of data that it can process. The speed of a CPU is rated in cycles per second, such as millions of cycles per second, called megahertz (MHz), or billions of cycles per second, called gigahertz (GHz). The amount of data that a CPU can process at one time depends on the size of the front side bus (FSB). This is also called the CPU bus or the processor data bus. Higher performance can be achieved when the width of the FSB increases, much like a roadway can carry more cars when it has many lanes. The width of the FSB is measured in bits. A bit is the smallest unit of data in a computer. Current processors use a 32-bit or 64-bit FSB.

Overclocking is a technique used to make a processor work at a faster speed than its original specification. Overclocking is not a recommended way to improve computer performance and can result in damage to the CPU. The opposite of overclocking is CPU throttling. CPU throttling is a technique used when the processor runs at less than the rated speed to conserve power or produce less heat. Throttling is commonly used on laptops and other mobile devices.

CPU virtualization is a hardware feature supported by AMD and Intel CPUs that enables a single processor to act as multiple processors. This hardware virtualization technology allows the operating system to support virtualization more effectively and efficiently than is possible through software emulation. With CPU virtualization multiple operating systems can run in parallel on their own virtual machines as if they were running on completely independent computers. CPU virtualization is sometimes disabled by default in the BIOS and will need to be enabled.

Refer to Online Course for Illustration

3.3.1.3   Multicore Processors

The latest processor technology has resulted in CPU manufacturers finding ways to incorporate more than one CPU core into a single chip. Multicore processors have two or more processors on the same integrated circuit. In some architectures, the cores have separate L2 and L3 cache resources, while in other architectures cache is shared among the different cores for better performance and resource allocation. The table in the figure describes the various types of multicore processors.

Integrating the processors on the same chip creates a very fast connection between them. Multicore processors execute instructions more quickly than single-core processors. Instructions can be distributed to all the processors at the same time. RAM is shared between the processors because the cores reside on the same chip. A multicore processor is recommended for applications such as video editing, gaming, and photo manipulation.

High-power consumption creates more heat in the computer case. Multicore processors conserve power and produce less heat than multiple single-core processors, thus increasing performance and efficiency.

Another feature found in some CPUs is an integrated graphics processing unit or GPU. The GPU is a chip that performs the rapid mathematical calculations required to render graphics. A GPU can be integrated or dedicated. Integrated GPUs are often directly embedded on the CPU and is dependent on system RAM while the dedicated GPU is a separate chip with its own video memory dedicated exclusively for graphical processing. The benefit of integrated GPUs is cost and less heat dissipation. This allows for cheaper computers and smaller form factors. The trade off is performance. Integrated GPUs are good at less complex tasks like watching videos and processing graphical documents but are not best suited for intense gaming applications.

CPUs have also been enhanced using the NX bit, also called the execute disable bit. This feature, when supported and enabled in the operating system, can protect areas of memory that contain operating system files from malicious attacks by malware.

Refer to
Interactive Graphic
in online course

3.3.1.4   CPU Cooling Mechanisms

Refer to
Interactive Graphic
in online course

3.3.1.5   Check Your Understanding - CPU Architectures and Operation

3.3.2   RAID

Refer to
Interactive Graphic
in online course

3.3.2.1   What Do You Already Know? - RAID

Refer to
Online Course
for Illustration

3.3.2.2   RAID Concepts

Storage devices can be grouped and managed to create large storage volumes with redundancy. To do so, computers can implement redundant array of independent disks (RAID) technology. RAID provides a way to store data across multiple storage devices for availability, reliability, capacity, and redundancy and/or performance improvement. In addition, it may be more economical to create an array of smaller devices than it is to purchase a single device of the combined capacity provided by the RAID, especially for very large drives. To the operating system, a RAID array appears as one drive.

The following terms describe how RAID stores data on the various disks:

- **Striping** - This RAID type enables data to be distributed across multiple drives. This provides a significant performance increase. However, since the data is distributed across multiple drives, the failure of a single drive means that all data is lost.

- **Mirroring** - This RAID type stores duplicate data on one or more other drives. This provides redundancy so that the failure of a drive does not cause the loss of data. The Mirror can be recreated by replacing the drive and restoring the data from the good drive.

- **Parity** - This RAID type provides basic error checking and fault tolerance by storing checksums separately from data. This enables the reconstruction of lost data without sacrificing speed and capacity, like mirroring.

- **Double Parity** - This RAID type provides fault tolerance up to two failed drives.

The figure shows a large drive enclosure that could be used in a data center with one or more RAID implementations. Drive enclosures can use hot swappable drives. This means that a drive that fails can be replaced without powering down the entire RAID. Powering down the RAID may make the data on the RAID unavailable to users for an extended period of time. Not all drives and RAID types support hot swapping.

Refer to
Online Course
for Illustration

3.3.2.3   RAID Levels

There are several levels of RAID available. These levels use mirroring, striping, and parity in different ways. Higher levels of RAID, such as RAID 5 or 6, use striping and parity in combination to provide speed and to create large volumes. The figure shows the details about the RAID levels. RAID levels higher than 10 combine lower RAID levels. For example. RAID 10 combines RAID 1 and RAID 0 functionalities.

Refer to
Interactive Graphic
in online course

3.3.2.4   Check Your Understanding - RAID Levels

3.3.3 Ports, Connectors, and Cables

Refer to **Interactive Graphic** in online course

3.3.3.1 Legacy Ports

Computers have many different types of ports to connect the computer to external peripheral devices. As computer technology has evolved, so have the types of ports used to connect peripheral devices. Legacy ports are typically found on older computers and have been mostly replaced by newer technologies such as USB.

3.3.3.2 Video and Graphic Ports

Refer to **Video** in online course

Video and Graphic Ports

Graphic ports are used to connect monitors and external video displays to desktop computers and laptops.

Refer to **Interactive Graphic** in online course

3.3.3.3 USB Cables and Connectors

Over the years, the USB protocol has evolved and the various standards can be confusing. USB 1.0 provided a low-speed transfer rate at 1.5 Mbps for keyboards and mice and a full-speed channel at 12 Mbps. USB 2.0 made a significant leap, increasing transfer rates up to High Speed at 480 Mbps. USB 3.0 increased the transfer rate to SuperSpeed 5 Gbps, and USB 3.2, the latest USB-C specification supports speeds of up to SuperSpeed+ 20 Gbps.

Refer to **Interactive Graphic** in online course

3.3.3.4 SATA Cables and Connectors

SATA is an interface type used connect SATA hard drives and other storage devices to the motherboard inside the computer. SATA cables are long (up to 1 meter) and thin with a flat and thin 7-pin connector on each end.

Refer to **Interactive Graphic** in online course

3.3.3.5 Twisted Pair Cables and Connectors

Twisted pair cable is used in wired Ethernet networks and in older telephone networks. Twisted pair cabling gets its name from the fact that pairs of wires inside the cable are twisted together. The twisting of wire pairs helps reduce crosstalk and electromagnetic induction.

Refer to **Interactive Graphic** in online course

3.3.3.6 Coax Cables and Connectors

Coaxial cable has an inner center conductor, usually made from copper or copper-clad-steel, which is surrounded by a non-conductive dielectric insulating material. The dielectric is surrounded by a foil shield which forms the outer conductor and shields against electromagnetic interference (EMI). The outer conductor/shield is encased in a PVC outer jacket.

Refer to
Interactive Graphic
in online course

3.3.3.7 SCSI and IDE Cables and Connectors

Small Computer Systems Interface (SCSI) is a standard for connecting peripheral and storage devices. SCSI is a bus technology, meaning that all devices connect to a central bus and are "daisy-chained" together. The cabling/connector requirements depend upon the location of the SCSI bus.

Integrated Drive Electronics (IDE) is a standard type of interface used to connect some hard drives and optical drives to each other and to the motherboard.

Refer to
Interactive Graphic
in online course

3.3.3.8 Check Your Understanding - Identify the External Connectors

3.3.4 Monitors

Refer to
Online Course
for Illustration

3.3.4.1 Monitor Characteristics

There are many types of computer monitors available. Some are designed for casual use, while others are for specific requirements, such as those used by architects, graphic designers, or even gamers.

Monitors vary by use, size, quality, clarity, brightness and more. Therefore, it is useful to understand the various terms used when discussing monitors.

Computer monitors are usually described by:

- **Screen size** - This is the diagonal measurement of the screen (i.e., top left to bottom right) in inches. Common sizes include 19 to 24 inches, to ultrawide monitors that are 30 or more inches wide. Larger monitors are usually better but are more expensive and require more desk space.

- **Resolution** - Resolution is measured by the number of horizontal and vertical pixels. For example, 1920 × 1080 (i.e., 1080p) is a common resolution. This means it has 1920 horizontal pixels and 1080 vertical pixels.

- **Monitor resolution** - This relates to the amount of information that can be displayed on a screen. A higher resolution monitor displays more information on a screen than a lower resolution monitor does. This is true even with monitors that have the same screen size.

- **Native resolution** - This identifies the best monitor resolution for the specific monitor. In Windows 10, the native resolution of a monitor is identified using the keyword (Recommended) beside the monitor resolution. For example, in the figure, the native resolution of the monitor is 1920 × 1080.

- **Native mode** - This term describes when the image sent to the monitor by the video adapter card matches the native resolution of the monitor.

- **Connectivity** - Older monitors used VGA or DVI connectors while newer monitors support HDMI and DisplayPort ports. DisplayPort is a connection found on newer monitors. It supports higher resolutions and high refresh rates.

Note   If you want to display more things on the screen, then select a higher resolution monitor. If you just want things to appear bigger, then select a larger screen size.

Refer to
Interactive Graphic
in online course

3.3.4.2   Monitor Terms

Refer to
Interactive Graphic
in online course

3.3.4.3   Display Standards

Refer to
Online Course
for Illustration

3.3.4.4   Using Multiple Monitors

Adding monitors can increase your visual desktop area and improve productivity. The added monitors enable you to expand the size of the monitor or duplicate the desktop so you can view additional windows. For example, the woman in Figure 1 is using multiple displays. She is using the right monitor to make changes to a website and the left monitor to display the resulting change. She is also using a laptop to display a library of images she is considering for inclusion in the website.

Many computers have built-in support for multiple monitors. To connect multiple monitors to a computer, you need the supporting cables. Then you need to enable your computer to support multiple monitors.

For example, on a Windows 10 host, right-click anywhere on the Desktop and choose **Display settings**. This should open the Display window as shown in Figure 2. In the example, the user has three monitors connected in the configuration displayed. The current monitor selected is in blue and has a resolution of 1920 x 1080. It is also the main display monitor. Clicking on monitor 2 or 3 would display their respective resolutions.

Refer to
Interactive Graphic
in online course

3.3.4.5   Check Your Understanding - Monitor Terminology

3.4   Computer Configuration

3.4.1   Upgrade Computer Hardware

Refer to
Online Course
for Illustration

3.4.1.1   Motherboard Upgrade

Computers need periodic upgrades for various reasons:

- User requirements change

- Upgraded software packages require new hardware

- New hardware offers enhanced performance

Changes to the computer may cause you to upgrade or replace components and peripherals. Research the effectiveness and cost of both upgrading and replacing.

If you upgrade or replace a motherboard, consider that you might have to replace other components including the CPU, heat sink and fan assembly, and RAM. A new motherboard must also fit into the old computer case and the power supply must support it.

When upgrading the motherboard, begin the upgrade by moving the CPU and the heat sink and fan assembly to the new motherboard if they will be reused. These items are much easier to work with when they are outside of the case. Work on an antistatic mat, and wear antistatic gloves or an antistatic wrist strap to avoid damaging the CPU. If the new motherboard requires a different CPU and RAM, install them at this time. Clean the thermal compound from the CPU and heat sink. Remember to re-apply thermal compound between the CPU and the heat sink.

In the figure, select the components that are impacted by a motherboard upgrade.

Refer to
Online Course
for Illustration

3.4.1.2   Steps to Upgrade a Motherboard

Before beginning an upgrade, ensure that you know where and how everything is connected. Always make notes in a journal to record how the current computer is set up. A quick way is to use a cell phone and take pictures of important items such as how components connect to the motherboard. These pictures may prove to be surprisingly helpful when re-assembling.

To upgrade a motherboard from a computer case, follow these steps:

Step 1. Record how the power supply, case fans, case LEDs, and case buttons attach to the old motherboard.

Step 2. Disconnect the cables from the old motherboard.

Step 3. Disconnect the expansion cards from the case. Remove each expansion card and place them in antistatic bags, or on an antistatic mat.

Step 4. Carefully record how the old motherboard is secured to the case. Some mounting screws provide support while some may provide an important grounding connection between the motherboard and chassis. In particular, pay attention to screws and standoffs that are non-metallic, because these may be insulators. Replacing insulating screws and supports with metal hardware that conducts electricity might damage electrical components.

Step 5. Remove the old motherboard from the case.

Step 6. Examine the new motherboard and identify where all of the connectors are such as power, SATA, fan, USB, audio, front panel connector, and any others.

Step 7. Examine the I/O shield located at the back of the computer case. Replace the old I/O shield with the I/O shield that comes with the new motherboard.

Step 8. Insert and secure the motherboard into the case. Be sure to consult the case and motherboard manufacturer user guides. Use the proper types of screws. Do not swap threaded screws with self-tapping metal screws, because they will damage the threaded screw holes and might not be secure. Make sure that the threaded screws are the correct length and have the same number of threads per inch. If the thread is correct, they fit easily. If you force a screw to fit, you can damage the threaded hole, and it will not hold the motherboard securely. Using the wrong screw can also produce metal shavings that can cause short circuits.

Step 9. Next, connect the power supply, case fans, case LEDs, front panel, and any other required cables. If the ATX power connectors are not the same size (some have more pins than others), you might need to use an adapter. Refer to the motherboard documentation for the layout of these connections.

Step 10. After the new motherboard is in place and the cables are connected, install and secure the expansion cards.

It is now time to check your work. Make sure that there are no loose parts or unconnected cables. Connect the keyboard, mouse, monitor, and power. If a problem is detected, shut the power supply off immediately.

Refer to Online Course for Illustration

3.4.1.3   CPU Upgrade

One way to increase the power of a computer is to increase the processing speed. You can do this by upgrading the CPU. However, the CPU must meet the requirements listed in the figure.

The new CPU might require a different heat sink and fan assembly. The assembly must physically fit the CPU and be compatible with the CPU socket. It must also be adequate to remove the heat of the faster CPU.

Caution   You must apply thermal compound between the new CPU and the heat sink and fan assembly.

View thermal settings in the BIOS to determine if there are any problems with the CPU and the heat sink and fan assembly. Third-party software applications can also report CPU temperature information in an easy-to-read format. Refer to the motherboard or CPU user documentation to determine if the chip is operating in the correct temperature range.

To install additional fans in the case to help cool the computer, follow these steps:

Step 1. Align the fan so that it faces the correct direction to either draw air in or blow air out.

Step 2. Mount the fan using the predrilled holes in the case. It is common to mount fans near the top of the case to blow hot air out, and near the bottom of the case to bring air in. Avoid mounting two fans close together that are moving air in opposite directions.

Step 3. Connect the fan to the power supply or the motherboard, depending on the case fan plug type.

Refer to Online Course for Illustration

3.4.1.4   Storage Device Upgrade

Instead of purchasing a new computer to get faster speed and more storage space, you might consider adding another hard drive. There are several reasons for installing an additional drive as listed in the figure.

After selecting the appropriate hard drive for the computer, follow these general guidelines during installation:

Step 1.   Place the hard drive in an empty drive bay, and tighten the screws to secure the hard drive.

Step 2.   Connect the drive to the motherboard using the correct cable.

Step 3.   Attach the power cable to the drive.

Refer to
Online Course
for Illustration

3.4.1.5   Peripheral Upgrades

Peripheral devices periodically need to be upgraded. For example, if the device stops operating or if you wish to improve performance and productivity, an upgrade might be necessary.

These are a few reasons for upgrading a keyboard and/or a mouse:

- Change the keyboard and mouse to an ergonomic design such as those shown in Figure 1. Ergonomic devices are made to be more comfortable to use and to help prevent repetitive motion injuries.

- Reconfigure the keyboard to accommodate a special task, such as typing in a second language with additional characters.

- To accommodate users with disabilities.

However, sometimes it is not possible to perform an upgrade using the existing expansion slots or sockets. In this case, you may be able to accomplish the upgrade using a USB connection. If the computer does not have an extra USB connection, you must install a USB adapter card or purchase a USB hub, as shown in Figure 2.

Refer to
Online Course
for Illustration

3.4.1.6   Power Supply Upgrade

Upgrading your computer hardware will most likely also change its power needs. If so, you may need to upgrade your power supply. You can find calculators on the internet to help you determine if you need to upgrade the power supply. Search for "power supply wattage calculator".

Refer to
Lab Activity
for this chapter

3.4.1.7   Lab - Research a Hardware Upgrade

In this lab, you will gather information about hardware components so you can upgrade your customer's hardware so they can play advanced video games.

Lab - Research a Hardware Upgrade

3.4.2   Configurations for Specialized Computers

Refer to
Online Course
for Illustration

3.4.2.1   What Do You Already Know? - Configure a CAx Workstation

Refer to
Online Course
for Illustration

3.4.2.2   What Do You Already Know? - Configure an Audio Video Editing Workstation

Refer to
Online Course
for Illustration

3.4.2.3   What Do You Already Know? - Configure a Virtualization Workstation

Refer to
Online Course
for Illustration

Refer to
Interactive Graphic
in online course

Refer to
Online Course
for Illustration

3.4.2.4   What Do You Already Know? - Configure a Gaming PC

3.4.2.5   Check Your Understanding - Specialized Computer Component Types

3.4.2.6   Thick and Thin Clients

Computers are sometimes referred to as:

- **Thick clients** - Sometimes called fat clients, these are standard computers that we have discussed in this chapter. The computers have their own operating system, a multitude of applications, and local storage. They are stand-alone systems and do not require a network connection to operate. All of the processing is performed locally on the computer.

- **Thin clients** - These are typically low-end network computers that rely on remote servers to perform all data processing. Thin clients require a network connection to a server and usually access resources using a web browser. However, the client can be a computer running thin client software or a small, dedicated terminal consisting of a monitor, keyboard, and mouse. Typically the clients do not have any internal storage and have very little local resources.

The table in the figure identifies differences between thick and thin clients.

Along with thick and thin clients, there are computers that are built for specific purposes. Part of the responsibilities of a computer technician is to evaluate, select appropriate components, and upgrade or custom-build specialized computers to meet the needs of customers.

This section identifies and discusses some of these specialized computers.

Refer to
Online Course
for Illustration

3.4.2.7   NAS

Network attached storage (NAS) devices are servers that are connected to a network to provide file-level data storage to clients. This specialized computer is sometimes single-purposed, running a stripped-down operating system to perform only the function of file serving. Sometimes the device can offer additional functionality such as media streaming, network services, automated backup functions, website hosting, and many other services.

Often, the NAS will offer high-speed networking through the use of a gigabit network interface card (NIC). This interface allows many connections to the network at very high speed simultaneously. Some NAS devices will have more than one gigabit NIC to allow many more connections.

It is recommended to use a special hard drive when deploying a NAS device. These drives are specially built to endure the always-on environment of a NAS system. It is very common to find multiple drives within a NAS not only to provide additional storage, but also to provide either increased speed or redundancy through the use of RAID.

3.5   Protecting the Environment

3.5.1   Safe Disposal of Equipment and Supplies

Refer to
Online Course
for Illustration

3.5.1.1   Safe Disposal Methods

After upgrading a computer, or replacing a broken device, what do you do with the leftover parts? If the parts are still good, they can be donated or sold. Parts that no longer work must be disposed of, but they must be disposed of responsibly.

The proper disposal or recycling of hazardous computer components is a global issue. Make sure to follow regulations that govern how to dispose of specific items. Organizations that violate these regulations can be fined or face expensive legal battles. Regulations for the disposal of the items on this page vary from state to state and from country to country. Check your local environmental regulatory agency.

Batteries

Batteries often contain rare earth metals that can be harmful to the environment. These metals do not decay and remain in the environment for many years. Mercury is commonly used in the manufacturing of batteries and is extremely harmful to humans.

Recycling batteries should be standard practice. All batteries are subject to disposal procedures that comply with local environmental regulations.

Monitors

Handle CRT monitors with care. Extremely high voltage can be stored in CRT monitors, even after being disconnected from a power source.

Monitors contain glass, metal, plastics, lead, barium, and rare earth metals. According to the U.S. Environmental Protection Agency (EPA), monitors can contain approximately 4 pounds (1.8 kg) of lead. Monitors must be disposed of in compliance with environmental regulations.

Toner Kits, Cartridges, and Developers

Used printer toner kits and printer cartridges must be disposed of properly in compliance with environmental regulations. They can also be recycled. Some toner cartridge suppliers and manufacturers take empty cartridges for refilling. Kits to refill inkjet printer cartridges are available but are not recommended, because the ink might leak into the printer, causing irreparable damage. Using refilled inkjet cartridges might also void the inkjet printer warranty.

Chemical Solvents and Aerosol Cans

Contact the local sanitation company to learn how and where to dispose of the chemicals and solvents used to clean computers. Never dump chemicals or solvents down a sink or dispose of them in a drain that connects to public sewers.

Cell Phones and tablets

The EPA recommends individuals check with local health and sanitation agencies for their preferred way to depose of electronics such as cell phones, tablets, and computers. Most computer equipment and mobile devices contain hazardous materials, such as heavy metals, that do not belong in a landfill because they contaminate the earth. Local communities may also have recycling programs.

Refer to
Interactive Graphic
in online course

3.5.1.2   Safety Data Sheets

Hazardous materials are sometimes called toxic waste. These materials can contain high concentrations of heavy metals such as cadmium, lead, or mercury. The regulations for the disposal of hazardous materials vary by state or country. Contact the local recycling or waste removal authorities in your community for information about disposal procedures and services.

A Safety Data Sheet (SDS), formerly known as a Material Safety and Data Sheet (MSDS), is a fact sheet that summarizes information about material identification, including hazardous ingredients that can affect personal health, fire hazards, and first-aid requirements. The SDS contains chemical reactivity and incompatibility information. It also includes protective measures for the safe handling and storage of materials and spill, leak, and disposal procedures. To determine if a material is classified as hazardous, consult the manufacturer's SDS which in the U.S. is required by OSHA when the material is transferred to a new owner.

The SDS explains how to dispose of potentially hazardous materials in the safest manner. Always check local regulations concerning acceptable disposal methods before disposing of any electronic equipment.

In the European Union, the regulation Registration, Evaluation, Authorization and restriction of Chemicals (REACH) came into effect on June 1, 2007, replacing various directives and regulations with a single system.

Refer to
Interactive Graphic
in online course

3.5.1.3   Check Your Understanding - Safe Disposal

Refer to
Online Course
for Illustration

3.6   Summary

In this chapter, you learned about the computer boot process and the role played by the BIOS which performs the POST on the main components of the computer. You also learned that the motherboard BIOS settings are saved in a CMOS memory chip. When a computer boots, the BIOS software reads the configured settings stored in CMOS to determine how to configure the hardware. In the lab, you installed Microsoft Windows operating system and third-party software.

After installing Windows, you learned about Wattage and Voltage and the basic equation of Ohm's Law, which expresses how voltage is equal to the current multiplied by the resistance: $V = IR$ and that power is equal to the voltage multiplied by the current: $P = VI$. You learned about the types of AC power fluctuations that can cause data loss or hardware failure like blackouts, brownouts, noise, spikes and power surges. You also learned about the devices that help shield against power fluctuation problems and protect the data and computer equipment. These devices include surge protectors, UPS, and SPS.

Next, you learned about multicore processors ranging from dual core CPUs with two cores inside a single CPU, to Octa-core CPUs with eight cores inside a single CPU, and different types of CPU cooling mechanisms like fans, heat sinks, and water cooling systems. In addition to multicore CPUs, you learned how multiple drives can be logically grouped and managed to create large storage volumes with redundancy using RAID technology. Striping, mirroring, parity, and double parity types of RAID were covered.

You learned about many different types of computer ports and connectors starting with legacy ports that are typically found on older computers such as serial, parallel, game, PS/2 and audio ports - most of which are replaced by newer technologies like USB. You also learned about various video and game ports like VGA, DVI, HDMI and display ports used to connect monitors and external video displays. The evolution of USB ports was covered as well and included comparisons of USB Type-A, mini-USB, micro-USB, USB Type-B, USB Type-C, and lightning connectors.

The characteristics that define computer monitors was covered. You learned that monitors vary by use, size, quality, clarity, and brightness. You also learned that monitors are described by their screen size as measured diagonally and screen resolution as measured by the number of pixels. Display standards of CGA, VGA, SVGA, HD, FHD, QHD and UHD were all defined as well.

The chapter concluded with a discussion on protecting the environment through safe disposal methods for computer components. You learned that their are regulations for the disposal of many of these components such as batteries, toner, printer cartridges, cell phones, and tablets. You also learned about the SDS which explains how to dispose of potentially hazardous materials in the safest manner. Always check local regulations concerning acceptable disposal methods before disposing of any electronic equipment.

Go to the online course to take the quiz and exam.

Chapter 3 Quiz

This quiz is designed to provide an additional opportunity to practice the skills and knowledge presented in the chapter and to prepare for the chapter exam. You will be allowed multiple attempts and the grade does not appear in the gradebook.

Chapter 3 Exam

The chapter exam assesses your knowledge of the chapter content.

Your Chapter Notes

Preventive Maintenance and Troubleshooting

Refer to
Online Course
for Illustration

4.0 Introduction

Preventive maintenance is something that is often overlooked, but good IT professionals understand the importance of regular and systematic inspection, cleaning, and replacement of worn parts, materials, and systems. Effective preventive maintenance reduces part, material, and system faults, and keeps hardware and software in good working condition.

Preventive maintenance doesn't just apply to hardware. Performing basic tasks like checking what programs run on start-up, scanning for malware, and removing unused programs helps a computer function more efficiently, and can keep it from slowing down. Good IT professionals also understand the importance of troubleshooting which requires an organized and logical approach to problems with computers and other components.

In this chapter, you will learn general guidelines for creating preventive maintenance programs and troubleshooting procedures. These guidelines are a starting point to help you develop your preventive maintenance and troubleshooting skills. You will also learn the importance of maintaining an optimal operating environment for computer systems that are clean, free of potential contaminants, and within the temperature and humidity range specified by the manufacturer.

At the end of the chapter you will learn the six step troubleshooting process and common problems and solutions for different computer components.

4.1 Preventive Maintenance

4.1.1 PC Preventive Maintenance Overview

Refer to
Online Course
for Illustration

4.1.1.1 Benefits to Preventive Maintenance

Preventive maintenance plans are developed based on at least two factors:

- **Computer location or environment** - Dusty environments, such as construction sites, requires more attention than an office environment.

- **Computer use** - High-traffic networks, such as a school network, might require additional scanning and removal of malicious software and unwanted files.

Regular preventive maintenance:

- Reduces potential hardware and software problems, computer downtime, repair costs, and the number of equipment failures.

- Improves data protection, equipment life and stability, and saves money.

Refer to
Online Course
for Illustration

4.1.1.2   Preventive Maintenance - Dust

The following are considerations to keep dust from damaging computer components:

- Clean/replace building air filters regularly to reduce the amount of dust in the air.
- Use a cloth or a duster to clean the outside of the computer case. If using a cleaning product, put a small amount onto a cleaning cloth and then wipe the outside of the case.
- Dust on the outside of a computer can travel through cooling fans to the inside.
- Accumulated dust prevents the flow of air and reduces the cooling of components.
- Hot computer components are more likely to break down.
- Remove dust from the inside of a computer using a combination of compressed air, a low-air-flow ESD vacuum cleaner, and a small lint-free cloth.
- Keep the can of compressed air upright to prevent the fluid from leaking onto computer components.
- Keep the compressed air can a safe distance from sensitive devices and components.
- Use the lint-free cloth to remove any dust left behind on the component.

Caution   When you clean a fan with compressed air, hold the fan blades in place. This prevents overspinning the rotor or moving the fan in the wrong direction.

Refer to
Online Course
for Illustration

4.1.1.3   Preventive Maintenance - Internal Components

This is a basic checklist of components to inspect for dust and damage:

- **CPU heat sink and fan assembly** - The fan should spin freely, the fan power cable should be secure, and the fan should turn when the power is on.
- **RAM modules** - The modules must be seated securely in the RAM slots. Ensure that the retaining clips are not loose.
- **Storage devices** - All cables should be firmly connected. Check for loose, missing, or incorrectly set jumpers. A drive should not produce rattling, knocking, or grinding sounds.
- **Screws** - A loose screw in the case can cause a short circuit.
- **Adapter cards** - Ensure that they are seated properly and secured with the retaining screws in their expansion slots. Loose cards can cause short circuits. Missing expansion slot covers can let dust, dirt, or living pests inside the computer.
- **Cables** - Examine all cable connections. Ensure that pins are not broken and bent and that cables are not crimped, pinched, or severely bent. Retaining screws should be finger-tight.
- **Power devices** - Inspect power strips, surge suppressors (surge protectors), and UPS devices. Make sure that the devices work properly and that there is clear ventilation.
- **Keyboard and mouse** - Use compressed air to clean the keyboard, mouse, and mouse sensor.

Refer to
Online Course
for Illustration

4.1.1.4   Preventive Maintenance - Environmental Concerns

An optimal operating environment for a computer is clean, free of potential contaminants, and within the temperature and humidity range specified by the manufacturer.

Follow these guidelines to help ensure optimal computer operating performance:

- Do not obstruct vents or airflow to the internal components.

- Keep the room temperature between 45 to 90 degrees Fahrenheit (7 to 32 degrees Celsius).

- Keep the humidity level between 10 and 80 percent.

- Temperature and humidity recommendations vary by computer manufacturer. Research the recommended values for computers used in extreme conditions.

Refer to
Online Course
for Illustration

4.1.1.5   Preventive Maintenance - Software

Verify that installed software is current.

- Follow the policies of the organization when installing security updates, operating system, and program updates.

Create a software maintenance schedule to:

- Review and install the appropriate security, software, and driver updates.

- Update the virus definition files and scan for viruses and spyware.

- Remove unwanted or unused programs.

- Scan hard drives for errors and defragment hard drives.

Refer to
Interactive Graphic
in online course

4.1.1.6   Check Your Understanding - Preventive Maintenance

4.2   Troubleshooting Process

4.2.1   Troubleshooting Process Steps

Refer to
Online Course
for Illustration

4.2.1.1   Introduction to Troubleshooting

Troubleshooting requires an organized and logical approach to problems with computers and other components. Sometimes issues arise during preventive maintenance. At other times, a customer may contact you with a problem. A logical approach to troubleshooting allows you to eliminate variables and identify causes of problems in a systematic order. Asking the right questions, testing the right hardware, and examining the right data helps you understand the problem and form a proposed solution.

Troubleshooting is a skill that you refine over time. Each time you solve a problem, you increase your troubleshooting skills by gaining more experience. You learn how and when to combine steps, or skip steps, to reach a solution quickly. The troubleshooting process is a guideline that is modified to fit your needs.

This section presents an approach to problem-solving that you can apply to both hardware and software.

Note   The term customer, as used in this course, is any user that requires technical computer assistance.

Before you begin troubleshooting problems, always follow the necessary precautions to protect data on a computer. Some repairs, such as replacing a hard drive or reinstalling an operating system, might put the data on the computer at risk. Make sure you do everything possible to prevent data loss while attempting repairs. If your work results in data loss for the customer, you or your company could be held liable.

Data Backup

A data backup is a copy of the data on a computer hard drive that is saved to another storage device or to cloud storage. Cloud storage is online storage that is accessed via the internet. In an organization, backups may be performed on a daily, weekly, or monthly basis.

If you are unsure that a backup has been done, do not attempt any troubleshooting activities until you check with the customer. Here is a list of items to verify with the customer that a backup has been performed:

- Date of the last backup
- Contents of the backup
- Data integrity of the backup
- Availability of all backup media for a data restore

If the customer does not have a current backup and you are not able to create one, ask the customer to sign a liability release form. A liability release form contains at least the following information:

- Permission to work on the computer without a current backup available
- Release from liability if data is lost or corrupted
- Description of the work to be performed

Refer to
Online Course
for Illustration

4.2.1.2   Troubleshooting Process Steps

Refer to
Online Course
for Illustration

4.2.1.3   Identify the Problem

The first step in the troubleshooting process is to identify the problem. During this step, gather as much information as possible from the customer and from the computer.

Conversation Etiquette

When you are talking to the customer, follow these guidelines:

- Ask direct questions to gather information.
- Do not use industry jargon.

- Do not talk down to the customer.
- Do not insult the customer.
- Do not accuse the customer of causing the problem.

Figure 1 lists some of the information to gather from the customer.

Open-Ended and Closed-Ended Questions

Open-ended questions allow customers to explain the details of the problem in their own words. Use open-ended questions to obtain general information.

Based on the information from the customer, you can proceed with closed-ended questions. Closed-ended questions generally require a yes or no answer.

Documenting Responses

Document the information from the customer in the work order, in the repair log, and in your repair journal. Write down anything that you think might be important for you or another technician. The small details often lead to the solution of a difficult or complicated problem.

Beep Codes

Each BIOS manufacturer has a unique beep sequence, a combination of long and short beeps, for hardware failures. When troubleshooting, power on the computer and listen. As the system proceeds through the POST, most computers emit one beep to indicate that the system is booting properly. If there is an error, you might hear multiple beeps. Document the beep code sequence, and research the code to determine the specific problem.

BIOS Information

If the computer boots and stops after the POST, investigate the BIOS settings. A device might not be detected or configured properly. Refer to the motherboard documentation to ensure that the BIOS settings are correct.

Event Viewer

When system, user, or software errors occur on a computer, the Event Viewer is updated with information about the errors. The Event Viewer application, shown in Figure 2, records the following information about the problem:

- What problem occurred
- Date and time of the problem
- Severity of the problem
- Source of the problem
- Event ID number
- Which user was logged in when the problem occurred

Although the Event Viewer lists details about the error, you might need to further research the problem to determine a solution.

Device Manager

The Device Manager, shown in Figure 3, displays all the devices that are configured on a computer. The operating system flags the devices that are not operating correctly with an error icon. A yellow triangle with an exclamation point indicates that the device is in a problem state. A red X means that the device is disabled, removed, or Windows can't locate the device. An arrow down means the device has been disabled. A yellow question mark indicates that the system does not know which driver to install for the hardware.

Task Manager

The Task Manager, shown in Figure 4, displays the applications and background processes that are currently running. With the Task Manager, you can close applications that have stopped responding. You can also monitor the performance of the CPU and virtual memory, view all processes that are currently running, and view information about the network connections.

Diagnostic Tools

Conduct research to determine which software is available to help diagnose and solve problems. There are many programs to help you troubleshoot hardware. Manufacturers of system hardware usually provide diagnostic tools of their own. For instance, a hard drive manufacturer might provide a tool to boot the computer and diagnose why the hard drive does not start the operating system.

Refer to
Interactive Graphic
in online course

4.2.1.4   Check Your Understanding - Identify the Problem

Refer to
Online Course
for Illustration

4.2.1.5   Establish a Theory of Probable Cause

The second step in the troubleshooting process is to establish a theory of probable cause. First, create a list of the most common reasons for the error. Even though the customer may think that there is a major problem, start with the obvious issues before moving to more complex diagnoses. List the easiest or most obvious causes at the top. List the more complex causes at the bottom. If necessary, conduct internal (logs, journal) or external (internet) research based on the symptoms. The next steps of the troubleshooting process involve testing each possible cause.

Refer to
Online Course
for Illustration

4.2.1.6   Test the Theory to Determine the Cause

You can determine an exact cause by testing your theories of probable causes one at a time, starting with the quickest and easiest. Figure 1 identifies some common steps to determine the cause of the problem. Once the theory is confirmed, you then determine the steps to resolve the problem. As you become more experienced at troubleshooting computers, you will work through the steps in the process faster. For now, practice each step to better understand the troubleshooting process.

If you cannot determine the exact cause of the problem after testing all your theories, establish a new theory of probable cause and test it. If necessary, escalate the problem to a technician with more experience. Before you escalate, document each test that you tried, as shown in Figure 2.

Refer to
Online Course
for Illustration

4.2.1.7   Establish a Plan of Action to Resolve the Problem and Implement the Solution

After you have determined the exact cause of the problem, establish a plan of action to resolve the problem and implement the solution. Sometimes quick procedures can correct the problem. If a quick procedure does correct the problem, verify full system functionality and, if applicable, implement preventive measures. If a quick procedure does not correct the problem, research the problem further and then return to Step 2 to establish a new theory of the probable cause.

Note   always consider corporate policies, procedures, and impacts before implementing any changes.

After you have established a plan of action, you should research possible solutions. The figure lists possible research locations. Divide larger problems into smaller problems that can be analyzed and solved individually. Prioritize solutions starting with the easiest and fastest to implement. Create a list of possible solutions and implement them one at a time. If you implement a possible solution and it does not correct the problem, reverse the action you just took and then try another solution. Continue this process until you have found the appropriate solution.

Refer to
Online Course
for Illustration

4.2.1.8   Verify Full Functionality and, If Applicable, Implement Preventive Measures

After the repairs to the computer have been completed, continue the troubleshooting process by verifying full system functionality and implementing the preventive measures needed. Verifying full system functionality confirms that you have solved the original problem and ensures that you have not created another problem while repairing the computer. Whenever possible, have the customer verify the solution and system functionality.

Refer to
Online Course
for Illustration

4.2.1.9   Document Findings, Actions, and Outcomes

After the repairs to the computer have been completed, finish the troubleshooting process with the customer. Explain the problem and the solution to the customer verbally and in writing. The figure shows the steps to take when you have finished a repair.

Verify the solution with the customer. If the customer is available, demonstrate how the solution has corrected the computer problem. Have the customer test the solution and try to reproduce the problem. When the customer can verify that the problem has been resolved, you can complete the documentation for the repair in the work order and in your journal. Include the following information in the documentation:

- Description of the problem
- Steps to resolve the problem
- Components used in the repair

Refer to
Interactive Graphic
in online course

4.2.1.10   Check Your Understanding - Number the Steps

4.2.2   Common Problems and Solutions for PCs

Refer to
Online Course
for Illustration

4.2.2.1   PC Common Problems and Solutions

Computer problems can be attributed to hardware, software, networks, or some combination of the three. You will resolve some types of problems more often than others.

These are some common hardware problems:

- **Storage Device** - Storage device problems are often related to loose, or incorrect cable connections, incorrect drive and media formats, and incorrect jumper and BIOS settings.

- **Motherboard and Internal Components** - These problems are often caused by incorrect or loose cables, failed components, incorrect drivers, and corrupted updates.

- **Power Supply** - Power problems are often caused by a faulty power supply, loose connections, and inadequate wattage.

- **CPU and Memory** - Processor and memory problems are often caused by faulty installations, incorrect BIOS settings, inadequate cooling and ventilation, and compatibility issues.

- **Displays** - Display problems are often caused by incorrect settings, loose connections, and incorrect or corrupted drivers.

Refer to
Interactive Graphic
in online course

4.2.2.2   Common Problems and Solutions for Storage Devices

Refer to
Interactive Graphic
in online course

4.2.2.3   Common Problems and Solutions for Motherboards and Internal Components

Refer to
Interactive Graphic
in online course

4.2.2.4   Common Problems and Solutions for Power Supplies

Refer to
Interactive Graphic
in online course

4.2.2.5   Common Problems and Solutions for CPUs and Memory

Refer to
Interactive Graphic
in online course

4.2.2.6   Common Problems and Solutions for Displays

4.2.3   Apply Troubleshooting Process to Computer Components and Peripherals

Refer to
Online Course
for Illustration

4.2.3.1   Personal Reference Tools

Good customer service includes providing the customer with a detailed description of the problem and the solution. It is important that a technician document all services and repairs and that this documentation is available to all other technicians. The documentation can then be used as reference material for similar problems.

Personal Reference Tools

Personal reference tools include troubleshooting guides, manufacturer manuals, quick reference guides, and repair journals. In addition to an invoice, a technician keeps a journal of upgrades and repairs:

- **Notes** - Make notes as you go through the troubleshooting and repair process. Refer to these notes to avoid repeating steps and to determine what needs to be done next.

- **Journal** - Include descriptions of the problem, possible solutions that have been tried to correct the problem, and the steps taken to repair the problem. Note any configuration changes made to the equipment and any replacement parts used in the repair. Your journal, along with your notes, can be valuable when you encounter similar situations in the future.

- **History of repairs** - Make a detailed list of problems and repairs, including the date, replacement parts, and customer information. The history allows a technician to determine what work has been performed on a specific computer in the past.

Refer to **Online Course** for Illustration

4.2.3.2   Internet Reference Tools

The internet is an excellent source of information about specific hardware problems and possible solutions:

- Internet search engines
- News groups
- Manufacturer FAQs
- Online computer manuals
- Online forums and chat
- Technical websites

Refer to **Interactive Graphic** in online course

4.2.3.3   Check Your Understanding - Reference Tools

Refer to **Interactive Graphic** in online course

4.2.3.4   Advanced Problems and Solutions for Hardware

Refer to **Lab Activity** for this chapter

4.2.3.5   Lab - Use a Multimeter and a Power Supply Tester

In this lab, you will learn how to use and handle a multimeter and a power supply tester.

Lab - Use a Multimeter and a Power Supply Tester

Refer to **Lab Activity** for this chapter

4.2.3.6   Lab - Troubleshoot Hardware Problems

In this lab, you will diagnose the cause of various hardware problems and solve them.

Lab - Troubleshoot Hardware Problems

4.3 Summary

In this chapter, you learned there are many benefits of preventive maintenance, such as fewer potential hardware and software problems, less computer downtime, lower repair costs, and less frequent equipment failures. You learned how to keep dust from damaging computer components by keeping building air filters clean, cleaning the outside of the computer case, and removing dust from the inside of the computer with compressed air.

Next you learned that there are components that should be regularly inspected for dust and damage. These components include the CPU heat sink and fan, RAM modules, storage devices, adapter cards, cables and power devices, and keyboards and mice. Guidelines for ensuring optimal computer operating performance, such as not obstructing vents or airflow and maintaining proper room temperature and humidity,

In addition to learning how to maintain the hardware of a computer, you also learned that it is important to perform regular maintenance on computer software. This is best accomplished with a software maintenance schedule that covers security software, virus definition files, unwanted and unused programs, and hard drive defragmenting.

At the end of the chapter, you learned the six steps in the troubleshooting process as they pertain to preventative maintenance.

Go to the online course to take the quiz and exam.

Chapter 4 Quiz

This quiz is designed to provide an additional opportunity to practice the skills and knowledge presented in the chapter and to prepare for the chapter exam. You will be allowed multiple attempts and the grade does not appear in the gradebook.

Chapter 4 Exam

The chapter exam assesses your knowledge of the chapter content.

Your Chapter Notes

Networking Concepts

Refer to **Online Course** for Illustration

5.0 Introduction

Computer networks allow users to share resources and to communicate. Can you imagine a world without emails, online newspapers, blogs, web sites and the other services offered by the Internet? Networks also allow users to share resources such as printers, applications, files, directories, and storage drives. This chapter provides an overview of network principles, standards, and purposes. IT professionals must be familiar with networking concepts to meet the expectations and needs of customers and network users.

You will learn the basics of network design and how devices on the network impact the flow of data. These devices include hubs, switches, access points, routers, and firewalls. Different Internet connection types such as DSL, cable, cellular and satellite are also covered. You will learn about the four layers of the TCP/IP model and the functions and protocols associated with each layer. You will also learn about many wireless networks and protocols. This includes IEEE 802.11 Wireless LAN protocols, wireless protocols for close proximity, like Frequency Identification (RFID), Near Field Communication (NFC), and smart home protocol standards like Zigbee and Z-wave. This knowledge will help you successfully design, implement, and troubleshoot networks. The chapter concludes with discussions on network cable types; twisted-pair, fiber-optic, and coaxial. You will learn how each type of cable is constructed, how they carry data signals, and appropriate use cases for each.

It is important to not only learn about computer network operation and components but also to build hands-on skills. In this chapter you will build and to test a straight-through Unshielded Twisted-Pair (UTP) Ethernet network cable.

5.1 Network Components and Types

5.1.1 Types of Networks

Refer to **Interactive Graphic** in online course

5.1.1.1 Network Icons

Networks are systems that are formed by links. Computer networks connect devices and users to one another. A variety of networking icons are used to represent different parts of a computer network.

Host Devices

The network devices that people are most familiar with are called end devices or host devices (Figure 1). They are called end devices because they are at the end or edge of a network. They are also called host devices because they typically host network applications, such as web browsers and email clients, that use the network to provide services to the user.

Intermediary Devices

Computer networks contain many devices that exist in between the host devices. These intermediary devices ensure that data flows from one host device to another host device. The most common intermediary devices are shown in Figure 2:

- **Switch** - connects multiple devices to the network.

- **Router** - forwards traffic between networks.

- **Wireless router** - connects multiple wireless devices to the network and may include a switch to connect wired hosts.

- **Access point (AP)** - connects to a wireless router and is used to extend the reach of a wireless network.

- **Modem** - connects a home or small office to the Internet.

Network Media

Communication across a network is carried on a medium. The medium provides the channel over which the message travels from source to destination. The plural for medium is media. The icons in Figure 3 represent different types of network media. Local area network (LANs), wide area networks (WANs), and wireless networks are discussed further in this topic. The cloud is typically used in network topologies to represent connections to the internet. The internet is often the medium for communications between one network and another network.

Refer to
Interactive Graphic
in online course

5.1.1.2   Network Topologies and Description

PAN

A **personal area network (PAN)** is a network that connects devices, such as mice, keyboards, printers, smartphones, and tablets within the range of an individual person. These devices are most often connected with Bluetooth technology. Bluetooth is a wireless technology that enables devices to communicate over short distances.

Refer to
Interactive Graphic
in online course

5.1.1.3   Check Your Understanding - Types of Networks

5.1.2   Internet Connection Types

Refer to
Online Course
for Illustration

5.1.2.1   Brief History of Connection Technologies

In the 1990s, internet speeds were slow compared to today, which now has the bandwidth to transmit voice and video, as well as data. A dial-up connection requires either an internal modem installed in the computer or an external modem connected by USB. The modem dial-up port is connected to a phone socket using an RJ-11 connector. Once the modem is physically installed it must be connected to one of the computer's software COM ports. The modem must also be configured with local dialing properties such as the prefix for an outside line and the area code.

The Set Up a Connection or Network Wizard is used to configure a link to the ISP server. Connecting to the internet has evolved from analog telephone to broadband:

Analog Telephone

Analog telephone internet access can transmit data over standard voice telephone lines. This type of service uses an analog modem to place a telephone call to another modem at a remote site. This method of connection is known as dialup.

Integrated Services Digital Network

Integrated Services Digital Network (ISDN) uses multiple channels and can carry different types of services; therefore, it is considered a type of broadband. ISDN is a standard that uses multiple channels to send voice, video, and data over normal telephone wires. ISDN bandwidth is larger than traditional dialup.

Broadband

Broadband uses different frequencies to send multiple signals over the same medium. For example, the coaxial cables used to bring cable television to your home can carry computer network transmissions at the same time as hundreds of TV channels. Your cell phone can receive voice calls while also using a web browser.

Some common broadband network connections include cable, digital subscriber line (DSL), ISDN, satellite, and cellular. The figure shows equipment used to connect to or transmit broadband signals.

Refer to **Online Course** for Illustration

5.1.2.2   DSL, Cable, and Fiber

Both DSL and cable use a modem to connect to the internet through an Internet Service Provider (ISP), as shown in the figure. A DSL modem connects a user's network directly to the digital infrastructure of the phone company. A cable modem connects the user's network to a cable service provider.

DSL

DSL is an always-on service, which means that there is no need to dial up each time you want to connect to the internet. Voice and data signals are carried on different frequencies on the copper telephone wires. A filter prevents DSL signals from interfering with phone signals.

Cable

A cable internet connection does not use telephone lines. Cable uses coaxial cable lines originally designed to carry cable television. A cable modem connects your computer to the cable company. You can plug your computer directly into the cable modem. However, connecting a routing device to the modem allows multiple computers to share the connection to the internet.

Fiber

Fiber optic cables are made of glass or plastic and use light to transmit data. They have a very high bandwidth, which enables them to carry large amounts of data. At some point in your connection to the internet, your data will cross a fiber network. Fiber is used in backbone networks, large enterprise environments and large data centers. Older copper cabling infrastructures closer to home and businesses are increasingly being replaced with fiber. For example, in the figure, the cable connection includes a hybrid fiber coaxial (HFC) network in which fiber is used in the last mile to the user's home. At the user's home, the network switches back to copper coaxial cable.

The choice of connection varies depending on geographical location and service provider availability.

Refer to
Online Course
for Illustration

5.1.2.3   Line of Sight Wireless Internet Service

Line of sight wireless internet is an always-on service that uses radio signals for transmitting internet access, as shown in the figure. Radio signals are sent from a tower to the receiver that the customer connects to a computer or network device. A clear path between the transmission tower and customer is required. The tower may connect to other towers or directly to an internet backbone connection. The distance the radio signal can travel and still be strong enough to provide a clear signal depends on the frequency of the signal. Lower frequency of 900 MHz can travel up to 40 miles (65 km), while a higher frequency of 5.7 GHz can only travel 2 miles (3 km). Extreme weather conditions, trees, and tall buildings can affect signal strength and performance.

Refer to
Online Course
for Illustration

5.1.2.4   Satellite

Broadband satellite is an alternative for customers who cannot get cable or DSL connections. A satellite connection does not require a phone line or cable, but uses a satellite dish for two-way communication. The satellite dish transmits and receives signals to and from a satellite that relays these signals back to a service provider, as shown in the figure. Download speeds can reach up to 10Mb/s or more, while upload speed ranges about 1/10th of download speeds. It takes time for the signal from the satellite dish to relay to your ISP through the satellite orbiting the Earth. Due to this latency, it is difficult to use time-sensitive applications, such as video gaming, Voice over Internet Protocol (VoIP), and video conferencing.

Refer to
Online Course
for Illustration

5.1.2.5   Cellular

Cell phone technology relies on cell towers distributed throughout the user's coverage area to provide seamless access to cell phone services and the internet. With the advent of the third-generation (3G) of cellular technology, smartphones could access the internet. Download and upload speeds continue to improve with each iteration of cell phone technology.

In some regions of the world, smartphones are the only way users access the internet. In the United States, users are increasingly relying on smartphones for internet access. According to the Pew Research Center, in 2018 20% of adults in the United States do not use broadband at home (28% for adults 18-29). Instead, they use a smartphone for personal internet access. Search for "pew internet research" for more interesting statistics.

Refer to
Online Course
for Illustration

5.1.2.6   Mobile Hotspot and Tethering

Many cell phones provide the ability to connect other devices, as shown in the figure. This connection, known as tethering, can be made using Wi-Fi, Bluetooth, or by using a USB cable. Once a device is connected, it is able to use the phone's cellular connection to access the Internet. When a cellular phone allows Wi-Fi devices to connect and use the mobile data network, it is called a mobile hotspot.

Refer to
Interactive Graphic
in online course

5.1.2.7   Check Your Understanding - Internet Connection Types

5.2   Networking Protocols, Standards, and Services

5.2.1   Transport Layer Protocols

Refer to **Video** in online course

5.2.1.1   Video Explanation - Transport Layer Protocols

Click Play in the figure to view a video about transport layer protocols.

Click here to read the transcript of this video.

Refer to **Interactive Graphic** in online course

5.2.1.2   Activity - Transport Layer Protocols

Refer to **Interactive Graphic** in online course

5.2.1.3   The TCP/IP Model

The TCP/IP model consists of layers that perform functions necessary to prepare data for transmission over a network. TCP/IP stands for two important protocols in the model: Transmission Control Protocol (TCP) and Internet Protocol (IP). TCP is responsible for tracking all the network connections between a user's device and multiple destinations. The Internet Protocol (IP) is responsible for adding addressing so that data can be routed to the intended destination.

The two protocols that operate at the transport layer are TCP and User Datagram Protocol (UDP), as shown in Figure 1. TCP is considered a reliable, full-featured transport layer protocol, which ensures that all of the data arrives at the destination. In contrast, UDP is a very simple transport layer protocol that does not provide for any reliability. Figure 2 highlights the TCP and UDP properties.

Refer to **Video** in online course

5.2.1.4   TCP

TCP transport is analogous to sending packages that are tracked from source to destination. If a shipping order is broken up into several packages, a customer can check online to see the order of the delivery.

With TCP, there are three basic operations of reliability:

- Numbering and tracking data segments transmitted to a specific device from a specific application

- Acknowledging received data

- Retransmitting any unacknowledged data after a certain period of time

Click Play in the figure to see how TCP segments and acknowledgments are transmitted between sender and receiver.

Refer to **Video** in online course

5.2.1.5   UDP

UDP is similar to placing a regular, non-registered, letter in the mail. The sender of the letter is not aware of the availability of the receiver to receive the letter. Nor is the post office responsible for tracking the letter or informing the sender if the letter does not arrive at the final destination.

UDP provides the basic functions for delivering data segments between the appropriate applications, with very little overhead and data checking. UDP is known as a best-effort delivery protocol. In the context of networking, best-effort delivery is referred to as unreliable because there is no acknowledgment that the data is received at the destination.

Click Play in the figure to see an animation of UDP segments being transmitted from sender to receiver.

Refer to Interactive Graphic in online course

5.2.1.6   Check Your Understanding - Transport Layer Protocols

5.2.2   Application Port Numbers

Refer to Video in online course

5.2.2.1   Video Explanation - Application Port Numbers

Click Play in the figure to view a video about application port numbers.

Click here to read the transcript of this video.

Refer to Interactive Graphic in online course

5.2.2.2   Classify Application Port Numbers

TCP and UDP use a source and destination port number to keep track of application conversations. The source port number is associated with the originating application on the local device. The destination port number is associated with the destination application on the remote device. These are not physical ports. They are numbers that are used by TCP and UDP to identify the applications that should handle the data.

The source port number is dynamically generated by the sending device. This process allows multiple conversations to occur at the same time for the same application. For example, when you use a web browser, you can have more than one tab open at a time. The destination port number is 80 for regular web traffic or 443 for secure web traffic. These are called well-known port numbers because they are consistently used by most webservers on the Internet. Source port numbers will be different for each tab opened. This is how your computer knows which browser tab to deliver the web content to. Similarly, other network applications like email and file transfer have their own assigned port numbers.

There are a number of different types of application layer protocols that are identified by TCP or UDP port numbers at the transport layer.

- World Wide Web related protocols (Figure 1)
- Email and identity management protocols. (Figure 2)
- File transport and management protocols (Figure 3)
- Remote access protocols. (Figure 4)
- Network operations protocols. (Figure 5)

Figure 6 shows a summary table of all of these application protocols listed in protocol order.

Refer to Interactive Graphic in online course

5.2.2.3   Check Your Understanding - Application Port Numbers

5.2.3 Wireless Protocols

Refer to
Online Course
for Illustration

5.2.3.1 WLAN Protocols

The Institute of Electrical and Electronic Engineers' (IEEE) standards for Wi-Fi as specified in the 802.11 collective group of standards that specify the radio frequencies, speeds, and other capabilities for WLANs. Various implementations of the IEEE 802.11 standards have been developed over the years, as shown in the figure.

The 802.11a, 802.11b, and 802.11g standards should be considered legacy. New WLANs should implement 802.11ac devices. Existing WLAN implementations should upgrade to 802.11ac when purchasing new devices.

Refer to
Online Course
for Illustration

5.2.3.2 Bluetooth, NFC, and RFID

Wireless protocols for close proximity connectivity include Bluetooth, Radio Frequency Identification (RFID), and Near Field Communication (NFC).

Bluetooth

A Bluetooth device can connect up to seven other Bluetooth devices, as shown in Figure 1. Described in the IEEE standard 802.15.1, Bluetooth devices operate in the 2.4 to 2.485 GHz radio frequency range and is typically used for PANs. The Bluetooth standard incorporates Adaptive Frequency Hopping (AFH). AFH allows signals to "hop" around using different frequencies within the 2.4 to 2.485 GHz range, thereby reducing the chance of interference when multiple Bluetooth devices are present.

RFID

RFID uses the frequencies within the 125 MHz to 960 MHz range to uniquely identify items, such as in a shipping department as shown in Figure 2. Active RFID tags that contain a battery can broadcast their ID up to 100 meters. Passive RFID tags rely on the RFID reader to use radio waves to activate and read the tag. Passive RFID tags are typically used for close scanning but have a range of up to 25 meters.

NFC

NFC uses frequency 13.56 MHz and is a subset of the RFID standards. NFC is designed to be a secure method to complete transactions. For example, a consumer pays for good or services by waving the phone near the payment system, as shown in Figure 3. Based on a unique ID, the payment is charged directly against a pre-paid account or bank account. NFC is also used in mass-transportation services, the public parking sector, and many more consumer areas.

Refer to
Online Course
for Illustration

5.2.3.3 Zigbee and Z-Wave

Zigbee and Z-Wave are two smart home standards that allow users to connect multiple devices in a wireless mesh network. Typically, the devices are then managed from a smartphone app, as shown in the figure.

Zigbee

Zigbee uses low-power digital radios based on the IEEE 802.15.4 wireless standard for low-rate wireless personal area networks (LR-WPANs) that is meant to be used by low-cost, low-speed devices. Zigbee operates within frequencies from 868 MHz to 2.4 GHz and is limited to 10 to 20 meters. Zigbee has a data rate from 40-250 kb/s and can support approximately 65,000 devices.

The ZigBee specification relies on a main device called a ZigBee Coordinator. Tasked with managing all ZigBee client devices, the ZigBee Coordinator is responsible for the creation and maintenance of the ZigBee network.

Although Zigbee is an open standard, software developers must be a paid member of the Zigbee Alliance to use and contribute to the standard.

Z-Wave

Z-Wave technology is a proprietary standard that is now owned by Silicon Labs. However, a public version of the interoperability layer of Z-Wave was open sourced in 2016. These open source Z-Wave standards include Z-Wave's S2 security, Z/IP for transporting Z-Wave signals over IP networks, and Z-Ware middleware.

Z-Wave operates within a variety of frequencies based on the country from 865.2 MHz in India to 922 - 926 MHz in Japan. Z-Wave operates at 908.42 MHz in the North America. Z-Wave can transmit data up to 100 meters but has a slower data rate than Zigbee at 9.6-100 kb/s. Z-Wave can support up to 232 devices in one wireless mesh network.

Search the internet for "Zigbee and Z-Wave" to learn the latest information about these two smart home standards.

The Smart Home Market

The market for smart home products continues to grow. According to Statista.com, the number of smart homes was 34.8 million in 2018, which was a 28.4% increase from 2017. The smart home market will continue to provide economic opportunities for individuals and companies.

Refer to
Interactive Graphic
in online course

5.2.3.4 Cellular Generations

Refer to
Interactive Graphic
in online course

5.2.3.5 Check Your Understanding - Wireless Protocols

5.2.4 Network Services

Refer to **Video**
in online course

5.2.4.1 Video Explanation - Network Services

Click Play in the figure to view a video about network services.

Click here to read the transcript of this video.

Refer to
Online Course
for Illustration

5.2.4.2 Client - Server Roles

All computers connected to a network that participate directly in network communication are classified as hosts. Hosts are also called end devices. Hosts on networks perform a certain role. Some of these hosts perform security tasks, while others provide web services. There are also many legacy or embedded systems that perform specific tasks such as file or print services. Hosts that provide services are called servers. Hosts that use these services are called clients.

Each service requires separate server software. For example, a server requires web server software in order to provide web services to the network. A computer with server software can provide services simultaneously to one or many clients. Additionally, a single computer can run multiple types of server software. In a home or small business, it may be necessary for one computer to act as a file server, a web server, and an email server.

Clients need software installed in order to request and display the information obtained from the server. An example of client software is a web browser, like Chrome or FireFox. A single computer can also run multiple types of client software. For example, a user can check email and view a web page while instant messaging and listening to Internet radio.

5.2.4.3 DHCP Server

Refer to Online Course for Illustration

A host needs IP address information before it can send data on the network. Two important IP address services are Dynamic Host Configuration Protocol (DHCP) and Domain Name Service (DNS).

DHCP is the service used by ISPs, network administrators, and wireless routers to automatically assign IP addressing information to hosts, as shown in the figure.

5.2.4.4 DNS Server

Refer to Online Course for Illustration

DNS is the method computers use to translate domain names into IP addresses. On the internet, domain names, such as http://www.cisco.com, are much easier for people to remember than 198.133.219.25, which is the actual numeric IP address for this server. If Cisco decides to change the numeric IP address of www.cisco.com, it is transparent to the user because the domain name remains the same. The new address is simply linked to the existing domain name and connectivity is maintained.

Figures 1 through 5 display the steps involved in DNS resolution.

5.2.4.5 Print Server

Refer to Online Course for Illustration

Print servers enable multiple computer users to access a single printer. A print server has three functions:

- Provide client access to print resources.
- Administer print jobs by storing them in a queue until the print device is ready for them and then feeding or spooling the print information to the printer.
- Provide feedback to users.

5.2.4.6 File Server

Refer to Online Course for Illustration

The File Transfer Protocol (FTP) provides the ability to transfer files between a client and a server. An FTP client is an application that runs on a computer that is used to push and pull files from a server running FTP as a service.

As the figure illustrates, to successfully transfer files, FTP requires two connections between the client and the server, one for commands and replies, the other for the actual file transfer.

FTP has many security weaknesses. Therefore, a more secure file transfer services should be used, such as one of the following:

- **File Transfer Protocol Secure (FTPS)** - An FTP client can request the file transfer session be encrypted. The file server can accept or deny the request.

- **SSH File Transfer Protocol (SFTP)** - As an extension to Secure Shell (SSH) protocol, SFTP can be used to establish a secure file transfer session.

- **Secure Copy (SCP)** - SCP also uses SSH to secure file transfers.

Refer to **Online Course** for Illustration

5.2.4.7   Web Server

Web resources are provided by a web server. The host accesses the web resources using the Hypertext Transfer Protocol (HTTP) or the secure HTTP (HTTPS). HTTP is a set of rules for exchanging text, graphic images, sound, and video on the World Wide Web. HTTPS adds encryption and authentication services using Secure Sockets Layer (SSL) protocol or the newer Transport Layer Security (TLS) protocol. HTTP operates on port 80. HTTPS operates on port 443.

To better understand how the web browser and web server interact, we can examine how a web page is opened in a browser. For this example, use the http://www.cisco.com/index.html URL.

First, as shown in Figure 1, the browser interprets the three parts of the URL:

1. **http** (the protocol or scheme)

2. **www.cisco.com** (the server name)

3. **index.html** (the specific filename requested)

The browser then checks with a Domain Name Server (DNS) to convert www.cisco.com into a numeric address, which it uses to connect to the server. Using HTTP requirements, the browser sends a GET request to the server and asks for the index.html file, as shown in Figure 2. The server sends the HTML code for this web page back to the client's browser, as shown in Figure 3. Finally, as shown in Figure 4, the browser interprets the HTML code and formats the page for the browser window.

Refer to **Online Course** for Illustration

5.2.4.8   Mail Server

Email requires several applications and services, as shown in the figure. Email is a store-and-forward method of sending, storing, and retrieving electronic messages across a network. Email messages are stored in databases on mail servers.

Email clients communicate with mail servers to send and receive email. Mail servers communicate with other mail servers to transport messages from one domain to another. An email client does not communicate directly with another email client when sending email. Instead, both clients rely on the mail server to transport messages.

Email supports three separate protocols for operation: Simple Mail Transfer Protocol (SMTP), Post Office Protocol (POP), and Internet Message Access Protocol (IMAP). The application layer process that sends mail uses SMTP. A client retrieves email using one of the two application layer protocols: POP or IMAP.

Refer to
Online Course
for Illustration

5.2.4.9 Proxy Server

Proxy servers have the authority to act as another computer. A popular use for proxy servers is to act as storage or cache for web pages that are frequently accessed by devices on the internal network. For example, the proxy server in the figure is storing the web pages for www.cisco.com. When any internal host sends an HTTP GET request to www.cisco.com, the proxy server completes the following steps:

1. It intercepts the requests.

2. It checks to see if the website content has changed.

3. If not, the proxy server responds to host with the web page.

In addition, a proxy server can effectively hide the IP addresses of internal hosts because all requests going out to the internet are sourced from the proxy server's IP address.

Refer to
Online Course
for Illustration

5.2.4.10 Authentication Server

Access to network devices is typically controlled through authentication, authorization, and accounting services. Referred to as AAA or "triple A", these services provide the primary framework to set up access control on a network device. AAA is a way to control who is permitted to access a network (authenticate), what they can do while they are there (authorize), and track what actions they perform while accessing the network (accounting).

In the figure, the remote client goes through a four-step process to authenticate with a AAA server and gain access to the network.

Refer to
Online Course
for Illustration

5.2.4.11 Syslog Server

Many networking devices support syslog, including routers, switches, application servers, firewalls, and other network appliances. The syslog protocol allows networking devices to send their system messages across the network to syslog servers.

The syslog logging service provides three primary functions:

- The ability to gather logging information for monitoring and troubleshooting

- The ability to select the type of logging information that is captured

- The ability to specify the destinations of captured syslog messages

Refer to
Interactive Graphic
in online course

5.2.4.12 Check Your Understanding - Network Services

5.3 Network Devices

5.3.1 Basic Network Devices

Refer to **Video**
in online course

5.3.1.1 Video Explanation - Basic Network Devices

Click Play in the figure to view a video about basic network devices.

Click here to read the transcript of this video.

Refer to
Online Course
for Illustration

5.3.1.2   Network Interface Card

A network interface card (NIC) provides the physical connection to the network at the PC or other end device. As shown in the figure, there are different types of NICs. Ethernet NICs are used to connect to Ethernet networks and wireless NICs are used to connect to 802.11 wireless networks. Most NICs in desktop computers are integrated into the motherboard or connected to an expansion slot. NICs are also available in a USB form factor.

A NIC also performs the important function of addressing data with the NIC's media access control (MAC) address and sending the data out as bits on the network. NICs found on most computers today are gigabit Ethernet (1000 Mbps) capable.

Note   Today's computers and motherboards typically have NICs built in including wireless capability. Refer to the manufacturer's specifications for more information.

Refer to
Online Course
for Illustration

5.3.1.3   Repeaters, Bridges, and Hubs

In the early days of networking, solutions like using repeaters, hubs, and bridges were created to add more devices to the network.

Repeater

Regenerating weak signals is the primary purpose of a repeater, as shown in Figure 1. Repeaters are also called extenders because they extend the distance a signal can travel. In today's networks, repeaters are most often used to regenerate signals in fiber-optic cables. Also, every networking device that receives and sends data regenerates the signal.

Hub

Hubs, shown in Figure 2, receive data on one port and then send it out to all other ports. A hub extends the reach of a network because it regenerates the electrical signal. Hubs can also connect to another networking device, such as a switch or router, which connects to other sections of the network.

Hubs are legacy devices and should not be used in today's networks. Hubs do not segment network traffic. When one device sends traffic, the hub floods that traffic to all other devices connected to the hub. The devices are sharing the bandwidth.

Bridge

Bridges were introduced to divide LANs into segments. Bridges keep a record of all the devices on each segment. A bridge can then filter network traffic between LAN segments. This helps reduce the amount of traffic between devices. For example, in Figure 3, if PC-A needs to send a job to the printer, the traffic will not be forward to Segment 2. However, the server will also receive this print job traffic.

Refer to
Online Course
for Illustration

5.3.1.4   Switches

Bridges and hubs are now considered legacy devices because of the benefits and low cost of switches. As shown in the figure, a switch microsegments a LAN. Microsegmenting means that switches filter and segment network traffic by sending data only to the device to which it is sent. This provides higher dedicated bandwidth to each device on the network. When PC-A sends a job to the printer, only the printer receives the traffic. Both switches and legacy bridges perform microsegmentation, however, switches perform this filtering and forwarding operation in hardware, and also include additional features.

Switch Operation

Every device on a network has a unique media access control (MAC) address. This address is hardcoded by the manufacturer of the NIC. As devices send data, switches enter the device's MAC address into a switching table that records the MAC address for each device connected to the switch, and records which switch port can be used to reach a device with a given MAC address. When traffic arrives that is destined for a particular MAC address, the switch uses the switching table to determine which port to use to reach the MAC address. The traffic is forwarded out the port to the destination. By sending traffic out of only one port to the destination, other ports are not affected.

Managed and Unmanaged Switches

In larger networks, network administrators typically install managed switches. Managed switches come with additional features that the network administrator can configure to improve the functionality and security of the network. For example, a managed switch can be configured with VLANs and port security.

In a home or small business network, you probably do not need the added complexity and expense of a managed switch. Instead, you might consider installing an unmanaged switch. These switches typically have no management interface. You simply plug them into the network and attach network devices to benefit from a switch microsegmentation features.

Refer to
Online Course
for Illustration

5.3.1.5   Wireless Access Points

Wireless access points (APs), shown in the figure, provide network access to wireless devices, such as laptops and tablets. The wireless AP uses radio waves to communicate with the wireless NIC in the devices and other wireless access points. An access point has a limited range of coverage. Large networks require several access points to provide adequate wireless coverage. A wireless access point provides connectivity only to the network, while a wireless router provides additional features.

Refer to
Online Course
for Illustration

5.3.1.6   Routers

Switches and wireless APs forward data within a network segment. Routers can have all the functionality of a switch or a wireless AP. However, routers connect networks, as shown in the figure. Switches use MAC addresses to forward traffic within a single network. Routers use IP addresses to forward traffic to other networks. In larger networks, routers connect to switches, which then connect to LANs, like the router on the right in the figure. The router serves as the gateway to outside networks.

The router on the left in the figure is also known as a multipurpose device or integrated router. It includes a switch and a wireless access point. For some networks, it is more convenient to purchase and configure one device that serves all your needs than to purchase a separate device for each function. This is especially true for the home or small office. Multipurpose devices may also include a modem for connecting to the internet.

Refer to
Interactive Graphic
in online course

5.3.1.7   Check Your Understanding - Basic Network Devices

5.3.2   Security Devices

Refer to **Video** in online course

5.3.2.1   Video Explanation - Security Devices

Click Play in the figure to view a video about security devices.

Click here to read the transcript of this video.

Refer to **Online Course** for Illustration

5.3.2.2   Firewalls

An integrated router typically contains a switch, a router, and a firewall, as shown in the figure. Firewalls protect data and equipment on a network from unauthorized access. A firewall resides between two or more networks. It does not use the resources of the computers it is protecting, so there is no impact on processing performance.

Firewalls use various techniques for determining what is permitted or denied access to a network segment, such as an Access Control List (ACL). This list is a file that the router uses which contains rules about data traffic between networks.

Note   On a secure network, if computer performance is not an issue, enable the internal operating system firewall for additional security. For example, in Windows 10 the firewall is called Windows Defender Firewall. Some applications might not operate properly unless the firewall is configured correctly for them.

Refer to **Online Course** for Illustration

5.3.2.3   IDS and IPS

Intrusion Detection Systems (IDSs) passively monitor traffic on the network. Stand-alone IDS systems have largely disappeared in favor of Intrusion Prevention Systems (IPSs). But the detection feature of an IDS is still part of any IPS implementation. Figure 1 shows that an IDS-enabled device copies the traffic stream and analyzes the copied traffic rather than the actual forwarded packets. Working offline, it compares the captured traffic stream with known malicious signatures, similar to software that checks for viruses.

An IPS builds upon IDS technology. However, an IPS device is implemented in inline mode. This means that all inbound and outbound traffic must flow through it for processing. As shown in Figure 2, an IPS does not allow packets to enter the target system without first being analyzed.

The biggest difference between IDS and IPS is that an IPS responds immediately and does not allow any malicious traffic to pass, whereas an IDS allows malicious traffic to pass before it is addressed. However, a poorly configured IPS can negatively affect the flow of traffic in the network.

Refer to **Online Course** for Illustration

5.3.2.4   UTMs

Unified Threat Management (UTM) is a generic name for an all-in-one security appliance. UTMs include all the functionality of an IDS/IPS as well as stateful firewall services. Stateful firewalls provide stateful packet filtering by using connection information maintained in a state table. A stateful firewall tracks each connection by logging the source and destination addresses, as well as source and destination port numbers.

In addition to IDS/IPS and stateful firewall services, UTMs also typically provide additional security services such as:

- Zero Day protection
- Denial of Service (DoS) and Distributed Denial of Service (DDoS) protection
- Proxy filtering of applications
- Email filtering for spam and phishing attacks
- Antispyware
- Network access control
- VPN services

These features can vary significantly, depending on the UTM vendor.

In the firewall market today, UTMs are now typically called next-generation firewalls. For example, the Cisco Adaptive Security Appliance in the figure offers the latest in next-generation firewall features.

Refer to **Online Course** for Illustration

5.3.2.5 Endpoint Management Server

An endpoint management server is typically responsible for monitoring all the end devices in your network including desktops, laptops, servers, tablets, and any device connected to your network. An endpoint management server can restrict an end device's connection to the network if the device does not meet certain predetermined requirements. For example, it can verify the devices has the latest operating system and anti-virus updates.

Cisco's Digital Network Architecture (DNA) Center is an example of a solution that provides endpoint management. However, Cisco DNA is much more. It is a comprehensive management solution for managing all devices connected to the network so that the network administrator can optimize network performance to deliver the best possible user and application experience. The tools for managing the network are available for the Cisco DNA Center interface, as shown in the figure.

Refer to **Interactive Graphic** in online course

5.3.2.6 Check Your Understanding - Security Devices

5.3.3 Other Network Devices

Refer to **Online Course** for Illustration

5.3.3.1 Legacy and Embedded Systems

Legacy systems are those computer and networking systems that are no longer supported but are still in operation in today's networks. Legacy systems range from industrial control systems (ICSs) to computer mainframe systems, and a wide variety of networking devices such as hubs and bridges. Legacy systems are inherently vulnerable to security breaches because they cannot be upgraded or patched. One solution to alleviate some of the security risk is to air gap these systems. Air gapping is the process of physically isolating legacy systems from other networks and particularly the internet.

Embedded systems are related to legacy systems in that many legacy systems have embedded microchips. These embedded microchips are typically programmed to provide dedicated input and output instructions to a specialized device. Examples of embedded systems in the home are things such as a thermostat, refrigerator, cooking range, dishwasher, washing machine, video game consoles, and smart TVs. Embedded systems are increasingly becoming connected to the internet. Security should be top of mind when the technician recommends and installs embedded systems.

Refer to
Online Course
for Illustration

5.3.3.2   Patch Panel

A patch panel is commonly used as a place to collect incoming cable runs from the various networking devices throughout a facility, as shown in the figure. It provides a connection point between PCs and the switches or routers. A patch panel can be unpowered or powered. A powered patch panel can regenerate weak signals before sending them on to the next device.

For safety, ensure that all cables are secured using cable ties or cable management products and are not crossing walkways or running under desks where they can be kicked.

Refer to
Online Course
for Illustration

5.3.3.3   Power over Ethernet and Ethernet over Power

Power over Ethernet (PoE) is a method for powering devices that do not have a battery or access to a power outlet. For example, a PoE switch (Figure 1) transfers small amounts of DC current over an Ethernet cable, along with the data, to power PoE devices. Low voltage devices that support PoE, such as wireless access points, surveillance video devices, and IP phones, can be powered from remote locations. Devices that support PoE can receive power over an Ethernet connection at distances up to 330 ft (100 m) away. Power can also be inserted in the middle of a cable run using a PoE injector, as shown in Figure 2.

Ethernet over Power, or more commonly called powerline networking, uses existing electrical wiring to connect devices, as shown in Figure 3. The concept of "no new wires" means the ability to connect a device to the network wherever there is an electrical outlet. This saves the cost of installing data cables and without any additional cost to the electrical bill. Using the same wiring that delivers electricity, powerline networking sends information by sending data on certain frequencies. Figure 3 is of a powerline networking adapter plugged into an electrical outlet.

Refer to
Online Course
for Illustration

5.3.3.4   Cloud-based Network Controller

A cloud-based network controller is a device in the cloud that allows network administrators to manage network devices. For example, a medium sized company with multiple locations might have hundreds of wireless APs. Managing these devices can be cumbersome without using some type of controller.

For example, Cisco Meraki provides cloud-based networking that centralizes the management, visibility, and control of all Meraki devices into one dashboard interface, as shown in the figure. The network administrator is able to manage the wireless devices in multiple locations with the click of a mouse button.

Refer to
Interactive Graphic
in online course

5.3.3.5   Check Your Understanding - Other Network Devices

5.4   Network Cables

5.4.1   Network Tools

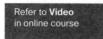

5.4.1.1   Video Explanation - Network Cable Tools

Click Play in the figure to view a video about network tools.

Click here to read the transcript of this video.

5.4.1.2   Network Tools and Descriptions

Refer to
Interactive Graphic
in online course

Wire cutters

Wire cutters are used to cut wires. Also known as side-cutters, these wire cutters are specifically designed to snip aluminum and copper wire.

Refer to
Interactive Graphic
in online course

5.4.1.3   Check Your Understanding - Network Tools

5.4.2   Copper Cables and Connectors

Refer to
Online Course
for Illustration

5.4.2.1   Cable Types

A wide variety of networking cables are available, as shown in the figure. Coaxial and twisted-pair cables use electrical signals over copper to transmit data. Fiber-optic cables use light signals to transmit data. These cables differ in bandwidth, size, and cost.

Refer to
Online Course
for Illustration

5.4.2.2   Coaxial Cables

Coaxial cable is usually constructed of either copper or aluminum. It is used by both cable television companies and satellite communication systems. Coaxial cable is enclosed in a sheath or jacket and can be terminated with a variety of connectors, as shown in the figure.

Coaxial cable (or coax) carries data in the form of electrical signals. It provides improved shielding compared to unshielded twisted-pair (UTP), so it has a higher signal-to-noise ratio allowing it to carry more data. However, twisted-pair cabling has replaced coax in LANs because, when compared to UTP, coax is physically harder to install, more expensive, and harder to troubleshoot.

Refer to
Online Course
for Illustration

5.4.2.3   Twisted-Pair Cables

Twisted-pair is a type of copper cabling used for telephone communications and most Ethernet networks. The pair is twisted to provide protection against crosstalk, which is the noise generated by adjacent pairs of wires in the cable. Unshielded twisted-pair (UTP) cabling is the most common variety of twisted-pair cabling.

As shown in Figure 1, UTP cable consists of four pairs of color-coded wires that have been twisted together and then encased in a flexible plastic sheath that protects from minor physical damage. UTP does not protect against electromagnetic interference (EMI) or radio frequency interference (RFI). EMI and RFI can be caused by a variety of sources including electric motors and fluorescent lights.

Shielded twisted-pair (STP) was designed to provide better protection against EMI and RFI. As shown in Figure 2, each twisted-pair is wrapped in a foil shield. The four pairs are then wrapped together in a metallic braid or foil.

Both UTP and STP cables are terminated with an RJ-45 connector and plug into RJ-45 sockets, as shown in Figure 3. Compared to UTP cable, STP cable is significantly more expensive and difficult to install. To gain the full benefit of the shielding, STP cables are terminated with special shielded STP RJ-45 data connectors (not shown). If the cable is improperly grounded, the shield may act as an antenna and pick up unwanted signals.

Refer to **Interactive Graphic** in online course

5.4.2.4   Twisted-Pair Category Ratings

Twisted-Pair Category Ratings

New or renovated office buildings often have some type of UTP cabling that connects every office. The distance limitation of UTP cabling used for data is 100 meters (330 feet). Click each UTP category for its speed rating and features.

Each category also comes in plenum rated versions, which are installed inside plenum areas of buildings. A plenum is any area that is used for ventilation, such as the area between the ceiling and a dropped ceiling. Plenum-rated cables are made from a special plastic that retards fire and produces less smoke than other cable types.

Click the buttons on the left to learn more about each type.

Refer to **Interactive Graphic** in online course

5.4.2.5   Twisted-Pair Wire Schemes

Refer to **Interactive Graphic** in online course

5.4.2.6   Activity - Cable Pinouts

Refer to **Video** in online course

5.4.2.7   Video Demonstration - Build and Test a Network Cable

Click Play in the figure to view a demonstration of how to build a straight-through Ethernet cable.

Click here to read the transcript of this video.

Refer to **Lab Activity** for this chapter

5.4.2.8   Lab - Build and Test a Network Cable

In this lab, you will build and test a straight-through UTP Ethernet network cable.

Lab - Build and Test a Network Cable

5.4.3   Fiber Cables and Connectors

Refer to **Online Course** for Illustration

5.4.3.1   Fiber-Optic Cables

Optical fiber is composed of two kinds of glass (core and cladding) and a protective outer shield (jacket). Click each component in the figure to learn more information.

Because it uses light to transmit signals, fiber-optic cable is not affected by EMI or RFI. All signals are converted to light pulses as they enter the cable, and converted back into electrical signals when they leave it. This means that fiber-optic cable can deliver signals that are clearer, can go farther, and have greater bandwidth than cable made of copper or other metals. Although the optical fiber is very thin and susceptible to sharp bends, the properties of the core and cladding make it very strong. Optical fiber is durable and is deployed in harsh environmental conditions in networks all around the world.

Refer to
Online Course
for Illustration

5.4.3.2   Types of Fiber Media

Fiber-optic cables are broadly classified into two types:

- **Single-mode fiber (SMF)** - Consists of a very small core and uses laser technology to send a single ray of light, as shown in Figure 1. Popular in long-distance situations spanning hundreds of kilometers, such as those required in long haul telephony and cable TV applications.

- **Multimode fiber (MMF)** - Consists of a larger core and uses LED emitters to send light pulses. Specifically, light from an LED enters the multimode fiber at different angles, as shown in Figure 2. Popular in LANs because they can be powered by low-cost LEDs. It provides bandwidth up to 10 Gb/s over link lengths of up to 550 meters.

Refer to
Online Course
for Illustration

5.4.3.3   Fiber-Optic Connectors

An optical fiber connector terminates the end of an optical fiber. A variety of optical fiber connectors are available. The main differences among the types of connectors are dimensions and methods of coupling. Businesses decide on the types of connectors that will be used, based on their equipment.

Click each connector in the figure to learn about the most popular types of fiber-optic connectors.

For fiber standards with FX and SX in the name, light travels in one direction over optical fiber. Therefore, two fibers are required to support the full duplex operation. Fiber-optic patch cables bundle together two optical fiber cables and terminate them with a pair of standard single fiber connectors. Some fiber connectors accept both the transmitting and receiving fibers in a single connector known as a duplex connector, as shown in the Duplex Multimode LC Connector in the figure.

For fiber standards with BX in the name, light travels in both directions on a single strand of fiber. It does this through a process called Wave Division Multiplexing (WDM). WDM is a technology that separates the transmit and receive signals inside the fiber.

For more information on fiber standards, search for "gigabit ethernet fiber-optic standards".

Refer to
Interactive Graphic
in online course

5.4.3.4   Check Your Understanding - Fiber Cables and Connectors

Refer to
Online Course
for Illustration

5.5   Summary

In this chapter, you learned about the different types of components, devices, services, and protocols that comprise a network. How all of these elements are arranged forms different network topologies such as PANs, LANs, VLANS, WLANs, and VPNs. There are also different ways in which computers and networks are connected to the Internet. For example, there are wired connections like DSL, cable, and fiber optics, and wireless connections such as satellite and cellular services. It is even possible to connect network devices to the Internet through a cell phone using tethering.

You learned about the four layers of the TCP/IP model; network access, internet, transport, and application. Each layer performs the functions necessary for data transmission over a network. Each layer also has specific protocols that are used to communicate between peers.

The chapter covered different wireless technologies and standards beginning with a comparison of the WLAN protocols and IEEE 802.11 standards. These standards use two radio frequency bands of 5 GHz (802.11a and 802.11ac) and 2.4GHz (802.11b, 802.11g, and 802.11n). Other wireless protocols for close proximity connectivity like Bluetooth, and NFC were discussed as well as standards for smart home applications, such as Zigbee, which is an open standard based on IEEE 802.15.4 and Z-Wave, which is a proprietary standard. You also learned about the evolution of the cellular generations from 1G, which supported only analog voice, through 5G which has enough bandwidth to support AR and VR.

Many types of network hardware devices were discussed. NICs provide physical connectivity for end devices, can be wired or wireless, and install inside the computer in an expansion slot or outside connected via USB. You learned that repeaters and hubs operate at layer 1and repeat network signals, and that switches and routers operate at Layers 2 and 3 respectively with switches forwarding frames based on MAC address and routers forwarding packets based on IP address.

Networks also include security devices such as firewalls, IDS, IPS, and UTM systems. Firewalls protect data and equipment on a network from unauthorized access. IDSs passively monitor traffic on the network while IPSs actively monitor traffic and respond immediately, not allowing any malicious traffic to pass. UTMs are all-in-one security appliances and include all the functionality of an IDS/IPS as well as stateful firewall services.

Finally in this chapter, you learned about network cables and connectors and the tools used by network technicians to test and repair them. Cables come in different sizes and costs and differ in the maximum bandwidth and distances that they support. Coax and twisted pair cables carry data in the form of electrical signals while fiber optic cables use light. Twisted pair cables use two different wiring schemes, T568A and T568B, which defines the order of the individual wire connections at the end of the cable. You built and tested a straight-through UTP Ethernet network cable using either the T568A or T568B standards.

Go to the online course to take the quiz and exam.

Chapter 5 Quiz

This quiz is designed to provide an additional opportunity to practice the skills and knowledge presented in the chapter and to prepare for the chapter exam. You will be allowed multiple attempts and the grade does not appear in the gradebook.

Chapter 5 Exam

The chapter exam assesses your knowledge of the chapter content.

Your Chapter Notes

Applied Networking

Refer to
Online Course
for Illustration

6.0 Introduction

Virtually all computers and mobile devices today are connected to some type of network and to the Internet. This means that configuring and troubleshooting computer networks is now a critical skill for IT professionals. This chapter focuses on applied networking with in-depth discussion on the format and architecture of media access control (MAC) addresses and Internet protocol (IP) addresses, both IPv4 and IPv6, that are used to connect computers to a network. Examples of how to configure static and dynamic addressing on computers are included. Also covered in this chapter is the configuration of both wired and wireless networks, firewalls, and IoT devices.

You will learn how to configure network interface cards (NICs), connect devices to a wireless router, and configure a wireless router for network connectivity. You will learn how to configure wireless network basic wireless settings, Network Address Translation (NAT), firewall settings, and Quality of Service (QoS). You will also learn about firewalls, Internet of Things (IoT) devices, and network troubleshooting. At the end of the chapter you will learn the six step troubleshooting process and common problems and solutions for computer networks.

Your networking skills should include the ability to configure wireless networks so that hosts can communicate, configure firewalls to filter traffic, verify network connectivity, and solve network connectivity problems. There are three labs included in this chapter where you will build these skills. In these labs you will configure basic settings on a wireless router and connect a PC to the wireless network, configure firewall settings to implement MAC address filtering, a DMZ, and single port forwarding, and finally, diagnose and solve network problems.

6.1 Device to Network Connection

6.1.1 Network Addressing

Refer to **Video**
in online course

6.1.1.1 Video Explanation - MAC Addressing

Click Play in the figure to view a video about Media Access Control (MAC) addresses.

Click here to read the transcript of this video.

Refer to **Video**
in online course

6.1.1.2 Video Explanation - IPv4 Addressing

Click Play in the figure to view a video about Internet Protocol (IP) v4 addressing.

Click here to read the transcript of this video.

Refer to **Video**
in online course

6.1.1.3 Video Explanation - IPv6 Addressing

Click Play in the figure to view a video about IPv6 addressing.

Click here to read the transcript of this video.

Refer to
Interactive Graphic
in online course

6.1.1.4   Two Network Addresses

Your fingerprint and mailing address are two ways to identify you and locate you. Your fingerprint usually does not change. Your fingerprint can be used to uniquely identify you, wherever your location. Your mailing address is different. It is your location. Unlike your fingerprint, your mailing address can change.

Devices that are attached to a network have two addresses that are similar to your fingerprint and mailing address, as shown in the figure. These two types of addresses are the Media Access Control (MAC) address and the Internet Protocol (IP) address.

The MAC address is hard-coded onto the Ethernet or wireless network interface card (NIC) by the manufacturer. The address stays with the device regardless of what network the device is connected to. A MAC address is 48 bits and can be represented in one of the three hexadecimal formats shown in Figure 2.

IP addressing is assigned by network administrators based on the location within the network. When a device moves from one network to another, its IP address will most likely change. An IP version 4 (IPv4) address is 32 bits and represented in dotted decimal notation. An IP version 6 (IPv6) address is 128 bits and is represented in hexadecimal format, as shown in Figure 3.

Figure 4 shows a topology with two local area networks (LANs). This topology demonstrates that MAC addresses do not change when a device is moved. But IP addresses do change. The laptop was moved to LAN 2. Notice that the laptop's MAC address did not change, but its IP addresses did change.

Note   Converting between decimal, binary, and hexadecimal numbering systems is beyond the scope of this course. Search the internet to learn more about these numbering systems.

Refer to
Online Course
for Illustration

6.1.1.5   Displaying the Addresses

Today, your computer probably has an IPv4 and an IPv6 address, as shown for the laptop in the figure. In the early 1990s, there was a concern about running out of IPv4 network addresses. The Internet Engineering Task Force (IETF) began to look for a replacement. This led to the development of IPv6. Currently, IPv6 is operating alongside IPv4 and is beginning to replace it.

The Figure shows output for the command **ipconfig /all** on the laptop. The output is highlighted to show the MAC address and two IP addresses.

Note   Windows OS calls the NIC an Ethernet adapter and the MAC address a physical address.

Refer to
Interactive Graphic
in online course

6.1.1.6   IPv4 Address Format

When you manually configure a device with an IPv4 address, you enter it in dotted decimal format, as shown for a Windows computer in Figure 1. Each number separated by a period is called an octet because it represents 8 bits. Therefore, the 32-bit address 192.168.200.8 has four octets.

An IPv4 address is composed of two parts. The first part identifies the network. The second part identifies this device on the network. The subnet mask is used by the device to determine the network. For example, the computer in Figure 1 uses the subnet mask 255.255.255.0 to determine that the IPv4 address 192.168.200.8 belongs to the 192.168.200.0 network. The .8 portion is this device's unique host portion on the 192.168.200 network. Any other device with that same 192.168.200 prefix will be on the same network but have a different value for the host portion. Devices with a different prefix will be on a different network.

To see this at the binary level, you can convert the 32-bit IPv4 address and subnet mask to their binary equivalents, as shown in Figure 2. A one bit in the subnet mask means that bit is part of the network portion. So, the first 24 bits of the 192.168.200.8 address are network bits. The last 8 bits are host bits.

When your device prepares data to send out on the network, it must first determine whether to send data directly to the intended receiver or to a router. It will send it directly to the receiver if the receiver is on the same network. Otherwise, it will send the data to a router. A router then uses the network portion of the IP address to route traffic between different networks.

For example, if the Windows computer in Figure 1 has data to send to a host at 192.168.200.25, it sends the data directly to that host because it has the same prefix of 192.168.200. If the destination's IPv4 address is 192.168.201.25, then the Window's computer will send the data to a router.

Refer to
Interactive Graphic
in online course

6.1.1.7   IPv6 Address Formats

IPv6 overcomes the address space limitations of IPv4. The 32-bit IPv4 address space provides approximately 4,294,967,296 unique addresses. The 128-bit IPv6 address space provides 340,282,366,920,938,463,463,374,607,431,768,211,456 addresses, or 340 undecillion addresses.

The 128 bits of an IPv6 addresses are written as a string of hexadecimal values, with letters expressed in lowercase. Every 4 bits is represented by a single hexadecimal digit for a total of 32 hexadecimal values. The examples shown in Figure 1 are fully expanded IPv6 addresses. Two rules help reduce the number of digits needed to represent an IPv6 address.

Rule 1 - Omit Leading Os

The first rule to help reduce the notation of IPv6 addresses is to omit any leading 0s (zeros) in any 16-bit section. For example, in Figure 1:

- **0db8** can be represented as **db8**, in the first IPv6 address

- **0123** can be represented as **123**, in the second IPv6 address

- **0001** can be represented as **1**, in the third IPv6 address

Note   IPv6 addresses must be represented in lowercase letters, but you may often see them as uppercase.

Rule 2 - Omit All 0 Segments

The second rule to help reduce the notation of IPv6 addresses is that a double colon (::) can replace any group of consecutive zeros. The double colon (::) can only be used once within an address, otherwise there would be more than one possible resulting address.

Figures 2 to 4 show examples of how to use the two rules to compress the IPv6 addresses shown in Figure 1.

Refer to
Interactive Graphic
in online course

6.1.1.8   Static Addressing

In a small network, you can manually configure each device with proper IP addressing. You would assign a unique IP address to each host within the same network. This is known as static IP addressing.

On a Windows computer, as shown in Figure 1, you can assign the following IPv4 address configuration information to a host:

- **IP address** - identifies this device on the network

- **Subnet mask** - is used to identify the network on which this device is connected

- **Default gateway** - identifies the router that this device uses to access the internet or another network

- **Optional values** - such as the preferred Domain Name System (DNS) server address and the alternate DNS server address

Similar configuration information for IPv6 addressing is shown in Figure 2.

Refer to
Online Course
for Illustration

6.1.1.9   Dynamic Addressing

Rather than manually configure every device, you can take advantage of implementing a Dynamic Host Configuration Protocol (DHCP) server. A DHCP server automatically assigns IP addresses, which simplifies the addressing process. Automatically configuring some of the IP addressing parameters also reduces the possibility of assigning duplicate or invalid IP addresses.

By default, most host devices are configured to request IP addressing from a DHCP server. The default setting for a Windows computer is shown in the figure. When a computer is set to obtain an IP address automatically, all other IP addressing configuration boxes are not available. This process is the same for a wired or wireless NIC.

A DHCP server can automatically assign the following IPv4 address configuration information to a host:

- IPv4 address

- Subnet mask

- Default gateway

- Optional values, such as a DNS server address

DHCP is also available for automatically assigning IPv6 addressing information.

Note   The steps to configure a Windows computer is beyond the scope of this topic.

Refer to
Online Course
for Illustration

6.1.1.10 Link-local IPv4 and IPv6 Addresses

Link-local addresses for IPv4 and IPv6 are used by a device to communicate with other computers connected to the same network within the same IP address range. The major difference between IPv4 and IPv6 is the following:

- An IPv4 device uses the link-local address if the device cannot obtain an IPv4 address.
- An IPv6 device must always be dynamically or manually configured with a link-local IPv6 address.

IPv4 Link-Local Address

If your Windows computer cannot communicate with a DHCP server to obtain an IPv4 address, then Windows automatically assigns an Automatic Private IP Addressing (APIPA) address. This link-local address is in the range of 169.254.0.0 to 169.254.255.255.

IPv6 Link-Local Address

Like IPv4, the IPv6 link-local address enables your device to communicate with other IPv6-enabled devices on the same network and only on that network. Unlike IPv4, every IPv6 enabled device is required to have a link-local address. IPv6 link-local addresses are in the range of fe80:: to febf::. For example, in the figure, the links to other networks are down (not connected) as notate by the red Xs. However, all the devices on the LAN can still use link-local IPv6 addresses to communicate with each other.

Note Unlike IPv4 link-local addresses, IPv6 link-local addresses are used in a variety of processes including network discovery protocols and routing protocols. This is beyond the scope of this course.

Refer to
Interactive Graphic
in online course

6.1.1.11 Check Your Understanding - Network Addressing

6.1.2 Configure a NIC

Refer to **Packet
Tracer Activity**
for this chapter

6.1.2.1 Packet Tracer - Add Computers to an Existing Network

In this Packet Tracer activity, you will configure the computers to use DHCP, configure static addressing, use **ipconfig** to retrieve host IPv4 information, and use **ping** to verify connectivity.

Packet Tracer - Add Computers to an Existing Network Instructions

Packet Tracer - Add Computers to an Existing Network PKA

Refer to
Online Course
for Illustration

6.1.2.2 Network Design

As a computer technician, you must be able to support the networking needs of your customers. Therefore, you must be familiar with:

- **Network components** - Includes wired and wireless network interface cards (NIC) and network devices such as switches, wireless access points (APs), routers, multipurpose devices, and more.

■ **Network design** - Involves knowing how networks are interconnected to support the needs of a business. For instance, the needs of a small business will differ greatly from the needs of a large business.

Consider a small business with 10 employees. The business has contracted you to connect their users. As shown in the figure, a home or small office wireless router could be used for such a small number of users. These routers are multiple purpose and typically provide router, switch, firewall, and access point capabilities. In addition, these wireless routers often provide a variety of other services including DHCP.

If the business was much larger, then you would not use a wireless router. Instead, you would consult with a network architect to design a network of dedicated switches, access points (AP), firewall appliances, and routers.

Regardless of network design, you must know how to install network cards, connect wired and wireless devices, and configure basic network equipment.

Note This chapter will focus on connecting and configuring a small office or home wireless router. The configurations will be demonstrated using Packet Tracer. However, the same functionality and similar graphical user interface (GUI) elements exist in all wireless routers. You can purchase a variety of low-cost wireless routers online and from consumer electronic stores. Search the internet for "wireless router reviews" to research current recommendations.

Refer to
Online Course
for Illustration

6.1.2.3   Selecting a NIC

A NIC is required to connect to the network. As shown in Figure 1, there are different types of NICs. Ethernet NICs are used to connect to Ethernet networks and wireless NICs are used to connect to 802.11 wireless networks. Most NICs in desktop computers are integrated into the motherboard or connected to an expansion slot. NICs are also available in a USB form factor.

Many computers purchased today come with a wired and wireless network interface integrated on the motherboard.

Refer to
Online Course
for Illustration

6.1.2.4   Installing and Updating a NIC

Follow the steps to install adapter cards if you are installing a NIC inside the computer. A wireless NIC for a desktop device has an external antenna connected to the back of the card or attached with a cable so that it can be positioned for the best signal reception. You must connect and position the antenna.

Sometimes a manufacturer publishes new driver software for a NIC. A new driver might enhance the functionality of the NIC, or it might be needed for operating system compatibility. The latest drivers for all supported operating systems are available for download from the manufacturer's website.

When installing a new driver, disable virus protection software to ensure that the driver installs correctly. Some virus scanners detect a driver update as a possible virus attack. Install only one driver at a time; otherwise, some updating processes might conflict. A best practice is to close all applications that are running so that they are not using any files associated with the driver update.

Note   An example of Windows Device Manager and the place to update a NIC's driver is shown in the figure. However, details of how to update drivers for specific devices and operating systems is beyond the scope of this topic.

Refer to
Online Course
for Illustration

6.1.2.5   Configure a NIC

After the NIC driver is installed, the IP address settings must be configured. For Windows computers, IP addressing is dynamic by default. After you physically connect a Windows computer to the network, it will automatically send out a request for IPv4 addressing the DHCP server. If a DHCP server is available, the computer will receive a message will all its IPv4 addressing information.

Note   Dynamic addressing for IPv6 can also use DHCP but is beyond the scope of this course.

This dynamic, default behavior is also typically for smartphones, tablets, gaming consoles, and other end-user devices. Static configuration is normally the job of a network administrator. However, you should be familiar with how to access the IP addressing configuration for any device you are asked to manage.

To find IP addressing configuration information, search the internet for "IP address configuration for device" where "device" is replaced with your device, such as "iPhone". For example, Figure 1 shows the dialog box for viewing and changing a Windows computer's IPv6 configuration. Figure 2 shows the setting screens for automatic and manual IPv4 configuration on an iPhone.

Refer to
Online Course
for Illustration

6.1.2.6   ICMP

Internet Control Message Protocol (ICMP) is used by devices on a network to send control and error messages. There are several different uses for ICMP, such as announcing network errors, announcing network congestion, and troubleshooting.

Ping is commonly used to test connections between computers. To see a list of options that you can use with the ping command, type **ping /?** in the Command Prompt window, as shown in Figure 1.

Ping works by sending an ICMP echo request to the IP address you entered. If the IP address is accessible, the receiving device then sends back an ICMP echo reply message to confirm connectivity.

You can also use the **ping** command to test connectivity to a website by entering the website's domain name. For example, if you enter **ping cisco.com** your computer will first use DNS to find the IP address and then send the ICMP echo request to that IP address, as shown in Figure 2.

Refer to
Lab Activity
for this chapter

6.1.2.7   Lab - Configure a NIC to Use DHCP in Windows

In this lab, you will configure an Ethernet NIC to use DHCP to obtain an IP address and test connectivity between two computers.

Lab - Configure a NIC to Use DHCP in Windows

6.1.3   Configure a Wired and Wireless Network

Refer to **Video**
in online course

6.1.3.1   Video Explanation - Configure a Wired and Wireless Network

Click Play in the figure to view a demonstration of how to configure a wired and wireless network.

Click here to read the transcript of this video.

Refer to
Interactive Graphic
in online course

6.1.3.2   Connecting Wired Devices to the Internet

The steps to connect a wired device to the internet in a home or small office are as follows:

Step 1.   Connect a network cable to the device.

To connect to a wired network, attach an Ethernet cable to the NIC port, as shown in Figure 1.

Step 2.   Connect the device to a switch port.

Connect the other end of the cable to an Ethernet port on the wireless router, such as one of the four yellow switch ports shown in Figure 2. In a SOHO network, the laptop would most likely connect to a wall jack which in turn connects to a network switch.

Step 3.   Connect a network cable to the wireless router internet port.

On the wireless router, connect an Ethernet cable to the port labeled Internet (blue port in Figure 2). This port might also be labeled WAN.

Step 4.   Connect the wireless router to the modem.

The blue port in Figure 2 is an Ethernet port that is used to connect the router to a service provider device such as a DSL or cable modem in Figure 3.

Step 5.   Connect to the service provider's network.

The modem is then connected to the service provider's network, as shown in Figure 3.

Note   A separate modem isn't necessary if the wireless router is a router/modem combination.

Step 6.   Power all devices and verify physical connections.

Turn on the broadband modem and plug in the power cord to the router. After the modem establishes a connection to the ISP, it will begin communicating with the router. The laptop, router, and modem LEDs will light up, indicating communication. The modem enables the router to receive the network information necessary to gain access to the internet from the ISP. This information includes public IPv4 addresses, subnet mask, and DNS server addresses. With the depletion of public IPv4 addresses, many ISPs are also providing IPv6 addressing information as well.

Figure 4 shows a topology depicting the physical connection of a wired laptop in the small office or home network.

Note Cable or DSL modem configuration is usually done by the service provider's representative either on-site or remotely through a walkthrough with you on the phone. If you buy the modem, it will come with documentation for how to connect it to your service provider which will most likely include contacting your service provider for more information.

Refer to
Online Course
for Illustration

6.1.3.3 Logging in to the Router

Most home and small office wireless routers are ready for service out of the box. They preconfigured to be connected to the network and provide services. For example, the wireless router uses DHCP to automatically provide addressing information to connected devices. However, wireless router default IP addresses, usernames, and passwords can easily be found on the internet. Just enter the search phrase "default wireless router IP address" or "default wireless router passwords" to see a listing of many websites that provide this information. Therefore, your first priority should be to change these defaults for security reasons.

To gain access to the wireless router's configuration GUI, open a web browser. In the address field, enter the default IP address for your wireless router. The default IP address can be found in the documentation that came with the wireless router or you can search the internet. The figure shows the IPv4 address 192.168.0.1, which is a common default for many manufacturers. A security window prompts for authorization to access the router GUI. The word admin is commonly used as the default username and password. Again, check your wireless router's documentation or search the internet.

Refer to
Interactive Graphic
in online course

6.1.3.4 Basic Network Setup

Refer to
Interactive Graphic
in online course

6.1.3.5 Basic Wireless Settings

Refer to
Online Course
for Illustration

6.1.3.6 Configure a Wireless Mesh Network

In a small office or home network, one wireless router may suffice to provide wireless access to all the clients. However, if you want to extend the range beyond approximately 45 meters indoors and 90 meters outdoors, you can add wireless access points. As shown in the wireless mesh network in the figure, two access points are configured with the same WLAN settings from our previous example. Notice that the channels selected are 1 and 11 so that the access points do not interfere with channel 6 configured previously on the wireless router.

Extending a WLAN in a small office or home has become increasingly easier. Manufacturers have made creating a wireless mesh network (WMN) simple through smartphone apps. You buy the system, disperse the access points, plug them in, download the app, and configure your WMN in a few steps. Search the internet for "best wi-fi mesh network system" to find reviews of current offerings.

Refer to
Online Course
for Illustration

6.1.3.7 NAT for IPv4

On a wireless router, if you look for a page like the Status page shown in the figure, you will find the IPv4 addressing information that the router uses to send data to the internet. Notice that the IPv4 address is 209.165.201.11 is a different network than the 10.10.10.1 address assigned to the router's LAN interface. All the devices on the router's LAN will get assigned addresses with the 10.10.10 prefix.

The 209.165.201.11 IPv4 address is publicly routable on the internet. Any address with the 10 in the first octet is a private IPv4 address and cannot be routed on the internet. Therefore, the router will use a process called Network Address Translation (NAT) to convert private IPv4 addresses to Internet-routable IPv4 addresses. With NAT, a private (local) source IPv4 address is translated to a public (global) address. The process is reversed for incoming packets. The router is able to translate many internal IPv4 addresses into public addresses, by using NAT.

Some ISPs use private addressing to connect to customer devices. However, eventually, your traffic will leave the provider's network and be routed on the internet. To see the IP addresses for your devices, search the internet for "what is my IP address." Do this for other devices on the same network and you will see that they all share the same public IPv4 address. NAT makes this possible by tracking the source port numbers for every session established by a device. If your ISP has IPv6 enabled, you will see a unique IPv6 address for each device.

Refer to
Online Course
for Illustration

6.1.3.8   Quality of Service

Many home and small office routers have an option for configuring Quality of Service (QoS). By configuring QoS, you can guarantee that certain traffic types, such as voice and video, are prioritized over traffic that is not as time-sensitive, such as email and web browsing. On some wireless routers, traffic can also be prioritized on specific ports.

The figure is a simplified mockup of a QoS interface based on a Netgear GUI. You will usually find the QoS settings in the advanced menus. If you have a wireless router available, investigate the QoS settings. Sometimes, these might be listed under "bandwidth control" or something similar. Consult the wireless router's documentation or search the internet for "qos settings" for your router's make and model.

Refer to **Packet Tracer Activity** for this chapter

6.1.3.9   Packet Tracer - Connect to a Wireless Network

In this activity, you will configure a wireless router and an access point to accept wireless clients and route IP packets.

Packet Tracer - Connect to a Wireless Network Instructions

Packet Tracer - Connect to a Wireless Network PKA

Refer to **Lab Activity** for this chapter

6.1.3.10   Lab - Configure a Wireless Network

In this lab, you will configure basic settings on a wireless router and connect a PC to router wirelessly.

Lab - Configure a Wireless Network

6.1.4   Firewall Settings

Refer to **Video** in online course

6.1.4.1   Video Explanation - Firewall Settings

Click Play in the figure to view a demonstration of how to configure a firewall.

Click here to read the transcript of this video.

Refer to
Online Course
for Illustration

6.1.4.2 UPnP

Universal Plug and Play (UPnP) is a protocol that enables devices to dynamically add themselves to a network without the need for user intervention or configuration. Although convenient, UPnP is not secure. The UPnP protocol has no method for authenticating devices. Therefore, it considers every device trustworthy. In addition, the UPnP protocol has numerous security vulnerabilities. For example, malware can use the UPnP protocol to redirect traffic to different IP addresses outside your network, potentially sending sensitive information to a hacker.

Many home and small office wireless routers have UPnP enabled by default. Therefore, check this configuration and disable it, as shown in the figure.

Search the internet for "vulnerability profiling tools" to determine if your wireless router is exposed to UPnP vulnerabilities.

Refer to
Interactive Graphic
in online course

6.1.4.3 DMZ

A demilitarized zone (DMZ) is a network that provides services to an untrusted network. An email, web, or FTP server is often placed into the DMZ so that the traffic using the server does not come inside the local network. This protects the internal network from attacks by this traffic but does not protect the servers in the DMZ in any way. It is common for a firewall to manage traffic to and from the DMZ.

On a wireless router, you can create a DMZ for one device by forwarding all traffic ports from the internet to a specific IP address or MAC address. A server, game machine, or web camera can be in the DMZ so that the device can be accessed by anyone. For example, the Web Server in Figure 1 is in the DMZ and is statically assigned the IPv4 address 10.10.10.50. Figure 2 shows a typical configuration where any traffic sources from the internet will be redirected to the Web Server's IPv4 address 10.10.10.50. However, the Web Server is exposed to attacks from hackers on the internet and should have firewall software installed.

Refer to
Online Course
for Illustration

6.1.4.4 Port Forwarding

Hardware firewalls can be used to block TCP and UDP ports to prevent unauthorized access in and out of a LAN. However, there are situations when specific ports must be opened so that certain programs and applications can communicate with devices on different networks. Port forwarding is a rule-based method of directing traffic between devices on separate networks.

When traffic reaches the router, the router determines if the traffic should be forwarded to a certain device based on the port number found with the traffic. Port numbers are associated with specific services, such as FTP, HTTP, HTTPS, and POP3. The rules determine which traffic is sent on to the LAN. For example, a router might be configured to forward port 80, which is associated with HTTP. When the router receives a packet with the destination port of 80, the router forwards the traffic to the server inside the network that serves web pages. In the figure, port forwarding is enabled for port 80 and is associated with the web server at IPv4 address 10.10.10.50.

Port triggering allows the router to temporarily forward data through inbound ports to a specific device. You can use port triggering to forward data to a computer only when a designated port range is used to make an outbound request. For example, a video game might use ports 27000 to 27100 for connecting with other players. These are the trigger ports. A chat client might use port 56 for connecting the same players so that they can interact with each other. In this instance, if there is gaming traffic on an outbound port within the triggered port range, inbound chat traffic on port 56 is forwarded to the computer that is being used to play the video game and chat with friends. When the game is over and the triggered ports are no longer in use, port 56 is no longer allowed to send traffic of any type to this computer.

Refer to
Online Course
for Illustration

6.1.4.5   MAC Address Filtering

MAC address filtering specifies exactly which device MAC addresses are allowed to or blocked from sending data on your network. Many wireless routers only give you the option of allowing or blocking MAC addresses, but not both. Technicians will typically configure allowed MAC addresses. The MAC address for your Windows computer can be found with the **ipconfig /all** command, as shown in Figure 1.

You may need to search the internet for where to find the MAC address on a specific device. Finding the MAC address is not always straight forward because not all devices call it a MAC address. Windows calls it a "Physical Address", as shown in Figure 1. On an iPhone it is called the "Wi-Fi Address" and on an Android it is called "Wi-Fi MAC address", as shown in Figure 2.

Additionally, your device may have two or more MAC addresses. For example, the PlayStation 4 in Figure 3 has two MAC addresses: one for wired networks and one for wireless networks. Similarly, a Windows PC might have multiple MAC addresses. As shown in Figure 4, the PC has three MAC addresses: wired, wireless, and virtual.

Note   The last half of the MAC addresses and other identifying information is blurred out in Figures 2 and 3. The last six hexadecimal numbers are replaced with an **X** in Figure 4.

Finally, consider the fact that new devices might be added to the network at any time. You can see how the technician responsible for manually configuring all these MAC addresses might be overwhelmed. Imagine having to manually enter and maintain dozens of MAC addresses in an interface such as the one shown in Figure 5.

However, MAC address filtering may be your only option. Better solutions, such as port security, require purchasing a more expensive router or a separate firewall device, and are beyond the scope of this course.

Refer to
Online Course
for Illustration

6.1.4.6   Whitelisting and Blacklisting

Whitelisting and blacklisting specify which IP addresses are allowed or denied on your network. Similar to MAC address filtering, you can manually configure specific IP addresses to allow or deny into your network. On a wireless router, this is typically done using an access list or access policy, as shown in the figure. Refer to your wireless router's documentation for specific steps or search the internet for a tutorial.

Whitelisting is a good tool for allowing your users, such as children or employees, access to those IP addresses you approve. You can also blacklist or explicitly block known sites. However, similar to MAC address filtering, this can become burdensome. Better solutions exist. Search the internet for "parental control software" and "content filters".

Refer to **Packet Tracer Activity** for this chapter

6.1.4.7   Packet Tracer - Configure Firewall Settings

In this Packet Tracer activity, you will configure a wireless router to rely on MAC filtering, allow access to a server in the DMZ, and disable the DMZ and configure support for Single Port Forwarding.

Packet Tracer - Configure Firewall Settings Instructions

Packet Tracer - Configure Firewall Settings PKA

Refer to **Lab Activity** for this chapter

6.1.4.8   Lab - Configure Firewall Settings

In this lab, you will configure firewall settings to use MAC address filtering, a DMZ, and single port forwarding on a wireless router to manage connections and traffic through the wireless router.

Lab - Configure Firewall Settings

6.1.5   IoT Device Configuration

Refer to **Online Course** for Illustration

6.1.5.1   Internet of Things

The internet of today is significantly different than the internet of past decades. The internet of today is more than email, web pages, and file transfers between computers. The evolving internet is becoming an Internet of Things (IoT). No longer will the only devices accessing the internet be computers, tablets, and smartphones. The sensor-equipped, internet-ready devices of tomorrow will include everything from automobiles and biomedical devices, to household appliances and natural ecosystems.

You may already have some IoT devices in your home. You can buy all kinds of connected devices including thermostats, light switches, security cameras, door locks, and voice-enabled digital assistants (such as Amazon Alexis and Google Home). These devices can all be connected to your network. In addition, many of them can be directly managed from a smartphone app, as shown in the figure.

Refer to **Online Course** for Illustration

6.1.5.2   IoT Devices in Packet Tracer

At this point in its infancy, the IoT market has not yet agreed upon a set of standards for IoT device installation and configuration. Configuring IoT devices is very much device specific. Consult the manufacturer's documentation or website for configuration guides.

In this course, you will use Packet Tracer to explore a basic IoT device configuration. The figure shows all the IoT devices in Packet Tracer. Packet Tracer also includes a number of sensors and actuators. In the figure, the sensors are shown in the bottom panel of the Packet Tracer interface.

Refer to **Packet Tracer Activity** for this chapter

6.1.5.3   Packet Tracer - Control IoT Devices

In this activity, you have just installed various IoT devices around the house and wish to configure them as a home security system. You will configure the home gateway to use a motion sensor, test and reset security features, and set the air conditioning.

Packet Tracer - Control IoT Devices Instructions

Packet Tracer - Control IoT Devices PKA

6.2   Basic Troubleshooting Process for Networks

6.2.1   Applying the Troubleshooting Process to

Refer to
Interactive Graphic
in online course

6.2.1.1   The Six Steps of the Troubleshooting Process

Refer to
Online Course
for Illustration

6.2.1.2   Identify the Problem

Network problems can be simple or complex, and can result from a combination of hardware, software, and connectivity issues. As a technician, you should develop a logical and consistent method for diagnosing network problems by eliminating one problem at a time.

For example, to assess the problem determine how many devices are experiencing the problem. If there is a problem with one device, start with that device. If problem with all devices, start the troubleshooting process in the network room where all the devices are connected.

The first step in the troubleshooting process is to identify the problem. Use the list of open-ended and closed-ended questions in the figure as a starting point to gather information from the customer.

Refer to
Online Course
for Illustration

6.2.1.3   Establish a Theory of Probable Cause

After you have talked to the customer, you can establish a theory of probable causes. The list in the figure provides some common probable causes for network problems.

Refer to
Online Course
for Illustration

6.2.1.4   Test the Theory to Determine the Cause

After you have developed some theories about what is wrong, test your theories to determine the cause of the problem. Once the theory is confirmed, determine the next steps to resolve the problem. The list above shows some quick procedures that you can use to determine the exact cause of the problem or even correct the problem. If a quick procedure does correct the problem, you can then verify full system functionality. If a quick procedure does not correct the problem, you might need to research the problem further to establish the exact cause.

Refer to
Online Course
for Illustration

6.2.1.5   Establish a Plan of Action to Resolve the Problem and Implement the Solution

After you have determined the exact cause of the problem, establish a plan of action to resolve the problem and implement the solution. The list in the figure shows some sources you can use to gather additional information to resolve an issue.

Refer to
Online Course
for Illustration

6.2.1.6   Verify Full Functionality and, If Applicable, Implement Preventive Measures

After you have corrected the problem, verify full functionality and, if applicable, implement preventive measures. The list in the figure shows a few steps to verify the solution.

Refer to
Online Course
for Illustration

6.2.1.7   Document Findings, Actions, and Outcomes

In the final step of the troubleshooting process, document your findings, actions, and outcomes, as shown in the list in the figure.

Refer to
Interactive Graphic
in online course

6.2.1.8   Check Your Understanding - Network Troubleshooting Process

6.2.2   Network Problems and Solutions

Refer to
Interactive Graphic
in online course

6.2.2.1   Common Problems and Solutions for Networking

Refer to
Interactive Graphic
in online course

6.2.2.2   Advanced Problems and Solutions for Network Connections

Refer to
Interactive Graphic
in online course

6.2.2.3   Advanced Problems and Solutions for FTP and Secure Internet Connections

Refer to
Interactive Graphic
in online course

6.2.2.4   Advanced Problems and Solutions Using Network Tools

Refer to
Lab Activity
for this chapter

6.2.2.5   Lab - Troubleshoot Network Problems

In this lab, you will diagnose the causes and solve the network problems.

Lab - Troubleshoot Network Problems

Refer to
Online Course
for Illustration

6.3   Summary

In this chapter, you learned how to configure NICs, connect devices to a wireless router, and configure a wireless router for network connectivity. You also learned about firewalls, IoT devices, and network troubleshooting. You learned about the 48-bit MAC addresses that identified devices connected to an Ethernet LAN, and the two types of IP addresses, IPv4 and IPv6. IPv4 addresses are 32-bits in length and are written in dotted decimal format while IPv6 addresses are 128-bits in length and written in hexadecimal format.

Configuring an IP address on a device can be done manually or dynamically by using DHCP. You learned that manual, or static addressing, is appropriate for small networks while DHCP is best suited for larger networks. In addition to an IP address, DHCP can also automatically assign the subnet mask, default-gateway, and address of DNS servers. You configured a NIC to use DHCP on a Windows computer through a lab exercise. You were able to verify network configuration using the ipconfig /all command in Windows and test connectivity by using ping.

You then learned how to configure a wireless network including the configuration of a wireless router with basic wireless settings, NAT, firewall settings, and QoS. You then completed two labs one about configuring a wireless network and then a lab on configuring firewall settings. The wireless network lab had you configure basic wireless settings on a wireless host and an access point and then test connectivity. In the firewall lab you configured MAC filtering, a DMZ, and port forwarding.

The internet today is becoming more than just computers, tablets, and smartphones. It is becoming an IoT. These things are sensor-equipped, internet-ready devices that include automobiles, biomedical devices, household appliances, and natural ecosystems. You used Packet Tracer to explore IoT devices and their basic configuration.

At the end of the chapter, you learned the six steps in the troubleshooting process as they pertain to networks.

Go to the online course to take the quiz and exam.

Chapter 6 Quiz

This quiz is designed to provide an additional opportunity to practice the skills and knowledge presented in the chapter and to prepare for the chapter exam. You will be allowed multiple attempts and the grade does not appear in the gradebook.

Chapter 6 Exam

The chapter exam assesses your knowledge of the chapter content.

Your Chapter Notes

Laptops and Other Mobile Devices

Refer to
Online Course
for Illustration

7.0 Introduction

The first laptops were used primarily by business people who needed to access and enter data when they were away from the office. The use of laptops was limited due to expense, weight, and limited capabilities compared to less expensive desktops. Improvements in technology have allowed the laptop to become lightweight, powerful, and much more affordable. Because of this, laptops are found in just about every setting today. Laptops run the same operating systems as desktop computers and most come with built-in Wi-Fi, webcam, microphone, speakers, and ports to attach external components.

A mobile device is any device that is hand-held, lightweight, and typically has a touchscreen for input. Like a desktop or laptop computer, mobile devices use an operating system to run applications (apps), games, and play movies and music. Mobile devices also have a different CPU architecture, designed to have a reduced instruction set when compared to laptop and desktop processors. With the increase in demand for mobility, the popularity of laptops and other mobile devices continues to grow. This chapter focuses on many features of laptops, mobile devices, and their capabilities.

You will learn the features and functionality of laptops and mobile devices, like smartphones and tablets, as well as how to remove and install internal and external components. At the end of the chapter, you will learn the importance of a preventive maintenance program for laptops and other mobile devices and apply the six steps in the troubleshooting process as they pertain to laptops and other mobile devices.

It is important to not only learn about laptops and mobile devices and their components but also to build hands-on skills. In this chapter, you will research and gather information about an Andriod and iOS mobile device. In other labs, you will research laptop screens, drives, and specifications. As an IT technician, asking the right questions is critical to solving customer problems. You need to be able to ask questions that will be recorded on a work order. You will create closed-ended and open-ended questions to ask a customer about a computer problem.

7.1 Characteristics of laptops and other mobile devices

7.1.1 Mobile Device Overview

Refer to
Interactive Graphic
in online course

7.1.1.1 What Do You Already Know? - Mobile Devices

Refer to
Online Course
for Illustration

7.1.1.2 Mobility

Mobility in information technology means the ability to access information electronically from different locations outside of the home or office. Mobile connectivity is limited only by the availability of cellular or data networks. Mobile devices have self-contained power in the form of rechargeable batteries, are generally small and lightweight, and do not rely on other connected peripheral devices, such as a mouse and keyboard, to operate.

Examples of mobile devices are laptops, tablets, smartphones, smartwatches, and wearables.

Refer to
Online Course
for Illustration

7.1.1.3   Laptops

Laptops are portable computers. They usually run full versions of operating systems such as Microsoft Windows, iOS or Linux.

Laptops can have the same computing power and memory resources as desktop computers. As shown in the figure, laptops integrate a screen, keyboard, and a pointing device, such as a touchpad, in one portable device. Laptops can be run from an internal battery or from an electrical outlet. They offer connectivity options such as wired or wireless Ethernet networking and Bluetooth.

Laptops offer device connection options such as USB and HDMI. Laptops frequently have speaker and microphone connections as well. Some laptops offer graphic connectivity using different types of graphics standards, similar to desktops. However, in order to make laptops more portable, some peripheral connection options may require additional hardware, such as a dock or port replicator.

In order to increase portability, laptops may sacrifice some of the advantages that are offered by desktop computers. For example, laptops may not use the fastest processors available due to cooling concerns and high power consumption. Laptop memory upgrades may be limited, and some types of laptop memory are more expensive than comparable desktop memory. Laptops lack the expansion capability of desktops as well. Special-purpose expansion cards and large volume storage often cannot be installed in laptops. For example, upgrading the graphics subsystem in a laptop is likely to be impossible.

Refer to
Online Course
for Illustration

7.1.1.4   Smartphone Characteristics

Smartphones differ from laptops in that they run special operating systems that are designed for mobile devices. Examples of these operating systems are Google's Android and Apple's iOS. Smartphones may have limited OS upgradeability, so they can become out-of-date and require a purchase of a new phone to take advantage of new features of the OS and apps that require a higher OS version. Software for smartphones is usually limited to apps that can be downloaded from stores such as Google Play or the Apple App Store.

Smartphones are very compact and quite powerful. They have small touch screens with no physical keyboard. The keyboard is displayed on the screen. Because they are so small, they are usually limited to only one or two types of physical connection such as USB and headphones.

Smartphones use cellular connectivity options for voice, text, and data services. Other data connections include Bluetooth and Wi-Fi.

Refer to
Online Course
for Illustration

7.1.1.5   Smartphone Features

An additional feature of smartphones is location services. Most phones include global positioning system (GPS) functionality. A GPS receiver in the phone uses satellites to determine the geographic location of the device. This allows the device location to be used by apps for various purposes such as social media updates or receiving offers from nearby businesses. Some apps allow a smartphone to act as a navigational GPS that provides guidance for driving, biking, or walking. If the GPS is off, most smartphones can still determine the location, in a less precise way, by using info coming from nearby mobile service antennas or nearby Wi-Fi access points.

Another feature of some smartphones is the ability to "tether", or share, the cellular data connection with other devices. The smartphone can be configured to act as a modem that provides other devices to the cellular data network over USB, Bluetooth, or Wi-Fi. Not all smartphone carriers permit tethering.

Refer to
Online Course
for Illustration

7.1.1.6   Tablets and E-Readers

Tablets are similar to smartphones in that they use special mobile operating systems like Android or iOS. However, most tablets do not have the ability to access cellular networks. Some higher-end models do allow access to cellular services.

Unlike smartphones, tablets normally have larger touch-screen displays. The displays are often quite vivid in their graphic rendering. Tablets usually offer Wi-Fi and Bluetooth connectivity and most have USB and audio ports. In addition, some tablets include GPS receivers that can be activated to provide location services, similar to smartphones. Most of the apps that work on phones are also available for tablets.

E-readers, such as the Amazon Kindle, are special purpose devices with black and white displays that have been optimized for reading text. Although they resemble tablets, they lack many of the features and functions that tablets provide. Web access is limited to eBook stores that may be operated by the e-reader manufacturer. Many have touch displays that make it easy to turn pages, change settings, and access eBooks online. Many E-readers can store 1,000 or more books. For connectivity, some offer free cellular data connections for downloading books from a specific store, but most rely on Wi-Fi. Bluetooth is also available and supports headphones for audio books. E-reader battery life is usually longer than tablets, at up 15-20 hours of reading time or more.

Refer to
Online Course
for Illustration

7.1.1.7   Wearables: Smartwatches and Fitness Trackers

Wearables are smart devices that are meant to be worn on the body or attached to clothing. Two popular wearables are smartwatches and fitness trackers.

Smartwatches

Smartwatches are a type of wearable that includes a microprocessor, a special operating systems, and apps. Sensors in the smartwatch can gather data about various aspects of the body, such as heart rate, and use Bluetooth to report this information back to another device, such as a smartphone. The smartphone then forwards the information to an application over the internet for storage and analysis. Some smartwatches can also connect directly to a cellular network, serve as convenient displays for notifications from apps, can include GPS location services, and the ability to store and play music and playlists.

Fitness Trackers

Fitness trackers are similar to smartwatches but are limited to monitoring the body such as physical activity, sleep, and exercise. FitBit is a popular example that monitors heart rate and the number of steps taken. Similar to fitness trackers are more sophisticated health monitoring devices that can detect heart attacks, monitor air quality, and detect oxygen levels in the blood. These devices can deliver hospital-quality data to healthcare practitioners.

Refer to
Interactive Graphic
in online course

7.1.1.8   Wearables: Augmented and Virtual Realities

In Augmented Reality (AR), computer graphics are integrated with what is seen in the real world, usually through the device camera, as shown for the tablet in Figure 1. The graphics overlays can range from cartoon characters in a game application to information for emergency management training for first responders. There are many potential uses for AR and it is one of the most promising areas for future product development.

Related to AR is virtual reality (VR). In VR a user wears a special headset which displays graphics from a separate computer, as shown in Figure 2. The graphics are immersive 3D and create very realistic worlds. The VR user's motions are detected by sensors which allow the user to interact with and move around in the virtual environment. VR is very popular in games but has applications in other fields such as education and training.

Refer to
Interactive Graphic
in online course

7.1.1.9   Check Your Understanding - Laptops and Other Mobile Devices

Refer to
Lab Activity
for this chapter

7.1.1.10   Lab - Mobile Device Information

In this lab, you will gather information about an Android and an iOS device.

Lab - Mobile Device Information

7.1.2   Laptop Components

Refer to **Video**
in online course

7.1.2.1   Video Explanation - External Features Unique to Laptops

Click Play in the figure to view an explanation of external features unique to laptops.

Click here to read the transcript of this video.

Refer to **Video**
in online course

7.1.2.2   Video Explanation - Common Input Devices and LEDs in Laptops

Click Play in the figure to view an explanation of common input devices and LEDs in laptops.

Click here to read the transcript of this video.

Refer to
Online Course
for Illustration

7.1.2.3   Motherboards

The compact nature of laptops requires a number of internal components to fit in a small amount of space. The size restrictions result in a variety of form factors for a number of laptop components, such as the motherboard, RAM, CPU, and storage devices. Some laptop components, such as the CPU, may be designed to use less power to ensure that the system can operate for a longer period of time when using a battery source.

Desktop motherboards have standard form factors. The standard size and shape allow motherboards from different manufacturers to fit into common desktop cases. In comparison, laptop motherboards vary by manufacturer and are proprietary. When you repair a laptop, you must often obtain a replacement motherboard from the laptop manufacturer. The figure shows a comparison between a desktop motherboard and a laptop motherboard.

Because laptop motherboards and desktop motherboards are designed differently, components designed for a laptop generally cannot be used in a desktop. Laptop and desktop designs are compared in the table.

Refer to **Interactive Graphic** in online course

7.1.2.4   Internal Components

Laptop internal components are designed to fit into the confined spaces of the laptop form factor.

- RAM
- CPUs
- SATA drives
- Solid-state drives

Refer to **Interactive Graphic** in online course

7.1.2.5   Check Your Understanding - External Laptop components

Refer to **Video** in online course

7.1.2.6   Special function keys

The purpose of the Function (Fn) key is to activate a second function on a dual-purpose key. The feature that is accessed by pressing the Fn key in combination with another key is printed on the key in a smaller font or different color. Function keys will vary on different laptop models but these are some examples of functions that can be accessed:

- Dual displays
- Volume settings
- Media options such as fast forward or rewind
- Keyboard backlight
- Screen orientation
- Screen brightness
- WiFi, cellular, and Bluetooth on or off
- Media options such as play or rewind
- Touchpad on or off
- GPS on or off
- Airplane mode

Note   Some laptops may have dedicated function keys that perform functions without requiring users to press the Fn key.

A laptop monitor is a built-in LCD or LED screen. You cannot adjust the laptop monitor for height and distance because it is integrated into the lid of the case. You can often connect an external monitor or projector to a laptop. Pressing the Fn key with the appropriate Function key on the keyboard toggles between the built-in display and the external display, as shown in the figure.

Do not confuse the Fn key with Function keys F1 through F12. These keys are typically located in a row across the top of the keyboard. Their function depends on the OS and application that is running when they are pressed. Each key can perform up to seven different operations by pressing it with one or more combinations of the Shift, Control, and Alt keys.

Refer to **Video**
in online course

7.1.2.7   Video Explanation - Docking Station Versus Port Replicator

Click Play in the figure to view an explanation of docking stations versus port replicators.

Click here to read the transcript of this video.

Refer to
Lab Activity
for this chapter

7.1.2.8   Lab - Research Docking Stations and Port Replicators

In this lab, you will use the internet, a newspaper, or a local store to gather information and then record the specifications for a laptop docking station and port replicators.

Lab - Research Docking Stations and Port Replicators

7.1.3   Laptop Display Components

Refer to
Interactive Graphic
in online course

7.1.3.1   LCD, LED, and OLED Displays

There are three types of laptop displays:

- Liquid-crystal display (LCD)
- Light-emitting diode (LED)
- Organic light-emitting diode (OLED)

Refer to
Interactive Graphic
in online course

7.1.3.2   Laptop Display Features

Some common laptop display features include:

- Detachable Screens
- Touch Screens
- Cutoff Switches

Refer to
Interactive Graphic
in online course

7.1.3.3   Backlights and Inverters

LCDs do not produce any light by themselves. A backlight shines through the screen and illuminates the display. Two common types of backlights are cold cathode fluorescent lamp (CCFL) and LED. With CCFL, fluorescent tubes are connected to an inverter, used to convert direct current (DC) to alternating current (AC).

Refer to
Interactive Graphic
in online course

7.1.3.4   Check Your Understanding - Laptop Display Components

Refer to
Interactive Graphic
in online course

7.1.3.5   Wi-Fi Antenna Connectors

Wi-Fi Components
Wi-Fi antennas transmit and receive data carried over radio waves.

Refer to
Online Course
for Illustration

7.1.3.6   Webcam and Microphone
Most laptops today have a webcam and microphone built in. The webcam is normally positioned at the top, center of the display, as shown in the figure. The internal microphone can often be found next to the webcam. Some manufacturers may place the microphone next to the keyboard, or on the side of the laptop.

7.2   Laptop Configuration

7.2.1   Power Settings Configuration

Refer to
Online Course
for Illustration

7.2.1.1   Power Management
Advances in power management and battery technology are increasing the amount of time that a laptop can be powered from a battery. Many batteries can power a laptop for 10 hours or more. Configuring laptop power settings to better manage power usage is important to ensure that the battery is used efficiently.

Power management controls the flow of electricity to the components of a computer. The Advanced Configuration and Power Interface (ACPI) creates a bridge between the hardware and the operating system and allows technicians to create power management schemes to get the best performance from a laptop. The ACPI states shown in the figure are applicable to most computers, but they are particularly important when managing power in laptops.

Refer to
Online Course
for Illustration

7.2.1.2   Managing ACPI Settings in the BIOS
Technicians are frequently required to configure power settings by changing the settings in the BIOS or UEFI setup. Configuring the power settings affects the following:

- System states
- Battery and AC modes
- Thermal management
- CPU PCI bus power management
- Wake on LAN (WOL)

Note   WOL might require a cable connection inside the computer from the network adapter to the motherboard.

The ACPI power management mode must be enabled in the BIOS or UEFI setup to allow the OS to configure the power management states, as shown in the figure.

To enable ACPI mode, follow these steps:

Step 1.   Enter BIOS or UEFI setup.

Step 2.   Locate and enter the Power Management settings menu item.

Step 3.   Use the appropriate keys to enable ACPI mode.

Step 4.   Save and exit.

Note   These steps are common to most laptops but be sure to check the laptop documentation for specific configuration settings. There is no standard name for each power management state. Different manufacturers might use different names for the same state.

Refer to
Interactive Graphic
in online course

7.2.1.3   Check Your Understanding - Match ACPI Standards

Refer to **Video**
in online course

7.2.1.4   Video Demonstration - Managing Laptop Power Options

Click Play in the figure to view a demonstration of managing laptop power options.

Click here to read the transcript of this video.

7.2.2   Wireless Configuration

Refer to
Online Course
for Illustration

7.2.2.1   Bluetooth

The Bluetooth technical specification is described by the Institute of Electrical and Electronics Engineers (IEEE) 802.15.1 standard. Bluetooth devices are capable of handling voice, music, videos, and data.

The distance of a Bluetooth personal area network (PAN) is limited by the amount of power used by the devices in the PAN. Bluetooth devices are broken into three classifications. The most common Bluetooth network is Class 2, which has a range of approximately 33 ft (10 m).

Five specifications of Bluetooth technology are capable of different transfer rates, ranges, and power consumption. Each subsequent version offers enhanced capabilities. For instance, Versions 1 - 3 are older technologies with limited capabilities and high power consumption. Later versions such as Version 4 and 5 are geared towards devices that have limited power and do not need high data transfer rates. Additionally, version 5 has four different data rates to accommodate a variety of transmission ranges.

Security measures are included in the Bluetooth standard. The first time that a Bluetooth device connects, the device is authenticated using a PIN. This is known as pairing. Bluetooth supports both 128-bit encryption and PIN authentication.

Refer to
Online Course
for Illustration

7.2.2.2   Bluetooth Laptop Connections

Windows activates connections to Bluetooth devices by default. If the connection is not active, look for a switch on the front face or on the side of the laptop. Some laptops may have a special function key on the keyboard to enable the connection. If a laptop does not feature Bluetooth technology, you can purchase a Bluetooth adapter that plugs into a USB port.

Before installing and configuring a device, make sure that Bluetooth is enabled in the BIOS.

Turn on the device and make it discoverable. Check the device documentation to learn how to make the device discoverable. Use the Bluetooth Wizard to search and discover Bluetooth devices that are in discoverable mode.

Refer to **Video** in online course

7.2.2.3   Video Demonstration - Bluetooth Configuration

Click Play in the figure to view a demonstration of Bluetooth configuration.

Click here to read the transcript of this video.

Refer to **Online Course** for Illustration

7.2.2.4   Cellular WAN

Laptops with integrated cellular WAN capabilities require no software installation and no additional antenna or accessories. When you turn on the laptop, the integrated WAN capabilities are ready to use. If the connection is not active, look for a switch on the front face or on the side of the laptop. Some laptops may have a special function key on the keyboard to enable the connection.

Many cell phones provide the ability to connect other devices. This connection, known as tethering, can be made using Wi-Fi, Bluetooth, or by using a USB cable. Once a device is connected, it is able to use the phone's cellular connection to access the internet. When a cellular phone allows Wi-Fi devices to connect and use the mobile data network, this is called a hotspot.

You can also access a cellular network by using a cellular hotspot device.

There are also wireless mini PCIe and M.2 adapters for laptops that can provide a combination of Wi-Fi, Bluetooth, and/or cellular data (4G/LTE) connectivity. Some of these adapters will require the installation of a new antenna kit which has wires that are usually routed around the screen in the laptop lid. When installing an adapter card with cellular functionality a SIM will need to be inserted as well.

Refer to **Interactive Graphic** in online course

7.2.2.5   Wi-Fi

Wireless Adapter Types

Laptops usually access the internet by using wireless adapters. Wireless adapters can be built in to the laptop or attached to the laptop through an expansion port. Three major types of wireless adapters are used in laptops.

Refer to **Video** in online course

7.2.2.6   Video Demonstration - Wi-Fi Configuration

Click Play in the figure to view a demonstration of Wi-Fi configuration on a mobile device.

Click here to read the transcript of this video.

Refer to **Interactive Graphic** in online course

7.2.2.7   Check Your Understanding - Wireless Configuration

7.3   Laptop Hardware and Component Installation and Configuration

7.3.1   Expansion Slots

7.3.1.1   Expansion Cards

Refer to **Online Course** for Illustration

One of the disadvantages of laptops in comparison to desktops is that their compact design might limit the availability of some functions. To address this problem, many laptops contain ExpressCard slots to add functionality. The figure shows a comparison of the two ExpressCard models: ExpressCard/34 and ExpressCard/54. The models are 34 mm and 54 mm in width, respectively.

Here are some examples of functionality that can be added when using ExpressCards:

- Additional memory card reader
- External hard drive access
- TV turner cards
- USB and FireWire ports
- Wi-Fi connectivity

To install a card, insert the card into the slot and push it all the way in. To remove the card, press the eject button to release it.

If the ExpressCard is hot-swappable, follow these steps to safely remove it:

Step 1.   Click the Safely Remove Hardware icon in the Windows system tray to ensure that the device is not in use.

Step 2.   Click the device that you want to remove. A message pops up to tell you that it is safe to remove the device.

Step 3.   Remove the hot-swappable device from the laptop.

Caution   ExpressCards and USB devices are commonly hot-swappable. However, removing a device that is not hot-swappable while the computer is powered on can cause damage to data and devices.

7.3.1.2   Flash Memory

Refer to **Online Course** for Illustration

You should be aware of the following types of external flash memory and readers.

External Flash Drive

An external flash drive is a removable storage device that connects to an expansion port such as USB, eSATA, or Firewire. External flash drives can be an SSD drive or a smaller device, such as the one shown in the figure. Flash drives provide fast access to data, high reliability, and reduced power usage. These drives are accessed by the operating system in the same way that other types of drives are accessed.

Flash Cards

A flash card is a data storage device that uses flash memory to store information. Flash cards are small, portable, and require no power to maintain data. They are commonly used in laptops, mobile devices, and digital cameras. A large variety of flash card models are available, and each varies in size and shape.

Flash Card Readers

Most modern laptops feature a flash card reader for Secure Digital (SD) and Secure Digital High Capacity (SDHC) flash cards.

Note   Flash memory cards are hot-swappable and should be removed by following the standard procedure for hot-swappable device removal.

Refer to
Online Course
for Illustration

7.3.1.3   Smart Card Reader

A smart card is similar to a credit card, but has an embedded microprocessor that can be loaded with data. It can be used for telephone calling, electronic cash payments, and other applications. The microprocessor on the smart card is there for security and can hold much more information than that of a magnetic stripe found on a credit card.

Smart cards have been around for more than a decade but were found mostly in Europe. Recently, their popularity has increased in the United States.

Smart card readers are used to read and write to smart cards and can be connected to a laptop using a USB port. There are two types of smart card readers:

- **Contact** - This type of reader requires a physical connection to the card, made by inserting the card into the reader, as shown in the figure.

- **Contactless** - This type of reader works on a radio frequency that communicates when the card comes close to the reader.

Many smart card readers support contact and contactless read operations all in one device. These cards are identified by an oval logo that shows radio waves pointing to a hand holding a card.

Refer to
Online Course
for Illustration

7.3.1.4   SODIMM Memory

The make and model of the laptop determines the type of RAM needed. It is important to select the memory type that is physically compatible with the laptop. Most desktop computers use memory that fits into a DIMM slot. Most laptops use a smaller profile memory module that is called SODIMM. SODIMM has 72-pin and 100-pin configurations for support of 32-bit transfers and 144-pin, 200-pin, and 204-pin configurations for support of 64-bit transfers.

Note   SODIMMs can be further classified by DDR version. Different laptop models require different types of SODIMMs.

Before purchasing and installing additional RAM, consult the laptop documentation or the website of the manufacturer for form-factor specifications. Use the documentation to find where to install RAM on the laptop. On most laptops, RAM is inserted into slots behind a cover on the underside of the case, as shown in Figure 1. On some laptops, the keyboard must be removed to access the RAM slots.

Consult the manufacturer of the laptop to confirm the maximum amount of RAM each slot can support. You can view the currently installed amount of RAM in the POST screen, BIOS, or System Properties window.

Figure 2 shows where the amount of RAM is displayed in the System utility.

To replace or add memory, determine if the laptop has available slots and that it supports the quantity and type of memory to be added. In some instances, there are no available slots for the new SODIMM.

Refer to **Video** in online course

7.3.1.5   Video Demonstration - Install SODIMM

Click Play in the figure to view a video on how to install SODIMM in a laptop.

Click here to read a transcript of this video.

Refer to **Interactive Graphic** in online course

7.3.1.6   Check Your Understanding - Expansion Modules

7.3.2   Replacing Laptop Components

Refer to **Interactive Graphic** in online course

7.3.2.1   Overview of Hardware Replacement

Some parts of a laptop, typically called customer-replaceable units (CRUs), can be replaced by the customer. CRUs include components such as the laptop battery and RAM. Parts that should not be replaced by the customer are called field-replaceable units (FRUs). FRUs include components such as the motherboard, LCD display, as shown in Figure 1, and keyboard, as shown in Figure 2. Replacing FRUs typically requires a considerable amount of technical skill. In many cases, the device may need to be returned to the place of purchase, a certified service center, or the manufacturer. There are special cases, such as the video card where a user may be able to replace it, but they may need a repair center to replace it due to power and cooling requirements and space limitations. When repairing a laptop or portable device, it is important to keep parts organized and cables labeled to aid in re-assembly.

A repair center might provide service on laptops made by different manufacturers or just specialize in a specific brand and be considered an authorized dealer for warranty work and repair. The following are common repairs performed at local repair centers:

- Hardware and software diagnostics
- Data transfer and recovery
- Keyboard and fan replacement
- Internal laptop cleaning
- Screen repair
- LCD inverter and backlight repair

Most repairs to displays must be performed in a repair center. The repairs include replacing the screen, the backlight, or the inverter.

If no local services are available, you might need to send the laptop to a regional repair center or to the manufacturer. If the laptop damage is severe or requires specialized software and tools, the manufacturer can decide to replace the laptop instead of attempting a repair.

Caution   Before attempting to repair a laptop or portable device, check the warranty to see if repairs during the warranty period must be done at an authorized service center to avoid invalidating the warranty. If you repair a laptop yourself, always back up the data and disconnect the device from the power source. Always consult the service manual before beginning a laptop repair.

Refer to Video in online course

7.3.2.2   Video Demonstration - Keyboard Replacement

Click Play to view a video about replacing the keyboard on a laptop.

Click here to read a transcript of this video.

Refer to Video in online course

7.3.2.3   Video Demonstration - Screen Replacement

Click Play to view a video about replacing the screen on a laptop.

Click here to read a transcript of this video.

Refer to Lab Activity for this chapter

7.3.2.4   Lab - Research Laptop Screens

In this activity, you will use the internet, newspaper, or a local store to gather information and then record the specifications for a laptop display onto this worksheet.

Lab - Research Laptop Screens

Refer to Online Course for Illustration

7.3.2.5   Power

These are some signs that the battery, as shown in Figure 1, may need to be replaced:

- The battery does not hold a charge.
- The battery overheats.
- The battery is leaking.

If you experience problems that you suspect are battery related, exchange the battery with a known, good battery that is compatible with the laptop. If a replacement battery cannot be located, take the battery to an authorized repair center for testing.

A replacement battery must meet or exceed the specifications of the laptop manufacturer. New batteries must use the same form factor as the original battery. Voltages, power ratings, and AC adapters must also meet manufacturer specifications.

Note   Always follow the instructions provided by the manufacturer when charging a new battery. The laptop can be used during an initial charge, but do not unplug the AC adapter.

Caution   Handle batteries with care. Batteries can explode if they are shorted, mishandled, or improperly charged. Be sure that the battery charger is designed for the chemistry, size, and voltage of your battery. Batteries are considered toxic waste and must be disposed of according to local laws.

Refer to **Video** in online course

7.3.2.6   Video Demonstration - DC Jack Replacement

Click Play to view a video about replacing a DC jack.

Click here to read a transcript of this video.

Refer to **Lab Activity** for this chapter

7.3.2.7   Lab - Research Laptop Batteries

In this lab, you will use the internet, newspaper, or a local store to gather information and then record the specifications for a laptop battery.

Lab - Research Laptop Batteries

Refer to **Online Course** for Illustration

7.3.2.8   Internal Storage and Optical Drive

The form factor of an internal storage device is smaller for a laptop than for a desktop computer. Laptop drives are 1.8 in. (4.57 cm.) or 2.5 in. (6.35 cm.) in width. Most storage devices are CRUs unless a warranty requires technical assistance.

Before purchasing a new internal or external storage device, check the laptop documentation or the website of the manufacturer for compatibility requirements. Documentation often contains FAQs that may be helpful. It is also important to research known laptop component issues on the internet.

On most laptops, the internal hard drive and the internal optical drive are inserted into bays that are protected by a removable cover on the case, as shown in the figures. On some laptops, the keyboard must be removed to access these drives. Optical drives might not be interchangeable in the laptop. Some laptops may not include optical drives at all.

To view the currently installed storage devices, check the POST screen or BIOS. If installing a second drive or an optical drive, confirm that there are no error icons next to the device in the Device Manager.

Refer to **Video** in online course

7.3.2.9   Video Demonstration - Internal Storage and Optical Drive Replacement

Click Play to view a video about replacing the internal storage and optical drive on a laptop.

Click here to read a transcript of this video.

Refer to **Lab Activity** for this chapter

7.3.2.10   Lab - Research Laptop Drives

In this lab, you will use the internet, newspaper, or a local store to gather information about data drives for a laptop.

Lab - Research Laptop Drives

Refer to **Video** in online course

7.3.2.11   Video Demonstration - Wireless Card Replacement

Click Play to view a video about replacing the wireless card on a laptop.

Click here to read a transcript of this video.

Refer to **Video**
in online course

7.3.2.12   Video Demonstration - Speakers Replacement

Click Play to view a video about replacing the speakers on a laptop.

Click here to read a transcript of this video.

Refer to **Video**
in online course

7.3.2.13   Video Demonstration - CPU Replacement

Click Play to view a video about replacing the CPU on a laptop.

Click here to read a transcript of this video.

Refer to **Video**
in online course

7.3.2.14   Video Demonstration - Motherboard Replacement

Click Play to view a video about replacing the motherboard on a laptop.

Click here to read a transcript of this video.

Refer to **Video**
in online course

7.3.2.15   Video Demonstration - Plastic Frames

Click Play to view a video about plastic frames on a laptop.

Click here to read a transcript of this video.

Refer to
Interactive Graphic
in online course

7.3.2.16   Check Your Understanding - Replacing Laptop Components

7.4   Other Mobile Device Hardware Overview

7.4.1   Other Mobile Device Hardware

Refer to
Online Course
for Illustration

7.4.1.1   Cell Phone Parts

Because of their small size, mobile devices usually do not have field-serviceable parts. Mobile devices consist of several compact components integrated into a single unit. When a mobile device malfunctions, it is usually sent to the manufacturer for repair or replacement.

The cell phone contains one or more of these field replaceable parts: memory, a SIM card, and a battery.

A Secure Digital (SD) card is used to add memory to many mobile devices.

A SIM card is a small card that contains information used to authenticate a device to mobile telephone and data providers. The card can also hold user data such as personal contacts and text messages. Some phones can have two SIM cards installed and are called a dual SIM device. This would allow a number for personal use and a number for professional use to be received and sent from the same phone, for example. The DUAL SIM could also hold SIM cards from different vendors.

Some mobile device batteries can be replaced like the battery shown outside the cell phone. Be sure to check the battery for bulging and avoid placing the mobile device in direct sunlight.

Refer to
Interactive Graphic
in online course

7.4.1.2   Wired connectivity

A mini-USB cable
A mini-USB cable is used to connect a mobile device to an electrical outlet charger or to connect to another device in order to charge and/or transfer data.

Refer to
Online Course
for Illustration

7.4.1.3   Wireless Connections and Shared Internet Connections
Besides Wi-Fi, mobile devices also use the following wireless connections:

- **Near field communication (NFC)** - NFC enables mobile devices to establish radio communications with other devices by placing the devices close together or by touching them together.

- **Infrared (IR)** - If a mobile device is IR enabled, it can be used to control other IR controlled devices remotely, such as a TV, set top box, or audio equipment.

- **Bluetooth** - This wireless technology allows data exchange over a short distance between two Bluetooth-enabled devices or connect to other Bluetooth-enabled peripheral devices, such as speakers or headphone

A smartphone's internet connection can be shared with other devices. There are two ways to share the smartphone's internet connection: tethering and mobile hotspot. The ability to share the connection depends on the cellular carrier and the plan with the carrier.

- **Tether** - This uses your cellular phone as a modem for another device, such as a tablet or laptop. The connection is made over a USB cable or Bluetooth.

- **Mobile hotspot** - A hotspot is where devices connect using WiFi to share a cellular data connection.

Refer to
Interactive Graphic
in online course

7.4.1.4   Check Your Understanding - Identify Connection Types

7.4.2   Specialty Mobile Devices

Refer to
Interactive Graphic
in online course

7.4.2.1   Wearable Devices
Wearable devices are clothing or accessories that have miniature computing devices. Smart watches, fitness monitors, and smart headsets are some examples.

Refer to
Interactive Graphic
in online course

7.4.2.2   Specialty Devices
There are many other types of smart devices. These devices benefit from network connectivity and advanced functions.

7.5   Network Connectivity and Email

7.5.1   Wireless and Cellular Data Networks

Refer to **Online Course** for Illustration

7.5.1.1   Wireless Data Networks

The ability of a laptop, tablet, or cell phone to wirelessly connect to the internet has provided people with the freedom to work, learn, communicate, and play wherever they want.

Mobile devices typically have two wireless internet connectivity options:

- **Wi-Fi** - Wireless network connection is provided using local Wi-Fi settings.

- **Cellular** - Wireless network connection is provided for a fee using cellular data. Cellular networks require cellular towers and satellites to create a mesh of global coverage. A cellular data network connection can become expensive without an appropriate service plan.

You may need to register a device with a carrier, or provide some kind of unique identifier. Every mobile device has an unique 15-digit number called an International Mobile Equipment Identity (IMEI). This number identifies the device to a carrier's network. The numbers come from a family of devices called the Global System for Mobile Communications (GSM). The number can often be found in the configuration settings of the device, or in a battery compartment, if the battery is removable.

The user of the device is also identified using an unique number called the International Mobile Subscriber Identity (IMSI). The IMSI is often programmed on the subscriber identity module (SIM) card, or can be programmed on the phone itself, depending on the network type.

Wi-Fi is usually preferred over a cellular connection because it is usually free. Wi-Fi radios use less battery power than cellular radios so the device battery should last longer using Wi-Fi.

Many businesses, organizations, and locations now also offer free Wi-Fi connections to attract customers. For example, coffee shops, restaurants, libraries, and even public transportation may offer free Wi-Fi access to users. Educational institutions have also adopted Wi-Fi connectivity. For instance, College campuses enable students to connect their mobile device to the college network and sign up for classes, watch lectures, and submit assignments.

It is important to secure home Wi-Fi networks. These precautions should be taken to protect Wi-Fi communications on mobile devices:

- Enable security on home networks. Always enable the highest Wi-Fi security framework possible. Currently, WPA2 security is the most secure.

- Never send login or password information using clear, unencrypted text.

- Use a secure VPN connection when possible.

Devices can connect automatically or manually to Wi-Fi networks. The figure displays the steps to take when manually connecting to a Wi-Fi network using an Android or an iOS mobile device.

Refer to
Lab Activity
for this chapter

7.5.1.2   Lab - Mobile Wi-Fi

In this lab, you will turn the Wi-Fi radio on and off, forget a found Wi-Fi network, and find and connect to a Wi-Fi network.

Lab - Mobile Wi-Fi

Refer to
Online Course
for Illustration

7.5.1.3   Cellular Communication Standards

Cell phones were introduced in the mid-1980s. Back then, cell phones were bigger and bulkier. It was also difficult and expensive to call people on another cellular network because there were few industry standards for cellular technology. Without standards, interoperability between cell phone manufacturers was very difficult.

Industry standards have simplified interconnectivity between cell providers. These standards have also made it less expensive to use cellular technology. However, cellular standards have not been adopted uniformly around the world. Therefore, some cell phones may only work in one country and not operate in other countries. Other cell phones are capable of using multiple standards and can operate in many countries.

Cellular technology has evolved approximately every 10 years. The figure represents the major cellular standards:

- **1G** - Introduced in the 1980s, first generation (1G) standards used analog standards. However, analog systems were prone to noise and interference which made it difficult to get a clear voice signal. Few 1G devices are in use today.

- **2G** - Introduced in the 1990s, the second generation (2G) standards switched from analog to digital standards. 2G provided speeds up to 1 Mb/s and supported higher call quality. 2G also introduced Short Message Service (SMS) which is used for text messaging and Multimedia Message Service (MMS) which is used for sending and receiving photos and videos.

- **3G** - Introduced in the late 1990s, third-generation (3G) standards enabled speeds up to 2 Mb/s to support mobile internet access, web browsing, video calls, video streaming, and picture sharing.

- **4G** - Introduced in the late 2000s, 4G standards enables speeds of 100 Mb/s and up to 1Gb/s. 4G supports gaming services, high-quality video conferencing, and high-definition television. 4G technology is commonly available with Long Term Evolution (LTE). LTE adds improvements to 4G.

- **5G** - Introduced in 2019, 5G is the latest standard. It is more efficient than previous standards and may support speeds up to 20 Gb/s.

Many cell phones can also support multiple standards to enable backward compatibility. For instance, many cell phones support 4G and 3G standards. The cell phone will use 4G when available. If a 4G network is no longer available, it will automatically switch to 3G without losing connection.

Refer to
Online Course
for Illustration

7.5.1.4   Airplane Mode

It may be required for you to disable your cellular access. For instance, airlines typically ask their passengers to disable cellular access. To simplify this process, most mobile devices have a setting called Airplane Mode. This setting turns off all cellular, as well as Wi-Fi and Bluetooth radios.

Airplane Mode is useful when traveling on an airplane or when located where accessing data is prohibited or expensive. Most mobile device functions are still usable, but communication is not possible.

Figure 1 displays the screen to turn Airplane Mode on or off on an iOS device.

You can also enable or disable cellular access. Figure 2 lists the steps to change cellular access settings on an Android and an iOS device. Figure 3 displays the screen to enable or disable cellular access on an iOS.

Refer to
Online Course
for Illustration

7.5.1.5   Hotspot

Another useful cellular feature is to use a cellular device as a hotspot. A hotspot is when a cellular device is used to provide an internet connection to other devices. The Wi-Fi devices could select the cellular device at its Wi-Fi connection. For instance, a user may need to connect a computer to the internet but no Wi-Fi or wired connection is available. A cell phone can be used as a bridge to the internet, through the cellular carrier's network.

To enable an iOS device to become a personal hotspot, touch Personal Hotspot as shown in the bottom of Figure 1. This opens the Personal Hotspot screen in Figure 2. Notice how the iOS Personal Hotspot feature can also connect Bluetooth or USB connected devices to the internet.

Note   A hotspot is sometimes referred to as tethering.

Finally, there are apps available for mobile devices that can be useful tools when diagnosing mobile device radio problems. For instance, a Wi-Fi analyzer can be used to display information about wireless networks, while a cell tower analyzer can be used on cellular networks.

Refer to
Interactive Graphic
in online course

7.5.1.6   Check Your Understanding - Wireless Technology

7.5.2   Bluetooth

Refer to
Interactive Graphic
in online course

7.5.2.1   Bluetooth for Mobile Devices

Refer to
Interactive Graphic
in online course

7.5.2.2   Bluetooth Pairing

Bluetooth is a networking standard that consists of two levels: the physical level and the protocol level. The physical level for Bluetooth is a radio frequency standard. Devices connect to other Bluetooth enabled devices at the protocol level. This is referred to as Bluetooth pairing. At the protocol level, devices agree on when bits are sent, how they are sent, and that what is received is the same as what was sent.

Specifically, Bluetooth pairing is when two Bluetooth devices establish a connection to share resources. In order for the devices to pair, the Bluetooth radios must be turned on, and one device begins searching for other devices. Other devices must be set to discoverable mode, also called visible, so that they can be detected.

When a Bluetooth device is in discoverable mode, it transmits Bluetooth and device information such as device name, services that the device can use, Bluetooth class and device name.

During the pairing process, a PIN may be requested to authenticate the pairing process, as shown in Figure 1. The PIN is often a number, but can also be a numeric code or passkey. The PIN is stored using pairing services, so it does not have to be entered the next time the device tries to connect. This is convenient when using a headset with a smartphone because they are paired automatically when the headset is turned on and within range.

Figure 2 lists the steps required to pair a Bluetooth device with an Android and an iOS device.

7.5.3   Configuring Email

Refer to
Interactive Graphic
in online course

7.5.3.1   Introduction to Email

We all use email but never really think about how email actually works. The email structure relies on email servers and email clients as displayed in Figure 1.

Note   This section focuses on email clients for mobile devices.

Email clients and servers use various protocols and standards to exchange emails. The most common are described in Figure 2.

Email servers require email software such as Microsoft Server Exchange. Exchange is also a contact manager and calendaring software. It uses a proprietary messaging architecture called Messaging Application Programming Interface (MAPI). MAPI is used by the Microsoft Office Outlook client to connect to Exchange servers, to provide email, calendar, and contact management.

Email clients have to be installed on a mobile device. Many clients are configurable using a wizard. However, you still need to know key information to set up an email account. Figure 3 lists the type of information required when setting up an email account.

Refer to
Interactive Graphic
in online course

7.5.3.2   Activity - Matching Email Protocols

Refer to
Online Course
for Illustration

7.5.3.3   Android Email Configuration

Android devices are capable of using advanced communication applications and data services. Many of these applications and features require the use of web services provided by Google.

When you configure an Android mobile device for the first time, you are prompted to sign in to your Google account with your Gmail email address and password. By signing in to your Gmail account, the Google Play store, data and settings backup, and other Google services become accessible. The device synchronizes contacts, email messages, apps, downloaded content, and other information from Google services. If you do not have a Gmail account, you can use the Google account sign-in page to create one.

Figure 1 lists the steps to add an email account on an Android device.

Note   If you want to restore Android settings to a tablet that you have previously backed up, you must sign in to the account when setting up the tablet for the first time. You cannot restore your Android settings if you sign in after the initial setup.

After the initial setup, access your mailbox by touching the Gmail app icon. Android devices also have an email app for connecting to other email accounts, but it simply redirects the user to the Gmail app in later versions of Android.

> Refer to
> **Online Course**
> for Illustration

7.5.3.4   iOS Email Configuration

iOS devices ship with a stock Mail app which can handle multiple email accounts simultaneously. The Mail app also supports a number of different email account types including iCloud, Yahoo, Gmail, Outlook and Microsoft Exchange.

An Apple ID is required to set up an iOS device. An Apple ID is used to access the Apple App Store, the iTunes Store, and iCloud. iCloud provides email and the ability to store content on remote servers. The iCloud email is free and comes with remote storage for backups, mail, and documents.

All of the iOS devices, apps, and content are linked to your Apple ID. When an iOS device is turned on for the first time, the Setup Assistant guides you through the process of connecting the device and signing in with or creating an Apple ID. The Setup Assistant also allows you to create an iCloud email account. You can restore settings, content, and apps from a different iOS device from an iCloud backup during the setup process.

The figure displays the steps to set up an email account on an iOS device.

> Refer to
> **Online Course**
> for Illustration

7.5.3.5   Internet Email

Many people have multiple email addresses. For instance, you may have a personal email account and a school or work account.

The email service is provided using either:

- **Local email** - The email server is managed by a local IT department such as a school network, business network, or organizational network.

- **Internet email** - The email service is hosted on the internet and controlled by a service provider such as Gmail.

Users can access their online mailboxes using:

- Default mobile email app included in the OS such as iOS Mail.

- Browser-based email client, such as Mail, Outlook, Windows Live Mail, and Thunderbird.

- Mobile email client apps, including Gmail and Yahoo.

Email client apps provide a better user experience when compared to the web interface.

7.5.4   Mobile Device Synchronization

Refer to **Online Course** for Illustration

7.5.4.1   Types of Data to Synchronize

Many people use a combination of desktop, laptop, tablet, and smartphone devices to access and store information. It is helpful when specific information is the same across multiple devices. For example, when scheduling appointments using a calendar program, each new appointment would need to be entered in each device to ensure that each device is up to date. Data synchronization eliminates the need to make changes to every device.

Data synchronization is the exchange of data between two or more devices while maintaining consistent data on those devices.

Synchronization methods include synchronization to the cloud, a desktop, and an automobile.

There are many different types of data to synchronize:

- Contacts
- Applications
- Email
- Pictures
- Music
- Videos
- Calendar
- Bookmarks
- Documents
- Location data
- Social media data
- E-books
- Passwords

Refer to **Interactive Graphic** in online course

7.5.4.2   Enabling Synchronization

Sync typically means data synchronization. However, the meaning of sync varies slightly between an Android and an iOS device.

Android devices can synchronize your contacts and other data including that from Facebook, Google, and Twitter. As a result, all devices using the same Google account will have access to the same data. This makes it easier to replace a damaged device without data loss. Android Sync also allows the user to choose the types of data to synchronize.

Android devices also support automatic synchronization with a feature called Auto Sync. This synchronizes the device with the service provider's servers automatically, without user intervention. To save on battery life, you can disable automatic synchronization for all or just some of the data.

Figure 1 lists various steps to synchronize an Android device. Figure 2 displays a sample Sync screen on an Android device.

iOS devices support two types of synchronizing:

- **Backup** - Copies your personal data from your phone to your computer. That includes application settings, text messages, voicemails, and other data types. Backup saves a copy of the all data created by the user and by apps.

- **Sync** - Copies new apps, music, video, or books from iTunes to your phone and from your phone to iTunes, resulting in full synchronization on both devices. Sync copies only media downloaded via the iTunes Store mobile app, respecting what was specified through iTunes' Sync definitions. For example, a user can keep movies from syncing to the phone if the user does not watch movies on the phone.

As a general rule, when connecting an iOS device to iTunes, always perform a Backup first, and then Sync. This order can be changed in iTunes' Preferences.

A few more useful options are available when performing Sync or Backup on iOS:

- **Backup storage location** - iTunes allows backups to be stored on the local computer hard drive or on the iCloud online service.

- **Backup straight from an iOS device** - In addition to backing up data from an iOS device to the local hard drive or iCloud through iTunes, users can configure the iOS device to upload a copy of its data directly to iCloud. This is useful as Backups can be performed automatically, eliminating the need to connect to iTunes. Similar to Android, the user can also specify what type of data is sent to the iCloud backup, as shown in Figure 3.

- **Sync over Wi-Fi** - iTunes can scan and connect to iOS on the same Wi-Fi network. When connected, the Backup process can be initiated automatically between iOS devices and iTunes. This is useful as Backups can be performed automatically every time iTunes and the iOS device are on the same Wi-Fi, eliminating the need for a wired USB connection.

When a new iPhone is connected to the computer, iTunes will offer to restore it using the most recent backup of data from other iOS devices, if available. Figure 4 shows the iTunes window on a computer.

7.5.4.3 Synchronization Connection Types

Refer to **Online Course** for Illustration

To synchronize data between devices, the devices either use USB and Wi-Fi connections.

Most Android devices do not have a desktop program for performing data synchronization, therefore most users sync with Google's different web services, even when synchronizing with a desktop or laptop computer. One benefit of synchronizing data using this method is that the data is accessible from any computer or mobile device at any time by signing in to a Google account. The disadvantage of this arrangement is that it can be difficult to synchronize data with programs that are installed locally on a computer, such as Outlook for email, calendar, and contacts.

iOS devices can also use Wi-Fi Sync to synchronize with iTunes. To use Wi-Fi Sync, the iOS device must first synchronize with iTunes using a USB cable. You must also turn on Sync over Wi-Fi Connection in the Summary pane of iTunes as shown in the figure.

After that, you can use Wi-Fi Sync or a USB cable. When the iOS device is on the same wireless network as the computer running iTunes and it is plugged into a power source, it automatically synchronizes with iTunes.

Microsoft also offers cloud storage for synchronizing data between devices through the use of OneDrive. OneDrive is also able to synchronize data between mobile devices and PCs.

7.6   Preventive Maintenance for Laptops and other Mobile Devices

7.6.1   Scheduled Maintenance for Laptops and other Mobile Devices

Refer to
Interactive Graphic
in online course

7.6.1.1   What Do You Already Know? - Preventive Maintenance

Refer to
Online Course
for Illustration

7.6.1.2   The Reason for Maintenance

Because laptops and mobile devices are portable, they are used in different types of environments. As a result, they are more likely than desktop computers to be exposed to harmful materials and situations, including dirt and contamination, spills, drops, excessive heat or cold, and excessive moisture. In a laptop, many components are placed in a very small area directly beneath the keyboard. Spilling liquid onto the keyboard can result in severe internal damage. It is important to keep a laptop clean. Proper care and maintenance can help laptop components run more efficiently and extend the life of the equipment.

Refer to
Online Course
for Illustration

7.6.1.3   Laptop Preventive Maintenance Program

A preventive maintenance program is important in addressing such issues and must include a routine schedule for maintenance. Maintenance should also be performed when usage demands it.

The preventive maintenance schedule for a laptop may include practices that are unique to a particular organization but should also include the standard procedures of cleaning, hard drive maintenance, and software updates.

To keep a laptop clean, be proactive, not reactive. Keep fluids and food away from the laptop. Close the laptop when it is not in use. When cleaning a laptop, never use harsh cleaners or solutions that contain ammonia. Use nonabrasive materials including compressed air, mild cleaning solutions, cotton swabs, and a soft, lint-free cloth .:

Caution: Before you clean a laptop, disconnect it from all power sources and remove the battery.

Routine maintenance includes the monthly cleaning of these laptop components:

- **Exterior case** - Wipe the case with a soft, lint-free cloth that is lightly moistened with water or mild cleaning solution.

- **Cooling vents and I/O ports** - Use compressed air or a non-electrostatic vacuum to clean out the dust from the vents and from the fan behind the vent. Use tweezers to remove any debris.

- **Display** - Wipe the display with a soft, lint-free cloth that is lightly moistened with a computer-screen cleaner.

- **Keyboard** - Wipe the keyboard with a soft, lint-free cloth that is lightly moistened with water or mild cleaning solution.

- **Touchpad** - Wipe the surface of the touchpad gently with a soft, lint-free cloth that is moistened with an approved cleaner. Never use a wet cloth.

Note   If it is obvious that the laptop needs to be cleaned, clean it. Do not wait for the next scheduled maintenance.

Refer to **Online Course** for Illustration

7.6.1.4   Mobile Device Preventive Maintenance Program

Mobile devices are often carried in pockets or purses. They can be damaged by drops, excess moisture, heat, or cold. Although mobile device screens are designed to prevent light scratching, the touchscreen should be protected using a screen protector if possible.

Preventative maintenance for mobile devices requires only three basic tasks: cleaning, backing up data and keeping the operating system and applications up to date.

- **Cleaning** - Use a soft, lint-free cloth and a cleaning solution designed for a touchscreen to keep the touchscreen clean. Do not use ammonia or alcohol to clean the touchscreen.

- **Backing up the data** - Keep a backup copy of the information on the mobile device to another source, such as a cloud drive. The information includes contact, music, photos, video, apps, and any customized settings.

- **Updating the system and applications** - When a new version of the operating system or applications is available, the device should be updated to ensure that the device is working at its best. An update can include new features, fixes, or improvements to performance and stability.

7.7   Basic Troubleshooting Process for Laptops and other Mobile Devices

7.7.1   Applying the Troubleshooting Process to Laptops and other Mobile Devices

Refer to **Interactive Graphic** in online course

7.7.1.1   The Troubleshooting Process

Refer to **Online Course** for Illustration

7.7.1.2   Identify the problem

Laptop and mobile device problems can result from a combination of hardware, software, and network issues. Technicians must be able to analyze the problem and determine the cause of the error to repair the device. This process is called troubleshooting.

The first step in the troubleshooting process is to identify the problem. The figure shows a list of open-ended and closed-ended questions to ask laptop and mobile device customers.

Refer to
Online Course
for Illustration

7.7.1.3   Establish a theory of probable cause

After you have talked to the customer, you can establish a theory of probable causes. The figure shows a list of some common probable causes for laptop and mobile device problems.

Refer to
Online Course
for Illustration

7.7.1.4   Test the Theory to Determine Cause

After you have developed some theories about what is wrong, test your theories to determine the cause of the problem. The figure shows a list of quick procedures that can determine the exact cause of the problem or even correct the problem. If a quick procedure does not correct the problem, research the problem further to establish the exact cause.

Refer to
Online Course
for Illustration

7.7.1.5   Establish a Plan of Action to Resolve the Problem and Implement the Solution

After you have determined the exact cause of the problem, establish a plan of action to resolve the problem and implement the solution. The figure shows some sources you can use to gather additional information to resolve an issue.

Refer to
Online Course
for Illustration

7.7.1.6   Verify Full System Functionality and if Applicable, Implement Preventative Measures

In the final step of the troubleshooting process, document your findings, actions, and outcomes. The figure shows a list of the tasks required to document the problem and the solution.

Refer to
Online Course
for Illustration

7.7.1.7   Document Findings, Actions, and Outcomes

In the final step of the troubleshooting process, document your findings, actions, and outcomes. The figure shows a list of the tasks required to document the problem and the solution.

7.7.2   Common Problems and Solutions for Laptops and Other Mobile Devices

Refer to
Online Course
for Illustration

7.7.2.1   Identify Common Problems and Solutions

Laptops and other mobile device problems can be attributed to hardware, software, networks, or some combination of the three. You will resolve some types of problems more often than others.

Refer to
Interactive Graphic
in online course

7.7.2.2   Common Problems and Solutions for Laptops

Refer to
Online Course
for Illustration

7.7.2.3   Common Problems and Solutions for Other Mobile Devices

7.7.2.4   Lab - Research Laptop Specifications

Laptops often use proprietary parts. To find information about the replacement parts, you may have to research the website of the laptop manufacturer.

Lab - Research Laptop Specifications

7.7.2.5   Lab - Gather Information from the Customer

In this lab, you will act as a call center technician and create closed-ended and open-ended questions to ask a customer about a laptop problem.

Lab - Gather Information from the Customer

7.7.2.6   Lab - Investigate Support Websites

In this lab, you will investigate the services provided by a local laptop repair company or a laptop manufacturer's support website. Use the internet or a local phone directory to locate a local laptop repair company or laptop manufacturer's support website.

Lab - Investigate Support Websites

7.8   Summary

In this chapter, you learned the features and functionality of laptops and other mobile devices, like smartphones and tablets, as well as how to remove and install internal and external components. Laptops are portable computers and usually run full versions of operating systems such as Microsoft Windows, macOS, or Linux while smartphones and tablets run special operating systems that are designed for mobile devices. Other small mobile devices that are popular are smartwatches, fitness trackers, and virtual and augmented reality headsets.

You learned that laptops use the same types of ports as desktop computers so that peripheral devices can be interchangeable. Mobile devices can also use some of the same peripheral devices. Essential input devices, such as a keyboard and track pad, are built into laptops to provide similar functionality as desktop computers. Some laptops and mobile devices use touchscreens as input devices. The internal components of laptops are typically smaller than desktop components because they are designed to fit into compact spaces and conserve energy. The internal components of mobile devices are usually connected to the circuit board to keep the device compact and lightweight.

Laptops feature function keys that can be pressed in combination with the Fn key. The functions performed by these keys are specific to the laptop model. Docking stations and port replicators can increase the functionality of laptops by providing the same types of ports that are featured on desktop computers. Some mobile devices use a docking station to charge or use peripheral devices. Laptops and mobile devices most commonly feature LCD or LED screens, many of which are touchscreen. Backlights illuminate LCD and LED laptop displays. OLED displays have no backlight.

Laptops and mobile devices can feature several wireless technologies, including Bluetooth, Infrared, Wi-Fi and the ability to access Cellular WANs. Laptops provide many expansion possibilities. Users can add memory to increase performance, make use of flash memory to increase storage capacity, or increase functionality by using expansion cards. Some mobile devices can add more storage capacity by upgrading or adding more flash memory, such as MicroSD cards.

At the end of the chapter, you learned the importance of a preventive maintenance program for laptops and other mobile devices. They are used in different types of environments, and as a result, they are more likely than desktop computers to be exposed to harmful materials and situations, including dirt and contamination, spills, drops, excessive heat or cold, and excessive moisture.

Finally, you learned the six steps in the troubleshooting process as they pertain to laptops and other mobile devices.

Go to the online course to take the quiz and exam.

Chapter 7 Quiz

This quiz is designed to provide an additional opportunity to practice the skills and knowledge presented in the chapter and to prepare for the chapter exam. You will be allowed multiple attempts and the grade does not appear in the gradebook.

Chapter 7 Exam

The chapter exam assesses your knowledge of the chapter content.

Your Chapter Notes

Printers

Refer to
Online Course
for Illustration

8.0 Introduction

Printers produce paper copies of electronic files. Government regulations and business policies often require that physical records be kept. This makes paper copies of digital documents as important today as they were when the paperless revolution began several years ago. This chapter provides essential information about printers.

You will learn how printers operate, what to consider when purchasing a printer, and how to connect printers to an individual computer or to a network. You will also learn the operation of various types of printers and how to install them, maintain them, and to troubleshoot common problems that arise. At the end of the chapter you will learn the importance of a preventive maintenance program for printers and apply the six steps in the troubleshooting process as they pertain to printers.

It is important to not only learn about the different types of printers and their components but also to build hands-on skills. In this chapter you will complete a lab performing preventive maintenance on an inkjet printer and a laser printer. You will also work labs on installing and sharing a printer in Windows

8.1 Common Printer Features

8.1.1 Characteristics and Capabilities

Refer to
Online Course
for Illustration

8.1.1.1 Characteristics of Printers

Computer technicians are often required to select, purchase, and install printers for the users. Technicians need to know how to configure, troubleshoot, and repair the most common types of printers. Most printers available today are usually either laser printers using imaging drums or inkjet printers using electrostatic spray technology. Dot matrix printers using impact technology are used in applications that require carbon copies. Thermal printers are commonly found in retail. Many are used to print receipts. 3D printers are used in design and manufacturing. The figure shows examples of these five types of printers.

Refer to
Online Course
for Illustration

8.1.1.2 Printer Speed, Quality, and Color

Speed and Quality

Printer speed is a factor to consider when selecting a printer. The speed of a printer is measured in pages per minute (PPM). Printer speed varies between makes and models. Speed is also affected by the complexity of the image and the quality desired by the user. The quality of printing is measured in dots per inch (dpi). The larger the dpi number, the better the image resolution. When the resolution is higher, text and images are clearer. To produce the best high-resolution images, use high-quality ink or toner and high-quality paper.

Color

The color printing process uses the primary colors cyan, magenta, and yellow (CMY). For inkjet printing, the color black serves as the base or key color. Thus, the acronym CMYK refers to the inkjet color printing process. The figure shows a CMYK color wheel.

Refer to
Online Course
for Illustration

8.1.1.3   Reliability and Total Cost of Ownership

A printer should be reliable. Because so many types of printers are on the market, research the specifications of several printers before selecting one. Here are some manufacturer options to consider:

- **Warranty** - Identify what is covered within the warranty.

- **Scheduled servicing** - Servicing is based on expected usage. Usage information is in the documentation or on the manufacturer's website.

- **Mean time between failures (MTBF)** - The printer should work without failing for an average length of time. This information is in the documentation or on the manufacturer's website.

When buying a printer, there is more than just the initial cost of the printer to consider. The total cost of ownership (TCO) includes a number of factors:

- Initial purchase price

- Cost of consumable supplies, such as paper and ink

- Pages per month

- Price per page

- Maintenance costs

- Warranty costs

When calculating the TCO, consider the amount of printing required and the expected lifetime of the printer.

Refer to
Online Course
for Illustration

8.1.1.4   Automatic Document Feeder

An automatic document feeder (ADF) can be found on some laser and inkjet printers which also have the capabilities of copy machines. The ADF is a slot where an existing document can be placed. The machine is then set to make copies of this document.

When started, the ADF pulls one page of the document onto the glass surface of the platen, where it is scanned and copies are made. The page on the platen is then automatically removed and the next page in the original document is pulled onto the platen. This process continues until the entire original document in the feeder has been pulled through. Some machines can make multiple copies. Usually these machines can also collate these copies.

Depending on the capabilities of the machine, the original document may be placed face up in the feeder or face down. The machine may have a limit as to how many pages can be in the original document.

Refer to
Interactive Graphic
in online course

8.1.1.5   Check Your Understanding - Printer Capabilities and Characteristics

8.1.2   Printer Connections

Refer to
Interactive Graphic
in online course

8.1.2.1   Printer Connection Types

A printer must have a compatible interface with the computer to print. Typically, printers connect to home computers using a USB or wireless interface. However, printers may also connect directly to a network using a network cable or a wireless interface.

Refer to
Interactive Graphic
in online course

8.1.2.2   Check Your Understanding - Printer Connections

8.2   Printer Type Comparison

8.2.1   Inkjet Printers

Refer to
Interactive Graphic
in online course

8.2.1.1   Inkjet Printer Characteristics

Inkjet printers are easy to use and usually less expensive than laser printers. The figure shows an all-in-one device that contains an inkjet printer.

Some advantages of an inkjet printer are initial low cost, high resolution, and they are quick to warm up. Some disadvantages of an inkjet printer are that the nozzles are prone to clogging, ink cartridges can be expensive, and the ink is wet for a few seconds after printing.

Refer to
Interactive Graphic
in online course

8.2.1.2   Inkjet Printer Parts

Ink Cartridges/Paper

Ink cartridges and paper are the primary consumable items in an inkjet printer. Ink cartridges are designed for specific makes and models of inkjet printers. Most inkjet printers use plain paper for printing. Some can also print images on high quality photo paper. Consult your printer's manual for the correct type of ink cartridges and paper to use.

If inkjet printer quality degrades, check the printer calibration by using the printer software.

Refer to
Interactive Graphic
in online course

8.2.1.3   Check Your Understanding - Inkjet Printers

8.2.2   Laser Printers

Refer to
Online Course
for Illustration

8.2.2.1   Laser Printer Characteristics

A laser printer is a high-quality, fast printer that uses a laser beam to create an image.

Some advantages of a laser printer are low cost per page, high ppm, high capacity, and prints come out dry. Some disadvantages of a laser printer are high cost of startup, and that toner cartridges can be expensive.

Refer to
Interactive Graphic
in online course

8.2.2.2   Laser Printer Parts

Imaging Drum

The central part of the laser printer is its imaging drum. The drum is a metal cylinder that is coated with a light-sensitive insulating material. When a beam of laser light strikes the drum, it becomes a conductor at the point where the light hits it.

Refer to
Interactive Graphic
in online course

8.2.2.3   Check Your Understanding - Laser Printers

8.2.3   Laser Printing Process

Refer to
Interactive Graphic
in online course

8.2.3.1   How Laser Printing Works

Laser Printing

The laser printer process involves seven steps to print information onto a single sheet of paper.

Refer to
Interactive Graphic
in online course

8.2.3.2   Check Your Understanding - The Laser Printing Process

8.2.4   Thermal Printers and Impact Printers

Refer to
Online Course
for Illustration

8.2.4.1   Thermal Printer Characteristics

Many retail cash registers and some older fax machines contain thermal printers. Thermal paper is chemically treated and has a waxy quality. Thermal paper becomes black when heated. After a roll of thermal paper is loaded, the feed assembly moves the paper through the printer. Electrical current is sent to the heating element in the print head to generate heat. The heated areas of the print head make the image on the paper.

Some advantages of thermal printers are that they last a long time because there are few moving parts, their operation is quiet and there is no cost for ink or toner. However, thermal paper is expensive, it must be stored at room temperature and can degrade over time. Thermal printer images are poor quality, and color printing is not available.

Refer to
Online Course
for Illustration

8.2.4.2   Impact Printer Characteristics

Impact printers have print heads that strike an inked ribbon, causing characters to be imprinted on the paper. Dot matrix and daisy wheel are examples of impact printers.

An advantage of impact printers is that the ribbon is less expensive than inkjet cartridges or laser printer toner cartridges. They can use continuous feed or normal sheets of paper and can print carbon copies. Disadvantages include the fact that they are noisy, the graphics are low-resolution, and they have limited color-printing capabilities.

A dot matrix printer has a print head containing pins that are surrounded by electromagnets. When energized, the pins push forward onto the ink ribbon, creating a character on the paper. The number of pins on a print head, 9 or 24, determines the quality of the print. The highest quality of print that is produced by the dot matrix printer is referred to as near letter quality (NLQ).

Most dot matrix printers use continuous-feed paper, also known as tractor feed. The paper has perforations between each sheet, and perforated strips on the side are used to feed the paper and to prevent skewing or shifting. Sheet feeders that print one page at a time are available for some higher quality printers. A large roller, called the platen, applies pressure to keep the paper from slipping. If a multiple-copy paper is used, you can adjust the platen gap to the thickness of the paper.

Refer to **Interactive Graphic** in online course

8.2.4.3 Check Your Understanding - Thermal Printers and Impact Printers

8.2.5 Virtual Printers

Refer to **Online Course** for Illustration

8.2.5.1 Virtual Printer Characteristics

Virtual printing does not send a print job to a printer within your local network. Instead, the print software either sends the job to a file or transmits the information to a remote destination in the cloud for printing.

Typical methods for sending a print job to a file include the following:

- **Print to file** - Originally, print to file saved your data in a file with the .prn extension. The .prn file then could be quickly printed at any time without opening the original document. Print to file can now save in other formats, as shown in the figure.

- **Print to PDF** - Adobe's Portable Document Format (PDF) was released as an open standard in 2008.

- **Print to XPS** - Introduced by Microsoft in Windows Vista, the XML Paper Specification (XPS) format was meant to be an alternative to PDF.

- **Print to image** - To prevent others from easily copying the content in a document, you can choose to print to an image file format, such as JPG or TIFF.

Refer to **Online Course** for Illustration

8.2.5.2 Cloud Printing

Cloud printing is sending a print job to a remote printer, as shown in the figure. The printer could be at any location within your organization's network. Some printing companies provide software that you can install and then send print jobs to their closest location for processing.

Another cloud printing example is Google Cloud Print, which allows you to connect your printer to the web. After it is connected, you can send print jobs to your printer from anywhere that has internet access.

Refer to **Interactive Graphic** in online course

8.2.5.3 Check Your Understanding - Virtual Printers

8.2.6 3D Printers

Refer to **Online Course** for Illustration

8.2.6.1 3D Printer Characteristics

3D printers are used to create three-dimensional objects. These objects are first designed using a computer. A variety of media is now available to create these objects. But for beginners, 3D printers that use plastic filament are the most commonly used. The plastic filament is added in layers to create the object that was programmed on the computer.

Traditionally, machines cut or drilled pieces out of raw material (e.g., stone, metal, wood) to create an object. This is known as subtractive manufacturing. 3D printers add the material used to create objects in layers or even small bits; therefore, they are known as additive manufacturing machines.

Refer to **Interactive Graphic** in online course

8.2.6.2 3D Printer Parts

Filament

Filament is the material used in 3D printers to create objects. Common types of filament are plastic-based: ABS, PLA, and PVA. There are even filaments made of nylon, metal, or wood. Check your 3D printer's manual to determine which type(s) of filament to use.

Refer to **Interactive Graphic** in online course

8.2.6.3 Check Your Understanding - 3D Printers

8.3 Installing and Configuring Printers

8.3.1 Installing and Updating a Printer

Refer to **Online Course** for Illustration

8.3.1.1 Installing a Printer

When you purchase a printer, the installation and configuration information is usually found on the manufacturer's website. Before you install a printer, remove all packing material. Remove anything that prevents moving parts from shifting during shipping. Keep the original packing material in case you need to return the printer to the manufacturer for warranty service.

Note Before connecting the printer to the computer, read the installation instructions. In some cases, the printer driver needs to be installed first before the printer is connected.

If the printer has a USB, FireWire, or parallel port, connect the corresponding cable to the printer port. Connect the other end of the data cable to the corresponding port on the back of the computer. If you are installing a network printer, connect the network cable to the network port.

After the data cable has been properly connected, attach the power cable to the printer. Connect the other end of the power cable to an available electrical outlet. When you turn on the power to the device, the computer determines the correct device driver to install.

Refer to **Online Course** for Illustration

8.3.1.2 Test Printer Functions

The installation of any device is not complete until you have successfully tested all its functions. Depending on the printer you have, functions might include:

- Print double-sided documents.
- Use different paper trays for different paper sizes.
- Change the settings of a color printer so that it prints in black and white or grayscale.

- Print in draft mode.

- Use an optical character recognition (OCR) application.

- Print a collated document.

Note   Collated printing is ideal when you need to print several copies of a multiple page document. The Collate setting will print each set, in turn, as shown in the figure. Some printers will even staple each printed set.

Functions for an all-in-one printer include the following:

- Fax to another known working fax.

- Create a copy of a document.

- Scan a document.

- Print a document.

8.3.1.3   Lab - Install a Printer in Windows

In this lab, you will install a printer. You will find, download, and update the driver and the software for the printer.

Lab - Install a Printer in Windows

8.3.2   Configuring Options and Default Settings

Refer to
Interactive Graphic
in online course

8.3.2.1   Common Configuration Settings

Configuration Options

Each printer may have different configurations and default options. Check the printer documentation for specific information about its configuration and default settings. The table shows some common configuration options available for printers. Click each button to see a table of options.

Refer to
Interactive Graphic
in online course

8.3.2.2   Check Your Understanding - Configuration Options

8.3.3   Optimizing Printer Performance

Refer to
Online Course
for Illustration

8.3.3.1   Software Optimization

With printers, most optimization is completed through the software that comes with the drivers.

The following tools optimize performance:

- **Print spool settings** - Cancel or pause current print jobs in the printer queue.

- **Color calibration** - Adjust settings to match the colors on the screen to the colors on the printed sheet.

- **Paper orientation** - Select landscape or portrait image layout.

Printers are calibrated using the printer driver software. Calibration makes sure that the print heads are aligned and that they can print on different kinds of media, such as cardstock, photographic paper, and optical discs. Some inkjet print heads are fitted to the ink cartridge, so you might have to recalibrate the printer each time you change a cartridge.

Refer to
Online Course
for Illustration

8.3.3.2   Hardware Optimization

Some printers can be upgraded to print faster and to accommodate more print jobs by adding hardware. The hardware may include additional paper trays, sheet feeders, network cards, and expansion memory.

Firmware

The procedure to upgrade firmware is similar to installing printer drivers. Because firmware updates do not take place automatically, visit the home page of the printer manufacturer to check the availability of new firmware.

Printer Memory

All printers have RAM, such as the chips shown in the figure. Printers usually arrive from the factory with enough memory to handle jobs that involve text. However, print jobs involving graphics, and especially photographs, run more efficiently if the printer memory is adequate to store the entire job before it starts. Upgrading the printer memory increases the printing speed and enhances complex print job performance.

Print job buffering is when a print job is captured in the internal printer memory. Buffering is a common feature in laser printers and plotters, as well as in advanced inkjet and dot matrix printers.

If you receive low memory errors, this can indicate that the printer is out of memory or has a memory overload. In this instance, you may need more memory.

Refer to
Interactive Graphic
in online course

8.3.3.3   Check Your Understanding - Printer Optimization

8.4   Sharing Printers

8.4.1   Operating System Settings for Sharing Printers

Refer to
Online Course
for Illustration

8.4.1.1   Configuring Printer Sharing

Windows allows computer users to share their printers with other users on the network.

Users who cannot connect to the shared printer might not have the required drivers installed. They might also be using different operating systems than the computer that is hosting the shared printer. Windows can automatically download the correct drivers to these users. Click the Additional Drivers button to select operating systems that the other users are using. When you close that dialog box by clicking OK, Windows will ask to obtain those additional drivers. If the other users are also using the same Windows OS, you do not need to click the Additional Drivers button.

Figures 1 and 2 show how to begin the process of printer sharing in Windows 10.

There are potential data privacy and security issues when sharing printers:

- **Hard drive caching** - Cached print files pose a privacy and security risk because someone with access to the device could recover this files and have access to confidential or personal information.

- **User authentication** - To prevent unauthorized use of a network or cloud-based printer, permissions and user authentication methods can be used to control access to the printer.

- **Data privacy** - Print jobs sent over a network could be intercepted and read, copied, or modified

Refer to
Online Course
for Illustration

8.4.1.2   Wireless Printer Connections

Wireless printers enable hosts to connect and print wirelessly using Bluetooth or a Wi-Fi connection. For wireless printers to use Bluetooth, both the printer and the host device must have Bluetooth capabilities and be paired. If necessary, you can add a Bluetooth adapter to the computer, usually in a USB port. Wireless Bluetooth printers also allow for printing from mobile devices.

Wireless printers that use Wi-Fi connect directly to a wireless router or access point. Setup is completed by connecting the printer to the computer with the supplied software or using the printer display panel to connect to the wireless router. The printer's wireless adapter will support an 802.11 standard. The devices connecting to the printer must also support the same standard.

In wireless infrastructure mode, the printer is configured to connect to an access point. Client connections to the printer go through the access point. In wireless ad-hoc mode, client devices connect directly to the printer.

Refer to
Lab Activity
for this chapter

8.4.1.3   Lab - Share a Printer in Windows

In this lab, you will share a printer, configure the printer on a networked computer, and print a test page from the remote computer.

Lab - Share a Printer in Windows

8.4.2   Print Servers

Refer to
Online Course
for Illustration

8.4.2.1   Purposes of Print Servers

Some printers require a separate print server to enable network connectivity because these printers do not have built-in network interfaces. Print servers let multiple computer users, regardless of device or operating system, to access a single printer. A print server has three functions:

- Provide client access to print resources.

- Administrate print jobs by storing them in a queue until the print device is ready for them and then feeding or spooling the print information to the printer.

- Provide feedback to users about the state of the printer.

Sharing a printer from a computer also has disadvantages. The computer sharing the printer uses its own resources to manage the print jobs coming to the printer. If the computer user on the desktop is working at the same time as a user on the network is printing, the desktop computer user might notice a performance slowdown. In addition, the printer is not available if the user reboots or powers off the computer with a shared printer.

Refer to
Online Course
for Illustration

8.4.2.2   Software Print Servers

In some instances, the computer sharing the printer is running an operating system that is not Windows, such as Mac OS. In this case, you can use print server software.

One example is Apple's free Bonjour Printer Server, which is a built-in service in Mac OS. It is automatically installed on a Windows computer if you install the Apple Safari Browser. You can also download the Bonjour Printer Server for Windows, as shown in the figure, for free from the Apple website.

When it is downloaded and installed, the Bonjour Printer Server operates in the background, automatically detecting any compatible printers connected to the network.

Refer to
Online Course
for Illustration

8.4.2.3   Hardware Print Servers

A hardware print server is a simple device with a network card and memory. It connects to the network and communicates with the printer to enable print sharing. The print server in the figure is connected to the printer by a USB cable. A hardware print server may be integrated with another device, such as a wireless router. In this case, the printer would connect directly to the wireless router, most likely through a USB cable.

Apple's AirPort Extreme is a hardware print server. Through the AirPrint service, the AirPort Extreme can share a printer with any device on the network.

A hardware print server can manage network printing through either wired or wireless connections. An advantage of using a hardware print server is that the server accepts incoming print jobs from devices, thereby freeing the computers for other tasks. A hardware print server is always available to users, unlike a printer shared from a user's computer.

Refer to
Online Course
for Illustration

8.4.2.4   Dedicated Print Servers

For larger networking environments with multiple LANs and many users, a dedicated print server is needed to manage printing services, as shown in the figure. A dedicated print server is more powerful than a hardware print server. It handles client print jobs in the most efficient manner and can manage more than one printer at a time. A dedicated print server must have the following resources to meet the requests of print clients:

- **Powerful processor** - Because the dedicated print server uses its processor to manage and route printing information, it must be fast enough to handle all incoming requests.

- **Adequate storage space** - A dedicated print server captures print jobs from clients, places them in a print queue, and sends them to the printer in a timely manner. This process requires the computer to have enough storage space to hold these jobs until completed.

- **Adequate memory** - The processor and RAM handle sending print jobs to a printer. If there is not enough memory to handle an entire print job, the document is stored on the drive in the print server and printed from there. This is generally is slower than printing directly from memory.

Refer to
Interactive Graphic
in online course

8.4.2.5   Check Your Understanding - Print Servers

8.5   Maintaining and Troubleshooting Printers

8.5.1   Printer Preventive Maintenance

Refer to
Online Course
for Illustration

8.5.1.1   Vendor Guidelines

A good preventive maintenance program helps to ensure good quality prints and uninterrupted operation. The printer documentation contains information on how to maintain and clean the equipment.

Read the information manuals that come with every new piece of equipment. Follow the recommended maintenance instructions. Use the supplies listed by the manufacturer. Less expensive supplies can save money, but may produce poor results, damage the equipment, or void the warranty.

As shown in the figure, most manufacturers sell maintenance kits for their printers. If you do not know how to maintain printing equipment, consult with a manufacturer-certified technician. When servicing toner kits and cartridges, wear air filter masks to avoid breathing in harmful particles

Refer to
Interactive Graphic
in online course

8.5.1.2   What Do You Already Know? Printer Operating Environment

8.5.2   Inkjet Printer Preventive Maintenance

Refer to **Video**
in online course

8.5.2.1   Video Demonstration - Inkjet Printer Preventive Maintenance

Always consult the manual before performing maintenance tasks. The manual gives instructions that are specific to your inkjet printer.

The type and quality of paper and ink used can affect the life of the printer. The printer manufacturer might recommend which type of paper to use for best results. Some paper, especially photo paper, transparencies, and multilayered carbon paper, have a right and wrong side. Load the paper according to the manufacturer's instructions.

The manufacturer recommends the brand and type of ink to use. If the wrong type of ink is installed, the printer might not work or the print quality might deteriorate. Avoid refilling ink cartridges because the ink can leak.

When an inkjet printer produces blank pages, the ink cartridges might be empty. Some inkjet printers may not print any pages if one of the ink cartridges is empty. You can set the printer software to draft quality to reduce the amount of ink that the printer uses. These settings also reduce the print quality and the time it takes to print a document.

Over time, the parts collect dust, dirt, and other debris. If not cleaned regularly, the printer may not work well or could stop working completely. On inkjet printers, clean the paper-handling machinery with a damp cloth.

Click Play in the video to see preventive maintenance performed on an inkjet printer. This video is interactive and has Check Your Understanding questions throughout.

Click here to read the transcript of this video.

Refer to
Lab Activity
for this chapter

8.5.2.2   Lab - Perform Preventive Maintenance on an Inkjet Printer

In this lab, you will perform preventive maintenance on an inkjet printer

Lab - Perform Preventive Maintenance on an Inkjet Printer

8.5.3   Laser Printer Preventive Maintenance

Refer to **Video**
in online course

8.5.3.1   Video Demonstration - Laser Printer Preventive Maintenance

Laser printers do not usually require much maintenance unless they are in a dusty area or are very old. When cleaning a laser printer, use only a vacuum cleaner with High Efficiency Particulate Air (HEPA) filtration. HEPA filtration catches microscopic particles within the filters.

Always consult the manual before performing maintenance tasks. The manual gives instructions that are specific to your laser printer. For some maintenance tasks done on a laser printer, you will need to disconnect the printer from its power source. Consult your manual for specific information. If you do not know how to maintain printing equipment, consult a manufacturer-certified technician.

Most manufacturers sell maintenance kits for their printers. For laser printers, the kit might contain replacement parts that often break or wear out such as the fuser assembly, transfer rollers and pickup rollers.

When you install new parts or replace toners and cartridges, visually inspect all internal components, remove bits of paper and dust, clean spilled ink or toner, and look for worn gears, cracked plastic, or broken parts.

Laser printers do not produce blank pages. Instead, they begin to print poor quality prints. Some printers have LCD message screens or LED lights that warn users when toner supplies are low. Some types of prints use more toner than others do. For example, a photograph uses more toner than a letter. You can set the printer software to toner save or draft quality to reduce the amount of toner that the printer uses. These settings also reduce the quality of laser prints.

When maintenance is completed, reset the counters to allow the next maintenance to be completed at the correct time. On many types of printers, the page count is viewed through the LCD display or a counter located inside the main cover.

Click Play in the video to see preventive maintenance performed on a laser printer. This video is interactive and has Check Your Understanding questions throughout.

Click here to read a transcript of this video.

Refer to
Lab Activity
for this chapter

8.5.3.2   Lab - Perform Preventive Maintenance on a Laser Printer

In this lab, you will perform preventive maintenance on a Laser Printer.

Lab - Perform Preventive Maintenance on a Laser Printer

8.5.4   Thermal Printer Preventive Maintenance

Refer to **Interactive Graphic** in online course

8.5.4.1   Preventive Maintenance on a Thermal Printer

Always consult the manual before performing maintenance tasks. The manual gives instructions that are specific to your thermal printer on how to replace the paper roll. Replacing the paper is shown in Figure 1.

Thermal printers use heat to create an image on special paper. To extend the life of the printer, dampen a cotton swab with isopropyl alcohol to clean the heating element. Do this on a regular basis. The heating element is located near the slot where the printed paper emerges, as shown in Figure 2. While the printer is open, use compressed air or a lint-free cloth to remove any debris.

Refer to **Interactive Graphic** in online course

8.5.4.2   Check Your Understanding - Thermal Printer Preventive Maintenance

8.5.5   Impact Printer Preventive Maintenance

Refer to **Interactive Graphic** in online course

8.5.5.1   Preventive Maintenance of an Impact Printer

Always consult the manual before performing maintenance tasks. The manual gives instructions that are specific to your impact printer.

An impact printer is similar to a typewriter because the print head strikes an inked ribbon to transfer ink to the paper. When the impact printer produces faded or light characters, the ribbon (Figure 1) is worn out and needs to be replaced. Consult your manual for instructions on how to replace the ribbon.

If a consistent flaw is produced in all characters, the print head (Figure 2) is stuck or broken and needs to be cleaned or even replaced. Search for procedures on dot matrix printhead cleaning to learn about this.

Refer to **Interactive Graphic** in online course

8.5.5.2   Check Your Understanding - Impact Printer Preventive Maintenance

8.5.6   3D Printer Preventive Maintenance

Refer to **Video** in online course

8.5.6.1   Video Demonstration - 3D Printer Preventive Maintenance

Always consult the manual before performing maintenance tasks. The manual gives instructions that are specific to your 3D printer.

Click Play in the video to see preventive maintenance performed on a 3D printer. This video is interactive and has Check Your Understanding questions throughout.

Click here to read a transcript of this video.

Refer to **Video** in online course

8.5.6.2   Video Demonstration - 3D Printer Printing a Component

Click Play in the video to watch a demonstration of a 3D printer printing a component.

Click here to read a transcript of the video.

8.5.7   Applying the Troubleshooting Process to Printers

Refer to
Interactive Graphic
in online course

8.5.7.1   The Six Steps of the Troubleshooting Process

8.5.7.2   Identify the Problem

Refer to
Online Course
for Illustration

Printer problems can result from a combination of hardware, software, and connectivity issues. A technician must be able to determine if the problem exists with the device, a cable connection, or the computer to which the printer is connected. Computer technicians must be able to analyze the problem and determine the cause of the error to repair the printer issues.

The first step in the troubleshooting process is to identify the problem. The figure shows a list of open-ended and closed-ended questions to ask the customer.

8.5.7.3   Establish a Theory of Probable Cause

Refer to
Online Course
for Illustration

After you have talked to the customer, you can establish a theory of probable cause. The figure shows a list of some common probable causes for printer problems. If necessary, conduct internal and external research based on the symptoms of the problem.

8.5.7.4   Test the Theory to Determine Cause

Refer to
Online Course
for Illustration

After you have developed some theories about what is wrong, test them to determine the cause of the problem. Once the theory is confirmed, you then determine the steps to resolve the problem. The figure shows a list of quick procedures that can determine the exact cause of the problem or even correct the problem. If a quick procedure does correct the problem, you can verify full system functionality. If a quick procedure does not correct the problem, you may need to research the problem further to establish the exact cause.

8.5.7.5   Establish a Plan of Action to Resolve the Problem and Implement the Solution

Refer to
Online Course
for Illustration

After you have determined the exact cause of the problem, establish a plan of action to resolve the problem and implement the solution. The figure shows some sources you can use to gather additional information to resolve an issue.

8.5.7.6   Verify Full System Functionality and, if Applicable, Implement Preventive Measures

Refer to
Online Course
for Illustration

After you have corrected the problem, verify full functionality and, if applicable, implement preventive measures. The figure shows a list of the steps to verify the solution.

8.5.7.7   Document Findings, Actions, and Outcomes.

Refer to
Online Course
for Illustration

In the final step of the troubleshooting process, document your findings, actions, and outcomes. The figure shows a list of the tasks required to document the problem and the solution.

8.5.8   Problems and Solutions

Refer to
Online Course
for Illustration

8.5.8.1   Identify Printer Problems and Solutions

Printer problems can be attributed to hardware, software, networks, or some combination of the three. You will resolve some types of problems more often than others.

Refer to
Interactive Graphic
in online course

8.5.8.2   Common Problems and Solutions for Printers

Refer to
Interactive Graphic
in online course

8.5.8.3   Advanced Problems and Solutions for Printers

Refer to
Online Course
for Illustration

8.6   Summary

In this chapter, you learned how printers operate, what to consider when purchasing a printer, and how to connect printers to an individual computer or to a network. There are many different types and sizes of printers, each with different capabilities, speeds, and uses. Printers can be connected directly to computers or shared across a network. The chapter also introduced the different types of cables and interfaces available to connect a printer.

Some printers have low output and are adequate for home use, whereas other printers have high output and are designed for commercial use. Printers can have different speeds and quality of print. Older printers use parallel cables and ports. Newer printers typically use USB or FireWire cables and connectors. With newer printers, the computer automatically installs the necessary drivers. If the device drivers are not automatically installed by the computer, download them from the manufacturer's website or use the supplied CD.

You learned important characteristics and components of the various printer types. The primary components of an inkjet printer are the ink cartridges, the print head, roller, and feeder. A laser printer is a high-quality, fast printer that uses a laser beam to create an image. The central parts of a laser printer are the imaging drum, toner cartridge, fuser assembly, and rollers. Thermal printers use a special thermal paper that becomes black where heated. Impact printers have print heads that strike an inked ribbon, causing characters to be imprinted on the paper. Dot matrix and daisy wheel are examples of impact printers. 3D printers are used to create three-dimensional objects. These objects are first designed using a computer. A variety of media is now available to create these objects.

You also learned about virtual printing and cloud printing. Virtual printing does not send a print job to a physical printing device but rather, the print software sends the job to a file or transmits the information to a remote destination in the cloud for printing. Common virtual printing options are print to file, PDF, XPS, or to an image. Cloud printing involves sending a print job to a remote printer that could be at any location connected to the internet.

You completed a lab installing a printer in Windows. In the lab you installed a print driver, downloaded and installed an updated print driver and if all was configured correctly, were able to print a test page. After you set up the printer, you had a lab where you shared the device in Windows with other users on the network.

At the end of the chapter, you learned the importance of a preventive maintenance program for Printers. A good preventive maintenance program extends the life of the printer and keeps it performing well. Always follow safety procedures when working with printers. Many parts inside printers contain high voltage or become very hot with use. There were labs where you performed preventive maintenance on inkjet and laser printers.

Finally, you learned the six steps in the troubleshooting process as they pertain to printers.

Go to the online course to take the quiz and exam.

Chapter 8 Quiz

This quiz is designed to provide an additional opportunity to practice the skills and knowledge presented in the chapter and to prepare for the chapter exam. You will be allowed multiple attempts and the grade does not appear in the gradebook.

Chapter 8 Exam

The chapter exam assesses your knowledge of the chapter content.

Your Chapter Notes

Virtualization and Cloud Computing

Refer to
Online Course
for Illustration

9.0 Introduction

Organizations, both large and small, are investing heavily in virtualization and cloud computing. It is therefore important for IT technicians and professionals to understand these two technologies. While the two technologies do overlap, they are, in fact, two different technologies. Virtualization software allows one physical server to run several individual computing environments. Cloud computing is a term used to describe the availability of shared computing resources, software or data, as a service and on-demand over the Internet.

In this chapter, you will learn about the advantages that virtualization has over the traditional use of dedicated servers, such as using fewer resources, requiring less space, reducing cost, and increasing server uptime. You will also learn the terms that are used when discussing client-side virtualization, like host computer, which refers to the physical computer controlled by a user. The host OS is the OS on the host computer, and the guest OS is the OS running in the virtual machine on the host computer.

You will learn about the two types of hypervisors: Type 1 (native) hypervisor, also called bare metal hypervisor, and Type 2 (hosted) hypervisor. You will also learn the minimum system requirements to run Windows Hyper-V, which is a type 2 hypervisor, in Windows 7, Windows 8, and Windows 10.

It is important to not only learn about virtualization and cloud technology but to also build hands-on skills. In this chapter you will complete a lab installing Linux in a virtual machine.

9.1 Virtualization

9.1.1 Virtualization

Refer to **Video**
in online course

9.1.1.1 Video Explanation - What is the Cloud?

Click Play in the figure to view a video about the cloud.

Click here to read the transcript of this video.

Refer to
Online Course
for Illustration

9.1.1.2 Cloud Computing and Virtualization

The terms "virtualization" and "cloud computing" are often used interchangeably although they mean different things.

Virtualization enables a single computer to host multiple independent virtual computers that share the host computer hardware. Virtualization software separates the actual physical hardware from the virtual machine (VM) instances. VMs have their own operating systems and connect to hardware resources through software running on the host computer. An image of a VM can be saved as a file and then be re-started when required.

It is important to remember that all the VMs share the resources of the host computer. Therefore, the limiting factor on the number of VMs that can run at the same time is directly related to the amount of processing power, memory, and storage.

Cloud computing separates the applications from the hardware. It provides organizations with on-demand delivery of computing services over the network. Service providers such as Amazon Web Services (AWS) own and manage the cloud infrastructure that includes the networking devices, servers, and storage devices and is usually housed in a data center.

Virtualization is the foundation which supports cloud computing. Providers such as AWS offer cloud services using powerful servers that can dynamically provision virtual servers as required.

Without virtualization, cloud computing, as it is most-widely implemented, would not be possible.

Refer to
Online Course
for Illustration

9.1.1.3   Traditional Server Deployment

To fully appreciate virtualization, it is first necessary to understand how servers are used in an organization.

Traditionally, organizations delivered applications and services to their users using powerful dedicated servers as shown in the figure. These Windows and Linux servers are high-end computers with large amounts of RAM, powerful processors, and multiple large storage devices. New servers are added if more users or new services are required.

Problems with the traditional server deployment approach include:

- **Wasted resources** - This occurs when dedicated servers sit idle for long periods waiting until they are needed to deliver their specific service. Meanwhile, these servers waste energy.

- **Single-point of failure** - This occurs when a dedicated server fails or goes offline. There are no backup servers to handle the failure.

- **Server sprawl** - This occurs when an organization does not have adequate space to physically house underutilized servers. The servers take up more space than is warranted by the services that they provide.

Virtualizing servers to use resources more efficiently addresses these problems.

Refer to
Online Course
for Illustration

9.1.1.4   Server Virtualization

Server virtualization takes advantage of idle resources to reduce the number of servers required to provide services to users.

A special program called the hypervisor is used to manage the computer resources and various VMs. It provides VMs access to all of the hardware of the physical machine such as CPUs, memory, disk controllers, and NICs. Each of these VMs runs a complete and separate operating system.

With virtualization, enterprises can now consolidate the number of servers. For example, it is not uncommon for 100 physical servers to be consolidated as virtual machines on top of 10 physical servers using hypervisors. In the figure, the previous eight dedicated servers have been consolidated into two servers using hypervisors to support multiple virtual instances of the operating systems.

Refer to
Interactive Graphic
in online course

9.1.1.5   Advantages of Server Virtualization

Better use of resources

Virtualization reduces the number of physical servers, networking devices, supporting infrastructure, and maintenance costs.

Refer to
Interactive Graphic
in online course

9.1.1.6   Check Your Understanding - Match the Advantages of Virtualization

9.1.2   Client-Side Virtualization

Refer to
Online Course
for Illustration

9.1.2.1   Client-Side Virtualization

Many organizations use server virtualization to optimize network resources and reduce equipment and maintenance costs. Organizations are also using client-side virtualization to enable users with specific needs to run VMs on their local computer.

Client-side virtualization is beneficial for IT staff, IT support people, software developers and testers, and for educational reasons. It provides users with resources to test new operating systems, software, or to run older software. It can also be used to sandbox and create a secure isolated environment to open or run a suspicious file.

Some terms that are used when discussing client-side virtualization include:

- **Host computer** - This is the physical computer controlled by a user. VMs use the system resources of the host machine to boot and run an OS.

- **Host operating system (host OS)** - This is the operating system of the host computer. Users can use a virtualization emulator such as VirtualBox on the host OS to create and manage VMs.

- **Guest operating system (guest OS)** - This is the operating system that is running in the VM. Drivers are required to run the different OS version.

The guest OS is independent of the host OS. For example, the host OS could be Windows 10 and the VM could have Windows 7 installed. This guest of the VM would be Windows 7. In this example, the guest OS (Windows 7) does not interfere with the host OS (Windows 10) on the host computer.

Host and guest operating systems do not need to be of the same family. For example, the host OS could be Windows 10, while the guest OS is Linux. This is of benefit for users that need to increase the functionality of their host computer by running multiple operating systems at the same time.

The figure displays a logical virtual machine diagram. The bottom gray box represents the physical computer with its host OS (e.g., Windows 10). Hyper-V, Virtual PC, and VirtualBox are examples of virtualization software or emulator that could be used to create and manage the three VMs shown in the top of the figure.

Refer to
Interactive Graphic
in online course

9.1.2.2   Type 1 and Type 2 Hypervisors

The hypervisor, also called the Virtual Machine Manager (VMM), is the brain of virtualization. The hypervisor is the software used on the host computer to create and manage VMs.

The hypervisor allocates the physical system resources, such as CPU, RAM, and storage, to each VM as needed. This ensures that the operation of one virtual machine does not interfere with another.

There are two types of hypervisors, as shown in Figure 1.

- **Type 1 (native) hypervisor** - Also called bare-metal hypervisor and typically used with server virtualization. It runs directly on the hardware of a host and manages the allocation of system resources to virtual operating systems.

- **Type 2 (hosted) hypervisor** - This is hosted by an OS and is commonly used with client-side virtualization. Virtualization software such as Windows Hyper-V and VMware Workstation are examples of a Type 2 hypervisor.

Type 1 hypervisors are common in data centers and in cloud computing. Examples of Type 1 hypervisors include VMware vSphere / ESXi, Xen, and Oracle VM Server.

Type 2 hypervisors such as VMware Workstation works with the host computer to create and use multiple VMs. Windows Hyper-V is also included in Windows 10 Pro and Windows Server (2012 and 2016).

Figure 2 displays a sample Type 1 and a Type 2 hypervisor implementation. In the Type 1 implementation, VMware vSphere runs directly on the server hardware with no operating system. VMware vSphere has been used to create a Windows Server VM and a Linux Server VM. In the Type 2 implementation, the host OS on the computer is Windows 10. Windows Hyper-V has been used to create and manage the Windows 7 VM and a Linux VM.

Client-side emulators can run software meant for a different guest OS or an OS meant for different hardware. For example, if the host OS was Linux and we are creating a VM using Windows 7 to run an application that only runs in Windows 7. The Linux host computer will pretend to be a Windows 7 computer.

Refer to **Interactive Graphic** in online course

9.1.2.3 Virtual Machine Requirements

Virtual computing requires more powerful hardware configurations because each installation needs its own resources.

All virtual machines share the following basic system requirements:

- **Processor support** - Processors, such as Intel VT and AMD-V, were specifically designed to support virtualization. The virtualization feature on these processors may need to be enabled. Processors with multiple cores are also recommended as the additional cores increase speed and responsiveness when running multiple VMs.

- **Memory support** - Consider that you need memory for your host OS and will now need enough RAM to meet the requirements of each VM and their guest OS.

- **Storage** - Each VM creates very large files to store operating systems, applications, and all of the VM data. You must also factor in that an active VM will require a few GB of storage space. Therefore, large and fast drives are recommended.

- **Network Requirements** - Network connection requirements depend on the type of VM. Some VMs do not require outside connections while others do. VMs can be configured in a bridged, NAT, host-only, or a special network to connect only to other VMs. To connect to the Internet, a VM uses a virtual network adapter that simulates the real host adapter. The virtual network adapter then connects through the physical NIC to establish a connection to the Internet.

The minimum system requirements for Windows Hyper-V for Windows 10 and Windows 8, and Windows Virtual PC for Windows 7 are displayed in Figures 1, 2, and 3, respectively.

Like a physical computer, VMs are susceptible to the same threats and malicious attacks. Although VMs are isolated from the host, they can share resources (e.g., NIC, folders, and files). Users should exercise the same security considerations as the host and install security software, enable firewall features, install patches, and update the operating system and programs. It is also important to keep the virtualization software updated.

Refer to
Interactive Graphic
in online course

9.1.2.4   Check Your Understanding - Virtualization Terminology

Refer to
Lab Activity
for this chapter

9.1.2.5   Lab - Install Linux in a Virtual Machine and Explore the GUI

In this lab, you will install a Linux OS in a virtual machine using a desktop virtualization application, such as VirtualBox. After completing the installation, you will explore the GUI interface.

Lab - Install Linux in a Virtual Machine and Explore the GUI

9.2   Cloud Computing

9.2.1   Cloud Computing Applications

Refer to
Interactive Graphic
in online course

9.2.1.1   How We Use the Cloud

Virtual application streaming / cloud-based applications

Organization are using cloud-based applications to provide on-demand software delivery. For example, Microsoft Office365 provides online versions of Microsoft Word, Excel, and PowerPoint. When a user requests an application, minimal application code is forwarded to client. The client pulls additional code from the cloud server as required. For offline use, the application may be saved locally on the host.

9.2.2   Cloud Services

Refer to
Online Course
for Illustration

9.2.2.1   Cloud Services

Cloud service providers can provide various services tailored to meet customer requirements. However, most cloud computing services can be categorized into three main cloud computing services as defined by the National Institute of Standards and Technology (NIST) in their Special Publication (800-145):

- **Software as a Service (SaaS)** - The cloud provider provides access to services, such as email, calendar, communication, and office tools over the Internet on a subscription basis. Users access the software using a browser. Advantages include minimal upfront costs for customers and immediate application availability. SaaS providers include Salesforce customer management relationship (CRM) software, Microsoft Office 365, MS SharePoint software, and Google G Suite.

- **Platform as a Service (PaaS)** - The cloud provider provides access to operating systems, development tools, programming languages, and libraries used to develop, test, and deliver applications. This is useful to application developers. The cloud provider manages the underlying network, servers, and cloud infrastructure. PaaS providers include Amazon Web Service, Oracle Cloud, Google Cloud Platform and Microsoft Azure.

- **Infrastructure as a Service (IaaS)** - The cloud provider manages the network and provides organizations access to network equipment, virtualized network services, storage, software, and supporting network infrastructure. There are many advantages for organizations to adopt IaaS. Organizations do not need to invest in capital equipment and only pay for usage on-demand. The provider network includes redundancy and eliminates a single point of failure in the provider network infrastructure. The network can also scale seamlessly based on current requirements. IaaS providers include Amazon Web Service, DigitalOcean, and Microsoft Azure.

Cloud service providers have extended the IaaS model to also provide IT as a service (ITaaS). ITaaS can extend the capability of IT without requiring investment in new infrastructure, training new personnel, or licensing new software. These services are available on demand and delivered economically to any device anywhere in the world without compromising security or function.

9.2.2.2   What Do You Already Know? - Cloud Models

9.2.2.3   Check Your Understanding - Cloud Service and Cloud Model Terminology

9.2.2.4   Cloud Computing Characteristics

On-demand (self-service)

Individuals can provision or make changes to computing services as needed without requiring human interaction with the service provider.

9.2.2.5   Check Your Understanding - Match the Cloud Characteristics

9.3   Summary

In this chapter, you learned that the terms virtualization and cloud computing are often used interchangeably although they actually mean different things. Virtualization is a technology that enables a single computer to host multiple virtual computers that share the same host computer hardware. Cloud computing is a technology that enables the separation of applications from the hardware. Virtualization is the foundation which supports cloud computing.

You learned that the traditional way of delivering applications and services to users by using dedicated servers is inefficient, unreliable, and not scalable. Dedicated servers can sit idle for long periods, they are a single point of failure, and they take up a lot of physical space. Virtualization solves these issues by consolidating many virtual servers onto a single physical server, taking advantage of idle resources and reducing the number of servers required to provide services to users. You learned the many advantages that virtualization has over the traditional use of dedicated servers, such as better use of resources, less space required, reduced cost, and increased server uptime.

Cloud computing provides users with on-demand delivery of computer services over the Internet. Most of us already use these services when we access online music services or online data storage. You learned about the types of cloud services offered by cloud service providers. SaaS which provides access to services, such as email, calendar, communication, and office tools over the Internet on a subscription basis. PaaS which provides access to operating systems, development tools, programming languages, and libraries used to develop, test, and deliver applications. And, IaaS which provides organizations access to network equipment, virtualized network services, storage, software, and supporting network infrastructure.

The chapter concluded with several exercises to test your understanding of cloud computing terminology and characteristics.

Go to the online course to take the quiz and exam.

Chapter 9 Quiz

This quiz is designed to provide an additional opportunity to practice the skills and knowledge presented in the chapter and to prepare for the chapter exam. You will be allowed multiple attempts and the grade does not appear in the gradebook.

Chapter 9 Exam

The chapter exam assesses your knowledge of the chapter content.

Your Chapter Notes

Windows Installation

Refer to
Online Course
for Illustration

10.0 Introduction

IT technicians and professionals need to understand the general functions of any operating system (OS) such as controlling hardware access, managing files and folders, providing a user interface, and managing applications. To make an OS recommendation the technician needs to understand budget constraints, how the computer will be used, and which types of applications will be installed, so they can help determine the best OS for a customer: This chapter focuses on the Windows 10, Windows 8.x, and Windows 7 operating systems. The components, functions, system requirements, and terminology related to each operating system are explored. The chapter will also detail the steps to install a Windows operating system and the Windows boot sequence.

You will learn how to prepare a hard drive for a Windows installation by formatting the drive into partitions. You will learn about the different types of partitions and logical drives as well as other terms relating to hard drive setup. You will also learn about the different file systems which are supported by Windows, such as File Allocation Table (FAT), New Technology File System (NTFS), Compact Disc File System (CDFS), and Network File System (NFS).

It is important to not only learn about virtualization and cloud technology but to also build hands-on skills. In this chapter, you will complete a lab creating a FAT 32 partition in Windows and then converting the partition to NTFS. You will also complete labs on installing Windows, performing basic Windows setup task, creating user accounts, and installing Windows updates.

10.1 Modern Operating Systems

10.1.1 Operating System Features

Refer to
Online Course
for Illustration

10.1.1.1 Terms

An operating system (OS) has a number of functions. One of its main tasks is to act as an interface between the user and the hardware connected to the computer. The operating system also controls other functions:

- Software resources

- Memory allocation and all peripheral devices

- Common services to computer application software

From digital watches to computers, almost all computers require an operating system before they can be operated.

To understand the capabilities of an operating system, it is important to first understand some basic terms. The following terms are often used when describing operating systems:

- **Multi-user** - Two or more users have individual accounts that allow them to work with programs and peripheral devices at the same time.

- **Multitasking** - The computer is capable of operating multiple applications at the same time.

- **Multiprocessing** - The operating system can support two or more CPUs.

- **Multithreading** - A program can be broken into smaller parts that are loaded as needed by the operating system. Multithreading allows different parts of a program to be run at the same time.

The OS boots the computer and manages the file system. Operating systems can support more than one user, task, or CPU.

Refer to
Interactive Graphic
in online course

10.1.1.2   Basic Functions of an Operating System

Regardless of the size and complexity of the computer and the operating system, all operating systems perform the same four basic functions:

- Control hardware access
- Manage files and folders
- Provide a user interface
- Manage applications

Refer to
Interactive Graphic
in online course

10.1.1.3   Windows Operating Systems

Windows 7

Windows 7 is an upgrade from Windows XP or Vista. It is designed to run on personal computers. This version provided an improved graphical user interface and better performance from the previous versions.

Refer to
Interactive Graphic
in online course

10.1.1.4   Check Your Understanding - Windows Terminology

10.1.2   Customer Requirements for an Operating System

Refer to
Online Course
for Illustration

10.1.2.1   Compatible System Software and Hardware Requirements

Understanding how a computer will be used is important when recommending an OS to a customer. The OS must be compatible with the existing hardware and the required applications.

To make an OS recommendation, a technician must review budget constraints, learn how the computer will be used, determine which types of applications will be installed, and whether a new computer may be purchased. These are some guidelines to help determine the best OS for a customer:

- **Does the customer use off-the-shelf applications for this computer?** Off-the-shelf applications specify a list of compatible operating systems on the application package.

- **Does the customer use customized applications that were programmed specifically for the customer?** If the customer is using a customized application, the programmer of that application specifies which OS to use.

Refer to
Online Course
for Illustration

10.1.2.2 Minimum Hardware Requirements and Compatibility with OS

Operating systems have minimum hardware requirements that must be met for the OS to install and function correctly.

Identify the equipment that your customer has in place. If hardware upgrades are necessary to meet the minimum requirements for an OS, conduct a cost analysis to determine the best course of action. In some cases, it might be less expensive for the customer to purchase a new computer than to upgrade the current system. In other cases, it might be cost effective to upgrade one or more of the following components:

- RAM
- Hard disk drive
- CPU
- Video adapter card
- Motherboard

Note   If the application requirements exceed the hardware requirements of the OS, you must meet the additional requirements for the application to function properly.

Microsoft lists the minimum system requirements for Windows versions on its website as shown in the figure.

Refer to
Online Course
for Illustration

10.1.2.3 32-bit vs. 64-bit Processor Architecture

The processor architecture of the CPU affects the performance of the computer.

The terms 32-bit and 64-bit refer to the amount of data a computer's CPU can manage. A 32-bit register can store 2^{32} different binary values. Therefore, a 32-bit processor can directly address 4,294,967,295 bytes. A 64-bit register can store 2^{64} different binary values. Therefore, a 64-bit can directly address 18,446,744,073,709,551,615 bytes.

The figure shows the main differences between the 32-bit and 64-bit architectures.

Refer to
Interactive Graphic
in online course

10.1.2.4 What Do You Already Know? Choosing a Windows Edition

Refer to
Interactive Graphic
in online course

10.1.2.5 Check Your Understanding - Choosing an Operating System

10.1.3   Operating System Upgrades

Refer to
Online Course
for Illustration

10.1.3.1   Checking OS Compatibility

An OS must be upgraded periodically to remain compatible with the latest hardware and software. It is also necessary to upgrade an OS when a manufacturer stops supporting it. Upgrading an OS can increase performance. New hardware products often require that the latest OS version be installed to operate correctly. While upgrading an OS may be expensive, you can gain enhanced functionality through new features and support for newer hardware.

Note   When newer versions of an OS are released, support for older versions is eventually withdrawn.

Before upgrading the operating system, check the minimum hardware requirements of the new OS to ensure that it can be installed successfully on the computer.

Refer to
Online Course
for Illustration

10.1.3.2   Windows OS Upgrades

The process of upgrading the OS can be quicker than performing a new installation. The upgrade process varies depending on the version of Windows being upgraded.

The version of an OS determines available upgrade options. For example, a 32-bit OS cannot be upgraded to a 64-bit OS. Also, Windows 7 and Windows 8 can be upgraded to Windows 10 but Windows Vista and Windows XP cannot.

Note   Prior to performing an upgrade, back up all data in case there is a problem with the installation. Also, the version of Windows being upgraded must be activated.

To upgrade Windows 7 or Windows 8 to Windows 10, use the Windows 10 Update Assistant available on the Download Windows 10 website shown in the figure. The Windows 10 update assistant installs and runs directly on the computer being upgraded. The tool will walk the user through all the steps in the Windows 10 setup process. It is designed to prepare your computer for upgrading by checking for compatibility issues and downloading all necessary files to start the install.

Computers running Windows XP or Windows Vista do not have an upgrade path to Windows 10 and require a clean installation. Windows 10 installation media can be created using the Create Windows 10 installation media tool. This tool creates installation media (USB flash, DVD, or ISO file) which can be used to perform a clean installation.

10.1.3.3   Data Migration

Refer to
Interactive Graphic
in online course

Data migration

When a new installation is required, user data must be migrated from the old OS to the new one. There are several tools available to transfer data and settings. The tool you select depends on your level of experience and your requirements.

Refer to
Interactive Graphic
in online course

10.1.3.4   Check Your Understanding - OS Upgrades

10.2   Disk Management

10.2.1   Disk Management

Refer to
Online Course
for Illustration

10.2.1.1   Storage Device Types

As a technician, you might have to perform a clean installation of an OS. Perform a clean install in the following situations:

- When a computer is passed from one employee to another
- When the OS is corrupt
- When the primary hard drive is replaced in a computer

The installation and initial booting of the OS is called the operating system setup. Although it is possible to install an OS over a network from a server or from a local hard drive, the most common installation method for a home or small business is through external media such as DVDs or USB drives.

Note   If the hardware is not supported by the OS, you may need to install third-party drivers when performing a clean installation.

Before the operating system can be installed, a storage media device must be chosen and prepared. Several types of storage devices are available and can be used to receive the new operating system. The two most common types of data storage devices used today are hard disk drives and flash memory-based drives such as solid-state hard drives and USB drives.

When the storage device type has been chosen, it must be prepared to receive the new operating system. Modern operating systems ship with an installer program. Installers usually prepare the disk to receive the operating system, but it is crucial for a technician to understand the terms and methods involved in this preparation.

Refer to
Online Course
for Illustration

10.2.1.2   Hard Drive Partitioning

A hard drive is divided into areas called partitions. Each partition is a logical storage unit that can be formatted to store information, such as data files or applications. If you imagine a hard drive as a wooden cabinet, the partitions would be the shelves. During the installation process, most operating systems automatically partition and format available hard drive space.

Partitioning a drive is a simple process, but to ensure a successful boot, the firmware must know what disk and partition on that disk has an operating system installed. The partition scheme has direct influence in the location of the operating systems on a disk. Finding and launching the operating system is one of the responsibilities of computer firmware. The partition scheme is very important to the firmware. Two of the most popular partition scheme standards are master boot record (MBR) and globally unique identifier (GUID) partition table (GPT).

Master Boot Record

Publicly introduced in 1983, the MBR contains information on how the hard drive partitions are organized. The MBR is 512 bytes long and contains the boot loader, an executable program that allows a user to choose from multiple operating systems. MBR has become the de facto standard but has limitations that had to be addressed. MBR is commonly used in computers with BIOS-based firmware.

GUID Partition Table

Also designed as a partition table scheme standard for hard drives, the GPT makes use of a number of modern techniques to expand on the older MBR partitioning scheme. GPT is commonly used in computers with UEFI firmware. Most modern operating systems now support GPT.

The figure shows a comparison between MBR and GPT.

Refer to Interactive Graphic in online course

10.2.1.3   Partitions and Logical Drives

Primary Partition

The primary partition contains the operating system files and is usually the first partition. A primary partition cannot be subdivided into smaller sections. On a GPT partitioned disk, all partitions are primary partitions. On an MBR partitioned disk, there can be a maximum of four partitions, with only one being primary.

Refer to Interactive Graphic in online course

10.2.1.4   Check Your Understanding - Disk Terminology

Refer to Interactive Graphic in online course

10.2.1.5   File Systems

A new installation of an OS proceeds as if the disk were brand new. No information that is currently on the target partition is preserved. The first phase of the installation process partitions and formats the hard drive. This process prepares the disk to accept the new file system. The file system provides the directory structure that organizes the user's operating system, application, configuration, and data files. There are many different kinds of file systems and each one has different structure and logic. Different file systems also differ in properties of speed, flexibility, security, size and more. Here are five common file systems:

- **File Allocation Table, 32 bit (FAT32)** - Supports partition sizes up to 2 TB or 2,048 GB. The FAT32 file system is used by Windows XP and earlier OS versions.

- **New Technology File System (NTFS)** - Supports partition sizes up to 16 exabytes, in theory. NTFS incorporates file system security features and extended attributes. Windows 8.1, Windows 7, and Windows 10 automatically create a partition using the entire hard drive. If a user does not create custom partitions using the New option, as shown in the figure, the system formats the partition and begins installing Windows. If users create a partition, they will be able to determine the size of the partition.

- **exFAT (FAT 64)** - Created to address some of the limitations of FAT, FAT32, and NTFS when formatting USB flash drives, such as file size and directory size. One of the primary advantages of exFAT is that it can support files larger than 4GB.

- **Compact Disc File System (CDFS)** - Created specifically for optical disk media.
- **NFS (Network File System)** - NFS is a network-based file system, that allows file access over the network. From the user's standpoint, there is no difference between accessing a file stored locally or on another computer on the network. NFS is an open standard which allows anyone to implement it.

Quick Format versus Full Format

The quick format removes files from the partition but does not scan the disk for bad sectors. Scanning a disk for bad sectors can prevent data loss in the future. For this reason, do not use the quick format for disks that have been previously formatted. Although it is possible to quick format a partition or a disk after the OS is installed, the quick format option is not available when installing Windows 8.1 and Windows 7.

The full format removes files from the partition while scanning the disk for bad sectors. It is required for all new hard drives. The full format option takes more time to complete.

Refer to **Video** in online course

10.2.1.6   Video Demonstration - Disk Management Utility and Disk Partitioning

Click Play in the figure to view a demonstration of the Disk Management utility and disk partitioning.

Click here to read the transcript of this video.

Refer to **Video** in online course

10.2.1.7   Video Demonstration - Multiboot Procedures

Sometimes it is necessary to have more than one operating system installed in the computer. In those situations, the user must perform the installation of one OS, install a boot manager and then install the second OS. A boot manager is a program that is located in the boot sector and allows the user to choose which OS to use at boot time. By tracking the partition where a specific OS was installed, a boot manager can direct the BIOS to the correct partition, allowing it to load the desired operating system.

A popular boot manager for Linux is **grub**. For macOS, a common boot manager is **boot camp.**

Click Play in the figure to view a demonstration of multiboot procedures.

Click here to read the transcript of this video.

Refer to **Lab Activity** for this chapter

10.2.1.8   Lab - Create a Partition in Windows

In this lab, you will create a FAT32 formatted partition on a disk. You will convert the partition to NTFS. You will then identify the differences between the FAT32 format and the NTFS format.

Lab - Create a Partition in Windows

10.3   Installation and Boot Sequence

10.3.1   Basic Windows Installation

Refer to
Lab Activity
for this chapter

10.3.1.1   Lab - Windows Installation

In this lab, you will install the Windows operating system.

Lab - Windows Installation

Refer to
Online Course
for Illustration

10.3.1.2   Account Creation

When users attempt to log on to a device or to access system resources, Windows uses the process of authentication to verify the identity of the users. Authentication occurs when users enter a username and password to access a user account. Windows uses Single-Sign On (SSO) authentication, which allows users to log in once to access all system resources versus requiring them to log in each time they need to access an individual one.

User accounts allow multiple users to share a single computer using their own files and settings. Windows 10 offers two account types: Administrator and Standard User, as shown in the Figure. In previous versions of Windows, there was also a Guest account, but that has been removed with Windows 10.

Administrator accounts have complete control over a computer. Users with this type of account can change settings globally, install programs, get through the User Account Control (UAC) when elevation to perform a task is required.

Standard user accounts have limited control over a computer. Users with this type of account can run applications, but they cannot install programs. A standard user account can change system settings but only settings that do not affect other user accounts.

Refer to
Online Course
for Illustration

10.3.1.3   Finalize the Installation

Windows Update

To update the OS after the initial installation, Microsoft Windows Update is used to scan for new software and install service packs and patches.

Device Manager

After installation, verify that all hardware is installed correctly. The Device Manager is used to locate device problems and install the correct or updated drivers in Windows.

The figure shows the Windows Update and Device Manager utilities on Windows 10.

Refer to
Lab Activity
for this chapter

10.3.1.4   Lab - Finalize the Windows Installation

In this lab, you will add user accounts and finalize an installation of Windows 10.

Lab - Finalize the Windows Installation

10.3.2   Custom Installation Options

Refer to
Online Course
for Illustration

10.3.2.1   Disk Cloning

Installing an OS on a single computer takes time. Imagine the time it would take to install operating systems on multiple computers, one at a time. To simplify this activity, administrators usually elect a computer to act as a base system and go through the regular operating system installation process. After the operating is installed in the base computer, a specific program is used to duplicate all the information on its disk, sector by sector, to another disk. This new disk, usually an external device, now contains a fully deployed operating system and can be used to quickly deploy a fresh copy of the base operating system and any installed applications and data without the lengthy installation process or user involvement. Because the target disk now contains a sector-to-sector mapping of the original disk, the contents of the target disk is an image of the original disk.

If an undesirable setting is accidentally included during the base installation, an administrator can use Microsoft's System Preparation (Sysprep) tool to remove it before creating the final image. Sysprep can be used to install and configure the same OS on multiple computers. Sysprep prepares the OS with different hardware configurations. With Sysprep, technicians can quickly install the OS, complete the last configuration steps, and then install applications.

To run Sysprep in Windows 10, open Windows Explorer and navigate to C:\Windows\System32\sysprep. You can also just type "sysprep" in the Run command and click "OK."

The figure shows the Sysprep tool in Windows.

Refer to
Online Course
for Illustration

10.3.2.2   Other Installation Methods

A standard installation of Windows is sufficient for most computers used in a home or small office environment but there are cases when a custom installation process is required.

Take, for example, an IT support department; technicians in these environments must deploy hundreds, even thousands of Windows systems. Performing this many installations in the standard way is not feasible.

A standard installation is done via the installation media (DVD or USB drive), shown in the figure, provided by Microsoft and is an interactive process; the installer prompts the user for settings such as time zone and system language.

A custom installation of Windows can save time and provide a consistent configuration across computers within a large organization. A popular technique to install Windows across many computers is to perform installation in one computer and use it as a reference installation. When the installation is completed, an image is created. An image is a file that contains all the data from a partition.

When the image is ready, technicians can perform a much shorter installation by simply replicating and deploying the image to all computers in the organization. If the new installation requires any adjustments, those can be done quickly after the image is deployed.

Windows has several different types of custom installations:

- **Network Installation** - This includes Preboot Execution Environment (PXE) Installation, Unattended Installation, and Remote Installation.

- **Image-based Internal partition Installation** - This is a Windows image stored on an internal (often hidden) partition that can be used to restore Windows to its original state when it was shipped from the factory.

- **Other Types of Custom Installations** - This includes Windows Advanced Startup Options, Refresh your PC (Windows 8.x only), System Restore, Upgrade, Repair installation, Remote network installation, Recovery partition, and Refresh/restore.

Refer to **Online Course** for Illustration

10.3.2.3   Remote Network Installation

A popular method for OS installation in environments with many computers is a remote network installation. With this method, the operating system installation files are stored on a server so that a client computer can access the files remotely to begin the installation. A software package such as Remote Installation Services (RIS) is used to communicate with the client, store the setup files, and provide the necessary instructions for the client to access the setup files, download them, and begin the operating system installation.

Because the client computer does not have an operating system installed, a special environment must be used to boot the computer, connect to the network, and communicate with the server to begin the installation process. This special environment is known as the Preboot eXecution Environment (PXE). For the PXE to work, the NIC must be PXE-enabled. This functionality may come from the BIOS or the firmware on the NIC. When the computer is started, the NIC listens for special instructions on the network to start PXE.

The figure shows the client loading setup files from the PXE server over TFTP.

Note   If the NIC is not PXE-enabled, third-party software may be used to load PXE from storage media.

Refer to **Online Course** for Illustration

10.3.2.4   Unattended Network Installation

Unattended installation, another network-based installation, allows a Windows system to be installed or upgraded with little user intervention. The Windows unattended installation is based on an answer file. This file contains simple text that instructs Windows Setup how to configure and install the OS.

To perform a Windows Unattended installation, setup.exe must be run with the user options found in the answer file. The installation process begins as usual but instead of prompting the user, Setup uses the answers listed in the answer file.

To customize a standard Windows 10 installation, the System Image Manager (SIM), shown in the figure, is used to create the setup answer file. You can also add packages, such as applications or drivers, to answer files.

The answer file is copied to the distribution shared folder on a server. At this point, you can do one of two things:

- Run the unattended.bat file on the client machine to prepare the hard drive and install the OS from the server over the network.

- Create a boot disk that boots the computer and connects to the distribution shared folder on the server. You then run a batch file containing a set of instructions to install the OS over the network.

Note   Windows SIM is part of the Windows Automated Installation Kit (AIK) and can be downloaded from the Microsoft website.

Refer to **Video** in online course

10.3.2.5   Video Demonstration - Windows Restore and Recovery

Click Play in the figure to view a demonstration of Windows restore and recovery.

Click here to read the transcript of this video.

Refer to **Online Course** for Illustration

10.3.2.6   Recovery Partition

Some computers that have Windows installed contain a section of the disk that is inaccessible to the user. This partition, called a recovery partition, contains an image that can be used to restore the computer to its original configuration.

The recovery partition is often hidden to prevent it from being used for anything other than restoration. To restore the computer using the recovery partition, you often must use a special key or key combination when the computer is starting. Sometimes, the option to restore from the factory recovery partition is located in the BIOS or a program from the manufacturer that is accessed in Windows. Contact the computer manufacturer to find out how to access the partition and restore the original configuration of the computer.

Note   If the operating system has been damaged because of a faulty hard drive, the recovery partition may also be corrupt and not able to recover the operating system.

Refer to **Online Course** for Illustration

10.3.2.7   Upgrade Methods

In-place upgrade

The simplest path to upgrade a PC that is currently running Windows 7 or Windows 8.1 to Windows 10 is through an in-place upgrade. This will update the operating system and migrate apps and settings to the new OS. The System Center Configuration Manager (Configuration Manager) task sequence can be used to completely automate the process. The figure shows the Configuration Manager upgrade task sequence for Windows 10.

When upgrading Windows 7 or Windows 8 to Windows 10, the Windows installation program (Setup.exe) will perform an in-place upgrade, which automatically preserves all data, settings, applications, and drivers from the existing operating system version. This saves effort because there is no need for complex deployment infrastructure.

Note   Any user data should be backed up before performing the upgrade.

Clean install

Another way to upgrade to a newer version of Windows is to perform a clean upgrade. Because a clean install will wipe the drive completely, all files and data should be saved to some form of backup drive.

Before a clean install of Windows can be performed, the installation media will need to be created. This can be on a disc or flash drive that the PC can boot from to run the setup. Windows 7, 8.1, and 10 can be downloaded directly from Microsoft. The download Windows web site includes the directions to create the installation media.

Note   A valid product key is needed for the particular Windows version and edition in order to activate Windows after the installation process.

Refer to
Interactive Graphic
in online course

10.3.2.8   Check your Understanding– Identify OS Installation Terminology

10.3.3   Windows Boot Sequence

Refer to
Online Course
for Illustration

10.3.3.1   Windows Boot Sequence

After POST, the BIOS locates and reads the configuration settings that are stored in the CMOS memory. The boot device priority, as shown in the figure, is the order in which devices are checked to locate the bootable partition. The boot device priority is set in the BIOS and can be arranged in any order. The BIOS boots the computer using the first drive that contains a valid boot sector. This sector contains the Master Boot Record (MBR). The MBR identifies the Volume Boot Record (VBR) which loads the boot manager, which for Windows is bootmgr.exe.

Hard drives, network drives, USB drives, and even removable media can be used in the boot order, depending on the capabilities of the motherboard. Some BIOS also have a boot device priority menu that is accessed with a special key during computer startup. You can use this menu to select the device to boot as shown in the figure.

Refer to
Online Course
for Illustration

10.3.3.2   Windows 7 Startup Modes

Some problems will prevent Windows from starting up. To troubleshoot and fix this kind of problem, use one of the many Windows Startup Modes.

Pressing the F8 key during the boot process opens the Windows Advanced Boot Options menu, as shown in the figure. This allows users to select how they wish to boot Windows. These are four commonly used startup options:

- **Safe Mode** - A diagnostic mode used to troubleshoot Windows and Windows startup issues. Functionality is limited as many device drivers are not loaded.

- **Safe Mode with** Networking - Starts Windows in Safe Mode with networking support.

- **Safe Mode with Command Prompt** - Starts Windows and loads the command prompt instead of the GUI.

- **Last Known Good Configuration** - Loads the configuration settings that were used the last time that Windows started successfully. It does this by accessing a copy of the registry that is created for this purpose.

Note   Last Known Good Configuration is not useful unless it is applied immediately after a failure occurs. If the machine is restarted and manages to open Windows, the registry is updated with the faulty information.

Refer to
Online Course
for Illustration

10.3.3.3 Windows 8 and10 Startup Modes

Both Windows 8 and Windows 10 boot too quickly to use F8 to access startup settings. Instead, hold the Shift key and select the Restart option in the Power menu. This will display the Choose an Option screen. To get the startup settings, select Troubleshoot, then from the next screen select Advanced options. Inside Advanced options select Startup settings, then on the next screen select Restart. The computer will then restart and display the Startup Settings menu shown in the figure. To choose a startup option use number or function keys F1-F9 that corresponds to the desired option.

Refer to
Interactive Graphic
in online course

10.3.3.4 Check Your Understanding - Windows Boot Sequence

Refer to
Online Course
for Illustration

10.4 Summary

In this chapter, you learned that all operating systems perform the same four basic functions: Control hardware access, manage files and folders, provide a user interface, and manage applications. You also learned there are three most commonly used desktop operating systems; Microsoft Windows, Apple macOS, and Linux. This chapter focused on Microsoft Windows operating systems, specifically Windows 7, Windows 8, and Windows 10. You learned about the minimum system requirements of each Windows operating system. These system requirements define the minimum amount of RAM, storage drive space, and CPU speed needed for the operating system to install and function properly.

Before the OS can be installed, a storage media device must be chosen and prepared to receive the operating system. You learned how to prepare a storage drive for a Windows installation by formatting the drive into partitions. You learned about the primary partition that contains the operating system files, the active partition that is used to store and boot the operating system, and extended partitions that can be created to hold logical drives. You completed a lab where you created a FAT 32 partition in Windows and then converted the partition to NTFS.

You also performed a Windows operating system installation though two labs. In these labs, you installed Windows, performed basic setup tasks, created user accounts, and installed updates.

The chapter concluded with a review of the Windows boot sequence and the startup modes for Windows 7, Windows 8, and Windows 10.

Go to the online course to take the quiz and exam.

Chapter 10 Quiz

This quiz is designed to provide an additional opportunity to practice the skills and knowledge presented in the chapter and to prepare for the chapter exam. You will be allowed multiple attempts and the grade does not appear in the gradebook.

Chapter 10 Exam

The chapter exam assesses your knowledge of the chapter content.

Your Chapter Notes

Windows Configuration

Refer to
Online Course
for Illustration

11.0   Introduction

The first version of the Microsoft Windows operating system was released in 1985. Since then, over 25 versions, subversions, and varieties have been released. As an IT technician and professional you should understand the features of the most prevalent Windows versions in use today, Windows 7, Windows 8, and Windows 10.

In this chapter, you will learn about the different Windows versions and the editions of each that are most suited for corporate and home users. You will learn how to configure the Windows operating system and to perform administrative tasks using the Control Panel in the GUI and commands in the Windows command line (CLI) application and the PowerShell command line utility. You will have an opportunity to put into practice what you learn by working through several labs that involve working with file system commands, disk CLI commands, task and system CLI commands, and others.

You will learn about the two methods for organizing and managing Windows computers on a network, the domain and the workgroup, and how to share local computer resources, such as files, folders, and printers on the network. You will also learn how to configure a wired network connection in Windows. You will perform labs creating and sharing folders on the network and setting access permissions. You will also connect a computer to a wireless router and test the wireless connection as well as configure Windows for remote access using the Remote Desktop and Remote Assistance tools.

You will learn how a preventive maintenance plan can decrease downtime, improve performance, improve reliability, and lower repair costs and that preventive maintenance should take place when it causes the least amount of disruption to users. Regular scans for viruses and malware are also an important part of preventive maintenance. You will perform several labs to schedule a task using the GUI and at the command line and to manage startup applications using the Run key in the Registry.

At the end of the chapter, you will learn how the six steps in the troubleshooting process are applied to Windows operating systems.

11.1   Windows Desktop and File Explorer

11.1.1   Comparing Windows Versions

Refer to
Online Course
for Illustration

11.1.1.1   Windows Versions

The first version of the Microsoft Windows operating system was released in 1985, over 30 years ago! Since then, over 25 versions, subversions, and varieties have been released. In addition, each version can also have editions, such as Home, Pro, Ultimate, or Enterprise, and come in either 32-bit or 64-bit versions. In the case of Windows 10, twelve editions were developed and released. However, only nine are currently offered.

Corporate and personal users of Windows operating system have different needs. On a corporate network it is usually necessary to manage user accounts and system policies centrally due to the number of devices on the network and higher security requirements. Centralized management is provided through joining an Active Directory domain where the user accounts and security policies are configured on a Domain Controller. Windows Professional, Pro, Enterprise, Ultimate, and Education editions can join an Active Directory domain.

Other corporate features include:

- **BitLocker** - A feature that enables a user to encrypt all data on a disk drive or removable drive. Found on Windows 7 Enterprise and Ultimate, Windows 8 Pro and Enterprise, and Windows 10 Pro, Enterprise, and Education Editions.

- **Encrypted file system (EFS)** - A feature found on Windows 7 Professional, Enterprise and Ultimate, Windows 8 Pro and Enterprise, and Windows 10 Pro, Enterprise, and Education Editions that allows the user to configure file and folder-level encryption.

- **Branch Cache** - Allows remote computers to share access to a single cache of data from shared folders and files or document portals such as SharePoint sites. This can reduce WAN traffic because the individual clients do not each need to download their own copy of cache data. Found on Windows 7 Enterprise and Ultimate, Windows 8 Enterprise, and Windows 10 Pro, Enterprise, and Education Editions.

There are some features of Windows that are aimed at personal use, such as Windows Media Center. This is a Microsoft app that allows the computer to be used as a home entertainment appliance for playing DVDs. Windows Media Center was included in Windows 7 Home Premium, Professional, Enterprise, and Ultimate editions. It was also a paid-for add-on to Windows 8 but was discontinued in Windows 10.

This chapter covers the various tools and applications that are available for configuring, maintaining, and troubleshooting Windows. The primary focus of this course will be Windows 10. When relevant, Windows 8 and Windows 7 will be discussed when major differences exist between them and Windows 10.

Refer to **Online Course** for Illustration

11.1.1.2   Windows 7

Windows 7 was released in October 2009. It offered improvements to the interface, performance, and File Explorer, including the first appearance of Libraries and HomeGroup file sharing. The taskbar offered many of the enhancements that change the look and feel of the desktop over Vista. It was quite successful and Microsoft offers extended support for it until January of 2020.

Refer to **Online Course** for Illustration

11.1.1.3   Windows 8

Released in October of 2012, Windows 8 included a major revision of the Windows interface that made it very different from Windows 7. This was done to make Windows more compatible with touch screen devices like tablets and phones. Although Windows 8 included improvements in security and performance, the interface changes were unpopular and made it difficult for some users to learn to use them. For example, Windows 8 lacked a Start button, which was a major problem for some users.

Refer to
Online Course
for Illustration

11.1.1.4   Windows 8.1

Because Windows 8 was not very well received, Microsoft quickly responded with an update that addressed some of the criticisms of that version. Windows 8.1 was released in October of 2013, only one year after Windows 8. It included a Start screen that is more familiar to users of earlier versions, including a full Start button on the Taskbar. It included other new functionalities and easier configuration options of the desktop interface.

Refer to
Interactive Graphic
in online course

11.1.1.5   Windows 10

Windows 10 is the most recent version of Windows at the time of this writing. There are nine editions of Windows 10 that are currently offered. The examples used in this course are from the Windows 10 Professional edition.

The retail version of Windows 10 became available in July 2015. Windows 10 offered a return to the desktop computer-oriented interface that had been replaced in Windows 8. It supports an easy transition between a point-and-click interface and the touch interfaces of tablets, phones, and embedded systems like Internet of Things (IoT) single-board computers. Windows 10 includes support for universal apps that run on desktop and mobile devices. It also introduces the Microsoft Edge web browser. It offers enhanced security features, faster logons, and encryption of system files to save disk space. Charms were replaced with a new Windows Action Center that provides notifications and quick settings.

Windows 10 uses a new update model. Twice a year, Microsoft offers feature updates. These updates add new features to Windows and also improve existing features. The updates are numbered, and the description of them is listed on the Microsoft website. It is entirely possible that you will notice changes to the interfaces of some Windows apps and tools after a feature update. Quality updates, or cumulative updates, usually install monthly. They contain patches to fix problems with Windows or they contain security updates to address new threats and vulnerabilities.

Figure 2 summarizes the important features of the Windows versions that are covered in this course.

Refer to
Interactive Graphic
in online course

11.1.1.6   Check Your Understanding - Windows Versions

11.1.2   The Windows Desktop

Refer to
Online Course
for Illustration

11.1.2.1   The Windows 7 Desktop

Windows 7 has a default theme called Aero. Aero has translucent window borders, numerous animations, and icons that are thumbnail images of the contents of a file.

Windows versions 7 and above include the following desktop features:

- **Shake** - Minimize all windows that are not being used by clicking and holding the title bar of one window and shaking it with the mouse. Repeat the action to maximize all of the windows.

- **Peek** - View the desktop icons that are behind open windows by placing your cursor over the Show desktop button found at the right edge of the taskbar. This makes the open windows transparent. Click the button to minimize all windows.

- **Snap** - Resize a window by dragging it to one of the edges of the screen. Dragging the window to the left edge of the desktop fits the window to the left half of the screen. Dragging the window to the right edge of the desktop fits the window to the right half of the screen. Dragging the window to the top of the screen will maximize the window.

In Windows 7, users can place Gadgets on the desktop. Gadgets are small applications, such as games, sticky notes, a calendar, or a clock. The figure displays the weather, calendar, and clock Gadgets on a Windows 7 desktop.

Note   Microsoft has retired the Gadgets feature in versions following Windows 7 because of security concerns.

To add gadgets to the Windows 7 desktop, follow these steps:

Step 1.   Right-click anywhere on the desktop and choose Gadgets.

Step 2.   Drag and drop the gadget from the menu to the desktop, or double-click the gadget to add it to the desktop, or right-click the gadget and choose Add.

Step 3.   To snap a gadget, drag it to the desired desktop location. The gadget aligns itself with the screen edges and other gadgets.

Refer to
Online Course
for Illustration

11.1.2.2   The Windows 8 Desktop

Windows 8 introduced a new desktop that used tiles on the Start screen, as shown in the figure. This environment is used on desktops and laptops, but it is optimized for mobile devices. Microsoft intended to unify the Windows interface across desktop and mobile devices. The Start screen displays a customizable array of tiles designed to access apps and other information, such as social media updates and calendar notifications. These tiles represent notifications, applications, or desktop programs. Some tiles can display dynamic content. They are called live tiles. Another new GUI element is a vertical bar of five icons known as charms. Charms can be accessed by placing the mouse cursor in the upper-right corner of the screen or swiping your finger in from the right side of the screen on a touchscreen. They provide quick access to common functions.

Windows 8 included a revised task manager, the addition of the ribbon menu to File Explorer (formerly known as Windows Explorer.), and the inclusion of anti-virus functionality directly in the OS called Windows Defender.

Refer to
Online Course
for Illustration

11.1.2.3   The Windows 8.1 Desktop

The figure shows the Windows 8.1 desktop interface including the Taskbar, Start button, and pinned program icons. Clicking the Start button displays the Start screen that is very similar to the Windows 8 Start screen.

Refer to
Interactive Graphic
in online course

11.1.2.4   Personalizing the Windows Desktop

Windows offers many settings that enable users to personalize the desktop and other aspects of the Windows GUI. The fastest way to get to these settings is to right-click an empty area of the desktop and select **Personalize**. This shows the **Background** settings. Drag the right-hand border of the settings box to widen it. This will reveal the **Personalization** settings menu. The fastest way to change the look and feel of the Windows GUI is to select from the available themes, as shown in Figure 1. Themes are a preset combination of GUI settings that go together. You can also create themes from settings that you have made so that they can be used later. Themes beyond those that are provided can be downloaded from the Microsoft Store. Many other changes can be made to Windows GUI from here.

In Windows 8 the Apps environment is highly customizable. To re-arrange the tiles, click and drag the tiles. To rename a tile group, right-click on any empty area of the screen and select Name groups. To add tiles to the main screen, right-click the desired Windows app after searching for it and select Pin to Start. To search for an app, click Search from the Charms bar. Alternatively, you can start typing the name of the app from the Windows Apps environment. Search will start automatically. Figure 2 shows the Windows 8 Apps environment and the Charms bar.

In Windows 7 and 8.1, to customize the desktop, right-click anywhere on the desktop and choose **Personalize**. In the Personalization window, you can change the desktop appearance, display settings, and sound settings. Figure 3 shows the Windows 8 Personalization window. It is very similar to the Personalization window in Windows 7.

Refer to **Video** in online course

11.1.2.5   Video Demonstration - The Windows 10 Desktop

After the OS has been installed, you can customize the computer desktop to suit individual needs. A computer desktop is a graphical representation of the workspace and is commonly called a graphical user interface, or GUI. The desktop has icons, toolbars, and menus that are used for a variety of purposes. You can add or change images, sounds, and colors to provide a more personalized look and feel, for example. Click Play in the figure to view a video demonstration of the Windows 10 desktop.

Click here to read the transcript of this video.

Refer to **Online Course** for Illustration

11.1.2.6   The Windows 10 Start Menu

The Windows 10 Start menu consists of three main parts. To the left, a strip of shortcuts to common libraries appears with a button that provides access to settings and the shutdown button. To the right of this is a menu of applications that are available, in alphabetical order, with areas for the most recently installed and most used applications at the top. To the right is an area containing tiles for Apps that are arranged by category, such as games, creative software, etc. The Windows 10 Start menu is shown in the figure.

Refer to **Interactive Graphic** in online course

11.1.2.7   The Windows 8.1 and 8.0 Start Menu

In Windows 8.0, with the introduction of the Windows Apps environment, Microsoft chose to remove the Start Button and Start Menu. The Start Menu was replaced by the Start Screen, as shown in Figure 1. Clicking the downward-pointing arrow reveals the alphabetized list of Apps that are available, as shown in Figure 2.

After many requests, Microsoft brought back a limited Start Button in Windows 8.1. The Start Screen still plays the role of the Start Menu but Windows 8.1 users now have a button to access the Start Screen. Other ways to access the Start Screen include pressing the Windows key on the keyboard or clicking the Start Button located on the Charms bar.

A limited Start Menu can be displayed in Windows 8.1 by right-clicking the Start Button, as shown in Figure 3.

Refer to
Interactive Graphic
in online course

11.1.2.8   The Windows 7 Start Menu

The Start Menu in Windows 7 is accessed by clicking the Windows icon at the bottom-left of the desktop. The Start Menu, shown in Figure 1, displays all of the applications installed on the computer, a list of recently opened documents, and a list of other elements, such as the search feature, Help and Support, and Control Panel. To customize Start Menu settings in Windows 7 use the following path:

Right-click an empty section of the taskbar and choose **Properties > Start Menu > Customize.**

Refer to
Interactive Graphic
in online course

11.1.2.9   The Taskbar

The Taskbar provides easy access to many important and commonly used features of Windows. Applications, files, tools, and settings can all be accessed from this one place. Right-clicking the Taskbar or opening the Taskbar and Navigation control panel leads you to a Settings screen that allows easy configuration of the Taskbar appearance, location, operation, and features. The Windows 10 Taskbar Settings screen is shown in figure 1. It is available from the Taskbar option in the Personalization Settings window.

These are some useful features of the Taskbar:

- **Jump lists** - To display a list of tasks that are unique to the application, right-click the application's icon in the taskbar.

- **Pinned applications** - To add an application to the taskbar for easy access, right-click the icon of an application and select Pin to taskbar.

- **Thumbnail previews** - To view a thumbnail image of a running program, hover the mouse over the program icon on the taskbar.

Changes to Taskbar settings vary slightly between windows versions.

Figure 2 shows Windows 8.1 Taskbar and Navigation Properties.

Figure 3 shows Windows 7 Taskbar and Navigation Properties.

Refer to
Lab Activity
for this chapter

11.1.2.10   Lab - Explore the Windows Desktop

In this lab, you will explore the Windows Desktop, Start Menu, and Taskbar.

Lab - Explore the Windows Desktop

Refer to
Interactive Graphic
in online course

11.1.2.11   Check Your Understanding - Identify Elements of the Windows Desktop

11.1.3   Windows Task Manager

Refer to **Video**
in online course

11.1.3.1   Video Demonstration - Working With Task Manager

The Windows Task Manager provides information about all of the applications, processes, and services that are running on the computer. This can be used to monitor system resources and the programs that are using them. Task Manager can also be used to terminate processes that are causing system issues or that have stopped responding to user input. Care must be taken when terminating processes because they may be required for system operation.

Task Manager is essentially the same in Windows 10 and Windows 8. The Windows 7 Task Manager has some essential differences.

Click Play in the figure to view a demonstration of how to use Task Manager in Windows 10.

Click here to read the transcript of this video.

Refer to
Interactive Graphic
in online course

11.1.3.2   Windows 10 Task Manager Functions

Refer to
Online Course
for Illustration

11.1.3.3   Task Manager in Windows 7

Task Manager is different in Windows 7. In many ways, the Windows 10 Task Manager is a significant upgrade from the Windows 7 Task Manager. The Windows 7 Task Manager has six tabs:

- **Applications** - This tab shows all running applications. From this tab, you can create, switch to, or close any applications that have stopped responding using the buttons at the bottom.

- **Processes** - This tab shows all running processes. From this tab, you can end processes or set process priorities.

- **Services** - This tab shows the available services, including their operational status. Services are identified by their PID.

- **Performance** - This tab shows the CPU and page file usage.

- **Networking** - This tab shows the usage of all network adapters.

- **Users** - This tab shows all users that are logged on the computer.

Several major differences exist between Task Manager in Windows 7 and Windows 10:

1. The Applications and Processes tabs have been combined in Windows 10.

2. The Networking tab is now included with the Performance tab in Windows 10.

3. The Users tab has been enhanced in Windows 10 to not only show the users that are connected but also the resources that they are using.

Refer to
Lab Activity
for this chapter

11.1.3.4   Lab - Work with Task Manager

In this lab, you will use Task Manager to monitor system performance.

Lab - Work with Task Manager

Refer to
Interactive Graphic
in online course

11.1.3.5   Check Your Understanding - Compare Task Manager in Windows 7 and 10

11.1.4   Windows File Explorer

Refer to
Online Course
for Illustration

11.1.4.1   File Explorer

File Explorer is a file management application in Window 8 and Windows 10. It is used to navigate the file system and manage the folders, subfolders, and applications on storage media. You can also preview some types of files.

In File Explorer, common tasks, such as copying and moving files and creating new folders, can be done using the Ribbon. The tabs at the top of the window change as different types of items are selected. In the figure, the Ribbon for the File tab is displayed for Quick Access. If the Ribbon is not displaying, click the **Expand the Ribbon** icon, represented by a down arrow, on the upper right corner of the window.

Windows Explorer is the name of the file management application in Windows 7 and earlier. Windows Explorer performs similar functions as File Explorer but lacks the Ribbon.

Refer to **Video**
in online course

11.1.4.2   Video Demonstration - Working with File Explorer

Click Play to learn about some of the functions of File Explorer.

Click here to read the transcript of this video.

Refer to
Interactive Graphic
in online course

11.1.4.3   This PC

In Windows versions 10 and 8.1, the This PC feature allows you to access the various Devices and drives installed in the computer. In Windows 7, this same feature is called Computer.

To open This PC, open File Explorer, and it will display the This PC feature by default, as shown in Figure 1.

In Windows 8.0, or 7, click **Start** and select **Computer**. Figure 2 shows the **Computer** feature in Windows 7.

Refer to
Online Course
for Illustration

11.1.4.4   Run as Administrator

Modern operating systems use a number of methods to improve security. One of these methods is file permissions. Depending on the file permission, only users with enough permission can access the file. System files, other user files, or files with elevated permissions are examples of files that could lead Windows to deny access to a user. To override this behavior and gain access to those files, you must open or execute them as the system administrator.

To open or execute a file using elevated permission, right-click the file and choose **Run as Administrator** as shown in the figure. Choose **Yes** in the User Account Control (UAC) window. UAC is the location where administrators can manage user accounts. In some cases, software will not install properly unless the installer is run with Administrator privileges.

Note   An administrator password is required to use these feature if the current user does not belong to the Administrator group.

Refer to
Online Course
for Illustration

11.1.4.5   Windows Libraries

Windows Libraries allow you to easily organize content from various storage devices on your local computer and network, including removable media, without actually moving the files. A library is a virtual folder that presents content from different locations within the same view. When Windows 10 is installed, each user has six default libraries, as shown in the figure.

You can search a library, and you can filter the content using criteria such as filename, file type, or date modified. In Windows 10 and Windows 8.1, the libraries are hidden by default. The context menu for the left pane of the File Explorer window contains an option that shows the libraries.

Refer to
Online Course
for Illustration

11.1.4.6   Directory Structures

In Windows, files are organized in a directory structure. A directory structure is designed to store system files, user files, and program files. The root level of the Windows directory structure, the partition, is usually labeled drive C, as shown in the figure. Drive C contains a set of standardized directories, called folders, for the operating system, applications, configuration information, and data files. Directories may contain additional directories, as shown in the figure. These additional directories are commonly called subfolders. The number of nested folders is essentially limited by the maximum length of the path to the folders. In Windows 10, the default limit is 260 characters. The figure shows several nested folders in File Explorer along with the equivalent path.

Windows creates a series of folders for each user account that is configured on the computer. These folders appear to be the same in File Explorer for each user, however, they are actually unique to each user account. In this way, users cannot access each other's files, applications, or data.

Note   It is a best practice to store files in folders and subfolders rather than at the root level of a drive.

Refer to
Interactive Graphic
in online course

11.1.4.7   User and System File Locations

Users Folder

By default, Windows stores most of the files created by users in the Users Folder, C:\Users\ User_name\. Each user's folder contains folders for music, videos, websites, and pictures, among others. Many programs also store specific user data here. If a single computer has many users, they have their own folders containing their favorites, desktop items, logs, among others.

Refer to
Interactive Graphic
in online course

11.1.4.8   File Extensions

Files in the directory structure adhere to a Windows naming convention:

- A maximum of 255 characters is allowed.

- Characters such as a slash or a backslash (/ \) are not allowed.

- An extension of three or four letters is added to the filename to identify the file type.

- Filenames are not case sensitive.

By default, file extensions are hidden. In Windows 10 and Windows 8.1, in the File Explorer ribbon, click the **View** tab. Then click to check **File name extensions,** as shown in Figure 1. To display the file extensions In Windows 7, you must disable the **Hide extensions for known file types** setting in the **FolderOptions** control panel utility, as shown in Figure 2.

The following filename extensions are commonly used:

- .docx - Microsoft Word (2007 and later)
- .txt - ASCII text only
- .jpg - Graphics format
- .pptx - Microsoft PowerPoint
- .zip - Compression format

Refer to
Online Course
for Illustration

11.1.4.9   File Attributes

The directory structure maintains a set of attributes for each file that controls how the file can be viewed or altered. These are the most common file attributes:

- **R** - The file is read-only.
- **A** - The file will be archived the next time that the disk is backed up.
- **S** - The file is marked as a system file, and a warning is given if an attempt is made to delete or modify the file.
- **H** - The file is hidden in the directory display.

The figure shows the file properties dialog box in which attributes can be viewed or set.

Refer to **Video**
in online course

11.1.4.10   Video Demonstration - File and Folder Properties

Click Play in the figure to view a demonstration of the file and folder properties in Windows 10 File Explorer.

Click here to read the transcript of this video.

Refer to
Lab Activity
for this chapter

11.1.4.11   Lab - Working with File Explorer

In this lab, you will use File Explorer to work with files and folders.

Lab - Working with File Explorer

Refer to
Interactive Graphic
in online course

11.1.4.12   Check Your Understanding - File Explorer

11.2   Configure Windows with Control Panels

11.2.1   Control Panel Utilities

Refer to
Interactive Graphic
in online course

11.2.1.1   Windows 10: Settings and Control Panels

Windows 10 offers two ways to configure the operating system. The first is the Settings app. It has an interface that follows the modern Windows interface design guidelines. Figure 1 shows the Settings App menu. From it you can access many system settings. The Settings App first appeared in Windows 8 as shown in Figure 2. It provided access to fewer settings than the Windows 10 version, which has now become robust. Note that a search field enables you to find settings without taking a lot of time clicking through menus.

In Windows 7, the Setting App was not present. The most efficient way to make system configuration changes was by using the Control Panel, as shown in Figure 3. While it appears that Microsoft is moving more and more functionality to the Settings App, the Control Panel is still present in Windows 8 and 10, and in some cases it is the only way to make changes to some configuration settings. In other cases, especially in regards to Personalization, the Settings app provides more configuration options than Control Panel.

For this course, you will focus on the Control Panel in Windows 10, and learn about the Settings App where necessary. If important differences exist between the Windows 7 and 8 Control Panels and Windows 10, you will learn about those differences. The Control Panel window looks very similar between Windows versions, however some Control Panel items differ between the versions.

Refer to
Online Course
for Illustration

11.2.1.2   Introduction to Control Panel

Windows 10 usually defaults to the Settings app for configuration changes. This is good for the casual user, however a PC technician frequently needs more configuration options than what is available in the Settings App. The Control Panel offers many configuration tools and its interface is preferred by many experienced Windows administrators. In fact, some Settings actually link to Control Panel items.

To start Control Panel, type Control Panel into the Search box and click the Control Panel Desktop app that appears in the results, as shown in the figure. If you right-click on the result, you can pin it to the Start menu to make it easier to find. You can also open it from the Command Prompt by typing **control**.

In Windows 7, the Control Panel has an entry on the Start menu. In Windows 8.1, it can be accessed by right-clicking the Start button. In Windows 8, it can be opened by searching for Control Panel and clicking the result.

Refer to
Interactive Graphic
in online course

11.2.1.3   Control Panel Views

The Windows 10 Control Panel opens to the Categories view by default, as shown in Figure 1. This helps to organize the forty or more Control Panel items and makes them easier to find. This view also provides a search box which will return a list of Control Panel items that are relevant to a search term.

The classic view of Control Panel is reached by changing the setting in the **View by:** dropdown menu to **Small icons,** as shown in Figure 2. Note that there will be variations in what is available in Control Panel depending on features of the individual computer.

Refer to
Interactive Graphic
in online course

11.2.1.4   Define Control Panel Categories

System and Security

In this category, you can view and configure security settings such as Windows Defender Firewall. You can also access administrative tools that enable you to configure a wide range of system functions such as general hardware, storage, and encryption settings and operations.

Refer to
Lab Activity
for this chapter

11.2.1.5   Lab - Explore Control Panel Categories

In this lab, you will investigate the options provided in the various commonly used Control Panel items.

Lab - Explore Control Panel Categories

Refer to
Interactive Graphic
in online course

11.2.1.6   Check Your Understanding - Control Panel Categories

11.2.2   User and Account Control Panel Items

Refer to
Online Course
for Illustration

11.2.2.1   User Accounts

An administrative account is created when Windows is installed. To create a user account afterwards, open the User Accounts Control Panel item, as shown in the figure.

Administrator accounts have the ability to change all system settings and access all files and folders on the computer. For that reason, administrator accounts should be carefully controlled. Standard user accounts can manage most configuration settings that don't affect other users. They can only access their own files and folders.

The User Accounts Control Panel item provides options to help you create, change, and delete user accounts. It is very similar between Windows versions.

Note   Some features of the User Accounts utility require administrative privileges and will not be accessible with a standard user account.

Refer to
Online Course
for Illustration

11.2.2.2   User Account Control Settings

The User Account Control (UAC) monitors programs on the computer and warns users when an action might present a threat to the computer. In Windows versions 7 through 10, you can adjust the level of monitoring that the UAC performs. When Windows is installed, the UAC for the primary account defaults to the setting "Notify me only when programs try to make changes to my computer," as shown in the figure. You are not notified when you make changes to these settings.

To change when you are notified about changes that programs may make to your computer, adjust the level of UAC.

Refer to
Lab Activity
for this chapter

11.2.2.3   Lab - User Accounts

In this lab, you will work with User Accounts Control Panel item create and modify users.

Lab - User Accounts

Refer to
Online Course
for Illustration

11.2.2.4   Credential Manager

Credential Manager helps you to manage passwords that are used for websites and Windows applications, as shown in the figure. These passwords and usernames are stored in a secure location. Credentials are automatically updated as they are created or changed. You can view, add, edit, or delete the credentials that are stored by Credential Manager.

Credential Manager has been enhanced since the Windows 7 version although the interface is similar.

Note   Web credentials are not saved for sites accessed by browsers other than Internet Explorer and Edge. Credentials created with other browsers must be managed from within that browser.

Refer to
Online Course
for Illustration

11.2.2.5   Sync Center

Sync Center allows files to be edited from multiple Windows devices. While accessing networked files from multiple devices is nothing new, Sync Center allows a form of version control. This means that changes made to the networked files by one device will be made on all devices that are configured to synchronize those files. With this synchronization service, there is no need to physically copy a new version of a file from the device on which the changes were made to the device that you are currently working on. The updated file is on the networked storage location and the local versions are updated to the latest version automatically. When changes are made, those changes will be made to networked file too. All devices must be able to connect to the same networked storage location.

Another value to Sync Center is that users can work on files on a device that is offline and the server copy can be updated over the network when the device reconnects.

Using Sync Center requires activation of the Offline Files feature. This sets up a local file location that will store the files to be synchronized. It also requires you to set up a sync partnership with the networked file location. Files can be synchronized manually and synchronization can also be scheduled to occur automatically.

Microsoft OneDrive offers a similar service. OneDrive is a cloud storage service that is available to Microsoft Windows users. Since OneDrive is reachable over the internet, work can be done on any device that can connect to OneDrive from any location with internet access. Sync Center requires access to a network server that may not be reachable from networks in other locations.

Refer to
Interactive Graphic
in online course

11.2.2.6   Check Your Understanding - User and Account Control Panels

11.2.3   Network and Internet Control Panels

Refer to
Online Course
for Illustration

11.2.3.1   Network Settings

Windows 10 has a new Settings app for network settings. It combines many different functions into one high-level app, as shown in the figure. The links in this app can point to new settings screens, Control Panel items, or even the Action Center. Some of the options, such as Airplane Mode, Mobile Hotspot, and Data Usage are more relevant to mobile devices than to desktop computers.

Mobile devices use Wireless Wide Area Network (WWAN) or cellular Internet access technology. WWAN requires using an adapter to link to a cellular provider's network through the nearest base station or transmitter. WWAN adapters can be internal or external connected by USB. The bandwidth available over WWAN connections is dependent on the technologies supported by the adapter and the transmitter, such as 3G or 4G. Connection to the WWAN is automatic once the adapter and adapter software are installed.

Refer to **Interactive Graphic** in online course

11.2.3.2 Internet Options

General

General - Configure basic internet settings, such as selecting the default home page, viewing and deleting browsing history, adjusting search settings, and customizing the browser appearance.

Refer to **Interactive Graphic** in online course

11.2.3.3 Network and Sharing Center

Network and Sharing Center allows an administrator to configure and review nearly all network settings on a Windows computer. With it, you can do everything from viewing network status to changing properties of the protocols and services that are running on a network adapter. Figures 1, 2, and 3 show the Network and Sharing Center for Windows 10, 8, and 7, respectively. Note that although they look very similar. Small differences exist between the versions.

Network and Sharing Center shows how your computer connects to a network. Internet connectivity, if present, will also be displayed here. The window displays and allows the configuration of shared network resources. Some useful and common network-related tasks are displayed on the left pane of the window.

Network and Sharing center allows the configuration of file and device sharing through the use of network profiles. The network profiles enable basic sharing settings to change depending on whether you are attached to a private or public network. This enables sharing to be inactive on an insecure public network but active on a private secure network.

Refer to **Interactive Graphic** in online course

11.2.3.4 HomeGroup

In Windows networking, a homegroup is a group of computers that are on the same network. Homegroups simplify sharing files on simple networks. They are intended to make networking in the home easier by requiring a minimum of configuration. You can share your library folders on the network, making it easy for other devices to access your music, videos, photos, and documents. Devices that are attached to computers in the homegroup can also be shared. Users will need the homegroup password in order to join the homegroup and access shared resources.

Homegroups were used in Windows 7 and 8. Microsoft has been phasing out the homegroup functionality. In Windows 8.1 homegroups cannot be created, however Windows 8.1 computers can join existing home groups. In newer versions of Windows 10 (version 1803 and higher), home group functionality is not available.

Figure 1 shows the Windows 8 home group configuration screen. In Windows 8, nothing is shared by default. Figure 2 shows the Windows 7 screen. Note that everything except for documents is shared by default.

Refer to
Lab Activity
for this chapter

11.2.3.5   Lab - Configure Browser Settings

In this lab, you will configure Internet settings in Internet Explorer.

Lab - Configure Browser Settings

Refer to
Interactive Graphic
in online course

11.2.3.6   Check Your Understanding - Network and Internet Control Panel

11.2.4   Display Settings and Control Panel

Refer to
Interactive Graphic
in online course

11.2.4.1   Display Settings and Configuration

In Windows 10, much of the Appearance and Personalization configuration has been moved to the Settings app, as shown in Figure 1. The Windows 10 display settings are reached by right-clicking an empty area of the desktop and selecting Display settings from the context menu. Alternatively, the Settings app can be opened. Display settings are available in the System category.

You can change the appearance of the desktop by modifying the resolution that is output by the graphics adapter. If the screen resolution is not set properly, you might get unexpected display results from different video cards and monitors. You can also change the magnification of the desktop and text size in Windows interface elements. The Windows 8.1 Display control panel item is shown in Figure 2. In Windows 7 and 8, the Display Control Panel item is found in the Hardware and Sound category.

When using an LCD screen, set the resolution to the recommended setting. This will set the resolution to the native resolution, which sets the video output to the same number of pixels that the monitor has. If you do not use native resolution, the monitor does not produce the best picture.

Refer to
Online Course
for Illustration

11.2.4.2   Display Features

You can adjust the following features in the Windows 8 and 7 Display control panel item:

- **Display** - A specific monitor can be configured if there is more than one monitor.

- **Screen resolution** - This specifies the number of pixels horizontally and vertically. A higher number of pixels provides better resolution. Typically expressed as horizontal pixels × vertical pixels or 1920 × 1080, for example.

- **Orientation** - This determines whether the display appears in Landscape, Portrait, flipped Landscape, or flipped Portrait orientation.

- **Refresh rate** - This sets how often the image in the screen is redrawn. The refresh rate is in Hertz (Hz). 60Hz means the screen is redrawn 60 times per second. The higher the refresh rate, the steadier the screen image appears. However, some monitors cannot handle all refresh rate settings.

- **Display colors** - In older systems, the number of colors to display, or the bit depth, needed to be set to a value that is compatible with graphics adapter and monitor. The higher the bit depth, the greater the number of colors. For example, the 24-bit color (True Color) palette contains 16 million colors. The 32-bit color palette contains 24-bit color and 8 bits for other data such as transparency.

■ **Multiple displays** - Some computers or graphics cards permit the attachment of two or more monitors to the same computer. The desktop can be extended, meaning the displays combine to make one large display, or mirrored, meaning the same image is shown on all displays.

Refer to
Interactive Graphic
in online course

11.2.4.3   Check Your Understanding - Display Features

11.2.5   Power and System Control Panels

Refer to
Online Course
for Illustration

11.2.5.1   Power Options

The Power Options Control Panel item allows you to change the power consumption of certain devices or the entire computer. Use Power Options to maximize battery performance or conserve energy by configuring a power plan. Power plans are a collection of hardware and system settings that manage the power usage of the computer. The figure shows the Power Options Control Panel item in Windows 10. It varies slightly in Windows 7 and 8. One important difference is that that the setting that requires a password when the computer wakes has been moved from Power Options to User Accounts in Windows 10. This is an important setting for data security.

Windows has preset power plans. These are default settings that were created when Windows was installed. You can use the default settings or create your own customized plans that are based on specific work or device requirements.

Note Windows automatically detects some devices that are part of the computer and creates power settings accordingly. Therefore, the Power Options settings will vary based on the hardware that is detected.

Refer to
Online Course
for Illustration

11.2.5.2   Power Options Settings

The Power Options Control Panel item is part of the System and Security Control Panel category. The Widows 8 Power Options are shown in the figure.

You can choose from the following options:

■ Require a password on wakeup (Windows 7 and 8 only)

■ Choose what the power buttons do

■ Choose what closing the lid does (for laptops only)

■ Create a power plan

■ Choose when to turn off the display

■ Change when the computer sleeps

Refer to
Online Course
for Illustration

11.2.5.3   Power Options Actions

Selecting **Choose what the power buttons do**, or **Choose what closing the lid does,** configures how a computer acts when power or sleep buttons are pressed, or the lid is closed. Some of these settings also appear as shutdown options for the Windows Start button or the Windows 10 Power button. If users do not want to completely shut down a computer, the following options may be available:

- **Do nothing** - The computer continues to run at full power.

- **Sleep** - Documents, applications, and the state of the operating system are saved in RAM. This allows the computer to power on quickly, but uses power to retain the information in RAM.

- **Hibernate** - Documents, applications, and the state of the operating system are saved to a temporary file on the hard drive. With this option, the computer takes a little longer to power on than the Sleep state, but does not use any power to retain the information on the hard drive.

- **Turn off the display** - The computer operates at full power. The display is turned off.

- **Shut down** - Shuts down the computer.

Refer to
Interactive Graphic
in online course

11.2.5.4 Check Your Understanding - Power Options

Refer to
Online Course
for Illustration

11.2.5.5 System Control Panel Item

The System Control Panel item allows all users to view basic system information, access tools, and configure advanced system settings. The System Control Panel item is found under the System and Security category. The Windows 10 System Control Panel item is shown in Figure 1. The System Control Panel item is very similar in Windows 7 and 8.

The various settings can be accessed by clicking the links on the left panel.

Refer to
Interactive Graphic
in online course

11.2.5.6 System Properties

Computer Name

View or modify the name and workgroup settings for a computer, as well as change the domain or workgroup.

Refer to
Online Course
for Illustration

11.2.5.7 Increasing Performance

To enhance the performance of the OS, you can change the virtual memory configuration settings, as shown in the figure. When Windows determines that system RAM is insufficient, it will create a paging file on the hard drive that contains some of the data from RAM. When the data is required back in RAM, it is read from the paging file. This process is much slower than accessing the RAM directly. If a computer has a small amount of RAM, consider purchasing additional RAM to reduce paging.

Another form of virtual memory is the use of an external flash device and Windows ReadyBoost to enhance system performance. Windows ReadyBoost enables Windows to treat an external flash device, such as a USB drive, as hard drive cache. ReadyBoost will not be available if Windows determines that no performance improvement will be gained.

To activate Windows ReadyBoost, insert a flash device and right-click the drive in File Explorer. Click Properties and select the ReadyBoost tab.

11.2.5.8   Lab - Manage Virtual Memory

In this lab, you will use the System Control Panel item to configure and manage virtual memory.

Lab - Manage Virtual Memory

11.2.5.9   Check Your Understanding - Power Options and System Properties

11.2.6   Hardware and Sound Control Panels

11.2.6.1   Device Manager

Device Manager, shown in Figure 1, displays a list of all the devices installed in the computer, allowing you to diagnose and resolve device problems. You can view details about the installed hardware and drivers, as well as perform the following functions:

- **Update a driver** - Change the currently installed driver.
- **Roll back a driver** - Change the currently installed driver to the previously installed driver.
- **Uninstall a driver** - Remove a driver.
- **Disable a device** - Disable a device.

Device Manager organizes devices by type. To view the actual devices, expand the appropriate category. You can view the properties of any device in the computer by double-clicking the device name.

The Device Manager utility uses icons to indicate the types of problems that may exist with a device, as indicated in the icons that are shown in Figure 2.

The devices that are available in Device Manager vary from computer to computer. Device Manager is very similar in Windows versions 7, 8, and 10.

11.2.6.2   Lab - Use Device Manager

In this lab you will investigate Device Manager.

Lab - Use Device Manager

11.2.6.3   Devices and Printers

Use the Devices and Printers Control Panel item for a high-level view of the devices connected to a computer, as shown in the figure. Devices displayed in the Devices and Printers Control Panel item are typically external devices you can connect to your computer through a port such as USB, or a network connection. Devices and Printers also allows you to quickly add a new device to the computer. In most cases, Windows will automatically install any necessary drivers that are required by the device. Note that the desktop computer device in the figure shows a yellow triangle alert, indicate that there is a problem with the driver. The green check mark next to a device indicates that is to be used as the default device. Right-click on a device to view its properties.

Devices typically shown in Devices and Printers include:

- Portable devices that you occasionally connect to your computer, such as mobile phones, personal fitness devices, and digital cameras.
- Devices you plug into a USB port on your computer, such as external USB hard drives, flash drives, webcams, keyboards, and mice.
- Printers connected to your computer or available on the network.
- Wireless devices connected to your computer, such as Bluetooth and wireless USB devices.
- Compatible network devices connected to your computer, such as network-enabled scanners, media extenders, or Network Attached Storage devices (NAS).

Devices and Printers is very similar in Windows versions 7, 8, and 10.

Refer to **Online Course** for Illustration

11.2.6.4   Sound

Use the Sound Control Panel item to configure audio devices or change the sound scheme of the computer. For example, you can change the email notification sound from a beep to a chime. Sound also allows a user to choose which audio device is to be used for playback or recording.

The Sound Control Panel utility is largely unchanged between Windows 7, 8, and 10.

Refer to **Interactive Graphic** in online course

11.2.6.5   Check Your Understanding - Device Manager Alerts

11.2.7   Clock, Region, and Language

Refer to **Online Course** for Illustration

11.2.7.1   Clock

Windows allows you to change the system time and date through the Date and Time control panel item, as shown in the figure. You can also adjust your time zone. Windows will automatically update the time settings when time changes occur. The Windows clock will automatically synchronize with a time authority on the internet. This ensures that the time value is accurate.

Time and Date is accessed through the Clock and Region Control Panel category in Windows 10. In Windows 7 and 8, it is accessed through the Clock, Language, and Region Control Panel category.

Refer to **Interactive Graphic** in online course

11.2.7.2   Region

Windows allows you to change the format of numbers, currencies, dates, and times by using the Region Control Panel item. In Windows 7 there were tabs available to allow changing the system keyboard layout and language, and the computer location. In Windows 8 the keyboard and language tab was removed. Windows 10 attempts to use location services to automatically detect the location of the computer. The location can also be set manually if the location can't be determined. The Windows 8 and Windows 10 Region Control Panel item are shown in Figures 1 and 2 respectively.

Date and time setting formats can be changed by changing the display patterns available in the Date and Time formats area. Click Additional settings to change number and currency formats and the measurement system used in the region. Additional date and time formats are also available.

Refer to
Interactive Graphic
in online course

11.2.7.3   Language

In Windows 7 and Windows 8, shown in Figure 1, Language can be configured through Control Panel items. This allowed users to install language packs that included fonts and other resources required by different languages.

In Windows 10, this was moved to the Region settings app, shown in Figure 2. When adding a language, you can even choose to install Cortana support for voice commands in that language, if available.

Refer to
Lab Activity
for this chapter

11.2.7.4   Lab - Region and Language Options

In this lab, you will examine region and language options in Windows.

Lab - Region and Language Options

Refer to
Interactive Graphic
in online course

11.2.7.5   Check Your Understanding - Clock, Region, and Language

11.2.8   Programs and Features Control Panels

Refer to
Online Course
for Illustration

11.2.8.1   Programs

Use the Program and Features Control Panel items to uninstall a program from your computer if you no longer use it or if you want to free up space on your hard disk, as shown in the figure. It is important that applications be uninstalled either through the Programs and Features Control Panel item or from an uninstallation menu choice that is associated with the application in the Start menu.

In addition, you can repair the installation of some programs that may have problems. You can also troubleshoot problems with programs that were made for older versions of Windows that are not running correctly.

Finally, you can choose to manually install software from the network. It is possible that your organization provides updates or patches that could require manual installation.

Refer to
Online Course
for Illustration

11.2.8.2   Windows Features and Updates

You can also activate or deactivate Windows features, as shown in the figure. Programs and Features also allows you to view the Windows updates that have been installed, and uninstall specific updates if they are causing problems and don't have dependencies with other installed updates or software.

Refer to
Online Course
for Illustration

11.2.8.3   Default Programs

The Default Programs Control Panel item provides the means to configure the way that Windows handles files and the applications that are used to work with them, as shown in the figure. For example, if you have multiple web browsers installed, you can choose which web browser will open to view a link that you have clicked on in an email or other file.

This can be done by choosing default applications, or by choosing which application opens for a specific file type. For example, you configure a JPEG graphics file to open in a browser, for viewing, or in a graphics editor.

Finally, you can choose how AutoPlay works. You can select how Windows will automatically open files of different types depending on the type of removable storage media that they are stored on. You can select to have audio CDs open automatically in Windows Media Player, or have a Windows File Explorer display a directory of the disk contents.

Windows 10 uses a settings app for all but the AutoPlay configuration. Windows 7 and 8 use Control Panel utilities.

Refer to
Interactive Graphic
in online course

11.2.8.4   Check Your Understanding - Programs and Features

11.2.9   Other Control Panels

Refer to
Online Course
for Illustration

11.2.9.1   Troubleshooting

The Troubleshooting Control Panel item has a number of built-in scripts that are used to identify and solve common problems with many Windows components, as shown in the figure. The scripts run automatically and can be configured to automatically make the changes to fix the problems that are found. You can also view when the troubleshooting scripts have been run in the past by using the View History feature.

Refer to
Online Course
for Illustration

11.2.9.2   BitLocker Drive Encryption

BitLocker is a service provided with Windows that will encrypt an entire volume of disk data so that it can't be read by unauthorized parties. Data can be lost if your computer or disk drives are stolen. In addition, when the computer is taken out of service, BitLocker can help insure that the hard drive can't be read when it has been removed from the computer and scrapped.

The BitLocker Control Panel item, shown in the figure, enables you to control the way BitLocker operates.

Refer to
Interactive Graphic
in online course

11.2.9.3   File Explorer and Folder Options

The Folder Option Control Panel item permits changing a variety of settings regarding the way files are displayed in Windows Explorer or File Explorer. This Control Panel item is called File Explorer Options in Windows 10, and Folder Options in Windows 7 and 8.1 The Windows 10 File Explorer Options Control Panel item is shown in Figure 1. The Windows 7 and 8 version is very similar. The Windows 8 version is shown in Figure 2.

In Windows 10, many of the most commonly used file and folder options can be found in the File Explorer ribbon. In Windows 8.1 some functions are present in the ribbon, but the selection is not as comprehensive as it is in Windows 10. In Windows 7, there is no ribbon, so the Control Panel must be used.

The functions of the tabs in Windows 10 are described below.

The **General** tab is used to adjust the following settings:

- **Browse folders** - Configures how a folder is displayed when it is opened.
- **Click items as follows** - Specifies the number of clicks required to open an item.
- **Privacy** - Determines which files and folders are shown in Quick Access. Also allows File History to be cleared.

The **View** tab is used to adjust the following settings:

- **Folder views** - Applies the view settings for a folder being viewed to all folders of the same type.

- **Advanced settings** - Customizes the viewing experience including the ability to view hidden files and file extensions.

The **Search** tab is used to adjust the following settings:

- **What to search (Windows 7)** - Configures search settings based on indexed and non-indexed locations to make files and folders easier to find.

- **How to search** - Choose whether an indexed search is used.

- **When searching non-indexed locations** - Determines whether system directories, compressed files and file contents are included when searching non-indexed locations.

Refer to
Interactive Graphic
in online course

11.2.9.4   Check Your Understanding - Other Control Panels

11.3   System Administration

11.3.1   Administrative Tools

Refer to
Online Course
for Illustration

11.3.1.1   Administrative Tools Control Panel Item

The Administrative Tools Control Panel item is a collection of tools that are used to monitor and configure Windows operation. This Control Panel item has evolved over time. In Windows 7 it was somewhat limited. Microsoft added many different utilities in Windows 8.1. In Windows 10, the available tools changed slightly.

The Administrative Tools Control Panel item is unusual in that it is a collection of shortcuts that open in File Explorer. Since each icon represents a shortcut to an application, investigate the properties of each shortcut to see the name of the application file that is run when the shortcut is clicked. You can start the same applications by typing the name of application at the command prompt. Once you become experienced with managing Windows, this may be the most efficient way for you to access the tools you need. The figure shows the Administrative Tools Control Panel item in Windows 10.

Refer to
Online Course
for Illustration

11.3.1.2   Computer Management

One of the Administrative Tools items is the Computer Management console, shown in the figure. It allows you to manage many aspects of your computer and remote computers in one tool.

The Computer Management console provides access to three groups of utilities. Here we will learn about the System Tools group.

Conveniently, the Computer Management tool can be accessed by right-clicking This PC in Windows 8.1 or 10, or by right-clicking Computer in Windows 7 and 8 and selecting Manage. Administrator privileges are required to open Computer Management.

To view the Computer Management console for a remote computer, follow these steps:

Step 1.   In the console tree, click **Computer Management (Local)** and select **Connect to another computer.**

Step 2.   Enter the name of the computer or click **Browse** to find the computer to manage on the network.

<table>
<tr><td>Refer to
Online Course
for Illustration</td></tr>
</table>

11.3.1.3 Event Viewer

Event Viewer, shown in the figure, allows viewing the history of application, security, and Windows system events. These events are stored in log files. They are a valuable troubleshooting tool because they provide information necessary to identify a problem. Event Viewer permits filtering and customization of log views to make it easier to find important information from the various log files that Windows compiles.

Windows logs many events that can originate from applications, the Windows OS, application setup, and security events, by default. Each message is identified by its type or level:

- **Information** - A successful event. A driver or program has executed successfully. Windows logs thousands of information level events.

- **Warning** - Indication of a potential problem with a software component that is not functioning ideally.

- **Error** - A problem exists, but no immediate action is required.

- **Critical** - Immediate attention is required. Usually related to system or software crashes or lockups.

- **Success Audit (security only)** - A security event has been successful. For example, a successful logon from a user will trigger an event with this level.

- **Failure Audit (security only)** - A security event has not been successful. Failed attempts by someone attempting to log on to a computer will trigger this event.

<table>
<tr><td>Refer to
Online Course
for Illustration</td></tr>
</table>

11.3.1.4 Local Users and Groups

Local Users and Groups, shown in the figure, provides an efficient way of managing users. You can create new users and assign those users to membership in Groups. Groups have rights and permissions assigned that are suitable for different types of users. Rather than configuring rights and permissions for each individual user, a user can be assigned an appropriate group. Windows provides default user accounts and groups to make managing users easier:

- **Administrators** - Full control of the computer and access to all folders.

- **Guests** - Guests can access the computer through a temporary profile that is created at logon and deleted on logoff. Guest accounts are disabled by default.

- **Users** - Users can perform common tasks such as running applications and accessing local or network printers. A user profile is created and persists on the system.

Refer to
Online Course
for Illustration

11.3.1.5   Performance Monitor

Performance Monitor allows customized performance graphs and reports to be created from a wide range of hardware and software components. Data Collector Sets are collections of metrics, called performance counters. Windows has a number of default Data Collector Sets and you can create your own. A wide range of counters can be graphed against time and reports can also be generated and read or printed. Data collection can be scheduled to occur at different times and for different durations and stop criterion for a monitoring session can also be set.

The Performance Monitor provided here is different from the performance information that is available through Task Manager and Resource Monitor. The purpose of the Performance Monitor administrative tool is the creation of detailed custom reports from very specific counters. The figure shows a graph derived from a selection of data counters that are available for the CPU.

Refer to
Online Course
for Illustration

11.3.1.6   Component Services and Data Sources

Component Services is an administrative tool used by administrators and developers to deploy, configure, and manage Component Object Model (COM) components. COM is a way to allow the use of software components in distributed environments such as in enterprise, internet, and intranet applications.

Refer to
Online Course
for Illustration

11.3.1.7   Services

The Services console (SERVICES.MSC) allows you to manage all the services on your computer and remote computers. A service is a type of application that runs in the background to achieve a specific goal, or to wait for service requests. To reduce security risks, only start the necessary services. You can use the following settings, or states, to control a service:

- **Automatic** - The service starts when the computer is started. This prioritizes the most important services.

- **Automatic (delayed)** - The service starts after services that are set to Automatic have started. The Automatic (delayed) setting is available only in Windows 7.

- **Manual** - The service must be started manually by the user or by a service or program that needs it.

- **Disabled** - The service cannot be started until it is enabled.

- **Stopped** - The service is not running.

To view the Services console for a remote computer right-click on **Services (Local)** in the Computer Management window and select **Connect to another computer.** Enter the name for the computer or click **Browse** to allow Windows to scan the network for connected computers.

Refer to
Online Course
for Illustration

11.3.1.8   Data Sources

Data Sources is a tool used by administrators to add, remove, or manage data sources using Open Database Connectivity (ODBC). ODBC is a technology that programs use to access a wide range of databases or data sources. The tool is shown in the figure.

Refer to
Online Course
for Illustration

11.3.1.9   Print Management

The Print Management utility, shown in the figure, provides a detailed view of all of the printers that are available to a computer. It is not available in all Windows editions. It is available in Windows servers, Pro, Enterprise, and Ultimate editions. It enables efficient configuration and monitoring of directly attached and network printers, including print queues for all printers to which it has access. It also allows the deployment of a printer configuration to multiple computers on a network through the use of group policies.

Refer to
Online Course
for Illustration

11.3.1.10   Windows Memory Diagnostics

The Windows Memory Diagnostics tool schedules a memory test that will be executed when the computer starts. It can be configured to automatically restart the computer or execute the test the next time the computer starts. After the tests are complete, Windows will restart. The type of diagnostics to be run can be configured by pressing F1 from the diagnostic as it runs, as shown in the figure. The results of the test can be viewed by finding the memory diagnostic test result in the Windows Log folder in Event Viewer.

Refer to
Lab Activity
for this chapter

11.3.1.11   Lab - Monitor and Manage System Resources

In this lab, you will use administrative tools to monitor and manage system resources.

Lab - Monitor and Manage System Resources

Refer to
Interactive Graphic
in online course

11.3.1.12   Check Your Understanding - Administrative Tools

11.3.2   System Utilities

Refer to
Online Course
for Illustration

11.3.2.1   System Information

Administrators can use the System Information tool, as shown in the figure, to collect and display information about local and remote computers. The System Information tool is designed to quickly find information about software, drivers, hardware configurations, and computer components. Support personnel can use this information to diagnose and troubleshoot a computer.

You can also create a file containing all the information about the computer to send to someone. To export a System Information file, select File > Export, type the filename, choose a location, and click Save. The System Information utility can also display the configuration of other machines on the network.

The System Information tool can be opened from the command prompt by typing **msinfo32**, or it can be found in the Administrative Tools Control Panel item.

Refer to
Interactive Graphic
in online course

11.3.2.2   System Configuration

System Configuration (MSCONFIG) is a tool used to identify problems that keep Windows from starting correctly. To help with isolating the issue, services and startup programs can be turned off and turned back on one at a time. After you have determined the cause, permanently remove or disable the program or service, or reinstall it.

Explore the tabs available in the msconfig System Configuration utility by clicking the buttons in the figure.

Refer to **Online Course** for Illustration

11.3.2.3   The Registry

The Windows Registry is a database that contains settings for Windows and for applications that use the Registry. The settings contained in the Registry are very low-level, meaning there are many, many of them. Values in the registry are created when new software is installed or new devices are added. Every setting in Windows, from the background of the desktop and the color of the screen buttons, to the licensing of applications, is stored in the Registry. When a user makes changes to the Control Panel settings, file associations, system policies, or installed software, the changes are stored in the Registry.

The registry consists of a hierarchical arrangement of keys and subkeys that are represented as a tree. Levels of the subkey tree can be deeply nested with a maximum of 512 levels permitted. Locating the key for the value you want to see is a matter of working through the hierarchy of trees and subtrees. There are five top- level, or root, keys, as shown in the figure.

The registry exists as multiple database files, called hives, that are associated with each of the top level registry keys. Each key has values. The values consist of the name of the value, its data type, and the setting or data that is associated with the value. The values tell Windows how to operate.

The Windows Registry keys are an important part of the Windows boot process. These keys are recognized by their distinctive names, which begin with HKEY_, as shown in the figure. The words and letters that follow HKEY_ represent the portion of the OS controlled by that key.

Refer to **Online Course** for Illustration

11.3.2.4   Regedit

The Registry Editor allows an administrator to view or make changes to the Windows Registry. Using the Registry Editor utility incorrectly could cause hardware, application, or operating system problems, including problems that require you to reinstall the operating system.

The registry editor can only be opened from a search or command prompt. You can search for **regedit** and open it from the search results, or you can open a command or PowerShell prompt and type **regedit**.

The figure shows the **regedit** utility with the value of the OneDrive subkey open for modification.

Refer to **Online Course** for Illustration

11.3.2.5   Microsoft Management Console

Microsoft Management Console (MMC) is an application that allows the creation of custom management consoles for collections of utilities and tools from Microsoft or other sources. The Computer Management console that was previously discussed is a premade MMC. When initially opened, the console is empty. Utilities and tools, known as snap-ins, can be added to the console. You can also add web page links, tasks, ActiveX controls, and folders.

The console can then be saved and reopened when needed. This allows the construction of management consoles for specific purposes. You can create as many customized MMCs as needed, each with a different name. This is useful when multiple administrators manage different aspects of the same computer. Each administrator can have an individualized MMC for monitoring and configuring computer settings.

The figure shows a new empty console with the dialog box for selecting and adding snap-ins.

Refer to
Online Course
for Illustration

11.3.2.6   DxDiag

DxDiag stands for DirectX Diagnostic Tool. It displays details for all DirectX components and drivers that are installed in a computer, as shown in the figure. DxDiag is run from a search or from the command line.

DirectX is a software environment and interface for multimedia applications, especially games. It defines interfaces for 2D and 3D graphics, audio, media encoders and decoders, etc.

Refer to
Lab Activity
for this chapter

11.3.2.7   Lab - System Utilities

In this lab, you will use Windows utilities to configure operating system settings.

Lab - System Utilities

Refer to
Lab Activity
for this chapter

11.3.2.8   Lab - Manage System Files

In this lab, you will use Windows utilities to gather information about the computer.

Lab - Manage System Files

Refer to
Interactive Graphic
in online course

11.3.2.9   Check Your Understanding - System Utilities

11.3.3   Disk Management

Refer to
Interactive Graphic
in online course

11.3.3.1   What Do You Already Know? - Disk Operations

Refer to
Online Course
for Illustration

11.3.3.2   Disk Management Utility

The Disk Management utility is part of the Computer Management console. It can be opened by right-clicking on **This PC** or **Computer** and selecting **Manage**. It can also be opened through the Computer Management Control Panel item or in its own Window by using the **Win+X** menu and selecting **Disk Management**.

In addition to extending and shrinking partitions, as demonstrated in the previous chapter, you can also use the Disk Management utility to complete the following tasks:

- View drive status
- Assign or change drive letters
- Add drives
- Add arrays
- Designate the active partition

The figure shows the Disk Management utility in Windows 10.

Refer to
Online Course
for Illustration

11.3.3.3   Drive Status

The Disk Management utility displays the status of each disk, as shown in the figure. The drives in the computer display one of the following conditions:

- **Foreign** - A dynamic disk that has been moved to a computer from another computer running Windows
- **Healthy** - A volume that is functioning properly

- **Initializing** - A basic disk that is being converted into a dynamic disk

- **Missing** - A dynamic disk that is corrupted, turned off, or disconnected

- **Not Initialized** - A disk that does not contain a valid signature

- **Online** - A basic or dynamic disk that is accessible and shows no problems

- **Online (Errors)** - I/O errors detected on a dynamic disk

- **Offline** - A dynamic disk that is corrupted or unavailable

- **Unreadable** - A basic or dynamic disk that has experienced hardware failure, corruption, or I/O errors

Other drive status indicators might be displayed when using drives other than hard drives, such as an audio CD that is in the optical drive, or a removable drive that is empty.

Refer to **Online Course** for Illustration

11.3.3.4 Mounting a Drive

Mounting a drive refers to making a disk image file readable as a drive. A good example of this is an ISO file. It is the entire contents of the disk represented as a single file. ISO images are used as archives of the contents of an optical disk. Disk writer software can take an ISO file and write its contents to the disk.

These ISO files can also be mounted on virtual drives. To mount an image, open File Explorer and locate and select an ISO file. In the ribbon, select the Manage menu under Disk Image Tools. Select Mount. The ISO file will be mounted as a removable media drive. The drive can be browsed and files opened. However, there is actually no drive. The drive is an ISO image mounted as a volume.

You can also create a mount point. A mount point is similar to a shortcut. You can create a mount point that makes an entire drive appear as a folder. This might provide an easy way for users to access files since the mounted folder can appear in their My Documents folder, for example.

Refer to **Interactive Graphic** in online course

11.3.3.5 Adding Arrays

In Windows disk management, you can create mirrored, spanned, or RAID 5 arrays from multiple dynamic disks. This is done by right-clicking a volume and selecting the type of multidisc volume that you want to create, as shown in Figure 1. Note that there must be two or more initialized dynamic drives available on the computer.

Storage Spaces became available in Windows 8 and 10. Storage Spaces can be configured from a Control Panel item as shown in Figure 2. Storage Spaces is the disk array technology that is recommended by Windows. It creates pools of physical hard drives from which virtual disks (storage spaces) can be created. Many different types of drives can be combined. Like other disk arrays, Storage Spaces offer mirrored, striped, and parity options.

Refer to **Interactive Graphic** in online course

11.3.3.6 Disk Optimization

To maintain and optimize disk storage, you can use various tools within Windows. Some of these tools include hard drive defragmentation, which consolidates files for faster access.

As files increase in size, some data is written to the next available cluster on the disk. In time, data becomes fragmented and spread over nonadjacent clusters on the hard drive. As a result, it takes longer to locate and retrieve each section of the data. A disk defragmenter gathers the noncontiguous data into one place, making the OS run faster.

Note   It is not recommended to perform disk defragmentation on SSDs. SSDs are optimized by the controller and firmware they use. It should not be harmful to defragment Hybrid SSDs (SSHD) because they use hard disks to store data, not solid-state ram.

In Windows 8 and 10, the option is called Optimize, as shown in Figure 1. In Windows 7, it is called Defragment Now. It can be accessed from the disk properties menu or from the File Explorer ribbon in Windows 8 and 10.

Figure 2 shows the Optimize Drives utility. It allows analysis of the drive prior to optimization. The analysis will display the degree of fragmentation of the drive.

You can also optimize the available space by doing a disk Cleanup operation. This will remove unnecessary files from the drive.

11.3.3.7   Disk Error - Checking

Refer to
Online Course
for Illustration

The Disk Error-Checking tool checks the integrity of files and folders by scanning the hard disk surface for physical errors.

If errors are detected, the tool attempts to repair them. In File Explorer or File Manager, right-click the drive and select **Properties**. Select the **Tools** tab and select **Check** or **Check Now** in Windows 7. In Windows 8, select **Scan Drive** to attempt to recover bad sectors. In Windows 7, select **Scan for and attempt recovery of bad sectors** and click **Start**. The tool fixes file system errors and checks the disk for bad sectors. It also attempts to recover data from bad sectors.

In Windows 8 and 10, if you want to see a detailed report of the results of the scan, click Check Results after the scan has completed. This will open an Event Viewer window that will allow you to view the log entry for the scan. In Windows 7, a report is displayed by the error-checking utility, as shown in the figure.

Note   Use the Disk Error-Checking tool whenever a sudden loss of power causes the system to shut down incorrectly.

11.3.3.8   Lab - Hard Drive Maintenance

Refer to
Lab Activity
for this chapter

In this lab, you will perform hard drive maintenance tasks including defragmentation and error checking.

Lab - Hard Drive Maintenance

Refer to
Interactive Graphic
in online course

11.3.3.9   Check Your Understanding - Disk Management

11.3.4   Application Installation and Configuration

Refer to
Online Course
for Illustration

11.3.4.1   System Requirements

Before purchasing or attempting to install an application, you should verify that the system requirements are met. System requirements are usually stated as the minimum requirements. The recommended system requirements may also be stated, as shown in the figure. The following requirements are normally defined in the software packaging or on the software download page:

- **Processor speed** - 32 or 64-bit, x86 or other.

- RAM, sometimes as minimum or recommended capacities

- Operating system and version

- Hard disk space available

- **Software dependencies** - runtime and other frameworks or environments may be required to be present in order for the software to run.

- Graphics and display

- Network access, if any

- Peripheral devices

Refer to
Online Course
for Illustration

11.3.4.2   Installation Methods

As a technician, you will be responsible for adding and removing software from your customers' computers. Most applications use an automatic installation process when the application disc is inserted in the optical drive. The user is required to click through the installation wizard and provide information when requested. Most Windows software installations are attended, meaning the user must be present to interact with the installer software to provide input about the options to use when installing the software. The various types of installations are defined in the figure.

Refer to
Online Course
for Illustration

11.3.4.3   Installing an Application

Local installation can occur from the hard drive, CD, DVD, or USB media. To perform a local, attended installation, insert the media or drive, or open the downloaded program file. Depending on autoplay settings, the software installation process may not automatically start. In that case, you will need to browse the installation media in order to find and execute the installer. Installer software usually has an EXE or MSI (Microsoft Silent Installer) file extension.

Note that the user must have the appropriate permissions in order to install the software. They must also not be blocked by group policies that prevent software installation.

After the application is installed, you can run it from the Start Menu or the shortcut icon that the application places on the desktop. Check the application to ensure that it is functioning properly. If there are problems, repair or uninstall the application. Some applications, such as Microsoft Office, provide a repair option within the installation program. In addition to the process described above, Windows 8 and 10 provide access to the Microsoft Store, as shown in the figure. The Microsoft Store allows a user to search for and install apps on Windows devices. To open the Windows Store app, search from the Start Screen taskbar by entering **Store**. Click the **Store** icon when it appears in the search results. The Windows Store app is not available in Windows 7.

Refer to
Online Course
for Illustration

11.3.4.4 Compatibility Mode

Older applications may not run properly on newer Windows operating systems. Windows provides a way that these programs can be configured to run. If older software is not running properly, locate the executable file for the application. This can be done by right-clicking a shortcut for the application and selecting **Open file location**. Right-click the executable file and choose Properties. From the **Compatibility** tab, shown in the figure, you can run the **Windows compatibility troubleshooter** or manually configure the environment for the application.

Refer to
Online Course
for Illustration

11.3.4.5 Uninstalling or Changing a Program

If an application is uninstalled incorrectly, you might be leaving files on the hard drive and unnecessary settings in the registry, which wastes hard drive space and system resources. Unnecessary files might also reduce the speed at which the registry is read. Microsoft recommends that you always use the Programs and Features Control Panel utility when removing, changing, or repairing applications. The utility guides you through the software removal process and removes every file that was installed, as shown in the figure.

Some applications may include an uninstall feature that is located in the Windows Start menu with the application.

Refer to
Lab Activity
for this chapter

11.3.4.6 Lab - Install Third-Party Software

In this lab, you will install and remove a third party software application.

Lab - Install Third-Party Software

Refer to
Online Course
for Illustration

11.3.4.7 Security Considerations

Allowing users to install software on computers that are owned by a business organization can be a security risk. Users can be tricked into downloading malicious software that can cause data loss, either through theft or destruction. Malicious software, known as malware, can infect all computers that are attached to a network and can cause widespread damage and loss. As a technician, it is important to enforce policies regarding software installation and ensure that antimalware software, such as Windows Defender is active and up to date.

Refer to
Interactive Graphic
in online course

11.3.4.8 Check Your Understanding - Application Installation and Configuration

11.4 Command-Line Tools

11.4.1 Using Windows CLI

Refer to
Online Course
for Illustration

11.4.1.1 PowerShell

The old Windows command line application was replaced in the Windows Power User menu Win+X with PowerShell. The original command line still exists in Windows 10, and can be opened by typing cmd into the search field on the Taskbar. You can also change which command line is displayed in the menu by changing a Taskbar setting.

PowerShell is a more powerful command line utility. It offers many advanced features, such as scripting and automation. It even comes with its own scripting development environment, called PowerShell ISE, to help with the task of writing scripts. PowerShell uses "cmdlets", or small applications, that represent the commands that are available. PowerShell also allows naming of cmdlets with aliases, so the same cmdlet can be run at the command line with any name that adheres to naming conventions that you choose to assign to it. Microsoft has created aliases for all of the old cmd commands so that it works much like the older command line.

The figure shows Windows ISE, with the PowerShell command line in the lower right window. PowerShell can also be opened as the command line shell alone.

Refer to
Online Course
for Illustration

11.4.1.2 The Command Shell

Windows has two command line utilities. One is the classic **command** application, known as **cmd**. This command line is a remnant of the very early days of Microsoft when DOS was the only operating system that Microsoft had to offer. Many users were experienced with using cmd, so it was retained when Windows was developed. It has persisted as the default command line for Windows until Windows 10 build 14791 when PowerShell became the default. To open the command shell, type **cmd** in the search box and click the app in the results. You can also use the **Win+R** key to open a run box. Type **cmd** in the run box and click **OK**. Press **Ctrl+Shift+Enter** to run the command prompt as an administrator. The title bar for the command window will indicate that the command window is open in Administrator mode. You can also use the **whoami** command to display the name of the computer that the prompt is open on and the user account, as shown in the figure.

Here we will focus on the **cmd** command line. All commonly used commands are supported by Windows 7, 8, and 10.

Refer to
Interactive Graphic
in online course

11.4.1.3 Basic Commands

Syntax and Info

Enter by itself to see all available commands. Type help followed by a specific command to see information about that command.

Refer to **Video**
in online course

11.4.1.4 Video Demonstration - Managing CLI Sessions

Working at a command line may be new to some people. Watch the video to see a demonstration of how it is done.

Click Play in the figure to view a demonstration of how to work in the Windows command line.

Click here to read the transcript of this video.

Refer to
Lab Activity
for this chapter

11.4.1.5   Lab - Work in the Windows Command Shell

In this lab, you will practice techniques for working in the Windows Command Shell.

Lab - Work in the Windows Command Shell

Refer to
Interactive Graphic
in online course

11.4.1.6   Check Your Understanding - Basic Command Line Commands

11.4.2   File System CLI Commands

Refer to
Online Course
for Illustration

11.4.2.1   Command Syntax Conventions

It is important to be able to use technical resources to learn how to use CLI commands. Different software vendors and organizations use different conventions to indicate syntax for commands. Microsoft provides an online command reference that can be found on the web. Many conventions used by Microsoft for CLI commands are summarized in the figure.

Special characters, called wildcards, can be substituted for characters or groups of characters in filenames. Wildcards can be used when you only know part of a filename that you are trying to find or when you want to perform a file operation on a group of files that share elements of a filename or extension. The two wildcards that can be used at the Windows command line are:

- **The asterisk (*)** - This character matches groups of characters, including entire filenames and file extensions. The asterisk (commonly called the star) will match any character that is permitted in a filename and will also match any group of characters. For example myfile.* will match files that are called myfile with any file extension. The asterisk can be used with a pattern of characters too. For example, my*.txt will match all filenames that start with my and have the .txt extension. Finally, *.* refers to any file name with any extension.

- **The question mark (?)** - This character stands for any single character. It does not stand for a group of characters. For example, to match myfile.txt using the question mark, you would need to use my????.txt. This will match filenames that start with my, any four characters, and that have a .txt file extension.

Refer to
Online Course
for Illustration

11.4.2.2   File System Navigation

When working at the command line, there is no File Explorer to help you get to the files and folders that you want to work with. Instead, you need to move through the folder structure using a combination of commands, normally displaying the contents of a drive or directory and changing directories until you find what you are looking for.

Refer to
Interactive Graphic
in online course

11.4.2.3   File System Navigation - Commands

Syntax and Info

Simply type the drive letter followed by a colon at the command prompt. The example shows directories displayed for the C: drive and then the drive is changed, and a directory is displayed for the D: drive

Refer to **Video**
in online course

11.4.2.4   Video Demonstration - Working with Files and Folders

Click Play in the figure to view a review of some basic CLI commands and a demonstration of CLI commands for manipulating files and folders. The operating system is Windows 7, however, the commands are the same as Window 8 and 10.

Click here to read the transcript of this video.

Refer to
Interactive Graphic
in online course

11.4.2.5   Manipulating Folders - Commands

Syntax and Info

md [<Drive>:]<Path>

Make a new directory at the location specified. If you don't provide a drive and path, the new directory is created at the current location.

Refer to
Interactive Graphic
in online course

11.4.2.6   Manipulating Files - Commands

Syntax and Info

Example: **dir > directory.txt** will send the output of the directory command to a text type file.

Because the output is redirected, it does not display on the screen.

Refer to
Lab Activity
for this chapter

11.4.2.7   Lab - File System Commands

In this lab, you will work with file system commands.

Lab - File System Commands

Refer to
Interactive Graphic
in online course

11.4.2.8   Check Your Understanding - File System CLI Commands

11.4.3   Disk CLI Commands

Refer to
Interactive Graphic
in online course

11.4.3.1   Disk Operations - Commands

Syntax and Info

chkdsk <Volume> <Path> <FileName>

- **/f** - fix disk errors, recovers bad sectors, and recovers readable information
- **/r** - same as /f but fixes physical errors if possible

Requires Administrator privilege.

Refer to
Lab Activity
for this chapter

11.4.3.2   Lab - Disk CLI Commands

In this lab, you will work with disk CLI commands.

Lab - Disk CLI Commands

Refer to
Interactive Graphic
in online course

11.4.3.3   Check Your Understanding - Disk Operations Commands

11.4.4   Task and System CLI Commands

Refer to
Interactive Graphic
in online course

11.4.4.1   System CLI Commands

Syntax and Info

tasklist

Options concern the format and filtering of the output of the command and connecting to other PCs on the network.

Running process are identified by their process IDs (PID).

Refer to
Lab Activity
for this chapter

11.4.4.2   Lab - Task and System CLI Commands

In this lab, you will work with task and system CLI commands.

Lab - Task and System CLI Commands

Refer to
Interactive Graphic
in online course

11.4.4.3   Check Your Understanding - Task and System Commands

11.4.5   Other Useful CLI Commands

Refer to
Interactive Graphic
in online course

11.4.5.1   Other Useful Commands

Syntax and Info

gpupdate

Group Policies can be set by an administrator and configured on all machines on a network from a central location. gpupdate is used to update a local machine and verify that the machine is getting Group Policy updates.

- **/target:computer** - force update of another computer
- **/force** - force and update even if Group Policy has not changed
- **/boot** - restart computer after update

Refer to
Online Course
for Illustration

11.4.5.2   Running System Utilities

The Windows run line utility can be opened by pressing the **Win+R** keys and entering **cmd** to open the command line window, as shown in the figure. The following windows utilities and tools can also be run by entering the commands shown in the run line utility.

- **EXPLORER** - Opens File Explorer or Windows Explorer.
- **MMC** - Opens Microsoft Management Console (MMC). Specify the path and .msc filename to open a saved console.

- **MSINFO32** - Opens the System Information window, which shows a summary of system components, including hardware components and software information.
- **MSTSC** - Opens the Remote Desktop utility.
- **NOTEPAD** - Opens the Notepad basic text editor.

Refer to
Lab Activity
for this chapter

11.4.5.3   Lab - Other Useful Commands

In this lab, you will work other useful commands.

Lab - Other Useful Commands

Refer to
Interactive Graphic
in online course

11.4.5.4   Check Your Understanding - Other Useful CLI Commands

11.5   Windows Networking

11.5.1   Network Sharing and Mapping Drives

Refer to
Online Course
for Illustration

11.5.1.1   Domain and Workgroup

Domain and workgroup are methods for organizing and managing computers on a network. They are defined as:

- **Domain** - A domain is a group of computers and electronic devices with a common set of rules and procedures administered as a unit. Computers in a domain can be located in different locations in the world. A specialized server called a domain controller manages all security-related aspects of users and network resources, centralizing security and administration. For example, within a domain, Lightweight Directory Access Protocol (LDAP) is a protocol used to allow computers to access data directories that are distributed throughout the network.

- **Workgroup** - A workgroup is a collection of workstations and servers on a LAN that are designed to communicate and exchange data with one another. Each individual workstation controls its user accounts, security information, and access to data and resources.

All computers on a network must be part of either a domain or a workgroup. When Windows is first installed on a computer, it is automatically assigned to a workgroup, as shown in the figure.

Refer to
Online Course
for Illustration

11.5.1.2   Homegroup

A homegroup was a feature introduced in Windows 7 and is also available in Windows 8 to simplify secure access to shared resources such as folders, pictures, music, videos, and printers on a home network. Homegroup has been removed from Windows 10 with the release of Windows 10 (1803).

All Windows computers that belong to the same workgroup can also belong to a homegroup. There can only be one homegroup per workgroup on a network. Computers can only be a member of one homegroup at a time. Homegroups are secured with a simple password. A homegroup can be a mix of Windows 7 and Windows 8 computers.

One user in the workgroup creates the homegroup. The other users can join the homegroup, provided they know the homegroup password. Homegroup availability depends on your network location profile:

- **Home Network** - allowed to create or join a homegroup
- **Work Network** - not allowed to create or join a homegroup, but you can view and share resources with other computers
- **Public Network** - homegroup not available

When a computer joins a homegroup, all user accounts on the computer, except the Guest account, become members of the homegroup. Being part of a homegroup makes it easy to share pictures, music, videos, documents, libraries, and printers with other people in the same homegroup. Users control access to their own resources.

Note   If a computer belongs to a domain, you can join a homegroup and access files and resources on other homegroup computers. You are not allowed to create a new homegroup or share your own files and resources with a homegroup.

11.5.1.3   Video Demonstration - Connecting to a Workgroup or Domain

Click Play in the figure to view a demonstration of how to connect to a Workgroup or domain.

Click here to read the transcript of this video.

11.5.1.4   Network Shares and Mapping Drives

Network file sharing and mapping network drives is a secure and convenient way to provide easy access to network resources. This is especially true when different versions of Windows require access to network resources. Click each button below for more information on network shares and mapping drives.

11.5.1.5   Administrative Shares

Administrative shares, also called hidden shares, are identified with a dollar sign ($) at the end of the share name. By default, Windows creates several hidden administrative shares. These include the root folder of any local drives (C$), the system folder (ADMIN$), and the print driver folder (PRINT$). Administrative shares are hidden from users and only accessible by members of the local administrators' group. The figure shows administrative shares on a Windows 10 PC. Note the $ after each share name making them hidden shares.

Adding a $ sign to the end of any local share name will cause it to become a hidden share. It will not be visible by browsing but can be accessed via the command-line by mapping a drive to the share name.

11.5.2   Sharing Local Resources with Others

Refer to
Online Course
for Illustration

11.5.2.1   Sharing Local Resources

Windows 10 controls which resources are shared and how they are shared by turning specific sharing features on and off. Advanced Sharing Settings, located in the Network and Sharing Center, manages the sharing options for three different network profiles; Private, Guest or Public, and All Networks. Different options can be chosen for each profile. The following items can be controlled:

- Network discovery
- File and printer sharing
- Public folder sharing
- Password protected sharing
- Media Streaming

To access Advanced Sharing Settings, use the following path:

Start > Control Panel > Network and Internet > Network and Sharing Center

To enable sharing resources between computers connected to the same workgroup, Network Discovery and File and printer sharing must be turned on, as shown in the figure.

There are simple file sharing mechanisms developed by OS vendors. Microsoft's file sharing mechanism is called Nearby Sharing. Nearby Sharing was introduced in Windows 10, partly replacing the previous Homegroup feature. Nearby Sharing provides the ability to share content with a nearby device using both Wi-Fi and Bluetooth.

AirDrop is supported by Apple iOS and macOS and uses Bluetooth to establish a Wi-Fi direct connection between devices for the file transfer to take place. There are also many third-party and open source alternatives, however, there is the potential for security vulnerabilities that allow unsolicited transfers.

Refer to
Interactive Graphic
in online course

11.5.2.2   Printer Sharing vs. Network Printer Mapping

Printer

Printing is one of the most common tasks for users in both home and business environments.

Refer to **Video**
in online course

11.5.2.3   Video Demonstration - Sharing Files and Folders on a Local Network

Click Play in the figure to view a demonstration of how to share a folder.

Click here to read the transcript of this video.

Refer to
Lab Activity
for this chapter

11.5.2.4   Lab - Share Resources

In this lab, you will work with another student. You will create and share a folder. You will also set permissions for the share so your partner will only have read access.

Lab - Share Resources

11.5.3 Configure a Wired Network Connection

Refer to
Online Course
for Illustration

11.5.3.1 Configuring Wired Network Interfaces in Windows 10

Windows 10 network settings are managed through the Network & Internet section in the Settings App. From the Network & Internet window, there are links to View network properties and to the Network and Sharing Center. Available network connections, both wired and wireless, can be viewed by selecting the Change Adapter Options link. From there, each network connection can be configured.

Network card properties are configured in the Advanced tab of the adapter properties window. Navigate to Device Manager. Locate and right click the network adapter. Choose **Properties > Advanced** tab. A list of properties allows configuration of features such as Speed & Duplex, QoS, Wake-on LAN, and many others. Click the desired feature in the **Property:** drop down list. Each property has configurable values in the Value: drop list.

The Windows Internet Protocol Version 4 (TCP/IPv4) Properties window includes an Alternate Configuration tab which allows an administrator to configure an alternative IP address for the PC to use if it is unable to contact a DHCP server. Note that this tab is not visible if a static IPv4 address configuration is configured in the General tab.

Refer to
Interactive Graphic
in online course

11.5.3.2 Configuring a Wired NIC

Configuring a Wired NIC

After the NIC driver is installed, the IP address settings must be configured. A computer can be assigned its IP configuration in one of two ways:

- **Manually** - The host is statically assigned a specific IP configuration.

- **Dynamically** - The host requests its IP address configuration from a DHCP server.

From the properties window of the wired NIC, both IPv4 and IPv6 addresses and other options such as the default gateway and DNS server address can be configured, as shown in the figure.

The default setting for both IPv4 and IPv6 is to obtain the IP settings automatically using DHCP in the case of IPv4 and Stateless Automatic Address Configuration (SLAAC) in the case of IPv6.

Note Most computers today come with an onboard NIC. If you are installing a new NIC, it is considered a best practice to disable the onboard NIC in BIOS settings.

Refer to
Online Course
for Illustration

11.5.3.3 Setting a Network Profile

The first time a computer with Windows 10 connects to a network, a network profile must be selected. Each network profile has different default settings. Depending on the profile selected, file and printer sharing, or network discovery can be turned off or on, and different firewall settings can be applied.

Windows 10 has two network profiles:

- **Public** - The public profile disables file and printer sharing and network discovery on the link. The PC is hidden from other devices.

- **Private** - The private profile allows the user to customize the sharing options. This profile is for use on trusted networks. The PC is discoverable by other devices.

Refer to
Online Course
for Illustration

11.5.3.4   Verify Connectivity with the Windows GUI

The easiest way to test for an internet connection is to open a web browser and see if the internet is available. To troubleshoot a connection, you can use the Windows GUI or CLI.

In Windows 10, the status of a network connection can be viewed under the General tab, as shown in the figure. Click the **Details** button to view IP addressing information, subnet mask, default gateway, MAC address, and other information. If the connection is not functioning correctly, close the Details window and click **Diagnose** to have the Windows Network Diagnostics troubleshooter attempt to troubleshoot and fix the issue.

Refer to
Online Course
for Illustration

11.5.3.5   ipconfig Command

The ipconfig command displays basic IP configuration information, to include the IP address, subnet mask, and default gateway for all network adapters to which TCP/IP is bound. There are several ipconfig switches and arguments which are useful to know. The table in the figure displays available command options. To use a command option, enter the ipconfig /option (e.g., ipconfig /all).

Refer to
Online Course
for Illustration

11.5.3.6   Network CLI Commands

There are several CLI commands that can be executed from the command prompt to test network connectivity.

- **ping** - The command tests basic connectivity between devices by using ICMP echo request and reply messages.

- **tracert** - The command traces the route that packets take from your computer to a destination host. At the command prompt, enter **tracert***hostname*. The first listing in the results is your default gateway. Each listing after that is the router that packets are traveling through to reach the destination. Tracert shows you where packets are stopping, indicating where the problem is occurring.

- **nslookup** - The command tests and troubleshoots DNS servers. It queries the DNS server to discover IP addresses or host names. At the command prompt, enter **nslookup***hostname*. Nslookup returns the IP address for the host name entered. A reverse nslookup command, **nslookup***IP_address* returns the corresponding host name for the IP address entered.

Refer to **Video**
in online course

11.5.3.7   Video Demonstration - Network Testing and Verification with CLI Commands

Click Play in the video to see a demonstration of network testing and verification using CLI commands.

Click here to read a transcript of this video.

11.5.4   Configure a Wireless Network Interfaces in Windows

Refer to
Online Course
for Illustration

11.5.4.1   Wireless Settings

Wireless networks can be added in Windows 10 by going to Settings > Network & Internet > Wi-Fi > Manage known networks, as shown in the figure. Enter the network name and select a security type that matches the configuration on the wireless router. There are four security type options:

- **No authentication (Open)** - Data is sent unencrypted and with no authentication

- **WEP** - Provides very weak security and should not be relied upon for confidentiality

- **WPA2**-Personal - Uses the Advanced Encryption Standard (AES) cipher and a Pre-shared Key (PSK) to encrypt communications.

- **WPA2-Enterprise** - Authentication is passed from the access point to a centralized authentication server running Remote Authentication Dial-in User Service (RADIUS)

Remote authentication for wireless devices can be provided by a scalable authentication architecture by using RADIUS or Terminal Controller Access Control System Plus (TACACS+). Both technologies use a separate server (an Authentication, Authorization, and Accounting (AAA) server) that performs the authentication on behalf of network devices. Rather than the network devices storing and validating user credentials directly, they pass the request to the AAA server and forward the response to the user.

Refer to
Lab Activity
for this chapter

11.5.4.2   Lab - Connect and Test the Wireless Connection

In this lab, you and your partner will connect your computers to a wireless router and test the wireless connection.

Lab - Connect and Test the Wireless Connection

11.5.5   Remote Access Protocols

Refer to
Interactive Graphic
in online course

11.5.5.1   VPN Access in Windows

To communicate and share resources over a network that is not secure, a Virtual Private Network (VPN) is used. A VPN is a private network that connects remote sites or users together over a public network, like the internet. The most common type of VPN is used to access a corporate private network.

The VPN uses dedicated secure connections, routed through the internet, from the corporate private network to the remote user. When connected to the corporate private network, users become part of that network and have access to all services and resources as if they were physically connected to it.

Remote-access users must install a VPN client on their computers to form a secure connection with the corporate private network. Special routers can also be used to connect computers connected to it to the corporate private network. The VPN software encrypts data before sending it over the internet to the VPN gateway at the corporate private network. VPN gateways establish, manage, and control VPN connections, also known as VPN tunnels. A VPN client software is shown in Figure 1.

A VPN in Windows 10 can be set up from the Network and Sharing Center is shown in Figure 2.

Windows supports several VPN types, however, for some VPNs, third-party software may be required.

Refer to
Online Course
for Illustration

11.5.5.2   Telnet and SSH

Telnet is a command-line terminal emulation protocol and program. The Telnet daemon listens for connections on TCP port 23. Telnet is sometimes used for troubleshooting services and for connecting to routers and switches for entering configurations. Telnet is not installed in Windows by default but can be added using Programs and Features. There are also third-party and free terminal emulation programs available that have support for Telnet. Telnet messages are sent in clear text. Anyone with a packet sniffer can capture and see the contents of Telnet messages. This is why it is advisable to use a secure connection rather than Telnet.

Secure Shell (SSH) is a secure alternative to Telnet and other file copy programs such as FTP. SSH communicates over TCP port 22 and uses encryption to protect the session. There are several methods in which a client can authenticate to an SSH server:

- **Username/Password** - The client sends credentials to the SSH host, which are then verified against a local user database or sent to a centralized authentication server.

- **Kerberos** - Networks which use Kerberos authentication protocol, such as Windows Active Directory, allow for Single Sign-On (SSO). SSO allows users to sign in to multiple systems with only one username and password.

- **Host-based authentication** - The client requests authentication with a public key. The server generates a challenge with this key which the client must decrypt with the matching private key to complete the authentication.

- **Public key authentication** - This provides additional protection over host-based authentication. The user must enter a passphrase to access the private key. This helps prevent the private key from becoming compromises.

Refer to **Packet Tracer Activity** for this chapter

11.5.5.3   Packet Tracer - Use Telnet and SSH

In this Packet Tracer activity, you will establish remote sessions to two routers, using Telnet and SSH. You may also install a third-party terminal emulation program and access a dedicated SSH server provided by your instructor.

Packet Tracer - Using Telnet and SSH Instructions

Packet Tracer - Using Telnet and SSH PKA

11.5.6   Remote Desktop and Assistance

Refer to **Video** in online course

11.5.6.1   Video Demonstration - Remote Desktop and Remote Assistance

Click Play in the figure to view a demonstration of how to use Remote Desktop and Remote Assistance in Windows.

Other operating systems can also perform these functions. For example, in macOS, remote access functionality is provided by the Screen Sharing feature, which is based on Virtual Network Computing (VNC). Any VNC client can connect to a Screen Sharing server. VNC is a freeware product that is similar in functionality to RDP and works over port 5900.

Click here to read the transcript of this video.

Refer to **Lab Activity** for this chapter

11.5.6.2   Lab - Windows Remote Desktop and Assistance

In this lab, you will partner with another student so you can configure a Remote Desktop connection for your partner and invite your partner to provide assistance on your computer via a Remote Assistance connection.

Lab - Windows Remote Desktop and Assistance

Refer to **Interactive Graphic** in online course

11.5.6.3   Check Your Understanding - Remote Desktop and Assistance

11.6   Common Preventive Maintenance Techniques for Operating Systems

11.6.1   OS Preventive Maintenance Plan

Refer to **Online Course** for Illustration

11.6.1.1   Preventive Maintenance Plan Contents

To ensure that an OS remains fully functional, you must implement a preventive maintenance plan. A preventive maintenance plan provides many benefits to users and organizations such as decreased downtime, improved performance, improved reliability, and lower repair costs.

Preventive maintenance plans should include detailed information about the maintenance of all computers and network equipment. The plan should prioritize equipment that would affect the organization the most if that equipment fails. Preventive maintenance for an OS includes automating tasks to perform scheduled updates. Preventive maintenance also includes installing service packs that help keep the system up to date and compatible with new software and hardware. Preventive maintenance includes the following important tasks:

- Hard drive error checking, defragmentation, and backup
- Updates to the operating system, applications, antivirus, and other protective software

Perform preventive maintenance regularly, and record all actions taken and observations made. A repair log helps you determine which equipment is the most or least reliable. It also provides a history of when a computer was last fixed, how it was fixed, and what the problem was.

Preventive maintenance should take place when it causes the least amount of disruption to the users. This often means scheduling tasks at night, early in the morning, or over the weekend. There are also tools and techniques that can automate many preventive maintenance tasks.

Security

Security is an important aspect of your preventive maintenance program. Install virus and malware protection software and perform regular scans on computers to help ensure that they remain free of malicious software. Use the Windows Malicious Software Removal Tool to check a computer for malicious software. If an infection is found, the tool removes it. Each time a new version of the tool is available from Microsoft, download it and scan your computer for new threats. This should be a standard item in your preventive maintenance program, along with regular updates to your antivirus and spyware removal tools.

Startup Programs

Some programs, such as antivirus scanners and spyware removal tools, do not automatically start when the computer boots. To ensure that these programs run each time the computer is booted, add the program to the Startup folder of the Start Menu. Many programs have switches to allow the program to perform a specific action such as starting without being displayed. Check the documentation to determine if your programs allow the use of special switches.

Refer to
Lab Activity
for this chapter

11.6.1.2   Lab - Manage the Startup Folder

In this lab, you will learn how to manage the Startup folder.

Lab - Manage the Startup Folder

Refer to
Interactive Graphic
in online course

11.6.1.3   Windows Updates

Windows Updates

Windows Update is a website located at update.microsoft.com. The site hosts maintenance updates, critical updates, and security patches as well as optional software and hardware updates for Microsoft Windows versions 7, 8 and 10. There is also a program called Microsoft Update which can keep Microsoft Office software patched at the same time. A control installed in Windows allows the OS to browse the update site and select updates for download and installation using the Background Intelligent Transfer Service, or BITS, protocol.

Microsoft releases updates on the second Tuesday of each month, unofficially known as Patch Tuesday.

Windows 10 automatically downloads and installs updates to make sure your device is secure and up to date. This means you receive the latest fixes and security updates, helping your device run efficiently and securely. In most cases, the only user interaction required is the restarting of your device to complete the update.

You can manually check for updates in Windows 10 via Settings > Update and Security as shown in the figure. You can choose which updates to apply and configure update settings.

A windowsupdate.log file stored in the %SystemRoot% directory contains records of update activity. If an update fails to install properly you can check the log file for an error code that can be referenced on the Microsoft Knowledge Base. If an update causes problems, it can be uninstalled from **Settings > Update and Security > View Update History**.

11.6.1.4   Video Demonstration - Scheduling Tasks

Click Play in the video to see a demonstration of scheduling tasks.

Click here to read a transcript of this video.

11.6.1.5   Lab - Schedule a Task using the GUI and the Command Line

In this lab, you will learn how to schedule a task using the GUI and at the command line.

Lab - Schedule a Task using the GUI and the Command Line

11.6.2   Backup and Restore

11.6.2.1   Restore Points

Sometimes installing an application or hardware driver can cause instability or create unexpected problems. Uninstalling the application or hardware driver usually corrects the problem. If not, you can restore the computer to a time before the installation with the System Restore utility.

Restore points contain information about the operating system, installed programs, and registry settings. If a computer crashes or if an update causes a problem, the computer can be rolled back to a previous configuration using a restore point. System restore does not back up personal data files, nor does it recover personal files that have been corrupted or deleted. Always use a dedicated backup system, such as a tape drive, optical disc, or USB storage device to back up personal files.

A technician should always create a restore point before making changes to a system in the following situations:

- When updating the OS
- When installing or upgrading hardware
- When installing an application
- When installing a driver

To open the System Restore utility in Windows 10, shown in the figure, open **System Properties** and click **System Restore**.

11.6.2.2   Hard Drive Backup

It is important to establish a backup strategy that includes data recovery of personal files. You can use the Microsoft Backup utility to perform backups as required. How the computer system is used, as well as organizational requirements, determines how often the data must be backed up and the type of backup to perform.

It can take a long time to run a backup. If the backup strategy is followed carefully, it is not necessary to back up all files every time. Only the files that have changed since the last backup need to be backed up.

The backup tool included with Windows 7 allowed users to back up files, or create and use a system image backup, or repair disc. Windows 8 and Windows 10 ship with **File History** which can be used to back up the files in the Documents, Music, Pictures, Videos, and Desktop folders. Over time, File History builds a history of your files, allowing you to go back and recover specific versions of a file. This is a helpful feature if there are damaged or lost files.

File History in Windows 10 is located in **Settings > Update&Security > Backup**, as shown in the figure.

Refer to **Video** in online course

11.6.2.3 Video Demonstration - Back up and Restore

Click Play in the figure to view a demonstration of how to use hard drive backup tools.

Click here to read the transcript of this video.

Refer to **Lab Activity** for this chapter

11.6.2.4 Lab - System Restore and Hard Drive Backup

In this lab, you will create a restore point and use it to restore your computer. You will also configure a hard drive backup.

Lab - System Restore and Hard Drive Backup

11.7 Basic Troubleshooting Process for Windows Operating Systems

11.7.1 Applying Troubleshooting Process to Windows Operating Systems

Refer to **Interactive Graphic** in online course

11.7.1.1 The Six Steps of the Troubleshooting Process

Refer to **Online Course** for Illustration

11.7.1.2 Identify the Problem

OS problems can result from a combination of hardware, software, and network issues. Computer technicians must be able to analyze the problem and determine the cause of the error to repair the computer. This process is called troubleshooting.

The first step in the troubleshooting process is to identify the problem. Click an option on the left side of the screen to see examples of open-ended and closed-ended questions.

Refer to **Online Course** for Illustration

11.7.1.3 Establish a Theory of Probable Cause

After you have talked to the customer, you can establish a theory of probable causes. The figure lists some common probable causes for OS problems.

Refer to **Online Course** for Illustration

11.7.1.4 Test the Theory to Determine the Cause

After you have developed some theories about what is wrong, test your theories to determine the cause of the problem. The figure shows a list of quick procedures that can help determine the exact cause of the problem or even correct the problem. If a quick procedure does correct the problem, you can jump to verifying the full system functionality. If a quick procedure does not correct the problem, you need to research the problem further to establish the exact cause.

Refer to
Online Course
for Illustration

11.7.1.5   Establish a Plan of Action to Resolve the Problem and Implement the Solution

After you have determined the exact cause of the problem, establish a plan of action to resolve the problem and implement the solution. The figure shows some sources you can use to gather additional information to resolve an issue.

Refer to
Online Course
for Illustration

11.7.1.6   Verify Full System Functionality and if Applicable Implement Preventive Measures

After you have corrected the problem, verify full system functionality and, if applicable, implement preventive measures. The figure lists the steps to verify full system functionality.

Refer to
Online Course
for Illustration

11.7.1.7   Document Findings, Actions, and Outcomes

In the final step of the troubleshooting process, you must document your findings, actions, and outcomes. The figure lists the tasks required to document the problem and the solution.

11.7.2   Common Problems and Solutions for Windows Operating Systems

Refer to
Interactive Graphic
in online course

11.7.2.1   Common Problems and Solutions for Windows Operating Systems

11.7.3   Advanced Troubleshooting for Windows Operating Systems

Refer to
Interactive Graphic
in online course

11.7.3.1   Advanced Problems and Solutions for Windows Operating Systems

Refer to
Lab Activity
for this chapter

11.7.3.2   Lab - Troubleshoot Operating System Problems

In this lab, you will diagnose the cause of various operating system problems and solve them.

Lab - Troubleshoot Operating System Problems

Refer to
Online Course
for Illustration

11.8   Summary

The focus of this chapter was on Windows 7, Windows 8, and Windows 10. Each version comes in several editions, such as Home, Pro, Ultimate, or Enterprise, and come in either 32-bit or 64-bit versions. The Windows editions are tailored for the needs of corporate and personal users. You explored the Windows Desktop, Start Menu, and Taskbar and to work with the Task Manager and File Explorer to monitor system performance and manage files and folders on a computer running Windows in labs.

You learned about the various system tools used to configure the Windows operating system and to change settings. You learned that Control Panel offers many configuration tools that are used to create and modify user accounts, configure updates and backups, personalize the look and feel of Windows, install and uninstall apps, and configure network settings. You performed several lab exercises using tools found in the control panel. In these labs, you used the User Accounts Control Panel to create and modify users, configured Internet settings in Internet Explorer, used the System Control Panel to configure and manage virtual memory, used device manager to display devices and monitor settings, changed region and language options, and many other administrative tasks.

In addition to using the Control Panel GUI, you also learned how to use the Windows CLI and PowerShell command line utility to perform administrative tasks. You also learned system commands that provide the same functions as those found in Task Manager and how to run system utilities from the Windows CLI. To practice what you learned you performed several labs that involved working with file system commands, disk CLI commands, task and system CLI commands, and other useful commands.

You also learned about the two methods for organizing and managing Windows computers on a network, the domain and the workgroup. You learned how to share local computer resources, such as files, folders, and printers on the network and how to configure a wired network connection. You performed labs related to Windows networking where you created and shared a folder and set permissions, connected your computer to a wireless router and tested the wireless connection, and configured Windows for remote access using Remote Desktop and Remote Assistance.

At the end of the chapter, you learned the importance of a preventive maintenance plan to decrease downtime, improve performance, improve reliability, and lower repair costs. A good preventive maintenance plan includes detailed information about the maintenance of all computers and network equipment. Preventive maintenance should take place when it causes the least amount of disruption to the users. This often means scheduling tasks at night, early in the morning, or over the weekend. You scheduled a task using the GUI and at the command line in the lab.

Regular scans for viruses and malware are an important part of preventive maintenance. Some programs, such as antivirus scanners and spyware removal tools, do not automatically start when the computer boots. To ensure that these programs do run each time the computer is booted, they can be added to the Startup folder of the Start Menu. You managed startup applications using the Run key in the Registry in the lab.

Finally, you learned the six steps in the troubleshooting process as they are applied to Windows operating systems.

Go to the online
course to take the
quiz and exam.

Chapter 11 Quiz

This quiz is designed to provide an additional opportunity to practice the skills and
knowledge presented in the chapter and to prepare for the chapter exam. You will be
allowed multiple attempts and the grade does not appear in the gradebook.

Chapter 11 Exam

The chapter exam assesses your knowledge of the chapter content.

Your Chapter Notes

Mobile, Linux, and macOS Operating Systems

Refer to **Online Course** for Illustration

12.0   Introduction

The use of mobile devices has grown very rapidly. IT technicians and professionals must be familiar with the operating systems on these devices. Like desktops and laptops, mobile devices also use operating systems to interface with the hardware and to run software. The two most commonly used mobile operating systems are Android and iOS. There are also desktop operating systems other than Windows, the two most popular being Linux and macOS.

In this chapter, you will learn about the components, functions, and terminology related to mobile, Linux, and macOS operating systems. First you will learn about the differences between the Android and iOS mobile operating systems, Linux being open source and customizable, and iOS being proprietary to Apple and closed source. You will also learn about common mobile device features like screen orientation, screen calibration, Wi-Fi calling, virtual assistants, and GPS. You will work with both the Android and iOS operating systems as part of lab exercises.

The portable nature of mobile devices makes them at risk for theft and loss. You will learn about mobile security features such as screen lock, biometric authentication, remote lock, remote wipe, and patching and upgrading. You also learned that mobile OSs can be configured to disable access if too many failed login attempts are made. This can prevent someone from trying to guess a passcode. Most mobile devices also have a remote lock and remote wipe feature that can be activated if the device is stolen. You will perform a lab exercise securing a mobile device using passcode locks.

Finally, you will learn the six steps in the troubleshooting process as they are applied to mobile, Linux, and macOS operating systems.

12.1   Mobile Operating Systems

12.1.1   Android vs. iOS

Refer to **Interactive Graphic** in online course

12.1.1.1   Open Source vs. Closed Source

Mobile Device Operating Systems

Like desktops and laptops, mobile devices use an operating system (OS) to run software. This chapter focuses on the two most commonly used mobile operating systems: Android and iOS. Android is developed by Google, and iOS is developed by Apple.

Before users can analyze and modify software, they must be able to see the source code. Source code is the sequence of instructions that is written in human readable language, before it is turned into machine language (zeroes and ones). The source code is an important component of free software as it allows the users to analyze and eventually modify the code. When the developer chooses to provide the source code, the software is said to be open source. If the program's source code is not published, the software is said to be closed source.

Refer to
Interactive Graphic
in online course

12.1.1.2   Applications and Content Sources

Applications

Apps are the programs that are executed on mobile devices. Apps are written and compiled for a specific mobile operating system such as Apple iOS, Android, or Windows. Mobile devices come with a number of different apps preinstalled to provide basic functionality. There are apps to make phone calls, send and receive email, listen to music, take pictures, and play video or video games.

Apps are used on mobile devices the same way that programs are used on computers. Instead of being installed from an optical disk, apps are downloaded from a content source. Some apps can be downloaded for free, and others must be purchased.

Refer to
Interactive Graphic
in online course

12.1.1.3   Check Your Understanding - Compare Android and iOS

12.1.2   Android Touch Interface

Refer to
Interactive Graphic
in online course

12.1.2.1   Home Screen Items

Icon and Widget Organization

Much like a desktop or laptop computer, mobile devices organize icons and widgets on multiple screens for easy access.

Refer to
Lab Activity
for this chapter

12.1.2.2   Lab - Working with Android

In this lab, you will work with the Android operating system.

Lab - Working with Android

12.1.3   iOS Touch Interface

Refer to
Interactive Graphic
in online course

12.1.3.1   Home Screen Items

iOS Interface

The iOS interface works in much the same way as the Android interface. Screens are used to organize apps, and apps are launched with a touch. There are some very important differences:

- **No navigation icons** - A physical button may have to be pressed instead of touching navigation icons.

- **No widgets** - Only apps and other content can be installed on iOS device screens.

- **No app shortcuts** - Each app on a home screen is the actual app, not a shortcut.

Refer to
Lab Activity
for this chapter

12.1.3.2   Lab - Working with iOS

In this lab, you will work with the iOS operating system.

Lab - Working with iOS

12.1.4   Common Mobile Device Features

Refer to
Interactive Graphic
in online course

12.1.4.1   Screen Orientation

Most mobile devices can be used in either portrait or landscape mode. A sensor inside the device known as an accelerometer, detects how it is being held and will change the screen orientation appropriately. Users can choose the viewing mode that is the most comfortable for them for different types of content or applications. Content is automatically rotated to the position of the device. This feature is useful, for example, when taking a photograph. When the device is turned to landscape mode, the camera app also turns to landscape mode. Also, when a user is writing a text, turning the device to landscape mode automatically turns the app to landscape mode, making the keyboard larger and wider.

Some devices also have gyroscopes to provide more accurate movement readings. Gyroscopes allow a device to be used as a control mechanism for driving games where the phone or tablet itself functions as a steering wheel.

Refer to
Interactive Graphic
in online course

12.1.4.2   Screen Calibration

When using a mobile device, you may need to adjust the brightness of the screen. When bright sunlight makes the screen difficult to read, increase the brightness level. Inversely, very low brightness is helpful when reading a book on a mobile device at night. Some mobile devices can be configured to auto-adjust the brightness depending on the amount of surrounding light. The device must have a light sensor to use auto-brightness.

The LCD screen for most mobile devices uses the most battery power. Lowering the brightness or using auto-brightness helps conserve battery power. Set the brightness to the lowest setting to get the most battery life from the device.

Refer to
Interactive Graphic
in online course

12.1.4.3   GPS

Another common feature of mobile devices is the Global Positioning System (GPS). GPS is a navigation system that determines the time and geographical location of the device by using messages from satellites in space and a receiver on Earth. A GPS radio receiver uses at least four satellites to calculate its position based on the messages. GPS is very accurate and can be used under most weather conditions. However, dense foliage, tunnels, and tall buildings can interrupt satellite signals. GPS receivers must have line-of-sight to GPS satellites and do not work indoors. Indoor Positioning Systems (IPS) can determine device location by triangulating its proximity to other radio signals such as Wi-Fi access-points.

GPS services allow app vendors and website to know the location of a device and offer location-specific services (such as local weather and advertising). This is called geotracking.

Refer to
Lab Activity
for this chapter

12.1.4.4   Lab - Mobile Device Features

In this lab, you will learn about mobile device features.

Lab - Mobile Device Features

Refer to
Interactive Graphic
in online course

12.1.4.5   Wi-Fi Calling

Instead of using the cellular carrier's network, modern smartphones can use the internet to transport voice calls by taking advantage of a local Wi-Fi hotspot. This is called Wi-Fi calling. Locations, such as coffee shops, work places, libraries, or homes, usually have Wi-Fi networks connected to the internet. The phone can transport voice calls through the local Wi-Fi hotspot. If there is no Wi-Fi hotspot within reach, the phone will use the cellular carrier's network to transport voice calls.

Wi-Fi calling is very useful in areas with poor cellular coverage because it uses a local Wi-Fi hotspot to fill the gaps. The Wi-Fi hotspot must be able to guarantee a throughput of at least 1Mbps to the internet for a good quality call. When Wi-Fi calling is enabled and in use during a voice call, the phone will display "Wi-Fi" next to the carrier name.

Refer to
Interactive Graphic
in online course

12.1.4.6   NFC Payment

Premium SMS based transactional payments

Consumers send an SMS message to a carrier's special phone number containing a payment request. The seller is informed the payment has been received and is cleared to release the goods. The charge is then added to the customer's phone bill. Slow speed, poor reliability, and poor security are a few shortcomings of this method.

Refer to
Interactive Graphic
in online course

12.1.4.7   Virtual Private Network

A Virtual Private Network (VPN) is a private network that uses a public network (usually the internet) to connect remote sites or users together. Instead of using a dedicated leased line, a VPN uses "virtual" connections routed through the internet from the company's private network to the remote site or employee.

Many companies create their own VPNs to accommodate the needs of remote employees and distant offices. With the proliferation of mobile devices, it was a natural move to add VPN clients to smartphones and tablets.

When a VPN is established from a client to a server, the client accesses the network behind the server as if it was connected directly to that network. Because VPN protocols also allow for data encryption, the communication between client and server is secure.

When the VPN information has been added to the device, that device must be started before traffic can be sent and received through it.

Refer to
Interactive Graphic
in online course

12.1.4.8   Virtual Assistants

A digital assistant, sometimes called a virtual assistant, is a program that can understand natural conversational language and perform tasks for the end user. Modern mobile devices are powerful computers, making them the perfect platform for digital assistants. Popular digital assistants currently include Google Now for Android, Siri for iOS, and Cortana for Windows Phone 8.1.

These digital assistants rely on artificial intelligence, machine learning, and voice recognition technology to understand conversational-style voice commands. As the end user interacts with these digital assistants, sophisticated algorithms predict the user's needs and fulfill requests. By pairing simple voice requests with other inputs, such as GPS location, these assistants can perform several tasks, including playing a specific song, performing a web search, taking a note, or sending an email.

12.2   Methods for Securing Mobile Devices

12.2.1   Screen Locks and Biometric Authentication

Refer to
Interactive Graphic
in online course

12.2.1.1   What Do You Already Know? - Locks

Refer to
Lab Activity
for this chapter

12.2.1.2   Lab - Passcode Locks

In this lab, you will use passcode locks.

Lab - Passcode Locks

Refer to
Interactive Graphic
in online course

12.2.1.3   Restrictions on Failed Login Attempts

When a passcode has been properly implemented unlocking a mobile device requires entering the correct PIN, password, pattern, or another passcode type. In theory, a passcode, such as a PIN, could be guessed given enough time and perseverance. To prevent someone from trying to guess a passcode, mobile devices can be set to perform defined actions after a certain number of incorrect attempts have been made.

For Android devices, the number of failed attempts before lockout depends on the device and version of Android OS. It is common that an Android device will lock when a passcode has failed from 4 to 12 times. After a device is locked, you can unlock it by entering the Gmail account information used to set up the device.

Refer to
Interactive Graphic
in online course

12.2.1.4   Check your Understanding - Screen Locks and Biometric Authentication

12.2.2   Cloud-Enabled Services for Mobile Devices

Refer to
Online Course
for Illustration

12.2.2.1   Remote Backup

Mobile device data can be lost due to device failures or the loss or theft of the device. Data must be backed up periodically to ensure that it can be recovered if needed. With mobile devices, storage is often limited and not removable. To overcome these limitations, remote backups can be performed. A remote backup is when a device copies its data to cloud storage using a backup app. If data needs to be restored, run the backup app and access the website to retrieve the data.

Most mobile operating systems come with a user account linked to the vendor's cloud services, such as iCloud for iOS, Google Sync for Android, and OneDrive for Microsoft. The user can enable automatic backups to the cloud for data, apps, and settings. There are also third-party back providers, such as Dropbox, that can be used. Mobile devices can also be backed up to a PC. iOS supports backups on iTunes running on a PC. Another option is to configure Mobile Device Management (MDM) software to automatically backup user devices.

Refer to
Online Course
for Illustration

12.2.2.2 Locator Applications

If a mobile device is misplaced or stolen, it is possible to find it using a locator app. A locator app should be installed and configured on each mobile device before it is lost. Both Android and iOS have apps for remotely locating a device.

Similar to Apple's Find My iPhone, Android Device Manager allows a user to locate, ring, or lock a lost Android device, or to erase data from the device. To manage a lost device, the user must visit Android Device Manager Dashboard hosted at https://www.google.com/android/devicemanager and log in with the Google account used on the Android device. Android Device Manager is included and enabled by default on Android 5.x and can be found under **Settings > Security > Device Administration**.

iOS users can use the Find My iPhone app, as shown in the figure. The first step is to install the app, start it, and follow the instructions to configure the software. The Find My iPhone app can be installed on different iOS devices to locate the lost device.

Note If the app is unable to locate the lost device, the device might be turned off or disconnected. The device must be connected to a cellular or wireless network to receive commands from the app, or to send location information to the user.

After the device is located, you might be able to perform additional functions, such as sending a message or playing a sound. These options are useful if you have misplaced your device. If the device is close by, playing a sound indicates exactly where it is. If the device is at another location, sending a message to display on the screen allows someone to contact you if it has been found.

Refer to
Interactive Graphic
in online course

12.2.2.3 Remote Lock and Remote Wipe

If attempts to locate a mobile device have failed, there are other security features that can prevent data on the device from being compromised. Usually, the same apps that perform remote location have security features. Two of the most common remote security features are remote lock and remote wipe.

Note For these remote security measures to function, the device must be powered on and connected to a cellular or Wi-Fi network.

Click each button to learn more.

Refer to
Interactive Graphic
in online course

12.2.2.4 Check Your Understanding - Cloud-Enabled Services for Mobile Devices

12.2.3 Software Security

Refer to
Online Course
for Illustration

12.2.3.1 Antivirus

All computers are vulnerable to malicious software. Smartphones and other mobile devices are computers and are also vulnerable. Antivirus apps are available for both Android and iOS. Depending on the permissions granted to antivirus apps when they are installed on an Android device, the app might not be able to scan files automatically or run scheduled scans. File scans must be initiated manually. iOS does not allow automatic or scheduled scans. This is a safety feature to prevent malicious programs from using unauthorized resources or contaminating other apps or the OS. Some antivirus apps also provide locator services, remote lock, or remote wipe.

Mobile device apps run in a sandbox. A sandbox is a location of the OS that keeps code isolated from other resources and other code. It is difficult for malicious programs to infect a mobile device because apps are run inside the sandbox. An Android app asks for permission to access certain resources upon installation. A malicious app has access to any resources that were allowed permission during installation. This is another reason why it is important to download apps only from trusted sources. A trusted app source is one that is authenticated and authorized by a service provider. The service provider issues the developer a certificate to use to sign their apps and identify them as trusted.

Due to the nature of the sandbox, malicious software does not usually damage mobile devices; it is far more likely for a mobile device to transfer a malicious program to another device, such as a laptop or desktop. For example, if a malicious program is downloaded from email, the Internet, or another device, the malicious program could be placed on a laptop the next time it is connected to the mobile device.

To prevent the malicious program from infecting additional devices, a firewall can be used. Firewall apps for mobile devices can Monitor app activity and prevent connections to specific ports or IP addresses. Because mobile device firewall must be able to control other apps they logically work at a higher (root) permission level. No root firewalls work by creating a virtual private network (VPN) and then controlling app access to the VPN.

Refer to
Online Course
for Illustration

12.2.3.2   Rooting and Jailbreaking

Mobile operating systems are usually protected by a number of software restrictions. An unmodified copy of iOS, for example, will only execute authorized code and allow very limited user access to its file system.

Rooting and Jailbreaking are two methods for removing restrictions and protections added to mobile operating systems. They are a means of circumventing the usual operating of the device operating system to gain super-user or root administrator permissions. Rooting is used on Android devices to gain privileged or root level access for modifying code or installing software that is not intended for the device. Jailbreaking is typically used on iOS devices to remove manufacturer restrictions allowing them to run arbitrary user-code, grant users full access to the file system and full access to kernel modules.

Rooting or jailbreaking a mobile device usually voids the manufacturer's warranty. It is not recommended that you modify a customer's mobile device in this way. Nevertheless, a large group of users choose to remove their own devices' restrictions. By rooting or jailbreaking a mobile device the GUI can be heavily customized, modifications can be made to the OS to improve the speed and responsiveness of the device, and apps can be installed from secondary or unsupported sources.

Jailbreaking exploits vulnerabilities in iOS. When a usable vulnerability is found, a program is written. This program is the actual jailbreak software and it is then distributed on the internet. Apple discourages jailbreaking, and actively works towards eliminating vulnerabilities that make jailbreaking possible on iOS. In addition to the OS updates and bug fixes, new iOS releases usually include patches to eliminate known vulnerabilities that allow jailbreaking. When iOS vulnerabilities are fixed by updates, it forces hackers to start over.

Note   The jailbreak process is completely reversible. To remove the jailbreak and bring the device back to its factory state, connect it to iTunes and perform a Restore.

Refer to
Online Course
for Illustration

12.2.3.3   Patching and Updating Operating Systems

Like the OS on a desktop or laptop, you can update or patch the OS on mobile devices. Updates add functionality or increase performance. Patches can fix security problems or issues with hardware and software.

Because there are so many different Android mobile devices, updates and patches are not released as one package for all devices. Sometimes a new version of Android cannot install on older devices where the hardware does not meet the minimum specifications. These devices might receive patches to fix known issues, but not receive OS upgrades.

Android updates and patches use an automated process for delivery. When a carrier or manufacturer has an update for a device, a notification on the device indicates that an update is ready, as shown in the figure. Touch the update to begin the download and installation process.

iOS updates also use an automated process for delivery, and devices that do not meet the hardware requirements are also excluded. To check for updates to iOS, connect the device to iTunes. A notice to download opens if updates are available. To manually check for updates, click the Check for Update button in the iTunes Summary pane.

There are two other types of updates for mobile device radio firmware that are important. These are called baseband updates and consist of the Preferred Roaming List (PRL) and the Primary Rate ISDN (PRI). The PRL is configuration information that a cellular phone needs to communicate on networks other than its own so that a call can be made outside of the carrier's network. The PRI configures the data rates between the device and the cell tower. This ensures that the device is able to communicate with the tower at the correct rate.

Refer to
Interactive Graphic
in online course

12.2.3.4   Check Your Understanding - Mobile Security Features

12.3   Linux and macOS Operating Systems

12.3.1   Linux and macOS tools and features

Refer to
Interactive Graphic
in online course

12.3.1.1   Introduction to Linux and macOS Operating Systems

Linux and macOS File Systems

Two file systems used on most Linux operating systems are ext3, which is a 64-bit file system with support for journaling, and ext4, which delivers significantly better performance than ext3. Linux can also support FAT and FAT32. In addition, Network File System (NFS), can be used to mount remote storage devices into the local file system.

Most installations of Linux also support creation of a swap partition to use as swap space. The swap partition is used by the operating system to supplement system RAM. If applications or data files use up all the available space in RAM, data is written to the swap space on a disk and is treated as if it were stored in RAM.

Apple Mac workstations have their own file system, Extended Hierarchical File System (HFS Plus). This file system supports many of the same features as NTFS in Windows, but not native file/folder encryption. In macOS High Sierra and later, HFS Plus updated to the Apple File System (APFS), which does support native file encryption. HFS Plus has a maximum volume and file size of 8 ExaBytes.

Refer to
Interactive Graphic
in online course

12.3.1.2 Overview of Linux GUI

Different Linux distributions ship with different software packages, but users decide what stays in their system by installing or removing packages. The graphical interface in Linux is comprised of a number of subsystems that can also be removed or replaced by the user. While the details about these subsystems and their interactions are beyond the scope of this course, it is important to know the Linux GUI as whole can be easily replaced by the user. Because there are so many Linux distributions, this chapter focuses on Ubuntu when covering Linux.

Ubuntu Linux uses Unity as its default GUI. The figure shows a breakdown of the main components of Ubuntu Unity Desktop. Another feature in the Linux GUI is the ability to have multiple desktops or workspaces. This allows the users to arrange the windows on a particular workspace.

Canonical has a website that simulates Unity's UI and also provides a tour through the Unity's main features. To experience Unity via Canonical's website visit http://tour.ubuntu.com/en.

Refer to
Interactive Graphic
in online course

12.3.1.3 Overview macOS GUI

Among the major differences between older versions of OS X and macOS is the addition of the Aqua GUI. Aqua was designed around the theme of water, with components resembling droplets and a deliberate use of reflection and translucency. The latest release of macOS at the time of writing is 10.14 Mojave. The figure shows a breakdown of the macOS Aqua desktop.

The Apple Magic Mouse and the Magic Trackpad of a MacBook both support gestures to control the user interface. Gestures are finger movements on a trackpad or mouse that enable a user to scroll, zoom, and navigate desktop, document, and application content. Available gestures can be viewed and changed under **System Preferences > Trackpad.**

With macOS, Mission Control is a quick way to see everything that is currently open on your Mac. Mission Control can be accessed by using a three or four finger swipe up gesture, depending on your touch pad or mouse settings. Mission Control allows you to organize your apps on multiple desktops. To navigate the file system, macOS includes Finder. Finder is very similar to the Windows File Explorer.

Most Apple laptops do not have an optical drive. To install software from optical media, Remote Disk can be used. Remote Disk is an app which lets the user access a CD/DVD drive on another Mac or Windows computer. Remote Disk sharing is set up in **System Preferences > Sharing** and then check the DVD or CD sharing check box.

macOS also allows screen sharing. Screen sharing is a feature that lets other people using Macs to be able to view your screen. They can even be allowed to take control of your computer. This is very useful when you may need help or wish to help someone else.

Refer to
Interactive Graphic
in online course

12.3.1.4   Overview of Linux and macOS CLI

Unix Diagram

In both Linux and macOS, the user can communicate with the operating system by using the command line interface (CLI). To add flexibility, commands (or tools) that support parameters, options and switches, are usually preceded by the dash (-) character. The options and switches supported by a command are also entered by the user along with the command.

Most operating systems include a graphical interface. Although a command line interface is still present, the OS often boots into the GUI by default, hiding the command line interface from the user. One way to access the command line interface in a GUI-based operating system is through a terminal emulator application. These applications provide user access to the command line interface and are often named as some variation of the word terminal.

Refer to
Online Course
for Illustration

12.3.1.5   Linux Backup and Recovery

The process of backing up data refers to creating a copy (or multiple copies) of data for safekeeping. When the backing up process is complete, the copy is called a backup. The primary goal is the ability to restore or recover the data in case of failure. Gaining access to an earlier version of the data is often seen as a secondary goal of the backing up process.

While backups can be achieved with a simple copy command, many tools and techniques exist to make the process automatic and transparent to the user.

Linux does not have a built-in backup tool. However, there are many commercial and open source backup solutions for Linux such as Amanda, Bacula, Fwbackups, and Déjà Dup. Déjà Dup is an easy and efficient tool for backing up data. Déjà Dup supports a number of features including local, remote, or cloud backup locations, data encryption compression, incremental backs up, periodic scheduled backups, and GNOME desktop integration. It also restores from any particular backup.

Refer to
Online Course
for Illustration

12.3.1.6   macOS Backup and Recovery

macOS includes a backup tool called Time Machine. With Time Machine, users choose an external drive to be used as a backup destination device and connect it to the Mac via USB, FireWire or Thunderbolt. Time Machine will prepare the disk to receive backups and, when the disk is ready, it performs incremental backups periodically.

If the user has not specified a Time Machine destination disk, Time Machine will ask if the newly connected external disk should be used as the destination backup disk. Time Machine stores some backups on your Mac, so if the Time Machine backup disk is not available, you may be able to restore a backup directly from your Mac. This type of back up is called a local snapshot.

To enable Time Machine, go to **System Preferences > Time Machine**, slide the switch **On** and select the disk where the backups are stored, as shown in the figure. Clicking the **Options** button allows the user to select or unselect the files, folders, or drives to backup. By default, Time Machine performs hourly backups for the past 24 hours, daily backups for a month, and weekly backups for all previous months. When the destination backup drive becomes full, Time Machine removes the oldest backup files to free up space.

To restore data from Time Machine, make sure the destination backup disk is connected to the Mac and click **Enter Time Machine** in the Time Machine menu. A timeline on the right-hand side of the screen will show the available backups. Time Machine allows the user to restore the data to any previous version currently available in the destination backup disk.

Refer to
Online Course
for Illustration

12.3.1.7   Overview of Disk Utilities

To help diagnose and solve disk-related problems, most modern operating systems include disk utility tools. Ubuntu Linux includes a disk utility called Disks. With Disks users can perform the most common disk-related tasks including partition management, mount or unmount, format disks and query Analysis and Reporting Technology, (S.M.A.R.T.). macOS includes Disk Utility. In addition to supporting the main disk maintenance tasks, Disk Utility also supports Verify Disk Permissions and Repair Disk Permissions. Repair Disk Permission is a common troubleshooting step in macOS. Disk Utility can also be used to backup disks to image files and perform an image recovery to disk from image files. These files contain the entire contents of a disk.

Below are a few common maintenance tasks that can be performed using disk utility software:

- **Partition management** - When working with computer disks, partitions may need to be created, deleted or resized.

- **Mount or Unmount disk partitions** - On Unix-like systems, mounting a partition relates to the process of binding a partition of a disk or a disk image file (usually a .iso) to a folder location.

- **Disk Format** - Before a partition can be used by the user or the system, it must be formatted.

- **Bad Sector Check** - When a disk sector is flagged as bad, it becomes harmless to the OS because it will no longer be used to store data. Many bad sectors could be an indicator of a failing disk. Disk utilities can salvage data stored in bad sectors by moving it to healthy disk sectors.

- **Query S.M.A.R.T. attributes** - S.M.A.R.T. can detect and report attributes about a disk's health. The goal of S.M.A.R.T. is to anticipate disk failure, allowing the user to move the data to a healthy disk before the failing disk becomes inaccessible.

Refer to
Interactive Graphic
in online course

12.3.1.8   Check your understanding - Linux and macOS Operating Systems

12.3.2   Linux and macOS Best Practices

Refer to
Interactive Graphic
in online course

12.3.2.1   Scheduled Tasks

Computer systems need periodic preventive maintenance to ensure best performance. Maintenance tasks should be scheduled and performed frequently to prevent or detect problems early. To avoid missing maintenance tasks due to human error, computer systems can be programmed to perform tasks automatically. Two tasks that should be scheduled and performed automatically are backups and disk checks.

Backups and disk checks are usually time-consuming tasks. An additional benefit of scheduled maintenance tasks is that it allows the computer to perform these tasks when no users are using the system. The CLI utility known as cron, can schedule these tasks during off-peak hours.

In Linux and macOS, the cron service is responsible for scheduled tasks. As a service, cron runs in the background and executes tasks at specific dates and times. cron uses a schedule table called a cron table that can be edited with the crontab command.

Refer to
Interactive Graphic
in online course

12.3.2.2   Operating System Updates

Despite continued efforts to create a perfectly secure operating system, vulnerabilities still exist. When a vulnerability is found, it can be used as basis for the creation of a virus or other malicious software.

Measures can be taken to help prevent malicious software from infecting a computer system. The most common of these are operating system updates, firmware updates, antivirus, and antimalware. Also known as patches, OS updates are released periodically by OS companies to address any known vulnerability in their operating systems. While companies have update schedules, the release of unscheduled OS updates is common when a major vulnerability is found in the OS code. Modern operating systems will alert the user when updates are available for download and installation, but the user can check for updates at any time. The figure shows an update alert window for Apple macOS.

Refer to
Interactive Graphic
in online course

12.3.2.3   Security

Security Credentials Manager

Usernames, passwords, digital certificates, and encryption keys are just a few of the security credentials associated to a user. Due to the increasing number of necessary security credentials, modern operating systems include a service to manage them. Applications and other services can then request and utilize the credentials stored by the security credentials manager service.

Refer to
Interactive Graphic
in online course

12.3.2.4   Check Your Understanding - Linux and macOS Best Practices

12.3.3   Basic CLI Commands

Refer to
Interactive Graphic
in online course

12.3.3.1   Syntax Checker - File and Directory Commands

Refer to
Interactive Graphic
in online course

12.3.3.2   Check Your Understanding - File and Directory commands

Refer to
Interactive Graphic
in online course

12.3.3.3   The ls -l command output

12.3.3.4   Basic Unix File and Directory Permissions

Refer to
Interactive Graphic
in online course

To organize the system and reinforce boundaries within the system, Unix uses file permissions. File permissions are built into the file system structure and provide a mechanism to define permissions to every file and directory. Every file and directory on Unix systems carries its permissions which define the actions that the owner, the group, and others can do with the file or directory.

The only user who can override file permissions in Unix is the root user. Having the power to override file permissions, the root user can write to any file. Because everything is treated as a file, the root user has full control over the Unix operating system. Root access is often required before performing maintenance and administrative tasks.

Note Because Linux and OS X are based on Unix, both operating systems are in full compliance with Unix file permissions.

Review the different permission values shown in the Figure 1. Note the differences of how the file and directory access is affected by the permissions. Figure 2 is a summary of the permissions.

Refer to **Interactive Graphic** in online course

12.3.3.5 Syntax Checker: File and Directory Permissions

Refer to **Interactive Graphic** in online course

12.3.3.6 Check Your Understanding - File and Directory Permission

Refer to **Interactive Graphic** in online course

12.3.3.7 Linux Administrative Commands

Administrators use the terminal to monitor and control users, processes, ip addresses, and other tasks. The commands on this page can be executed by users without any special privileges.

If you have an Ubuntu distribution, click Activities in the upper left hand corner and type "terminal". Opening the terminal in other Linux distributions varies depending on the interface.

Refer to **Interactive Graphic** in online course

12.3.3.8 Linux Administrative Commands Requiring Root Access

Commands Requiring Root Access

Some commands may be used without special privileges. Other commands require root access some of the time or all of the time. Typically, a user can manipulate the files within their own home directory, but changing files and settings throughout the server requires either sudo (Super User DO) or root access.

Refer to **Interactive Graphic** in online course

12.3.3.9 Check Your Understanding: - Administrative Commands

Refer to **Interactive Graphic** in online course

12.3.3.10 Syntax Checker - File Ownership and Permission

12.4   Basic Troubleshooting Process for Mobile, Linux, and macOS Operating Systems

12.4.1   Applying the Troubleshooting Process to Mobile, Linux, and macOS Operating Systems

Refer to Interactive Graphic in online course

12.4.1.1   The Six Steps of the Troubleshooting Process

Refer to Online Course for Illustration

12.4.1.2   Identify the Problem

When troubleshooting problems with mobile devices, find out if the device is under warranty. If it is, it can often be returned for repair or an exchange. If the device is no longer under warranty, determine if a repair is cost-effective. To determine the best course of action, compare the cost of the repair with the replacement cost of the mobile device. Because many mobile devices change rapidly in design and functionality, they are often more expensive to repair than to replace. For this reason, mobile devices are usually replaced.

Mobile device problems can result from a combination of hardware, software, and network issues. Mobile technicians must be able to analyze the problem and determine the cause of the error to repair the mobile device. This process is called troubleshooting.

The first step in the troubleshooting process is to identify the problem. The figure shows a list of open-ended and closed-ended questions to ask the customer for mobile device operating systems and on Linux and macOS.

Refer to Online Course for Illustration

12.4.1.3   Establish a theory of Probable Cause

After you have talked to the customer, you can establish a theory of probable causes. The figure shows a list of some common probable causes for mobile device operating systems, Linux, and macOS problems.

Refer to Online Course for Illustration

12.4.1.4   Test the Theory to Determine the Cause

After you have developed some theories about what is wrong, test your theories to determine the cause of the problem. Once the theory is confirmed, you then determine the steps to resolve the problem. The figure shows a list of quick procedures that can determine the exact cause of the problem or even correct the problem. If a quick procedure corrects the problem, you can then verify full system functionality. If a quick procedure does not correct the problem, you might need to research the problem further to establish the exact cause.

Refer to Online Course for Illustration

12.4.1.5   Establish a Plan of Action to Resolve the Problem and Implement the Solution

After you have determined the exact cause of the problem, establish a plan of action to resolve the problem and implement the solution. The figure shows some sources you can use to gather additional information to resolve an issue.

12.4.1.6   Verify Full System Functionality and if Applicable, Implement Preventive Measures

After you have corrected the problem, verify full functionality and, if applicable, implement preventive measures. The figure shows a list of the steps to verify the solution.

12.4.1.7   Document Findings, Actions, and Outcomes.

In the final step of the troubleshooting process, you must document your findings, actions, and outcomes. The figure lists the tasks required to document the problem and the solution.

12.4.2   Common Problems and Solutions for Other Operating Systems

12.4.2.1   Common Problems and Solutions for Mobile Operating Systems

12.4.2.2   Common Problems and Solutions for Mobile OS Security

12.4.2.3   Common Problems and Solutions for Linux and macOS Operating Systems

12.4.2.4   Lab - Troubleshoot Mobile Devices

In this lab, you will learn how to troubleshoot mobile devices.

Lab - Troubleshoot Mobile Devices

12.5   Summary

In this chapter, you learned that, like desktops and laptops, mobile devices also use operating systems to interface with the hardware and to run software. The two most commonly used mobile operating systems are Android and iOS. You learned that Android is an open source operating system and is customizable while iOS is closed source and cannot be modified or redistributed without permission from Apple. Both platforms use apps to provide functionality. You worked with both the Android and iOS operating systems as part of lab exercises.

Mobile devices are easily lost or stolen, therefore as an IT professional, you need to be familiar with mobile security features such as screen locks, biometric authentication, remote lock and remote wipe, and patching and upgrading. You learned that mobile devices can be unlocked using facial recognition, fingerprints, passcodes, and swipe patterns. You also learned that mobile OSs can be configured to disable access if too many failed login attempts are made to prevent someone from trying to guess a passcode. Another measure of security is provided by remote lock and remote wipe for devices that have been lost or stolen. These features allow the device to be remotely wiped or locked to prevent data on the device from being compromised. You configured passcode locks on a mobile device in the lab.

You learned about the Linux and macOS operating systems and some of the differences between them. Linux supports ext3, ext4, FAT, and NFS file systems while macOS supports HFS and APFS. Also, macOS includes a backup tool called Time Machine while Linux does not have a built-in backup tool. Another major difference is the Linux GUI can be easily replaced by the user.

It is important to not only learn about other operating systems but to also build hands-on skills. In this chapter there was a lab to install Linux in a virtual machine and explore the GUI.

Finally, you learned the six steps in the troubleshooting process as they are applied to mobile, Linux, and macOS operating systems.

Go to the online course to take the quiz and exam.

Chapter 12 Quiz

This quiz is designed to provide an additional opportunity to practice the skills and knowledge presented in the chapter and to prepare for the chapter exam. You will be allowed multiple attempts and the grade does not appear in the gradebook.

Chapter 12 Exam

The chapter exam assesses your knowledge of the chapter content.

Your Chapter Notes

Security

Refer to
Online Course
for Illustration

13.0 Introduction

This chapter reviews the types of attacks that threaten the security of computers and the data contained on them. An IT technician is responsible for the security of data and computer equipment in an organization. To successfully protect computers and the network, a technician must understand the threats to physical equipment, such as servers, switches, and wiring, and threats to data such as authorized access, theft, or loss.

In this chapter, you will learn about the many types of threats to computers and networks, the greatest and most common being malware. You will learn about common types of computer malware such as viruses, trojan horses, adware, ransomware, rootkits, spyware, and worms and the techniques to protect against them. You will also learn about TCP/IP attacks like denial of service, spoofing, syn flood, and man-in-the-middle. Cybercriminals often use social engineering techniques to deceive and trick unsuspecting individuals to reveal confidential information or account login credentials. You will learn about the many forms of social engineering attacks such as phishing, pretexting, baiting, and dumpster diving and how to protect against these attacks.

You will also learn about the importance of having a security policy which is a set of security objectives that ensure the security of a network, the data, and the computers in an organization. You will learn that a good security policy should specify the persons authorized to access network resources, the minimum requirements for passwords, acceptable uses for network resources, how remote users can access the network, and how security incidents will be handled. You will learn about host-based firewalls like Windows Defender how to configure it to allow or deny access to specific programs or ports. You will explore the Windows Defender Firewall in a lab and configure firewall advanced settings. You will also learn about wireless security and configure wireless security in a packet tracer activity.

Finally, you will learn the six steps in the troubleshooting process as they are applied to security.

13.1 Security Threats

13.1.1 Malware

Refer to
Online Course
for Illustration

13.1.1.1 Malware

There are many types of threats created to disrupt computers and networks. The greatest and most common threat for computers and the data contained on them is malware.

Malware is software developed by cybercriminals to perform malicious acts. In fact, the word malware is an abbreviation of **mal**icious soft**ware**.

Malware is typically installed on a computer without user knowledge. Once a host is infected, the malware could:

- Change the computer configuration.

- Delete files or corrupt hard drives.

- Collect information stored on the computer without the user's consent.

- Open extra windows on the computer or redirect the browser.

How does malware get on your computer? Cybercriminals use a variety of methods such as those listed in the figure to infect hosts.

Depending on their goals, cybercriminals will use different types of malware. The choice of malware depends on the target and what they are after.

Non-compliant and legacy systems are especially vulnerable to software exploitations. A non-compliant system is one which has not been updated with operating system or application patches or missing antivirus and firewall security software. Legacy systems are those which the vendor no longer provides support or fixes for vulnerabilities.

Refer to
Interactive Graphic
in online course

Refer to
Interactive Graphic
in online course

13.1.1.2   What Do You Already Know? - Malware

13.1.1.3   Viruses and Trojan Horses

The first and most common type of computer malware is a **virus**. Viruses require human action to propagate and infect other computers. For example, a virus can infect a computer when a victim opens an email attachment, opens a file on a USB drive, or downloads a file.

The virus hides by attaching itself to computer code, software, or documents on the computer. When opened, the virus executes and infects the computer. Figure 1 lists examples of what can happen once a virus has infected a host. Modern viruses are developed for specific nefarious intent such as those listed in Figure 2.

Cybercriminals also use **Trojan horses** to compromise hosts. A Trojan horse is a program that looks useful but also carries malicious code. Trojan horses are often provided with free online programs such as computer games. Unsuspecting users download and install the game, installing the Trojan malware.

There are several types of Trojan horses as described in Figure 3.

Viruses and Trojan horses are only two types of malware that cybercriminals use. There are many other types of malware that have been designed for specific purposes.

To fix some issues caused by viruses, it may be necessary to boot the computer using the Windows product disk and then use the Windows Recovery Console, which replaces the recovery console from Windows 2000, to run commands from a "clean" command environment. The Recovery Console is able to perform functions such as repairing the boot file and writing a new master boot record or volume boot record.

Refer to
Interactive Graphic
in online course

13.1.1.4   Types of Malware

Adware

- Adware is usually distributed by downloading online software.

- Adware can display unsolicited advertising using pop-up web browser windows, new toolbars, or unexpectedly redirect a webpage to a different website.

- Pop-up windows may be difficult to control as new windows can pop-up faster than the user can close them.

Refer to
Interactive Graphic
in online course

13.1.1.5   Check Your Understanding - Malware

13.1.2   Preventing Malware

Refer to
Interactive Graphic
in online course

13.1.2.1   Anti-Malware Programs

Malware is designed to invade privacy, steal information, damage the operating system, or allow hackers to take control of a computer. It is important that you protect computers and mobile devices using reputable antivirus software.

This is the seven-step best practice procedure for malware-removal:

1. Identify and research malware symptoms

2. Quarantine the infected systems

3. Disable System Restore (in Windows)

4. Remediate infected systems

5. Schedule scans and run updates

6. Enable System Restore and create restore points (in Windows)

7. Educate the end user

Today, antivirus programs are commonly referred to as anti-malware programs because many of them can also detect and block Trojans, rootkits, ransomware, spyware, keyloggers, and adware programs, as shown in Figure 1.

Anti-malware programs are the best line of defense against malware because they continuously look for known patterns against a database of known malware signatures. They can also use heuristic malware identification techniques which can detect specific behavior associated with some types of malware.

Anti-malware programs are started when a computer boots checking the system resources, drives, and memory for malware. It then runs continuously in the background scanning for malware signatures. When a virus is detected, the anti-malware software displays a warning similar as shown in the figure. It may automatically quarantine or delete the malware depending on software settings.

Anti-malware programs are available for Windows, Linux, and macOS by many reputable security organizations such as McAfee, Symantec (Norton), Kaspersky, Trend Micro, Bitdefender and more.

Note   Using two or more anti-malware solutions simultaneously can negatively impact computer performance.

The most common method of malware delivery is through email. Email filters are a line of defense against email threats, such as spam, viruses, and other malware, by filtering email messages before they reach the user's inbox. File attachments can also be scanned before they are opened.

Email filtering is available on most email applications or it can be installed at the organization's email gateway. In addition to detecting and filtering out spam messages, email filters also allow the user to create blacklists of known spammer domains and to whitelist known trusted or safe domains.

Malware can also be delivered through applications that are installed. Installation of software from untrusted sources can lead to the spread of malware such as Trojans. To mitigate this risk vendors implement various methods to restrict the ability of users to install untrusted software. Windows uses the system of Administrator and Standard user accounts along with User Account Control.(UAC) and system policies to help prevent installation of untrusted software.

Be cautious of malicious rogue antivirus products that may appear while browsing the Internet. Most of these rogue antivirus products display an ad or pop-up that looks like an actual Windows warning window, as shown in Figure 2. They usually state that the computer is infected and must be cleaned. Clicking anywhere inside the window may begin the download and installation of the malware.

When faced with a warning window that is suspect, never click inside the warning window. Close the tab or the browser to see if the warning window goes away. If the tab or browser does not close, press ALT+F4 to close the window or use the task manager to end the program. If the warning window does not go away, scan the computer using a known, good antivirus or adware protection program to ensure that the computer is not infected.

Click here to read a blog about rogue antivirus malware.

In Linux, users are prompted if they attempt to install untrusted software. The software is signed with a cryptographic private key and requires the public key for the repository to install the software. 4

Mobile OS vendors use the walled garden model to prevent installation of untrusted software. Under this model, apps are distributed from an approved store, such as the App Store for Apple or the Windows Store for Microsoft.

Refer to
Online Course
for Illustration

13.1.2.2   Signature File Updates

New malware is always being developed therefore anti-malware software must be updated regularly. This process is often enabled by default. However, a technician should know how to manually update anti-malware software signatures.

To update the signature file manually follow the suggested step in the figure.

Always download the signature files from the manufacturer's website to make sure the update is authentic and not corrupted by malware. This can put great demand on the manufacturer's website, especially when new malware is released. To avoid creating too much traffic at a single website, some manufacturers distribute their signature files for download to multiple download sites. These download sites are called mirrors.

Caution   When downloading signature files from a mirror, ensure that the mirror site is a legitimate site. Always link to the mirror site from the manufacturer's website.

Refer to **Video** in online course

13.1.2.3   Video Explanation - Protecting Against Malware

Click Play in the figure to view an explanation of protecting against malware.

Click here to read the transcript of this video.

Refer to **Online Course** for Illustration

13.1.2.4   Remediating Infected Systems

When a malware protection program detects that a computer is infected, it removes or quarantines the threat. However, the computer is most likely still at risk.

When malware is discovered on a home computer, you should update your anti-malware software and perform full scans of all your media. Many anti-malware programs can be set to run on system start before loading Windows. This allows the program to access all areas of the disk without being affected by the operating system or any malware.

When malware is discovered on a business computer, you should remove the computer from the network to prevent other computers from becoming infected. Unplug all network cables from the computer and disable all wireless connections. Next, follow the incident response policy that is in place. This may include notifying IT personnel, saving log files to removable media, or turning off the computer.

Removing malware may require that the computer be rebooted into Safe Mode. This prevents most drivers from loading. Some malware may require that a special tool from the anti-malware vendor be used. Be sure that you download these tools from a legitimate site.

For really stubborn malware, it may be necessary to contact a specialist to ensure that the computer has been completely cleaned. Otherwise, the computer may need to be reformatted, the operating system reinstalled, and recover your data from the most recent backups.

The OS system restore service may include infected files in a restore point. Therefore, once a computer has been cleaned of any malware, the system restore files should be deleted, as shown in the figure.

After remediation, you may need to fix some issues caused by viruses, it may be necessary to boot the computer using the Windows product disk and then use the Windows Recovery Console, which replaces the recovery console from Windows 2000, to run commands from a "clean" command environment. The Recovery Console can perform functions such as repairing the boot file and writing a new master boot record or volume boot record.

Refer to **Video** in online course

13.1.2.5   Video Explanation - Remediating an Infected System

Click Play in the figure to view an explanation of how to remediate an infected system.

Click here to read the transcript of this video.

Refer to **Interactive Graphic** in online course

13.1.2.6   Check Your Understanding - Preventing Malware

13.1.3   Network Attacks

Refer to
Interactive Graphic
in online course

13.1.3.1   Networks Are Targets

Perform an information query of a target

Attacker is looking for network information about a target using various tools including Google search, organizations website, whois, and more.

Refer to
Interactive Graphic
in online course

13.1.3.2   Types of TCP/IP Attacks

Denial of Service (DoS)

- In a DoS attack, the attacker completely overwhelms a target device with false requests to create a denial of service for legitimate users.

- An attacker could also cut or unplug a network cable to a critical network device to cause a network outage.

- DoS attacks may be caused for malicious reasons or used in conjunction with another attack.

Refer to
Interactive Graphic
in online course

13.1.3.3   Check Your Understanding - Identify the TCP/IP Attack

Refer to
Online Course
for Illustration

13.1.3.4   Zero-Day

The following two terms are commonly used to describe when a threat is detected:

- **Zero-day** - Sometimes also referred to as zero-day attacks, zero-day threat, or zero-day exploit. This is the day that an unknown vulnerability has been discovered by the vendor. The term is a reference to the amount of time that a vendor has had to address the vulnerability.

- **Zero-hour** - This is the moment when the exploit is discovered.

A network remains vulnerable between the zero-day and the time it takes a vendor to develop a solution.

In the example in the figure, a software vendor has learned of a new vulnerability. The software can be exploited until a patch that addresses the vulnerability is made available. Notice that in the example, it took several days and a few software patch updates to mitigate the threat.

How can networks be protected against all of the threats and zero-day attacks?

Refer to
Interactive Graphic
in online course

13.1.3.5   Protecting Against Network Attacks

Many network attacks are fast moving, therefore, network security professionals must adopt a more sophisticated view of the network architecture. There is no one solution to protect against all TCP/IP or zero-day attacks.

One solution is to use a defense-in-depth approach also known as a layered approach to security. This requires a combination of networking devices and services working together in tandem.

Consider the network in the figure. There are several security devices and services implemented to protect its users and assets against TCP/IP threats.

All network devices including the router and switches are also hardened as indicated by the combination locks on their respective icons. This indicates that they have been secured to prevent attackers from tampering with the devices.

13.1.4   Social Engineering Attacks

Refer to
Online Course
for Illustration

13.1.4.1   Social Engineering

To secure networks and hosts, organizations often deploy the network security solutions and latest anti-malware solutions for their hosts. However, they still have not addressed the weakest link ... the users.

Social engineering is likely the single most serious threat to a well-configured and well-secured network.

Cybercriminals use social engineering techniques to deceive and trick unsuspecting targets to reveal confidential information or violate security gain information. Social engineering is an access attack that attempts to manipulate individuals into performing actions or divulging confidential information.

Social engineers prey on people's weaknesses and often rely on human nature and people's willingness to be helpful.

Note   Social engineering is often used in conjunction with other network attacks.

Refer to
Interactive Graphic
in online course

13.1.4.2   What Do You Already Know? - Social Engineering Techniques

Refer to
Interactive Graphic
in online course

13.1.4.3   Social Engineering Techniques

There are many different ways to use social engineering techniques. Some social engineering techniques are used in-person while others may use the telephone or Internet.

For example, a hacker could call an authorized employee with an urgent problem that requires immediate network access. The hacker could appeal to the employee's vanity, invoke authority using name-dropping techniques, or appeal to the employee's greed.

Click the **+** sign in the figure to learn about social engineering techniques.

Refer to
Online Course
for Illustration

13.1.4.4   Protecting Against Social Engineering

Enterprises must train and educate their users about the risks of social engineering, and develop strategies to validate identities over the phone, via email, or in person.

The figure lists recommended practices that should be followed by all users.

Refer to
Interactive Graphic
in online course

13.1.4.5   Check Your Understanding - Personal and Corporate Social Engineering Techniques

13.2   Security Procedures

13.2.1   Security Policy

Refer to
Online Course
for Illustration

13.2.1.1   What is a Security Policy

A security policy is a set of security objectives that ensure the security of a network, the data, and the computers in an organization. The security policy is a constantly evolving document based on changes in technology, business, and employee requirements.

The security policy is usually created by a committee with members consisting of management and IT staff. Together they create and manage a document that should answer the questions listed in the figure.

A security policy typically addresses the items described in the figure. This list is not exhaustive and would include other items related specifically to the operation of an organization.

It is up to the IT staff to implement security policy specifications in the network. For example, to implement recommendations on a Windows host, IT staff could use the Local Security Policy feature.

Refer to
Interactive Graphic
in online course

13.2.1.2   Security Policy Category

Specifies authorized persons that can have access to network resources and outlines verification procedures.

Refer to
Online Course
for Illustration

13.2.1.3   Securing Devices and Data

The goal of the security policy is to ensure a safe network environment and to protect assets. As shown in the figure, an organization's assets include their data, employees, and physical devices such as computers and network equipment.

The security policy should identify hardware and equipment that can be used to prevent theft, vandalism, and data loss.

13.2.2   Protecting Physical Equipment

Refer to
Online Course
for Illustration

13.2.2.1   Physical Security

Physical security is as important as data security. For example, if a computer is taken from an organization, the data is also stolen or worse, lost.

Physical security involves securing:

- Access to an organization's premise
- Access to restricted areas
- The computing and network infrastructure

The level of physical security implemented depends on the organization as some have higher physical security requirements than others.

For example, consider how data centers, airports, or even military installations are secured. These organizations use perimeter security including fences, gates, and checkpoints posted with security guards.

Entrance to a building premise and restricted areas is secured using one or more locking mechanism. Building doors typically use self-closing and self-locking mechanisms. The type of locking mechanism required varies based on the level of security required.

A visitor accessing a secure building may have to pass through a security checkpoint manned by security guards. They may scan you and your belongings, and have you sign in an entry control roster when you enter the building and sign out when you leave.

Higher security organizations have all employees wear identification badges with photographs. These badges could be smart cards containing the user information and security clearance to access restricted areas. For additional security requirements, RFID badges can also be used with proximity badge readers to monitor the location of an individual.

Refer to
Interactive Graphic
in online course

13.2.2.2   Types of Secure Locks

Refer to
Interactive Graphic
in online course

13.2.2.3   Mantraps

In high-security environments, mantraps are often used to limit access to restricted areas and to prevent tailgating. A mantrap is a small room with two doors, one of which must be closed before the other can be opened.

Typically, a person enters the mantrap by unlocking one door. Once inside the mantrap, the first door closes and then the user must unlock the second door to enter the restricted area.

The figure illustrates how a mantrap is used to secure access to a restricted area.

Refer to
Online Course
for Illustration

13.2.2.4   Securing Computers and Network Hardware

Organizations must protect their computing and network infrastructure. This includes cabling, telecommunication equipment, and network devices.

There are several methods of physically protecting computer and networking equipment as listed in the figure.

Network equipment should only be installed in secured areas. As well, all cabling should be enclosed within conduits or routed inside walls to prevent unauthorized access or tampering. Conduit is a casing that protects the infrastructure media from damage and unauthorized access.

Access to physical switch ports and switch hardware should be restricted to authorized personnel by using a secure server room and locking hardware cabinets. To prevent the attachment of rogue or unauthorized client devices, switch ports should be disabled through the switch management software.

Factors that determine the most effective security equipment to use to secure equipment and data include:

- How the equipment is used

- Where the computer equipment is located

- What type of user access to data is required

For instance, a computer in a busy public place, such as a library, requires additional protection from theft and vandalism. In a busy call center, a server may need to be secured in a locked equipment room. Server locks can provide physical chassis security by preventing access to power switches, removable drives, and USB ports. Where it is necessary to use a laptop computer in a public place, a security dongle and key fob ensure that the computer locks if the user and laptop are separated. Another tool for physical security is the USB lock which is locked into place in a USB port and requires a key to be removed.

Security policies can be applied to mobile devices in a corporate network through Mobile Device Management software. MDM software can manage corporate-owned devices and Bring Your Own Device (BYOD). The software logs use of devices on the network and determines if it should be allowed to connect, known as onboarding, or not based on administrative policies.

Refer to Interactive Graphic in online course

13.2.2.5 Check Your Understanding - Locking Mechanisms

13.2.3 Protecting Data

Refer to Interactive Graphic in online course

13.2.3.1 Data - Your Greatest Asset

Data is likely to be an organization's most valuable assets. Organizational data can include research and development data, sales data, financial data, human resource and legal data, employee data, contractor data, and customer data.

Data can be lost or damaged in circumstances such as theft, equipment failure, or a disaster. Data loss or data exfiltration are terms used to describe when data is intentionally or unintentionally lost, stolen, or leaked to the outside world.

Data loss can negatively affect an organization in multiple ways as listed in Figure 1. Losing data regardless of circumstances can be detrimental or even catastrophic to an organization.

Data can be protected from data loss using the methods listed in Figure 2.

Data loss prevention (DLP) is preventing data loss or leakage. DLP software uses a dictionary database or algorithm to identify confidential data and block the transfer of that data to removable media or email if it does not conform to predefined policy.

Refer to **Interactive Graphic** in online course

13.2.3.2   Data Backups

Backing up data is one of the most effective ways of protecting against data loss. A data backup stores a copy of the information on a computer to removable backup media that can be kept in a safe place. If the computer hardware fails, the data can be restored from the backup to functional hardware.

Data backups should be performed on a regular basis as identified in the security policy. Data backups are usually stored offsite to protect the backup media if anything happens to the main facility. Windows hosts have a backup and restore utility. This is useful for users to backup their data to another drive or to a cloud-based storage provider. The macOS includes the **Time Machine** utility to perform backup and restore functions.

Click each **+** button in the figure to learn about backup consideration.

Refer to **Online Course** for Illustration

13.2.3.3   File and Folder Permissions

Permissions are rules you configure to limit folder or file access for an individual or for a group of users. The figure lists the permissions that are available for files and folders.

To configure file- or folder-level permissions in all versions of Windows, right-click the file or folder and select **Properties > Security > Edit...**

Users should be limited to only the resources they need in a computer or on a network. For example, they should not be able to access all files on a server if they only need access to a single folder. It may be easier to provide users access to the entire drive, but it is more secure to limit access to only the folder that is needed to perform their job. This is known as the principle of least privilege. Limiting access to resources also prevents malicious programs from accessing those resources if the user's computer becomes infected.

Folder redirection allows a user with administrative privileges to redirect the path of a local folder to a folder on a network share. This makes the folder's data available to the user when they log into any computer on the network where the network share is located. With user data redirected from local to network storage, administrators can back up the user data when the network data folders are backed up.

File and network share permissions can be granted to individuals or through membership within a group. These share permissions are much different than file and folder level NTFS permissions. If an individual or a group is denied permissions to a network share, this denial overrides any other permissions given. For example, if you deny someone permission to a network share, the user cannot access that share, even if the user is the administrator or part of the administrator group. The local security policy must outline which resources and the type of access allowed for each user and group.

When the permissions of a folder are changed, you are given the option to apply the same permissions to all sub-folders. This is known as permission propagation. Permission propagation is an easy way to apply permissions to many files and folders quickly. After parent folder permissions have been set, folders and files that are created inside the parent folder inherit the permissions of the parent folder.

Also, the location of the data and the action performed on the data determine how the permissions are propagated:

- **Data is moved to the same volume** - It will keep the original permissions

- **Data is copied to the same volume** - It will inherit new permissions

- **Data is moved to a different volume** - It will inherit new permissions

- **Data is copied to a different volume** - It will inherit new permissions

Refer to
Online Course
for Illustration

13.2.3.4 File and Folder Encryption

Encryption is often used to protect data. Encryption is where data is transformed using a complicated algorithm to make it unreadable. A special key must be used to return the unreadable information back into readable data. Software programs are used to encrypt files, folders, and even entire drives.

Encrypting File System (EFS) is a Windows feature that can encrypt data. EFS is directly linked to a specific user account. Only the user that encrypted the data will be able to access it after it has been encrypted using EFS. To encrypt data using EFS in all Windows versions, follow these steps:

Step 1.   Select one or more files or folders.

Step 2.   Right-click the selected data **>Properties**.

Step 3.   Click **Advanced...**

Step 4.   Select the **Encrypt contents to secure data** check box and click **OK**. Windows will display an informational message stating that it is applying attributes.

Step 5.   Files and folders that have been encrypted with EFS are displayed in green, as shown in the figure.

Refer to
Interactive Graphic
in online course

13.2.3.5 Windows BitLocker and BitLocker To Go

You can also choose to encrypt an entire hard drive using a feature called BitLocker. To use BitLocker, at least two volumes must be present on a hard disk. A system volume is left unencrypted and must be at least 100 MB. This volume holds the files required by Windows to boot.

Note   BitLocker is built into the Windows Enterprise editions, Windows 7 Ultimate, Windows 8 Pro, and Windows 10 Professional.

Before using BitLocker, the Trusted Platform Module (TPM) must be enabled in BIOS. The TPM is a specialized chip installed on the motherboard. The TPM stores information specific to the host computer, such as encryption keys, digital certificates, and passwords. Applications, like BitLocker, that use encryption can make use of the TPM chip. Figure 1 lists the steps to enable TPM on a Lenovo laptop.

To turn on BitLocker full disk encryption in all versions of Windows, follow the steps listed in Figure 2.

Once the steps are completed, the **Encryption in Progress** status bar is displayed. After the computer reboots, you can verify BitLocker is active as shown in Figure 3. You can click **TPM Administration** to view the TPM details, as shown in Figure 4.

BitLocker encryption can also be used with removable drives by using **BitLocker To Go**. **BitLocker To Go** does not use a TPM chip, but still provides encryption for the data and requires a password.

Refer to **Video** in online course

13.2.3.6   Video Demonstration - Bitlocker and Bitlocker To Go

Click Play in the figure to view a demonstration of how to use Bitlocker and Bitlocker To Go.

Click here to read the transcript of this video.

Refer to **Lab Activity** for this chapter

13.2.3.7   Lab - Bitlocker and Bitlocker To Go

In this lab, you will enable BitLocker encryption on a removable data drive and on the computer system drive.

Lab- Bitlocker and Bitlocker To Go

13.2.4   Data Destruction

Refer to **Online Course** for Illustration

13.2.4.1   Data Wiping Magnetic Media

Protecting data also includes removing files from storage devices when they are no longer needed. Simply deleting files or reformatting the drive may not be enough to ensure your privacy.

For example, deleting files from a magnetic hard disk drive does not remove them completely. The operating system removes the file reference in the file allocation table but the actual data remains on the drive. This deleted data is only overwritten when the hard drive stores new data in the same location.

Software tools can be used to recover folders, files, and even entire partitions. This could be a blessing if the erasure was accidental. But it could also be disastrous if the data is recovered by a malicious user.

For this reason, storage media should be fully erased using one or more of the methods listed in the figure.

Note   Data wiping and degaussing techniques are irreversible, and the data can never be recovered.

Refer to **Online Course** for Illustration

13.2.4.2   Data Wiping Other Media

SSDs are comprised of flash memory instead of magnetic platters. Common techniques used for erasing data such as degaussing are not effective with flash memory. Perform a secure erase to fully ensure that data cannot be recovered from an SSD and hybrid SSD.

Other storage media and documents (e.g., optical disks, eMMC, USB sticks) must also be destroyed. Use a shredding machine or incinerator that is designed to destroy documents and each type of media. For sensitive documents that must be kept, such as those with classified information or passwords, always keep them locked in a secure location.

When thinking about what devices must be wiped or destroyed, remember that devices besides computers and mobile devices store data. Printers and multifunction devices may also contain a hard drive that caches printed or scanned documents. This caching feature can be turned off in some instances, or the device needs to be wiped on a regular basis to ensure data privacy. It is a good security practice to set up user authentication on the device, if possible, to prevent an unauthorized person from changing any settings that concern privacy.

Refer to
Online Course
for Illustration

13.2.4.3   Hard Drive Recycling and Destruction

Companies with sensitive data should always establish clear policies for storage media disposal. There are two choices available when a storage media is no longer needed.

The media can either be:

- **Recycled** - Hard drives that have been wiped can be reused in other computers. The drive can be reformatted, and a new operating system installed. Two types of formatting can be performed as described in the figure.

- **Destroyed** - Destroying the hard drive fully ensures that data cannot be recovered from a hard drive. Specifically designed devices such as hard drive crushers, hard drive shredders, incinerators, and more can be used for large volumes of drives. Otherwise physically damaging the drive with a hammer is effective.

A company may choose an outside contractor to destroy their storage media. These contractors are typically bonded and follow strict governmental regulations. They may also offer a certificate of destruction to provide evidence that the media has been completely destroyed.

Refer to
Interactive Graphic
in online course

13.2.4.4   Check Your Understanding - Data Protection

13.3   Securing Windows Workstations

13.3.1   Securing a Workstation

Refer to
Online Course
for Illustration

13.3.1.1   Securing a Computer

Computers and workstations should be secured from theft. This is a standard practice in a company as computers are typically secured in locked rooms.

To prevent unauthorized users from stealing or accessing local computers and network resources, lock your workstation, laptop, or server when you are not present. This includes physical security as well as password security.

If you must leave a computer in an open public area, cable locks should be used to deter theft.

Data displayed on your computer screen should also be protected. This is especially true when using a laptop in a public location such as an airport, coffee house, or customer site. Use a privacy screen to protect the information displayed on your laptop screen from prying eyes. A privacy screen is a clear plastic panel attached to the computer screen that only permits the user in front of the screen to see the information displayed.

Access to your computer must also be protected. There are three levels of password protection that can be used on a computer as described in the figure.

Refer to
Online Course
for Illustration

13.3.1.2   Securing BIOS

A Windows, Linux, or Mac login password can be bypassed. Your computer may be booted from a CD or flash drive with a different operating system. After it is booted, the malicious user could access or erase your files.

Setting a BIOS or UEFI password can prevent someone from booting the computer. It also prevents someone from altering the configured settings. In the figure, for example, a user would have to enter the configured BIOS password to access the BIOS configuration.

All users, regardless of user account, share BIOS passwords. UEFI passwords can be set on a per-user basis. However, an authentication server is required.

Caution   A BIOS or UEFI password is relatively difficult to reset, therefore be sure you remember it.

Refer to
Interactive Graphic
in online course

13.3.1.3   Securing Windows Login

The most common type of password protection is the computer login. This is typically where you enter a password and sometimes a username as shown in Figure 1.

Depending on your computer system, Windows 10 may also support other sign-in options. Specifically, Windows 10 supports the following sign-in options:

- **Windows Hello** - Feature that enables Window you to use facial recognition or use your fingerprint to access Windows.
- **PIN** - Enter a pre-configured PIN number to access Windows.
- **Picture password** - You choose a picture and gestures to use with the picture to create a unique password.
- **Dynamic lock** - Feature makes Windows lock when a pre-paired device such as a cell phone goes out of range of the PC.

Figure 2 displays a sample PIN authentication screen instead of the password login option. In this example, a user could change the sign-in option to either password, fingerprint, or facial recognition. If a user chose to authenticate using their fingerprint, they would then scan their finger as shown in Figure 3.

To change sign-in options on a Windows 10 computer, use **Start > Settings > Accounts > Sign-in options** as shown in Figure 4. In this window, you could also change your password, set a PIN number, enable picture password, and dynamic lock.

Refer to
Interactive Graphic
in online course

13.3.1.4   Local Password Management

Password management for stand-alone Windows computers can be set locally using the Windows **User Accounts** tool. To create, remove, or modify a password in Windows, use **Control Panel > User Accounts** as shown in Figure 1.

It is also important to make sure that computers are secure when users are away. A security policy should contain a rule about requiring a computer to lock when the screensaver starts. This will ensure that after a short time away from the computer, the screen saver will start and then the computer cannot be used until the user logs in.

In all versions of Windows, use **Control Panel > Personalization > Screen Saver** as shown in Figure 2. Choose a screen saver and a wait time, and then select the **On resume, display logon screen** option.

Refer to
Online Course
for Illustration

13.3.1.5   Usernames and Passwords

The system administrator usually defines a naming convention for usernames when creating network logins. A common example of a username is the first letter of the person's first name and then the entire last name. Keep the naming convention simple so that people do not have a hard time remembering it. Usernames, like passwords, are an important piece of information and should not be revealed.

Password guidelines are an important component of a security policy. Any user that must log on to a computer or connect to a network resource should be required to have a password. Passwords help prevent theft of data and malicious acts. Passwords also help to confirm that the logging of events is valid by ensuring that the user is the correct person.

The figure lists guidelines to create strong passwords.

Refer to
Interactive Graphic
in online course

13.3.1.6   Check your Understanding - Secure a Workstation

13.3.2   Windows Local Security Policy

Refer to
Online Course
for Illustration

13.3.2.1   The Windows Local Security Policy

In most networks that use Windows computers, Active Directory is configured with Domains on a Windows Server. Windows computers are members of a domain. The administrator configures a Domain Security Policy that applies to all computers that join. Account policies are automatically set when a user logs in to Windows.

For stand-alone computers that are not part of an Active Directory domain, the Windows Local Security Policy can be used to enforce security settings.

To access Local Security Policy in Windows 7 and Vista, use **Start > Control Panel > Administrative Tools > Local Security Policy.**

In Windows 8, 8.1, and Windows 10, use **Search > secpol.msc** and then click **secpol.**

The Local Security Policy Tool opens, as shown in the figure.

Note   In all versions of Windows, you can use the **Run** command **secpol.msc** to open the Local Security Policy tool.

Refer to
Interactive Graphic
in online course

13.3.2.2   Account Policies Security Settings

The security policy will identify the password policies required. The Windows local security policy could be used to set implement the password policies. When assigning passwords, the level of password control should match the level of protection required.

Note   Use strong passwords whenever possible.

Use **Account Policies > Password Policy** to enforce password requirements as shown in Figure 1. Click on the hotspots to learn about the currently configured Password Policy settings.

Use **Account Policies > Account Lockout Policy** to prevent brute-force attacks as shown in Figure 2. In a brute force attack, software attempts to break a password by trying every possible combination of characters. Click on the hotspots to learn about the currently configured Account Lockout Policy settings. This Account Lockout Policy would also protect against a dictionary attack. This is a type of brute-force attack that attempts every word in a dictionary hoping to gain access. An attacker may also use a rainbow table. Rainbow tables are a refinement of the dictionary attack approach and involves a precomputed lookup table of all probably plaintext passwords and their matching hashes. The hash value of a stored password can be looked up in the table and the corresponding plaintext discovered.

Refer to
Online Course
for Illustration

13.3.2.3   Local Policies Security Settings

The Local Policy in the Local Security Policy is used to configure audit policies, user rights policies, and security policies.

It is useful to log successful and unsuccessful login attempts. Use the **Local Policies > Audit Policy** to enable auditing as shown in the figure. In this example, the **Audit account login events** auditing is being enabled for all logon events.

The **User Rights Assignment** and **Security Options** provide a wide variety of security options beyond the scope of this course. However, some settings will be explored in the lab.

Refer to
Online Course
for Illustration

13.3.2.4   Exporting the Local Security Policy

An administrator may need to implement an extensive local policy for user rights and security options. This policy most likely would need to be replicated on each system. To help simplify this process, the **Local Security Policy** can be exported and copied to other Windows hosts.

The steps to replicate a Local Security Policy on other computers are:

1. Use the **Action > Export List...** feature as shown in the figure to export the policy of a secure host.

2. Save the policy with a name, such as **workstation.inf**. to external media.

3. Then import the Local Security Policy file to other stand-alone computers.

Refer to
Lab Activity
for this chapter

13.3.2.5   Lab - Configure Windows Local Security Policy

In this lab, you will configure Windows Local Security Policy. You will modify password requirements, enable auditing, configure some user rights, and set some security options. You will then use Event Manager to view logged information.

Lab - Configure Windows Local Security Policy

Refer to
Interactive Graphic
in online course

13.3.2.6   Check Your Understanding- Local Security Policy

13.3.3   Managing Users and Groups

Refer to
Interactive Graphic
in online course

13.3.3.1   Maintaining Accounts

Refer to
Online Course
for Illustration

13.3.3.2   Managing Users Account Tools and User Account Tasks

A regular maintenance task for administrators is to create and remove users from the network, change account passwords, or change user permissions. You must have administrator privileges to manage users.

To accomplish these tasks, you can use either User Account Control (UAC) or Local Users and Group Manager. The figure shows how to access these.

Managing user account tasks allows you to create an account, reset the account password, disable or activate an account, delete an account, rename an account, assign a login script to an account, and assign a home folder to an account.

Refer to
Interactive Graphic
in online course

13.3.3.3   Local Users and Groups Manager

The Local Users and Groups tool can limit the ability of users and groups to perform certain actions by assigning rights and permissions as described in Figure 1.

To configure all of the users and groups on a computer using the **Local Users and Groups Manager** tools type **lusrmgr.msc** in the Search box, or Run Line utility.

The **Local Users and Groups > Users** window displays current user accounts on the computer. It includes the built-in administrator and built-in guest accounts as described in Figure 2.

Double-clicking a user or right-clicking and choosing **Properties** opens the user properties window, as shown in Figure 3. This window allows you to change the user options defined when the user was created. Additionally, it permits you to lock an account. The window also lets you assign a user to a group using the **Member of** tab, or controlling which folders the user has access to using the **Profile** tab.

To add a user, click the **Action** menu and select **New User**. This opens the New User window, as shown in Figure 4. From here you can assign a username, full name, description, and account options.

Note   Some versions of Windows also include the built-in Power User account which possesses most of the power of an administrator but for security reasons, lacks some of the privileges of an administrator.

Refer to
Interactive Graphic
in online course

13.3.3.4 Managing Groups

Users can be assigned to groups for easier management. Tasks used to manage local groups are listed in Figure 1.

The Local Users and Groups Manager tool is used to manage local groups on a Windows computer. Use **Control Panel > Administrative Tools > Computer Management > Local Users and Groups** to open the Local Users and Groups Manager.

From the Local Users and Groups window, double-click **Groups**.to list all of the local groups on the computer. There are many built-in groups available, as shown in Figure 2. However, the three most commonly used groups are described in the figure.

It is important to note that running your computer as a member of the Administrators group makes the system vulnerable to Trojan horses and other security risks. It is recommended that you add your domain user account only to the Users group (and not to the Administrators group) to perform routine tasks, including running programs and visiting internet sites. When it becomes necessary to perform administrative tasks on the local computer, use **Run as Administrator** to start a program using administrative credentials.

Double click a group to view its properties. Figure 3 for example, is displaying the properties of the Guest group.

To create a new group, click the **Action > New Group** to open the **New Group** window as shown in Figure 4. From here you can create new groups and assign users to them.

Refer to
Online Course
for Illustration

13.3.3.5 Active Directory Users and Computers

While local accounts are stored in the in the Local Security Accounts database of a local machine, domains accounts are stored in the Active Directory on a Windows Server Domain Controller (DC) and are accessible from any computer joined to the domain. Only domain administrators can create domain accounts on a Domain Controller.

The Active Directory is a database of all computers, users, and services in an Active Directory domain. The Active Directory Users and Computers console on Windows server is used to manage Active Directory users, groups, and Organizational Units (OUs). Organizational units provide a way to subdivide a domain into smaller administrative units. The Active Directory Users and Computers, an administrator can create more OUs in which to place accounts or add accounts to existing OUs.

To create a new user account, right-click the container or OU which will contain the account and choose **New User**. Enter the user's information such as name, last name and logon name, then click **Next**, and then set an initial password for the user. By default, the option to force the user to reset their password on first sign in is selected. If a user should lock themselves out of their account with too many password attempts, the administrator can open Active Directory Users and Computers, right-click on the user object, select **Properties**, and check **Unlock account.**

To delete a user account simply right-click the user object and select **Delete**. Note however that once an account is deleted it may not be retrievable. Another option is to disable an account rather than to delete it. Once an account is disabled, the user is denied access to the network until the administrator re-enables the account.

To create a new group account in active directory is similar to creating a new user. Open Active directory Users and Computers select the container that will house the group, click **Action**, click **New** and then click **Group.** Fill in the group details and click **OK.**

Refer to
Lab Activity
for this chapter

13.3.3.6   Lab - Configure Users and Groups in Windows

In this lab, you will create users and groups and delete users using the Local Users and Groups Manager. You will also assign group and user permission to the folders.

Lab - Configure Users and Groups in Windows

Refer to
Interactive Graphic
in online course

13.3.3.7   Check your Understanding - User Account Tools and User Account Tasks

13.3.4   Windows Firewall

Refer to
Interactive Graphic
in online course

13.3.4.1   Firewalls

A firewall protects computers and networks by preventing undesirable traffic from entering internal networks. For instance, the top topology in Figure 1 illustrates how the firewall enables traffic from an internal network host to exit the network and return to the inside network. The bottom topology illustrates how traffic initiated by the outside network (i.e., the internet) is denied access to the internal network.

A firewall could allow outside users controlled access to specific services. For instance, servers accessible to outside users are usually located on a special network referred to as the demilitarized zone (DMZ) as shown in Figure 2. The DMZ zone enables a network administrator to apply specific policies for hosts connected to that network. For example, click play in Figure 3 to see how the DMZ server provides web, FTP, and email services (i.e, SMTP and IMAP) to external users. Notice how the firewall only permits access to those server services and denies all other outside requests.

Firewall services can be provided as follows:

- **Host-based firewall** - Using software such as Windows Defender Firewall.

- **Small office home office (SOHO)** - Network-based solution using a home or small office wireless router. These devices not only provide routing and WI-FI services, but they also provide NAT, DHCP, and firewall services. Many routers also provide settings listed in Figure 4.

- **Small to medium-sized organization** - Network-based solution using a dedicated device such as a Cisco Adaptive Security Appliance (ASA) or enabled on a Cisco Integrated Services Router (ISR). These devices use access control lists (ACLs) and advanced features to filter packets based on their header information including source and destination IP address, protocol, source and destination TCP/UDP ports, and more.

The focus of this section is on the host-based firewall solution using Windows Firewall.

Refer to
Online Course
for Illustration

13.3.4.2   Software Firewalls

A software firewall is a program that provides firewall services on a computer to allow or deny traffic to the computer. The software firewall applies a set of rules to data transmissions through inspection and filtering of data packets.

Windows Firewall is an example of a software firewall that helps prevent cybercriminals and malware from gaining access to your computer. It is installed by default when the Windows OS is installed.

Note   In Windows 10 the Windows Firewall was renamed to Windows Defender Firewall. In this section, Windows Firewall includes Windows Defender Firewall.

Windows Firewall settings are configured using the Windows Firewall window. To change Windows Firewall settings, you must have administrator privileges to open the Windows Firewall window.

To open the Windows Firewall window, use **Control Panel > Windows Firewall**. The example in the figure displays the Windows 10 Windows Defender Firewall window.

Refer to
Online Course
for Illustration

13.3.4.3   Windows Firewall

Software firewall features are applied to a network connection. Software firewalls have a standard set of inbound and outbound rules that are enabled depending on the location of the connected network.

In the example in Figure 1, firewall rules are enabled for a private network, a guest or public network, or a corporate domain network. The window displays the settings for the private network as it is the currently connected network. To display the settings for the domain or guest networks, click on the drop-down arrow beside the **Not connected** label.

From this Windows Firewall window, you can enable or disable Windows Firewall, change notification settings, allow apps through the firewall, configure advanced settings, or restore firewall defaults.

To disable or re-enable Windows Firewall or change notifications for a network, click on either **Change notifications settings** or **Turn Windows Defender Firewall on or off** to open the Customize Settings window shown in Figure 2.

If you wish to use a different software firewall, you will need to disable Windows Firewall. To disable the Windows Firewall in Windows 7 through Windows 10, follow the steps listed in Figure 3.

Note   Windows Firewall is enabled by default. Do not disable Windows Firewall on a Windows host unless another firewall software is enabled.

Refer to
Online Course
for Illustration

13.3.4.4   Configuring Exceptions in Windows Firewall

You can allow or deny access to specific programs or ports from the Windows Firewall window. To configure exceptions and allow or block applications or ports, click on **Allow an app or feature through the Windows Firewall** to open the Allowed apps window shown in Figure 1.

From this window, you can add, change, or remove the allowed programs and ports on the different networks. Figure 2 lists the steps required to add programs through the Windows Firewall.

Refer to
Online Course
for Illustration

13.3.4.5   Windows Firewall with Advanced Security

Another Windows tool that is available to provide even greater access control with Windows Firewall policies is the Windows Firewall with Advanced Security. It is called Windows Defender Firewall with Advanced Security in Windows 10.

To open it, from the Windows Firewall window, click on **Advanced settings** to open it as shown in the figure.

Note   Alternatively, you can enter **wf.msc** in the search box and press enter.

Windows Defender Firewall with Advanced Security provides these features:

- **Inbound and Outbound Rules** - You can configure inbound rules that are applied to incoming internet traffic and outbound rules which are applied to traffic leaving your computer going to the network. These rules can specify ports, protocols, programs, services, users, or computers.

- **Connection Security Rules** - Connection security rules secure traffic between two computers. It requires that both computers have the same rules defined and enabled.

- **Monitoring** - You can display the firewall inbound or outbound active rules or any active connection security rules.

Refer to
Lab Activity
for this chapter

13.3.4.6 Lab - Configure Windows Firewall

In this lab, you will explore the Windows Firewall and configure some advanced settings.

Lab - Configure Windows Firewall

Refer to
Interactive Graphic
in online course

13.3.4.7   Check your Understanding - Windows Firewall

13.3.5   Web Security

Refer to
Online Course
for Illustration

13.3.5.1   Web Security

Web browsers are not only used for web browsing, they are also now used to run other applications including Microsoft 365, Google docs, interface for remote access SSL users, and more. To help support these additional features, browsers use plug-ins to support other content. However, some of these plug-ins may also introduce security problems.

Browsers are targets and should be secured. The figure lists some features to secure web browsers.

When browsing, many websites and services require the use of authentication for access. Recently, it has become common to require multifactor authentication over a traditional username and password. Multifactor authentication involves using a combination of different technologies, such as a password, a smart card, and biometrics, to authentication a user. For example, two-factor authentication combines something a user has, such as a smart card with something they know like a password or pin. Three-factor authentication combines all three, something a user knows, something they have, and some type of biometric component like a thumb or eye retina scan.

Recently, authenticator applications have become a popular method for multifactor authentication. For example, the service may require both a password and a registered phone or email address. To access the service an authenticator application sends a code called a one-time password (OTP) to the registered phone or email address. The user must supply their account username and password plus the OTP code to authenticate.

Once authenticated, the system may grant a software token to the application or device which was used to authenticate with. The software token allows the user to perform actions on the system without the need to repeatedly authenticate. If the token system is not secure, a third party may be able to capture it and act as the user. This is known as a replay attack. The token should be designed to prevent replay attacks, being time limited or being used only once.

Refer to
Interactive Graphic
in online course

13.3.5.2 InPrivate Browsing

Web browsers retain information about the web pages that you visit, the searches that you perform, and other identifiable information including usernames, passwords, and more. Although convenient on a personal computer, this is a concern when using a public computer such as a computer in a library, hotel business center, or an internet café. The information retained by web browsers can be recovered and exploited to steal your identity, your money, or change your passwords on important accounts.

To improve security when using a public computer, always:

- **Clear your browsing history** - All web browser have a way to clear their browsing history, cookies, files, and more. Figure 1 lists the steps to clear the browsing history in Microsoft Edge. Notice that you also have the option to always clear the browsing data when the browser is closed.

- **Use the InPrivate mode** - All web browsers provide the ability to browse the web anonymously without retaining information. Using an InPrivate browser temporarily stores files and cookies and deletes them when the InPrivate session is ended.

Figure 2 lists the steps to open an InPrivate window in Microsoft Edge. Notice that the new window is identified with an InPrivate label on the top left-hand corner of the browser. For Internet Explorer 11, use **Tools > InPrivate Browsing** as shown in Figure 3.

Note As an alternative, you could press **Ctrl+Shift+P** to open an InPrivate window.

Refer to
Online Course
for Illustration

13.3.5.3 Pop-up Blocker

A pop-up is a web browser window that opens on top of another web browser window. Some pop-ups are initiated while browsing, such as a link on a page that opens a pop-up to deliver additional information or a close-up of a picture. Other pop-ups are initiated by a website or advertiser and are often unwanted or annoying, especially when multiple pop-ups are opened at the same time on a web page.

Most web browsers offer the ability to block pop-up windows. This enables a user to limit or block most of the pop-ups that occur while browsing the web.

The figure lists the steps to enable the Internet Edge Pop-up Blocker feature. Figure

To enable the Internet Explorer 11 Pop-up Blocker feature, use **Tools > Pop-up Blocker > Turn on Pop-up Blocker.**

Refer to
Interactive Graphic
in online course

13.3.5.4 SmartScreen Filter

Web browsers may also offer additional web filtering capabilities. For instance, Internet Explorer 11 provides the SmartScreen Filter feature. This feature detects phishing websites, analyzes websites for suspicious items, and checks downloads against a list that contains sites and files that are known to be malicious.

The figure lists the steps to enable SmartScreen filter in Microsoft Edge.

In Internet Explorer 11, use **Tools > Smartscreen Filter > Turn on Smartscreen Filter.**

Refer to
Online Course
for Illustration

13.3.5.5 ActiveX Filtering

Some web browsers may require you to install an ActiveX control. The problem is that ActiveX controls can be used for malicious reasons.

ActiveX filtering allows for web browsing without running ActiveX controls. After an ActiveX control has been installed for a website, the control runs on other websites as well. This may degrade performance or introduce security risks. When ActiveX filtering is enabled, you can choose which websites are allowed to run ActiveX controls. Sites that are not approved cannot run these controls, and the browser does not show notifications for you to install or enable them.

To enable ActiveX filtering in Internet Explorer 11, use **Tools > ActiveX Filtering**. The example in the figure displays that ActiveX filtering is enabled. Clicking the **ActiveX Filtering** again would disable ActiveX.

To view a website that contains ActiveX content when ActiveX filtering is enabled, click the blue **ActiveX Filtering** icon in the address bar, and click **Turn off ActiveX Filtering.**

After viewing the content, you can turn ActiveX filtering for the website back on by following the same steps.

Note Microsoft Edge does not support ActiveX filtering.

Refer to
Interactive Graphic
in online course

13.3.5.6 Check Your Understanding - Web Security

13.3.6 Security Maintenance

Refer to
Online Course
for Illustration

13.3.6.1 Restrictive Settings

Devices often come with security features that are not enabled or the security features left to their defaults. For example, many home users leave the wireless routers with default passwords and open wireless authentication because it is "easier".

Some devices are shipped with permissive settings. This enables access through all ports, except those explicitly denied. The problem is that the default permissive settings leave many devices exposed to attackers.

Many devices now ship with restrictive settings. They must be configured to enable access. Any packet not explicitly permitted is denied.

It is your responsibility to secure devices and configure restrictive settings whenever possible.

Refer to
Interactive Graphic
in online course

13.3.6.2   Disable Auto-Play

Older Windows hosts used AutoRun to simplify the user experience. When new media (e.g., flash drive, CD, or DVD drive) is inserted into the computer, AutoRun would automatically look for a special file called **autorun.inf** and execute it. Malicious users have taken advantage of this feature to quickly infect hosts.

Newer Windows hosts now use a similar feature called AutoPlay. With AutoPlay, you can determine which media will run automatically. AutoPlay provides additional controls and can prompt the user to choose an action based on the content of the new media.

Use the **Control Panel > AutoPlay** window, shown in Figure 1, to open the AutoPlay window and configure the actions associated with specific media. However, you are still just one click away from unknowingly running malware through the AutoPlay dialog.

Therefore, the most secure solution is to turn off AutoPlay. Figure 2 lists the steps to disable AutoPlay.

Refer to
Online Course
for Illustration

13.3.6.3   Operating System Service Packs and Security Patches

Patches are code updates that manufacturers provide to prevent a newly discovered virus or worm from making a successful attack. From time to time, manufacturers combine patches and upgrades into a comprehensive update application called a service pack.

It is critical to apply security patches and OS updates whenever possible. Many devastating virus attacks could have been much less severe if more users had downloaded and installed the latest service pack.

Windows routinely checks the Windows Update website for high-priority updates that can help protect a computer from the latest security threats. These updates include security updates, critical updates, and service packs. Depending on the setting you choose, Windows automatically downloads and installs any high-priority updates that your computer needs or notifies you as these updates become available.

Refer to
Interactive Graphic
in online course

13.3.6.4   Check your Understanding - Security Maintenance

13.4   Wireless Security

13.4.1   Configure Wireless Security

Refer to
Interactive Graphic
in online course

13.4.1.1   What Do You Already Know? - Wireless Security

Refer to
Interactive Graphic
in online course

13.4.1.2 Common Communication Encryption Types

Hash encoding

Hash encoding, or hashing, ensures the integrity of the message. This means that the message is not corrupt, nor has it been tampered with during transmission. Hashing uses a mathematical function to create a numeric value, called a message digest that is unique to the data. If even one character is changed, the function output will not be the same. The function can only be used one way. Knowing only the message digest does not allow an attacker to recreate the original message, and changed message would have a completely different hash output. Hash encoding is illustrated in Figure 1. The most popular hashing algorithm is now Secure Hash Algorithm (SHA) which is replacing the older Message Digest 5 (MD5) algorithm.

Refer to
Online Course
for Illustration

13.4.1.3 Wi-Fi Configuration Best Practices

Radio waves used to transmit data in wireless networks make it easy for attackers to monitor and collect data without physically connecting to a network. Attackers gain access to an unprotected wireless network simply by being within range of it. A technician needs to configure access points and wireless NICs with an appropriate level of security.

A robust wireless network with sufficient coverage for users in all locations requires the proper placement of antenna and access points. If placing the access point in proximity of the provider's cabling does not provide enough coverage, then extenders and repeaters can be used to boost the wireless signals to locations where it is weak. A site survey can also be performed to identify signal dead zones.

Reducing the power output on an Access Point may help to prevent war driving, however it may also result in insufficient wireless coverage for legitimate users.

Increasing the power output of an Access Point can increase coverage, however it can also increase the chance of signal bouncing and interference. There may also be legal restrictions on wireless power levels. Because of these potential issues it is usually best to set power levels to auto negotiate.

When installing wireless services, apply wireless security techniques immediately to prevent unwanted access to the network. Wireless access points should be configured with basic security settings that are compatible with the existing network security. When setting up the access point on a Wi-Fi network, the management software will prompt for a new administrator password. There may also be an option to change the default username of the administrator account, which is slightly more secure that using the default name configured. Also, on smaller networks, you can assign IP addresses statically instead of using DHCP. This prevents any computer from connecting to the access point unless it is configured with the correct IP address.

Additional security, such as parental controls or content filtering are services that may be available in a wireless router. Internet access times can be limited to certain hours or days, specific IP addresses can be blocked, and key words can be blocked. The location and depth of these features varies depending on the manufacturer and model of the router.

One way to provide a level of security on Wi-Fi networks is to change the default Service Set ID (SSID) and to disable broadcast of the SSID. Access point vendors use a default SSIDs for their devices based on the devices brand and model. These should be changed to something users will recognize and will not get confused with other nearby networks. Most access points broadcast the SSID by default. A level of privacy can be gained by disabling the broadcast of the SSID. This will prevent wireless network adapters form finding the network unless they are specifically configured with the name of the network SSID. Disabling the SSID broadcast provides very little security. Someone who knows the SSID of that network can simply enter it manually. A wireless network will also broadcast the SSID during a computer scan. The SSID can be easily intercepted in transit.

Refer to **Interactive Graphic** in online course

13.4.1.4 Authentication Methods

Refer to **Interactive Graphic** in online course

13.4.1.5 Wireless Security Modes

WPA2

Use a wireless encryption system to encode the information being sent to prevent unwanted capture and use of data. Most wireless access points support several different security modes As discussed in a previous chapter, always implement the strongest security mode (WPA2) possible.

Refer to **Online Course** for Illustration

13.4.1.6 Firmware Updates

Most wireless routers offer upgradable firmware. Firmware releases may contain fixes for common problems reported by customers as well as security vulnerabilities. You should periodically check the manufacturer's website for updated firmware. After it is downloaded, you can use the GUI to upload the firmware to the wireless router, as shown in the figure. Users will be disconnected from the WLAN and the Internet until the upgrade finishes. The wireless router may need to reboot several times before normal network operations are restored.

Refer to **Interactive Graphic** in online course

13.4.1.7 Firewalls

A hardware firewall is a physical filtering component that inspects data packets from the network before they reach computers and other devices on a network. A hardware firewall is a freestanding unit that does not use the resources of the computers it is protecting, so there is no impact on processing performance. The firewall can be configured to block multiple individual ports, a range of ports, or even traffic specific to an application. Most wireless routers also include an integrated hardware firewall.

A hardware firewall passes two different types of traffic into your network:

- Responses to traffic that originates from inside your network
- Traffic destined for a port that you have intentionally left open

Hardware and software firewalls protect data and equipment on a network from unauthorized access. A firewall should be used in addition to security software. Figure 2 compares hardware and software firewalls.

Refer to **Interactive Graphic** in online course

13.4.1.8 Port Forwarding and Port Triggering

Hardware firewalls can be used to block ports to prevent unauthorized access in and out of a LAN. However, there are situations when specific ports must be opened so that certain programs and applications can communicate with devices on different networks. Port forwarding is a rule-based method of directing traffic between devices on separate networks.

Refer to
Interactive Graphic
in online course

13.4.1.9   Universal Plug and Play

Universal Plug and Play (UPnP) is a protocol that enables devices to dynamically forward traffic through network ports without the need for user intervention or configuration. Port forwarding is often used for streaming media, hosting games, or providing services from home and small business computers to the internet.

Refer to Packet
Tracer Activity
for this chapter

13.4.1.10   Packet Tracer - Configure Wireless Security

In this Packet Tracer activity, you will configure a wireless router to use WPA2 personal as a security method, rely on MAC filtering to increase security, and support single port forwarding.

Packet Tracer - Configure Wireless Security - Instructions

Packet Tracer - Configure Wireless Security - Activity

13.5   Basic Troubleshooting Process for Security

13.5.1   Applying the Troubleshooting Process to Security

Refer to
Online Course
for Illustration

13.5.1.1   The Six Steps of the Troubleshooting Process

Refer to
Online Course
for Illustration

13.5.1.2   Identify the Problem

Security-related issues can be as simple as preventing shoulder surfing or it can be more complex, such as having to remove infected files from multiple networked computers. Use the troubleshooting steps in the figure as guidelines to help you diagnose and repair security related problems.

Computer technicians must be able to analyze a security threat and determine the appropriate method to protect assets and repair damage. The first step in the troubleshooting process is to identify the problem. The figure shows a list of open-ended and closed-ended questions to ask the customer.

Refer to
Online Course
for Illustration

13.5.1.3   Establish a Theory of Probable Cause

After you have talked to the customer, you can begin to establish a theory of probable causes. You may need to conduct additional internal or external research based on the customer's description of the symptoms. The figure shows a list of some common probable causes for security problems.

Refer to
Online Course
for Illustration

13.5.1.4   Test the Theory to Determine Cause

After you have developed some theories about what is wrong, test your theories to determine the cause of the problem. The figure shows a list of quick procedures that can determine the exact cause of the problem or even correct the problem. If a quick procedure corrects the problem, you can verify full system functionality. If a quick procedure does not correct the problem, you might need to research the problem further to establish the exact cause.

Refer to
Online Course
for Illustration

13.5.1.5   Establish a Plan of Action to Resolve the Problem and Implement the Solution

After you have determined the exact cause of the problem, establish a plan of action to resolve the problem and implement the solution. The figure shows some sources you can use to gather additional information to resolve an issue.

Refer to
Online Course
for Illustration

13.5.1.6   Verify Full System Functionality and, If Applicable Implement Preventive Measures

After you have corrected the problem, verify full functionality and, if applicable, implement preventive measures. The figure shows a list of the steps to verify the solution.

Refer to
Online Course
for Illustration

13.5.1.7   Document Findings, Actions, and Outcomes

In the final step of the troubleshooting process, you must document your findings, actions, and outcomes. The figure shows a list of the tasks required to document the problem and the solution.

13.5.2   Common Problems and Solutions for Security

Refer to
Interactive Graphic
in online course

13.5.2.1   Common Problems and Solutions for Security

Refer to
Lab Activity
for this chapter

13.5.2.2   Lab - Document Customer Information in a Work Order

In this lab, you will document customer information in a work order.

Lab - Document Customer Information in a Work Order

13.6   Summary

In this chapter, you learned that there are many types of threats created to disrupt computers and networks, the greatest and most common being malware. Malware is software developed by cybercriminals to perform malicious acts. Malware is typically installed on a computer without user knowledge. You learned about common types of computer malware such as viruses, trojan horses, adware, ransomware, rootkits, spyware, and worms and mitigation techniques to project against them. You also learned about types of TCP/IP attacks like denial of service, spoofing, syn flood, and man-in-the-middle.

Organizations often deploy network security solutions and the latest anti-malware solutions to secure their networks. However, this does not address what is likely the single most serious threat to a well-configured and well-secured network, social engineering. You learned that Cybercriminals use social engineering techniques to deceive and trick unsuspecting individuals to reveal confidential information or account login credentials. Social engineering attacks take many forms such as phishing, pretexting, baiting, and dumpster diving.

You learned about the importance of a security policy in defining security objectives that ensure the security of the network, the data, and the computers in an organization. You learned that the policy should specify the persons authorized to access network resources, the minimum requirements for passwords, acceptable uses for network resources, how remote users can access the network, and how security incidents will be handled. Part of the security policy addresses protecting physical equipment. You learned about different types of secure locks and mantraps that can limit access to restricted areas and prevent tailgating.

Data can be easily lost or damaged in circumstances such as theft, equipment failure, or a disaster. The risk of data loss can be mitigated by using data backups, file and folder permissions, and file and folder encryption. You completed a lab using BitLocker encryption to encrypt the data on a removable USB data drive and on the OS drive of a Windows PC.

You learned how to secure a Windows workstation by setting passwords on the BIOS to prevent the operating system from booting and changing BIOS settings, setting login passwords to prevent access to the local computer, and setting network passwords to prevent access to network resources. You also learned how to set local security policies in Windows.

You completed a lab configuring a Windows Local Security Policy to modify password requirements, enable auditing, configure some user rights, and set security options. You also used Event Manager to view logged information in the lab.

You learned about the Windows Defender host-based firewall included with Windows 10 and how to configure Windows Defender to allow or deny access to specific programs or ports. You also learned about Windows Defender Firewall with Advanced Security that provides even greater access control with Windows Firewall policies such as inbound and outbound rules, connection security rules, and monitoring. You explored the Windows Firewall and configure advanced settings in the lab.

Wireless networks are particularly vulnerable to attack and must be properly secured. Radio waves used to transmit data in wireless networks make it easy for attackers to monitor and collect data without physically connecting to a network. One way to provide a level of security on Wi-Fi networks is to change the default SSID and to disable broadcast of the SSID. Further levels of security can be gained through authentication and encryption. You practiced configuring wireless security in a packet tracer activity.

Finally, you learned the six steps in the troubleshooting process as they are applied to security.

Go to the online course to take the quiz and exam.

Chapter 13 Quiz

This quiz is designed to provide an additional opportunity to practice the skills and knowledge presented in the chapter and to prepare for the chapter exam. You will be allowed multiple attempts and the grade does not appear in the gradebook.

Chapter 13 Exam

The chapter exam assesses your knowledge of the chapter content.

Your Chapter Notes

The IT Professional

Refer to
Online Course
for Illustration

14.0 Introduction

An IT professional must be familiar with the legal and ethical issues that are inherent in this industry. There are privacy and confidentiality concerns that you must take into consideration during every customer encounter as you interact with customers in the field, in the office, or over the phone. If you become a bench technician, although you might not interact with customers directly, you will have access to their private and confidential data. This chapter discusses some common legal and ethical issues.

Call center technicians work exclusively over the phone with customers. This chapter covers general call center procedures and the process of working with customers.

As an IT professional, you will troubleshoot and fix computers, and you will frequently communicate with customers and co-workers. In fact, troubleshooting is as much about communicating with the customer as it is about knowing how to fix a computer. In this chapter, you learn to use good communication skills as confidently as you use a screwdriver.

You will also learn about scripting to automate processes and tasks on various operating systems. For example, a script file might be used to automate the process of performing a backup of a customer's data or run a list of standard diagnostics on a broken computer. The script file can save the technician a lot of time, especially when the same tasks need to be performed on many different computers. You will learn about scripting languages and some basic Windows and Linux script commands. You will also learn key scripting terms like conditional variables, conditional statements, and loops. You will perform a lab writing very basic scripts.

14.1 Communication Skills and the IT Professional

14.1.1 Communication Skills, Troubleshooting, and Professional Behavior

Refer to
Online Course
for Illustration

14.1.1.1 Relationship Between Communication Skills and Troubleshooting

Think of a time when you had to call a repair person to get something fixed. Did it feel like an emergency to you? Perhaps you had a bad experience with a repair person. Are you likely to call that same person to fix a problem again? What could that technician have done differently in their communication with you? Did you have a good experience with a repair person? Did that person listen to you as you explained your problem and then ask you a few questions to get more information? Are you likely to call that person to fix a problem again?

Speaking directly with the customer is usually the first step in resolving the computer problem. To troubleshoot a computer, you need to learn the details of the problem from the customer. Most people who need a computer problem fixed are probably feeling some stress. If you establish a good rapport with the customer, the customer might relax a bit. A relaxed customer is more likely to be able to provide the information that you need to determine the source of the problem and then fix it.

Follow these guidelines to provide great customer service:

- Set and meet expectations, adhere to the agreed upon timeline, and communicate the status with the customer.

- If necessary, offer different repair or replacement options.

- Provide documentation on the services provided.

- Follow up with customers and users after services are rendered to verify their satisfaction.

Refer to
Lab Activity
for this chapter

14.1.1.2   Lab - Technician Resources

A technician's good communication skills are an aid in the troubleshooting process. It takes time and experience to develop good communication and troubleshooting skills. As your hardware, software, and OS knowledge increases, your ability to quickly determine a problem and find a solution will improve. The same principle applies to developing communication skills. The more you practice good communication skills, the more effective you will become when working with customers. A knowledgeable technician who uses good communication skills will always be in demand in the job market.

As a technician, you also have access to several communication and research tools. All these resources can be used to help gather information for the troubleshooting process.

In this lab, you will use the internet to find resources for a specific computer component. Search online for resources that can help you troubleshoot the component.

Lab - Technician Resources

Refer to
Online Course
for Illustration

14.1.1.3   Relationship Between Communication Skills and Professional Behavior

Whether you are talking with a customer on the phone or in person, it is important to communicate well and to present yourself professionally.

If you are talking with a customer in person, that customer can see your body language. If you are talking with a customer over the phone, that customer can hear your tone and inflection. Customers can also sense whether you are smiling when you are speaking with them on the phone. Many call center technicians use a mirror at their desk to monitor their facial expressions.

Successful technicians control their own reactions and emotions from one customer call to the next. A good rule for all technicians to follow is that a new customer call means a fresh start. Never carry your frustration from one call to the next.

14.1.2   Working with a Customer

Refer to
Interactive Graphic
in online course

14.1.2.1   Know, Relate, and Understand

Refer to
Online Course
for Illustration

14.1.2.2   Active Listening

To better enable you to determine the customer's problem, practice active listening skills. Allow the customer to tell the whole story. During the time that the customer is explaining the problem, occasionally interject some small word or phrase, such as "I understand," "Yes," "I see," or "Okay." This behavior lets the customer know that you are there and that you are listening.

However, a technician should not interrupt the customer to ask a question or make a statement. This is rude, disrespectful, and creates tension. Many times in a conversation, you might find yourself thinking of what to say before the other person finishes talking. When you do this, you are not actively listening. Instead, listen carefully when your customers speak, and let them finish their thoughts.

You asked the customer to explain the problem to you. This is known as an open-ended question. An open-ended question rarely has a simple answer. Usually it involves information about what the customer was doing, what they were trying to do, and why they are frustrated.

After you have listened to the customer explain the whole problem, summarize what the customer has said. This helps convince the customer that you have heard and understand the situation. A good practice for clarification is to paraphrase the customer's explanation by beginning with the words, "Let me see if I understand what you have told me." This is a very effective tool that demonstrates to the customer that you have listened and that you understand.

After you have assured the customer that you understand the problem, you will probably have to ask some follow-up questions. Make sure that these questions are pertinent. Do not ask questions that the customer has already answered while describing the problem. Doing this only irritates the customer and shows that you were not listening.

Follow-up questions should be targeted, closed-ended questions based on the information that you have already gathered. Closed-ended questions should focus on obtaining specific information. The customer should be able to answer a closed-ended question with a simple "yes" or "no" or with a factual response, such as "Windows 10."

Use all the information that you have gathered from the customer to complete a work order.

Refer to
Interactive Graphic
in online course

14.1.2.3   Check Your Understanding - Closed-Ended and Open-Ended Questions

Refer to **Video**
in online course

14.1.2.4   Video Demonstration - Active Listening and Summarizing

Click Play in the figure to hear a recording. The recording contains an example of a technician not using active listening skills and needlessly interrupting the customer. In the second half of this recording, the technician uses active listening skills and does not interrupt the customer.

Tips for Using Active Listening with a Customer

- Do allow the customer to tell their problem.

- Do occasionally interject some small word or phrase such as "I understand," "Yes," "I see," or "Okay." to let the customer know that you are listening.

- Do summarize the customer's problem when they are done so that you both are certain that you understand.

- Do ask clarifying questions.

- Do not interrupt the customer the moment you realize you have a question.

Click here to read the transcript of this video.

14.1.3 Professional Behavior

Refer to
Online Course
for Illustration

14.1.3.1 Using Professional Behavior with the Customer

Be positive when communicating with the customer. Tell the customer what you can do. Do not focus on what you cannot do. Be prepared to explain alternative ways that you can help them, such as emailing information and step-by-step instructions, or using remote control software to solve the problem.

When dealing with customers, it is sometimes easier to explain what you should not do. The following list describes things that you should not do when talking with a customer:

- Do not minimize a customer's problems.

- Do not use jargon, abbreviations, acronyms, and slang.

- Do not use a negative attitude or tone of voice.

- Do not argue with customers or become defensive.

- Do not say culturally insensitive remarks.

- Do not disclose any experiences with customers on social media.

- Do not be judgmental or insulting or call the customer names.

- Avoid distractions and do not interrupt when talking with customers.

- Do not take personal calls when talking with customers.

- Do not talk to co-workers about unrelated subjects when talking with the customer.

- Avoid unnecessary holds and abrupt holds.

- Do not transfer a call without explaining the purpose of the transfer and getting customer consent.

- Do not use negative remarks about other technicians to the customer.

If a technician is not going to be on time, then the customer should be informed as soon as possible

Refer to
Interactive Graphic
in online course

14.1.3.2   Tips for Hold and Transfer

When dealing with customers, it is necessary to be professional in all aspects of your role. You must handle customers with respect and prompt attention. When on a telephone, make sure that you know how to place a customer on hold, as well as how to transfer a customer without losing the call.

Refer to **Video**
in online course

14.1.3.3   Video Demonstration - Hold and Transfer

Click Play in the figure to view a demonstration of how to place a customer on hold, as well as how to transfer a customer.

Click here to read the transcript of this video.

Refer to
Interactive Graphic
in online course

14.1.3.4   What Do You Already Know? - Netiquette

14.1.4   The Customer Call

Refer to
Online Course
for Illustration

14.1.4.1   Keeping the Customer Call Focused

Part of your job is to focus the customer during the phone call. When you focus the customer on the problem, it allows you to control the call. These practices make the best use of your time and the customer's time:

- **Use proper language** - Be clear and avoid technical language that the customer might not understand.

- **Listen and question** - Listen carefully to the customer and let them speak. Use open and closed ended questions to learn details about the customer's problem.

- **Give feedback** - Let the customer know that you understand the problem and develop a friendly and positive conversational manner.

Just as there are many different computer problems, there are many different types of customers. By using active listening skills, you may be given some hints as to what type of customer is on the phone with you. Is this person very new to computers? Is the person very knowledgeable about computers? Is your customer angry? Do not take any comments personally, and do not retaliate with any comments or criticism. If you stay calm with the customer, finding a solution to the problem will remain the focal point of the call. Recognizing certain customer traits can help you manage the call accordingly.

The videos on the following pages will demonstrate strategies for dealing with different types of difficult customers. The list is not comprehensive, and often, a customer will display a combination of traits. Each video contains a recording of a technician handling a difficult customer type incorrectly, followed by a recording of the same technician handling the customer professionally. A quiz is embedded at the end of each example.

Refer to **Video**
in online course

14.1.4.2   Video Demonstration - The Talkative Customer

Click Play in the figure to view a demonstration of inappropriate and appropriate IT professional behavior with a talkative customer.

Tips for helping a talkative customer

- Do allow the customer to talk for about one minute.

- Do gather as much information about the problem as possible.

- Do politely step in to refocus the customer. This is the one exception to the rule of never interrupting a customer.

- Do ask as many closed-ended questions as you need to after you have regained control of the call.

- Do not encourage non-problem related conversation by asking social questions such as "How are you today?"

Click here to read the transcript of this video.

Refer to **Video** in online course

14.1.4.3   Video Demonstration - The Rude Customer

Click Play in the figure to view a demonstration of inappropriate and appropriate IT professional behavior with a rude customer.

Tips for helping a rude customer

- Do listen very carefully, as you do not want to ask the customer to repeat any information.

- Do follow a step-by-step approach to determining and solving the problem.

- Do try to contact the customer's favorite technician, if they have one, to see if that technician can take the call. Tell the customer, "I can help you right now, or see if your preferred technician is available." If the customer wants the preferred technician and they are available, politely transfer the call. If the technician is not available, ask the customer if he or she will wait. If they will wait, note that in the ticket.

- Do apologize for the wait time and the inconvenience, even if there has been no wait time.

- Do reiterate that you want to solve their problem as quickly as possible.

- Do not ask the customer to do any obvious steps if there is any way you can determine the problem without that information.

- Do not be rude to the customer, even if they are rude to you.

Click here to read the transcript of this video.

Refer to **Video** in online course

14.1.4.4   Video Demonstration - The Knowledgeable Customer

Click Play in the figure to view a demonstration of inappropriate and appropriate IT professional behavior with a knowledgeable customer.

Tips for helping a knowledgeable customer

- Do consider setting up a call with a level two technician, if you are a level one technician.

- Do give the customer the overall approach to what you are trying to verify.

- Do not follow a step-by-step process with this customer.

- Do not ask to check the obvious, such as the power cord or the power switch. Consider suggesting a reboot instead.

Click here to read the transcript of this video.

Refer to **Video** in online course

14.1.4.5   Video Demonstration - The Angry Customer

Click Play in the figure to view a demonstration of inappropriate and appropriate IT professional behavior with a talkative customer.

Tips for helping a talkative customer

- Do let the customer tell their problem without interrupting, even if they are angry. This allows the customer to release some of their anger before you proceed.

- Do sympathize with the customer's problem.

- Do apologize for the wait time or inconvenience.

- Do not, if at all possible, put this customer on hold or transfer the call.

- Do not spend the call time talking about what caused the problem. It is better to redirect the conversation to solving the problem.

Click here to read the transcript of this video.

Refer to **Video** in online course

14.1.4.6   Video Demonstration - The Inexperienced Customer

Click Play in the figure to view a demonstration of inappropriate and appropriate IT professional behavior with an inexperienced customer.

Tips for helping an inexperienced customer

- Do allow the customer to talk for about one minute.

- Do gather as much information about the problem as possible.

- Do politely step in to refocus the customer. This is the one exception to the rule of never interrupting a customer.

- Do ask as many closed-ended questions as you need to after you have regained control of the call.

- Do not encourage non-problem related conversation by asking social questions such as "How are you today?"

Click here to read the transcript of this video.

14.2 Operational Procedures

14.2.1 Documentation

14.2.1.1 Documentation Overview

Refer to
Online Course
for Illustration

Different types of organizations have different operating procedures and processes that govern business functions. Documentation is the main way of communicating these processes and procedures to employees, customers, suppliers, and others.

Purposes for documentation include:

- Providing descriptions for how products, software, and hardware function through the use of diagrams, descriptions, manual pages and knowledgebase articles.

- Standardizing procedures and practices so that they can be repeated accurately in the future.

- Establishing rules and restrictions on the use of the organization's assets including acceptable use policies for internet, network, and computer usage.

- Reducing confusion and mistakes saving time and resources.

- Complying with governmental or industry regulations.

- Training new employees or customers.

Keeping documentation up to date is just as important as creating it. Updates to policies and procedures are inevitable, especially in the constantly changing environment of information technology. Establishing a standard timeframe for reviewing documents, diagrams, and compliance policies ensures that the correct information is available when it is needed.

14.2.1.2 IT Department Documentation

Refer to
Interactive Graphic
in online course

Keeping documentation current is a challenge for even the best managed IT departments. IT documentation can come in many different forms, including diagrams, manuals, configurations and source code. In general, IT documentation falls into four broad categories: Policies, Operations, Projects and User Documentation. Click each category in the figure for more information.

14.2.1.3 Regulatory Compliance Requirements

Refer to
Online Course
for Illustration

Federal, state, local, and industry regulations can have documentation requirements over and above what is normally documented in the company's records. Regulatory and compliance policies often specify what data must be collected and how long it must be retained. A few of the regulations may have implications on internal company processes and procedures. Some regulations require keeping extensive records regarding how the data is accessed and used.

Failure to comply with laws and regulations can have severe consequences, including fines, termination of employment, and even incarceration of offenders. It is important to know how laws and regulations apply to your organization and to the work you perform.

Refer to
Interactive Graphic
in online course

14.2.1.4 Check Your Understanding - Documentation

14.2.2   Change Management

Refer to
Online Course
for Illustration

14.2.2.1   Change Control Process

Controlling changes in an IT environment can be difficult. Changes can be as minor as replacing a printer, or as important as upgrading all the enterprise servers to the latest operating system version. Most larger enterprises and organizations have change management procedures in place to ensure that installations and upgrades go smoothly,

A good change management process can prevent business functions from being negatively impacted by the updates, upgrades, replacements, and reconfigurations that are a normally part of IT operations. Change management usually starts with a change request from a stakeholder or from within the IT organization itself. Most change management processes include the following:

- **Identification** - What is the change? Why is it needed? Who are the stakeholders?

- **Assessment** - What business processes are impacted by this change? What are the costs and resources necessary for implementation? What risks are associated with making (or not making) this change?

- **Planning** - How long will this change take to implement? Is there downtime involved? What is the roll back or recovery process if the change fails?

- **Approval** - Who must authorize this change? Has approval to proceed with the change been obtained?

- **Implementation** - How are stakeholders notified? What are the steps to complete the change, and how will the results be tested?

- **Acceptance** - What is the acceptance criteria and who is responsible for accepting the results of the change?

- **Documentation** - What updates are required to change logs, implementation steps, or IT documents because of this change?

All the results of the process are recorded on a change request or change control document that becomes part of the IT documentation. Some expensive or complex changes that impact necessary business functions may require the approval of a change board or committee before work can begin.

Click here to view an example of a Change Control Worksheet.

14.2.3   Disaster Prevention and Recovery

Refer to
Online Course
for Illustration

14.2.3.1   Disaster Recovery Overview

We often think of a disaster as being something catastrophic, such as the destruction caused by an earthquake, tsunami or wildfire. In information technology, a disaster can include anything from natural disasters that affect the network structure to malicious attacks on the network itself. The impact of data loss or corruption from unplanned outages caused by hardware failure, human error, hacking, or malware can be significant.

A disaster recovery plan is a comprehensive document that describes how to restore operation quickly and keep critical IT functions running during or after a disaster occurs.

The disaster recovery plan can include information such as offsite locations where services can be moved, information on replacing network devices and servers, and backup connectivity options.

Some services may even need to be available during the disaster in order to provide information to IT personnel and updates to others in the organization. Services that might need to be available during or immediately after a disaster include:

- Web services and internet connectivity.
- Data stores and backup files.
- Directory and authentication services.
- Database and application servers.
- Telephone, email and other communication services.

In addition to having a disaster recovery plan, most organizations take steps to ensure they are ready in case a disaster occurs. These preventive measures can ease the impact of unplanned outages on the operation of the organization.

Refer to **Online Course** for Illustration

14.2.3.2   Preventing Downtime and Data Loss

Some business applications cannot tolerate any downtime. They use multiple data centers capable of handling all data processing needs, which run in parallel with data mirrored or synchronized between the centers. Often, these businesses run their applications from cloud servers to minimize the impact of physical damage to their sites.

Data and Operating System Backup

Even the best disaster recovery procedures cannot restore services quickly if there are no current backups of data and operating system environments. It is much easier to restore data from a reliable backup than it would be to recreate it. There are generally two types of backup done for disaster recovery purposes: image backups and file backups. Image backups record all the information stored on the computer at the time the image is created while file backups store only the specific files indicated at the time the backup is run no matter which type of backup is made, it is critical that the restore process is tested frequently to ensure that it will function when it is needed.

Backup files need to be available to the people who will be responsible for restoring and recovering the systems after an unplanned outage. Backup media can be stored securely off-site or backup files can be stored in an online location, such as a cloud service provider. Locally stored files may be accessible if communication service outages prevent accessing the Internet. Backup files stored online have the benefit of being accessible from anywhere the Internet is available.

Power and Environment Controls

Keeping the power on for a data center or for critical communications infrastructure can prevent data loss caused by interruptions or spikes in the electrical power delivery. Sometimes even minor natural disasters can cause power outages that last for longer than 24 hours. Small surge protectors and uninterrupted power supplies (UPS) can prevent damage from minor power problems, but for larger outages, a generator might be required. Data centers require power not only for the computing equipment but also for air conditioning and fire suppression. Large UPS units can keep a data center operational until a fuel-powered generator comes online.

Refer to
Online Course
for Illustration

14.2.3.3 Elements of a Disaster Recovery Plan

The first step in creating a disaster recovery plan is to identify the most critical services and applications that will need to be restored quickly. That information should be used to create a disaster recovery plan. There are five major phases of creating and implementing a disaster recovery plan:

Phase 1 - Network Design Recovery Strategy

Analyze the network design. Some aspects of the network design that should be included in the disaster recovery are:

- Is the network designed to survive a major disaster? Are there backup connectivity options and is there redundancy in the network design?

- Availability of offsite servers or cloud providers that can support applications such as email and database services.

- Availability of backup routers, switches, and other network devices.

- Location of services and resources that the network needs. Are they spread over a wide geography? Are backups easily accessible in an emergency?

Phase 2 - Inventory and Documentation

Create an inventory of all locations, devices, vendors, used services, and contact names. Verify cost estimates that are created in the risk assessment step.

Phase 3 - Verification

Create a verification process to prove that the disaster recovery strategy works. Practice disaster recovery exercises to ensure that the plan is up to date and workable.

Phase 4 - Approval and Implementation

Obtain senior management approval and develop a budget to implement and maintain the disaster recovery plan.

Phase 5 - Review

After the disaster recovery plan has been implemented for a year, review the plan. Information in the plan must be kept up to date, or critical services may not be restored in the case of a disaster.

Refer to
Interactive Graphic
in online course

14.2.3.4 Check Your Understanding - Disaster Recovery

14.3   Ethical and Legal Considerations

14.3.1   Ethical and Legal Considerations in the IT Profession

Refer to
Online Course
for Illustration

14.3.1.1   Ethical and Legal Considerations in IT

When you are working with customers and their equipment, there are some general ethical customs and legal rules that you should observe. These customs and rules often overlap.

You should always have respect for your customers, as well as for their property. Computers and monitors are property, but property also includes any information or data that might be accessible, for example:

- Emails
- Phone lists and contact lists
- Records or data on the computer
- Hard copies of files, information, or data left on a desk

Before accessing computer accounts, including the administrator account, get the permission of the customer. During the troubleshooting process, you might have gathered some private information, such as usernames and passwords. If you document this type of private information, you must keep it confidential. Divulging customer information to anyone else is not only unethical but might be illegal. Do not send unsolicited messages to a customer. Do not send unsolicited mass mailings or chain letters to customers. Never send forged or anonymous emails. Legal details of customer information are usually covered under the service-level agreement (SLA). The SLA is a contract between a customer and a service provider that defines the service or goods the customer will receive and the standards to which the provider must comply.

Refer to
Online Course
for Illustration

14.3.1.2   Personal Identifiable Information (PII)

Take particular care to keep personally identifiable information (PII) confidential. PII is any data that could potentially identify a specific individual. NIST Special Publication 800-122 defines PII as, "any information about an individual maintained by an agency, including (1) any information that can be used to distinguish or trace an individual's identity, such as name, social security number, date and place of birth, mother's maiden name, or biometric records; and (2) any other information that is linked or linkable to an individual, such as medical, educational, financial, and employment information".

Examples of PII include, but are not limited to:

- Names, such as full name, maiden name, mother's maiden name, or alias
- Personal identification numbers, such as social security number (SSN), passport number, driver's license number, taxpayer identification number, or financial account or credit card number, address information, such as street address or email address
- Personal characteristics, including photographic images (especially of the face or other identifying characteristics), fingerprints, handwriting, or other biometric data (e.g., retina scan, voice signature, facial geometry)

PII violations are regulated by several organizations in the United States, depending on the type of data. The EU General Data Protection Regulation (GDPR) also regulates how data is handled for personal data, including financial and healthcare information. To learn more about GDPR visit www.eugdpr.org.

Refer to
Online Course
for Illustration

14.3.1.3   Payment Card Industry (PCI)

Payment Card Industry (PCI) information is considered personal information that needs to be protected. We hear about countless breaches of credit card information on the news that impact millions of users. Often it is days or weeks before a merchant realizes there is a breach. All businesses and organizations, large or small, need to adhere to strict standards to protect the consumer's information.

The PCI Security Standards Council was formed in 2005 by the 5 major credit card companies in an effort to protect account numbers, expiration dates, magnetic strip and chip data for transactions around the globe. The PCI council partners with organizations, including NIST, to develop standards and security procedures around these transactions.

In one of the worst breaches in history, malware infected the point of sale system of a major retailer, impacting millions of consumers. This may have been prevented with adequate software and policies for data breach prevention. As an IT professional you should be aware of PCI compliance standards.

For more information on PCI, visit www.pcisecuritystandards.org.

Refer to
Online Course
for Illustration

14.3.1.4   Protected Health Information (PHI)

Protected Health Information (PHI) is another form of PII that needs to be secured and protected. PHI includes patient names, addresses, dates of visits, telephone and fax numbers, and email addresses. With the move from paper copy records to electronic records, Electronic Protected Health Information (ePHI) is also regulated. Penalties for breaches of PHI and ePHI are very severe and regulated by the Health Insurance Portability and Accountability Act (HIPAA).

Examples of these types of breaches are easily found with an internet search. Unfortunately, the breach may be undetected for months. Some breaches have occurred from one person giving out information to an unauthorized person. Human error can cause violations. For example, accidentally faxing health information to the wrong party is a violation. Other examples are sophisticated attacks. Recent phishing attacks on a California-based health plan went undetected for almost a month before they recognized it and then notified 37,000 patients that their data had been breached. As an IT professional, you should be aware of protecting PHI and ePHI.

For more information about PHI and ePHI, visit www.hhs.gov and search for PHI.

Search the internet for the regulatory agencies in your state, country, or province.

Refer to
Lab Activity
for this chapter

14.3.1.5   Lab - Investigate Breaches of PII, PHI, PCI

In this lab, you will investigate breaches of PII, PHI and PCI.

Lab - Investigate Breaches of PII, PHI, PCI

Refer to
Online Course
for Illustration

14.3.1.6   Legal Considerations in IT

The laws in different countries and legal jurisdictions vary, but generally, actions such as the following are considered to be illegal:

- It is not permissible to make any changes to system software or hardware configurations without customer permission.

- It is not permissible to access a customer's or co-worker's accounts, private files, or email messages without permission.

- It is not permissible to install, copy, or share digital content (including software, music, text, images, and video) in violation of copyright and software agreements or the applicable law. Copyright and trademark laws vary between states, countries, and regions.

- It is not permissible to use a customer's company IT resources for commercial purposes.

- It is not permissible to make a customer's IT resources available to unauthorized users.

- It is not permissible to knowingly use a customer's company resources for illegal activities. Criminal or illegal use typically includes obscenity, child pornography, threats, harassment, copyright infringement, Internet piracy, university trademark infringement, defamation, theft, identity theft, and unauthorized access.

- It is not permissible to share sensitive customer information. You are required to maintain the confidentiality of this data.

This list is not exhaustive. All businesses and their employees must know and comply with all applicable laws of the jurisdiction in which they operate.

Refer to
Interactive Graphic
in online course

14.3.1.7   Licensing

Licensing

As an IT technician, you may encounter customers who are using software illegally. It is important that you understand the purpose and types of common software licenses, should you determine that a crime has been committed. Your responsibilities are usually covered in your company's corporate end-user policy. In all instances, you must follow security best practices, including documentation and chain of custody procedures.

A software license is a contract that outlines the legal use, or redistribution, of that software. Most software licenses grant end-user permission to use one or more copies of software. They also specify the end-user's rights and restrictions. This ensures that the software owner's copyright is maintained. It is illegal to use licensed software without the appropriate license.

Refer to
Interactive Graphic
in online course

14.3.1.8   Check Your Understanding - Licensing

14.3.2   Legal Procedures Overview

Refer to
Online Course
for Illustration

14.3.2.1   Computer Forensics

Data from computer systems, networks, wireless communications, and storage devices may need to be collected and analyzed in the course of a criminal investigation. The collection and analysis of data for this purpose is called computer forensics. The process of computer forensics encompasses both IT and specific laws to ensure that any data collected is admissible as evidence in court.

Depending on the country, illegal computer or network usage may include:

- Identity theft

- Using a computer to sell counterfeit goods

- Using pirated software on a computer or network

- Using a computer or network to create unauthorized copies of copyrighted materials, such as movies, television programs, music, and video games

- Using a computer or network to sell unauthorized copies of copyrighted materials

- Pornography

This is not an exhaustive list. Becoming familiar with the signs of illegal computer or network usage can help you to identify a situation where you suspect illegal activity and report it to the authorities.

Refer to
Online Course
for Illustration

14.3.2.2   Data Collected in Computer Forensics

Two basic types of data are collected when conducting computer forensics procedures:

- **Persistent data** - Persistent data is stored on a local drive, such as an internal or external hard drive, or an optical drive. When the computer is turned off, this data is preserved.

- **Volatile data** - RAM, cache, and registries contain volatile data. Data in transit between a storage medium and a CPU is also volatile data. If you are reporting illegal activity or are part of an incident response team, it is important to know how to capture this data, because it disappears as soon as the computer is turned off.

Refer to
Online Course
for Illustration

14.3.2.3   Cyber Law

There is no single law known as a cyber law. Cyber law is a term to describe the international, regional, country, and state laws that affect computer security professionals. IT professionals must be aware of cyber law so that they understand their responsibility and their liability as it relates to cybercrimes.

Cyber laws explain the circumstances under which data (evidence) can be collected from computers, data storage devices, networks, and wireless communications. They can also specify the manner in which this data can be collected. In the United States, cyber law has three primary elements:

- Wiretap Act

- Pen/Trap and Trace Statute

- Stored Electronic Communication Act

IT professionals should be aware of the cyber laws in their country, region, or state.

Refer to
Online Course
for Illustration

14.3.2.4   First Response

First response is the term used to describe the official procedures employed by those people who are qualified to collect evidence. System administrators, like law enforcement officers, are usually the first responders at potential crime scenes. Computer forensics experts are brought in when it is apparent that there has been illegal activity.

Routine administrative tasks can affect the forensic process. If the forensic process is improperly performed, evidence that has been collected might not be admissible in court.

As a field or a bench technician, you may be the person who discovers illegal computer or network activity. If this happens, do not turn off the computer. Volatile data about the current state of the computer can include programs that are running, network connections that are open, and users who are logged in to the network or to the computer. This data helps to determine a logical timeline of the security incident. It may also help to identify those responsible for the illegal activity. This data could be lost when the computer is powered off.

Be familiar with your company's policy regarding cybercrimes. Know who to call, what to do and, just as importantly, know what not to do.

Refer to
Online Course
for Illustration

14.3.2.5   Documentation

The documentation required by a system administrator and a computer forensics expert is extremely detailed. They must document not only what evidence was gathered, but how it was gathered and with which tools. Incident documentation should use consistent naming conventions for forensic tool output. Stamp logs with the time, date, and identity of the person performing the forensic collection. Document as much information about the security incident as possible. These best practices provide an audit trail for the information collection process.

Even if you are not a system administrator or computer forensics expert, it is a good habit to create detailed documentation of all the work that you do. If you discover illegal activity on a computer or network on which you are working, at a minimum, document the following:

- Initial reason for accessing the computer or network
- Time and date
- Peripherals that are connected to the computer
- All network connections
- Physical area where the computer is located
- Illegal material that you have found
- Illegal activity that you have witnessed (or you suspect has occurred)
- Which procedures you have executed on the computer or network

First responders want to know what you have done and what you have not done. Your documentation may become part of the evidence in the prosecution of a crime. If you make additions or changes to this documentation, it is critical that you inform all interested parties.

Refer to
Online Course
for Illustration

14.3.2.6 Chain of Custody

For evidence to be admitted, it must be authenticated. A system administrator may testify about the evidence that was collected. But he or she must also be able to prove how this evidence was collected, where it has been physically stored, and who has had access to it between the time of collection and its entry into the court proceedings. This is known as the chain of custody. To prove the chain of custody, first responders have documentation procedures in place that track the collected evidence. These procedures also prevent evidence tampering so that the integrity of the evidence can be ensured.

Incorporate computer forensics procedures into your approach to computer and network security to ensure the integrity of the data. These procedures help you capture necessary data in the event of a network breach. Ensuring the viability and integrity of the captured data helps you prosecute the intruder.

Refer to
Interactive Graphic
in online course

14.3.2.7 Check Your Understanding - Legal Procedures Overview

14.4 Call Center Technicians

14.4.1 Call Centers, Level One and Level Two Technicians

Refer to
Interactive Graphic
in online course

14.4.1.1 Call Centers

A call center environment is usually very organized and professional. Customers call in to receive help for a specific computer-related problem. The typical workflow of a call center starts with calls from customers displayed on a callboard. Level one technicians answer these calls in the order that the calls arrive. If the level one technician cannot solve the problem, it is escalated to a level two technician. In all instances, the technician must supply the level of support that is outlined in the customer's Service Level Agreement (SLA).

A call center might exist within a company and offer service to the employees of that company as well as to the customers of that company's products. Alternatively, a call center might be an independent business that sells computer support as a service to outside customers. In either case, a call center is a busy, fast-paced work environment, often operating 24 hours a day.

Refer to
Online Course
for Illustration

14.4.1.2 Level One Technician Responsibilities

Call centers sometimes have different names for level one technicians. These technicians might be known as level one analysts, dispatchers, or incident screeners. Regardless of the title, the level one technician's responsibilities are fairly similar from one call center to the next.

The primary responsibility of a level one technician is to gather pertinent information from the customer. The technician has to accurately enter all information into the ticket or work order. Examples of the type of information that the level one technician must obtain is shown in the figure.

Some problems are very simple to resolve, and a level one technician can usually take care of these without escalating the work order to a level two technician.

When a problem requires the expertise of a level two technician, the level one technician must describe a customer's problem on a work order using a succinct sentence or two. An accurate description is important because it helps other technicians quickly understand the situation without having to ask the customer the same questions again.

Refer to
Online Course
for Illustration

14.4.1.3   Level Two Technician Responsibilities

As with level one technicians, call centers sometimes have different names for level two technicians. These technicians might be known as product specialists or technical-support personnel. The level two technician's responsibilities are generally the same from one call center to the next.

The level two technician is usually more knowledgeable and experienced than the level one technician or has been working for the company for a longer period of time. When a problem cannot be resolved within a predetermined amount of time, the level one technician prepares an escalated work order, as shown in the figure. The level two technician receives the escalated work order with the description of the problem and then calls the customer back to ask any additional questions and resolve the problem.

Level two technicians can also use remote access software to connect to the customer's computer to update drivers and software, access the operating system, check the BIOS, and gather other diagnostic information to solve the problem.

Refer to
Lab Activity
for this chapter

14.4.1.4   Lab - Remote Technician - Fix a Hardware Problem

In this lab, you will gather data from the customer, and then instruct the customer to fix a computer that does not boot.

Lab - Remote Technician - Fix a Hardware Problem

Refer to
Lab Activity
for this chapter

14.4.1.5   Lab - Remote Technician - Fix an Operating System Problem

In this lab, you will gather data from the customer, and then instruct the customer to fix a computer that does not connect to the network.

Lab - Remote Technician - Fix an Operating System Problem

Refer to
Lab Activity
for this chapter

14.4.1.6   Lab - Remote Technician - Fix a Network Problem

In this lab, you will gather data from the customer, and then instruct the customer to fix a computer that does not connect to the network.

Lab - Remote Technician - Fix a Network Problem

Refer to
Lab Activity
for this chapter

14.4.1.7   Lab - Remote Technician - Fix a Security Problem

In this lab, you will gather data from the customer and instruct the customer to fix a computer that cannot connect to a workplace wireless network.

Lab - Remote Technician - Fix a Security Problem

14.4.2   Basic Scripting and the IT Professional

Refer to
Interactive Graphic
in online course

14.4.2.1   Script Examples

As an IT professional, you will be exposed to many different types of files. One very important type of file is the script file. A script file is a simple text file written in scripting languages to automate processes and tasks on various operating systems. In the field, a script file might be used to automate the process of performing a backup of a customer's data or run a list of standard diagnostics on a broken computer. The script file can save the technician a lot of time, especially when the same tasks need to be performed on many different computers. You should also be able to identify the many different types of script files because a script file may be causing a problem at startup or during a specific event. Often, preventing the script file from running may eliminate the problem that is occurring.

The commands in a script file might be written on the command line one at a time but, is more effectively done in a script file. The script is designed to be executed line by line using a command line interpreter in order to perform various commands. The script can be created using a text editor such as Notepad but, an IDE (Integrated Development Environment) is often used to write and execute the script. Figure 1 is an image of a Windows batch script. Figure 2 is an image of a Linux shell script.

Refer to
Interactive Graphic
in online course

14.4.2.2   Scripting Languages

A scripting language is different than a compiled language because each line is interpreted and then executed when the script is run. Examples of scripting languages include Windows batch files, PowerShell, Linux shell script, VBScript, JavaScript, and Python. Compiled languages such as C, C++, C#, and Java, need to be converted into executable code using a "compiler". Executable code is directly readable by the CPU while scripting languages are interpreted into code that the CPU can read one line at a time by a command interpreter or by the operating system. This makes scripting languages unsuitable for situations where performance is a significant factor. The table in Figure 1 shows a list of scripting languages and their extensions. Figure 2 is a table of various comments found in scripts.

Refer to
Interactive Graphic
in online course

14.4.2.3   Basic Script Commands

Various commands are available at the terminals of each operating system. Some Windows commands are based on DOS and accessible through the command prompt. Other Windows commands are accessible through PowerShell. Linux commands are written to be compatible with UNIX commands and are often accessed through BASH (Bourne Again SHell). **Figure 1** is a table of various DOS commands. **Figure 2** is a table of various BASH commands.

Refer to
Interactive Graphic
in online course

14.4.2.4   Variables / Environmental Variables

Variables

Variables are designated places to store information within a computer. A primary function of computers is to manipulate variables. The figure shows a script where a user is prompted for their last name (LNAME) and where they are from (PLACE). The script then shows the execution and output of the script.

Refer to
Interactive Graphic
in online course

14.4.2.5   Conditional Statements

Conditional statements are needed for scripts to make decisions. These statements usually come in the form of an if-else or a case statement. In order for these statements to make a decision, a comparison must be made using operators. The syntax of these commands will vary, depending on the Operator language.

Click each button to learn more.

Refer to
Interactive Graphic
in online course

14.4.2.6   Loops

In order to repeat commands or tasks a loop can be used. The three main types of loops found in scripts are the For loop, the While loop, and the Do-While loop.

The For loop repeats a section of code a specified number of times. The While loop checks a variable to verify that it is true (or false) before repeating a section of code. This is known as a pre-test loop. Finally, the Do-While loop repeats a section of code, then checks a variable to verify that it is true (or false). This is known a s a post-test loop.

Refer to
Lab Activity
for this chapter

14.4.2.7   Lab - Write Basic Scripts in Windows and Linux

In this lab, you will write some basic scripts in different scripting languages to help understand how each language handles automating tasks

Lab - Write Basic Scripts in Windows and Linux

Refer to
Online Course
for Illustration

14.5   Summary

In this chapter, you learned about the relationship between communication skills and troubleshooting skills. These two skills need to be combined to make you a successful IT technician. You learned about the legal aspects and ethics of dealing with computer technology and the property of the customer.

You learned that you should always conduct yourself in a professional manner with your customers and co-workers. Professional behavior increases customer confidence and enhances your credibility. You learned how to recognize the signs of a difficult customer and learn what to do and what not to do when you are on a call with this customer.

You must understand and comply with your customer's SLA. If the problem falls outside the parameters of the SLA, find positive ways of telling the customer what you can do to help, rather than what you cannot do. In addition to the SLA, you must follow the business policies of the company. These policies include how your company prioritizes calls, how and when to escalate a call to management, and when you can take breaks and lunch. You performed several labs on how to fix hardware, operating system, network, and security problems.

You learned about the ethical and legal aspects of working in computer technology. You should be aware of your company's policies and practices. In addition, you might need to familiarize yourself with your local or country's trademark and copyright laws. A software license is a contract that outlines the legal use, or redistribution, of that software. You learned about the many different types of software licenses including Personal, Enterprise, Open Source and Commercial.

Cyber laws explain the circumstances under which data (evidence) can be collected from computers, data storage devices, networks, and wireless communications. First response is the term used to describe the official procedures employed by those people who are qualified to collect evidence. You learned that even if you are not a system administrator or computer forensics expert, it is a good habit to create detailed documentation of all the work that you do. Being able to prove how evidence was collected and where it has been between the time of collection and its entry into the court proceeding is known as the chain of custody.

Finally, you learned about script files which are files written in scripting languages to automate processes and tasks on various operating systems. The script file can save the technician a lot of time, especially when the same tasks need to be performed on many different computers. You learned about scripting languages and some basic Windows and Linux script commands. You learned about variables which are designated places to store information within a computer, conditional statements, which are needed for scripts to make decisions, and loops, which repeat commands or tasks.

Learning about scripting is important and so is experience practicing writing scripts. In this chapter you performed a lab writing some very basic scripts in different scripting languages to help understand how each language handles automating tasks.

Go to the online course to take the quiz and exam.

Chapter 14 Quiz

This quiz is designed to provide an additional opportunity to practice the skills and knowledge presented in the chapter and to prepare for the chapter exam. You will be allowed multiple attempts and the grade does not appear in the gradebook.

Chapter 14 Exam

The chapter exam assesses your knowledge of the chapter content.

Your Chapter Notes

Index

SYMBOLS

* (asterisk), in Windows commands, 205
$ (dollar sign), administrative shares, 209
:: (double colon), in IPv6 addresses, 88
? (question mark), in Windows commands, 205
1G cellular standard, 120
2G cellular standard, 120
3D printers
  characteristics, 137–138
  component printing, 145
  parts, 138
  preventive maintenance, 145
3G cellular standard, 120
4G cellular standard, 120
5G cellular standard, 120
32-bit processor architecture, 161
64-bit processor architecture, 161

A

AAA (authentication, authorization, accounting), 73
access points (APs), 64, 75
Account Policies, 257
accounts (Windows), creating, 166, 184
AC/DC converters, 3
ACPI (Advanced Configuration and Power Interface),
  109–110
Active Directory, 174, 259–260
active listening, 275–276
ActiveX filtering, 264
adapter cards, 8
  installing, 23–25
  preventive maintenance, 52
  selecting, 23–24
  types of, 23
adapters, 11
addresses
  dynamic addressing, 88
  ICMP, 91
  IPv4 addresses, 85–86
    format, 86–87
    NAT, 93
  IPv6 addresses, 85–86
    format, 87–88
  link-local addressing, 89
  MAC addresses, 85–86
    filtering, 96

  static addressing, 88
  viewing, 86
ADF (automatic document feeder), 134
administrative commands, Linux and macOS, 235
administrative shares, 209
Administrative Tools (Control Panel), 194
Advanced Configuration and Power Interface (ACPI),
  109–110
Advanced Technology (AT), 3
Advanced Technology eXtended (ATX), 3, 5
adware, 243
Aero, 175
aerosol cans, safe disposal, 47
Airplane Mode, 120–121
analog telephone Internet access, 65
Android devices
  email configuration, 122–123
  iOS devices versus
    apps and content sources, 224
    open source versus closed source, 223–224
    touch interfaces, 224
  synchronizing, 124–125
angry customers, 279
anti-malware programs, 228–229, 243–244
APs (access points), 64, 75
application port numbers, 68
applications
  installing
    compatibility mode, 203
    installation methods, 202–203
    security considerations, 203
    system requirements, 202
  uninstalling, 203
applied networking. *See* networking
apps for mobile devices, 224
AR (augmented reality), 12–13, 106
arrays, adding, 200
assembly of computers
  adapter card installation, 23–25
  adapter card selection, 23–24
  case and fan selection, 18
  case reassembly and external cable installation, 28
  CPU selection, 20
  external storage selection, 26
  front panel cable installation, 26–28
  general and fire safety, 17
  hard drive installation, 22
  hard drive selection, 21

internal data cable installation, 26
internal power cable installation, 26
media reader selection, 25
motherboard component installation, 19
motherboard selection, 19–20
optical drive installation, 22
optical drive selection, 21–22
power supply installation, 17
power supply selection, 18
RAM selection, 20–21
storage device installation, 21
asterisk (*), in Windows commands, 205
AT (Advanced Technology), 3
attacks. *See* threats
ATX (Advanced Technology eXtended), 3, 5
ATX12V, 3
audio ports, 27
augmented reality (AR), 12–13, 106
authentication
for mobile devices, 227
SSH (Secure Shell), 214
in web browsers, 262–263
Windows account creation, 166
wireless security, 267
authentication servers, 73
automatic document feeder (ADF), 134
AutoPlay, disabling, 265

B

backlights in laptops, 108
backups. *See* data backups
basic input/output system chip. *See* BIOS (basic input/output system) chip
batteries
replacing in laptops, 115
safe disposal, 47
BD (Blu-ray Disc), 11
beep codes, 55
best practices
Linux, 233–234
macOS, 233–234
wireless security, 266–267
biometric authentication for mobile devices, 227
BIOS (basic input/output system) chip, 4
ACPI settings, 109–110
BIOS/UEFI menus, 31
CMOS and, 32
configuring, 33
firmware updates, 34–35
security, 33–34, 255
in troubleshooting, 55
BitLocker, 174, 193, 252–253
BitLocker To Go, 252–253
blacklisting, 96

blackouts, 36
Bluetooth, 69, 118
in laptops, 110–111
for mobile devices, 121–122
pairing, 121–122
Blu-ray Disc (BD), 11
boot camp boot manager, 165
boot managers, 165
boot process
BIOS and CMOS, 32
BIOS/UEFI configuration, 33
BIOS/UEFI menus, 31
BIOS/UEFI security, 33–34
firmware updates, 34–35
POST (power-on self-test), 31–32
UEFI, 32–33
Windows, 170
Windows 7 startup modes, 170
Windows 8 and 10 startup modes, 171
Branch Cache, 174
bridges, 74
broadband Internet access, 65
brownouts, 36
browsers. *See* web browser security

C

cable Internet access, 65
cables, 11
building and testing, 80
coax, 40, 79
external cables, installing, 28
fiber optic, 80–81
front panel cables, installing, 26–28
internal data cables, installing, 26
internal power cables, installing, 26
mini-USB, 118
preventive maintenance, 52
SATA, 40
SCSI and IDE, 41
tools for, 79
twisted pair, 40, 79–80
types of, 79
USB, 40
call center technicians
call centers, 289
level one responsibilities, 289–290
level two responsibilities, 290
call centers, 289
capture cards, 8, 23
case (for PCs), 2–3
reassembly, 28
selecting, 18
categories (Control Panel), 184
category ratings for twisted pair cabling, 80

CD (Compact Disc), 11
CDFS (Compact Disc File System), 165
cell phones, 104–105. *See also* Android devices;
  iOS devices
  Airplane Mode, 120–121
  communication standards, 120
  components, 117
  email configuration
    for Androids, 122–123
    Internet email, 123
    for iOS devices, 123
  hotspots, 121
  safe disposal, 48
  Wi-Fi calling, 226
cellular generations, 70, 120
cellular Internet access, 66
cellular WAN in laptops, 111
Central Processing Unit (CPU). *See* CPU (Central
  Processing Unit)
chain of custody, 289
change management, 281
charms, 176
chemical solvents, safe disposal, 47
chipsets, 4–5
chkdsk command, 206
CISC (Complex Instruction Set Computer), 37
Cisco DNA (Digital Network Architecture) Center, 77
clean Windows installs, 169–170
cleaning
  dust, 52
  internal components, 52
  laptops, 126–127
  mobile devices, 127
CLI (command-line interface)
  Linux, 232, 234–235
  macOS, 232, 234–235
  Windows
    cmd command, 204
    disk operations, 206
    file manipulation, 206
    file system navigation, 205–206
    folder manipulation, 206
    gpupdate command, 207
    network commands, 212
    PowerShell, 204
    run line utility, 207–208
    session management, 204–205
    syntax and help, 204–205
    task and system commands, 207
    whoami command, 204
    wildcards, 205
  client-server roles, 70–71
  client-side virtualization, 153
  Clock (Control Panel), 191
  closed-ended questions, 55

closed source, open source versus, 223–224
cloud computing, 151
  applications, 155
  characteristics, 156
  cloud services, 155–156
  virtualization and, 151–152
cloud printing, 137
cloud services, 155–156, 227–228
cloud-based network controllers, 78
cmd command, 204
CMOS (Complementary Metal Oxide Semiconductor)
  chip, 32
coax cables and connectors, 40, 79
collated printing, 139
color process of printers, 134
command-line interface (CLI). *See* CLI (command-line
  interface)
commands, scripting, 291
common problems/solutions, 58
  for Linux, macOS, mobile operating systems, 237
  for mobile devices, 128
  in networking, 99
  for printers, 147
  for security issues, 269
  for Windows, 219
communication encryption, 266
communication skills
  active listening, 275–276
  during customer calls, 277–279
  hold and transfer, 277
  professional behavior and, 274, 276
  troubleshooting and, 273–274
communication standards for cell phones, 120
Compact Disc (CD), 11
Compact Disc File System (CDFS), 165
CompactFlash, 25
compatibility mode, application installation, 203
compatibility of operating system, 162
Complementary Metal Oxide Semiconductor (CMOS)
  chip, 32
Complex Instruction Set Computer (CISC), 37
Component Services, 196
Computer (Windows 7), 180
computer forensics, 287
Computer Management console, 194–195
computer name, 189
conditional statements, scripting, 292
configuring
  BIOS, 33
  email, 122
    for Androids, 122–123
    Internet email, 123
    for iOS devices, 123
  firewalls, 94
    DMZ, 95

exceptions, 261–262
MAC address filtering, 96
port forwarding, 95–96
UPnP, 95
whitelisting and blacklisting, 96
IoT devices, 97
laptops
  Bluetooth, 110–111
  cellular WAN, 111
  power management, 109–110
  Wi-Fi, 111
Local Security Policy, 257
NICs, 91, 211
printers, 139
shared printers, 140–141
Windows. *See* Control Panel
wired networks, 92–93, 211–212
  connectivity verification, 212
  ipconfig command, 212
  network profiles, 211–212
  NICs, 211
  nslookup command, 212
  ping command, 212
  tracert command, 212
  in Windows 10, 211
wireless networks, 92–93
  best practices, 266–267
  in Windows 10, 213
connections (Internet). *See* Internet connections
connections (network). *See* networking
connections (printer), 135, **141**
connectors
  coax, 40
  fiber optic, 81
  monitors, 41
  for power supplies, 3
  SATA, 40
  SCSI and IDE, 41
  system panel connectors, types of, 26–27
  twisted pair, 40
  USB, 40
content sources for mobile devices, 224
Control Panel
  Administrative Tools, 194
  BitLocker, 193
  categories, 184
  Clock, 191
  computer name, 189
  Credential Manager, 185
  Default Programs, 192–193
  Device Manager, 190
  Devices and Printers, 190–191
  display settings, 187–188
  Folder Options, 193–194
  homegroups, 186

Internet Options, 186
Language, 192
Network and Sharing Center, 186
network settings, 185–186
Power Options, 188–189
Programs, 192
Region, 191
Settings app versus, 183
Sound, 191
starting, 183
Sync Center, 185
System, 189
System Properties, 189
Troubleshooting, 193
User Account Control (UAC), 184
user account creation, 184
views, 183
virtual memory, 189
Windows Features and Updates, 192
conversation etiquette, 54–55
converters
  AC/DC, 3
  connections, 11
cooling systems, 6, 39
CPU (Central Processing Unit), 4, 6
  32-bit versus 64-bit, 161
  architectures, 37
  common problems/solutions, 58
  cooling systems, 39
  installing, 19
  multicore processors, 38
  performance enhancement, 37–38
  preventive maintenance, 52
  replacing in laptops, 117
  selecting, 20
  upgrading, 44
Credential Manager, 185
CRUs (customer-replaceable units), 114
custom Windows installation, 167–168
customer relations. *See* **communication skills**
customer-replaceable units (CRUs), 114
cyber law, 287

D

data backups, 54, 251
  disaster recovery, 282
  Linux, 232
  macOS, 232–233
  for mobile devices, 127, 227
  Windows
    backup tools, 217–218
    restore points, 217
data cables, installing internal cables, 26
data loss prevention (DLP), 251, 282–283

data migration, 162
data privacy in shared printers, 141
data protection, 250–251
  backups, 251
  BitLocker and BitLocker To Go, 252–253
  encryption, 252
  hard drive recycling, 254
  magnetic media data wiping, 253
  permissions, 251–252
  storage device destruction, 253–254
Data Sources tool, 196
data storage devices. *See* storage devices
data wiping, 253
date changes, 191
DC jacks, replacing in laptops, 116
dedicated print servers, 142
Default Programs (Control Panel), 192–193
demilitarized zone (DMZ), 95
denial of service (DoS), 246
desktops
  personalizing, 176–177
  Windows 7, 175–176
  Windows 8, 176
  Windows 8.1, 176
  Windows 10, 177
destroying
  hard drives, 254
  storage devices, 253–254
device form factors, 3
Device Manager
  in Control Panel, 190
  in troubleshooting, 56
  Windows installation, 166
Devices and Printers (Control Panel), 190–191
DHCP (Dynamic Host Configuration Protocol)
  servers, 71, 88
diagnostic tools, 56
digital assistants, 226
digital subscriber line (DSL), 65
Digital Versatile Disc (DVD), 11
DIP (dual inline package) chips, 7
dir command, 206
directories, creating, 206
directory permissions, Linux and macOS, 234–235
directory structures in Windows, 181
DirectX Diagnostic Tool (DxDiag), 199
disabling AutoPlay, 265
disassembly of computers, 13
disaster recovery, 281–282
  downtime and data loss prevention, 282–283
  steps in, 283
disc drive form factor (SSDs), 10
disk cloning, 167
Disk Error-Checking tool, 201

Disk Management, 165, 199
  array creation, 200
  Disk Error-Checking tool, 201
  disk optimization, 200–201
  drive status indicators, 199–200
  mounting drives, 200
disk operation commands, 206
disk optimization, 200–201
disk utility tools
  Linux, 233
  macOS, 233
display colors, 187
displays. *See also* monitors
  Control Panel settings, 187–188
  in laptops, 108
disposal methods, 47–48
DLP (data loss prevention), 251, 282–283
DMZ (demilitarized zone), 95
DNS (Domain Name Service) servers, 71
docking stations, port replicators versus, 108
documentation
  in IT department, 280
  legal considerations, 288
  purpose, 280
  regulatory compliance requirements, 280
  in troubleshooting, 55, 57
    Linux, macOS, mobile operating systems, 237
    mobile devices, 128
    networking, 99
    printers, 146
    security, 269
    Windows, 219
dollar sign ($), administrative shares, 209
Domain Name Service (DNS) servers, 71
domains, 208–209
DoS (denial of service), 246
double colon (::), in IPv6 addresses, 88
double parity, 39
downtime, preventing, 282–283
DRAM (dynamic RAM), 7
drive activity LED, 27
drive encryption, 34
drive mapping, 209
drive status indicators, 199–200
drives. *See* storage devices
DSL (digital subscriber line), 65
dual inline package (DIP) chips, 7
dust, 52
DVD (Digital Versatile Disc), 11
DxDiag (DirectX Diagnostic Tool), 199
dynamic addressing, 88
Dynamic Host Configuration Protocol (DHCP)
  servers, 71, 88
dynamic RAM (DRAM), 7

E

EFS (encrypted file system), 174, 252
EIDE (Enhanced Integrated Drive Electronics), 9
electrical safety, 1–2
electrostatic discharge (ESD), 1–2
email, configuring, 122
  for Androids, 122–123
  Internet email, 123
  for iOS devices, 123
email filtering, 244
embedded systems, 77–78
enabling mobile device synchronization, 124–125
encrypted file system (EFS), 174, 252
encryption, 252, 266. *See also* BitLocker
endpoint management servers, 77
Enhanced Integrated Drive Electronics (EIDE), 9
enhancing CPU performance, 37–38
environmental concerns, 53
EPS12V, 3
e-readers, 105
error-checking storage devices, 201
eSATA cards, 8
ESD (electrostatic discharge), 1–2
Ethernet over Power, 78
ethical considerations, 284
  PCI, 285
  PHI, 285
  PII, 284–285
Event Viewer, 55, 195
exceptions, firewall configuration, 261–262
exFAT (FAT 64), 164
expansion cards, 10, 112
expansion slots, 4, 8, 24. *See also* adapter cards
exporting Local Security Policy, 257
ExpressCards, 112
external cables, installing, 28
external storage
  for laptops, 112–113
  selecting, 26

F

failed login attempts, restrictions, 227
fans, 3
  preventive maintenance, 52
  selecting, 18
FAT 64 (exFAT), 164
FAT32 (File Allocation Table, 32 bit), 164
fiber optic cables, 80–81
fiber optic connectors, 81
fiber optic Internet access, 65
field-replaceable units (FRUs), 114
File Allocation Table, 32 bit (FAT32), 164
file attributes, 182

file encryption, 252
File Explorer, 180
  in Control Panel, 193–194
  directory structures, 181
  file attributes, 182
  file extensions, 181–182
  file locations, 181
  libraries, 181
  Run as Administrator, 180
  This PC, 180
  Users Folder, 181
file extensions, 181–182
File History, 217–218
file permissions, 251–252
  Linux and macOS, 234–235
  Run as Administrator, 180
file servers, 71–72
file sharing, 210
file synchronization, 185
file systems
  Linux, 230–231
  macOS, 230–231
  navigation commands, 205–206
  Windows, 164–165
File Transfer Protocol (FTP), 71–72
File Transfer Protocol Secure (FTPS), 72
fire safety, 17
firewalls, 76, 260
  advanced security, 262
  configuring, 94
    DMZ, 95
    exceptions, 261–262
    MAC address filtering, 96
    port forwarding, 95–96
    UPnP, 95
    whitelisting and blacklisting, 96
  for mobile devices, 229
  software, 261
  wireless networks, 267
firmware updates
  BIOS, 34–35
  printers, 140
  wireless networks, 267
first response, 288
fitness trackers, 105
flash memory in laptops, 112–113
folder encryption, 252
Folder Options (Control Panel), 193–194
folder permissions, 251–252
folder redirection, 251
formatting hard drives, 165
front panel cables, installing, 26–28
FRUs (field-replaceable units), 114
FTP (File Transfer Protocol), 71–72
FTPS (File Transfer Protocol Secure), 72

full format, 165
function keys in laptops, 107–108

G

Gadgets, 176
GPS (Global Positioning System), 225
GPT (GUID partition table), 164
GPU (graphic processing unit), 38
gpupdate command, 207
graphic ports, 40
graphics cards, 23
grounding electrical devices, 2
group management, 258–260
Group Policies, 207
grub boot manager, 165
guest operating systems (guest OS), 153
GUI (graphical user interface)
    Linux, 231
    macOS, 231
GUID (globally unique identifier) partition
    table (GPT), 164

H

Hard Disk Drives (HDDs). *See* HDDs (Hard Disk Drives)
hard drive caching in shared printers, 141
hardware
    operating system requirements, 160–161
    physical security, 249–250
    print servers, 142
    printer optimization, 140
hardware upgrades
    CPU, 44
    motherboards, 42–44
    peripherals, 45
    power supplies, 45
    storage devices, 44–45
hash encoding, 266
HDDs (Hard Disk Drives), 9
    formatting, 165
    installing, 22
    partitioning, 163–164
    recycling, 254
    selecting, 21
headphones, 12
hidden shares, 209
history of Internet connection types, 64
hold and transfer customers, 277
homegroups, 186, 208–209
host-based authentication, 214
host computers, 153
host devices, 63, 70
host operating systems (host OS), 153
hosted (Type 2) hypervisors, 153–154

hotspots. *See* mobile hotspot Internet access
HTTP (Hypertext Transfer Protocol), 72
HTTPS (secure HTTP), 72
hubs, 74
Hyper-Threading, 37
hypervisors, 153–154

I

IaaS (Infrastructure as a Service), 156
ICMP (Internet Control Message Protocol), 91
icons, networking icons, 63–64
IDE (Integrated Drive Electronics), 9, 41
identifying problems in troubleshooting, 54–56
    Linux, macOS, mobile operating systems, 236
    mobile devices, 127
    networking, 98
    printers, 146
    security, 268
    Windows, 218
IDSs (Intrusion Detection Systems), 76
IMAP (Internet Message Access Protocol), 72
impact printers
    characteristics, 136–137
    preventive maintenance, 145
inexperienced customers, 279
infrared (IR), 118
Infrastructure as a Service (IaaS), 156
inkjet printers
    characteristics, 135
    parts, 135
    preventive maintenance, 143
in-place Windows upgrades, 169
InPrivate Browsing, 263
input devices, 12, 106
input/output (I/O) cards, 23
input/output (I/O) ports, 11
installing
    adapter cards, 23–25
    applications
        compatibility mode, 203
        installation methods, 202–203
        security considerations, 203
        system requirements, 202
    CPU, 19
    external cables, 28
    front panel cables, 26–28
    hard drives, 22
    internal data cables, 26
    internal power cables, 26
    laptop hardware
        expansion cards, 112
        flash memory, 112–113
        smart card readers, 113
        SODIMM memory, 113–114

motherboards, 19
NICs, 90–91
operating systems
  boot managers, 165
  file systems, 164–165
  hard drive partitioning, 163–164
  storage device types, 163
optical drives, 22
power supplies, 17
printers, 138
RAM, 19
storage devices, 21
Windows
  account creation, 166
  custom installation, 167–168
  disk cloning, 167
  file systems, 164–165
  hard drive partitioning, 163–164
  recovery partition, 169
  remote network installation, 168
  steps in, 166
  storage device types, 163
  unattended network installation, 168–169
Integrated Drive Electronics (IDE), 9, 41
Integrated Services Digital Network (ISDN), 65
interfaces for storage devices, 9
intermediary devices, 64
internal components
  common problems/solutions, 58
  in laptops, 107
internal data cables, installing, 26
internal power cables, installing, 26
Internet connections
  analog telephone, 65
  broadband, 65
  cable, 65
  cellular, 66
  DSL, 65
  fiber optic, 65
  history of, 64
  ISDN, 65
  line of sight wireless, 66
  for mobile devices, 118–119
  mobile hotspot, 66
  satellite, 66
  wired networks, 92–93
Internet Control Message Protocol (ICMP), 91
Internet email, configuring, 123
Internet Message Access Protocol (IMAP), 72
Internet of Things (IoT), device configuration, 97
Internet Options (Control Panel), 186
Internet Protocol v4. *See* IPv4 addresses
Internet Protocol v6. *See* IPv6 addresses
Internet reference tools for troubleshooting, 59
Intrusion Detection Systems (IDSs), 76

Intrusion Prevention Systems (IPSs), 76
inverters in laptops, 108
I/O (input/output) cards, 23
I/O (input/output) ports, 11
iOS devices
  Android devices versus
    apps and content sources, 224
    open source versus closed source, 223–224
    touch interfaces, 224
  email configuration, 123
  synchronizing, 125–126
IoT (Internet of Things), device configuration, 97
ipconfig command, 212
ipconfig/all command, 86
IPSs (Intrusion Prevention Systems), 76
IPv4 addresses, 85–86
  dynamic addressing, 88
  format, 86–87
  link-local addressing, 89
  NAT, 93
  static addressing, 88
IPv6 addresses, 85–86
  dynamic addressing, 88
  format, 87–88
  link-local addressing, 89
  static addressing, 88
IR (infrared), 118
ISDN (Integrated Services Digital Network), 65
ISO files, 200
IT as a service (ITaaS), 156
IT department, documentation in, 280
IT professionals
  call center technicians
    call centers, 289
    level one responsibilities, 289–290
    level two responsibilities, 290
  change management, 281
  communication skills
    active listening, 275–276
    during customer calls, 277–279
    hold and transfer, 277
    professional behavior and, 274, 276
    troubleshooting and, 273–274
  disaster recovery, 281–282
    downtime and data loss prevention, 282–283
    steps in, 283
  documentation
    in IT department, 280
    purpose, 280
    regulatory compliance requirements, 280
  ethical and legal considerations, 284
    chain of custody, 289
    computer forensics, 287
    cyber law, 287
    documentation, 288

first response, 288
licensing, 286
PCI, 285
PHI, 285
PII, 284–285
types of laws, 286
scripting
  commands, 291
  conditional statements, 292
  examples, 291
  languages, 291
  loops, 292
  variables, 291
ITaaS (IT as a service), 156
ITX, 5

J

jailbreaking mobile devices, 229–230
jump lists, 178

K

Kerberos, 214
keyboards
  preventive maintenance, 52
  replacing in laptops, 115
knowledgeable customers, 278–279

L

LANs. *See* networking
Land Grid Array (LGA), 6
Language (Control Panel), 192
languages, scripting, 291
laptops, 104
  components
    backlights and inverters, 108
    displays, 108
    docking stations versus port replicators, 108
    expansion cards, 112
    external features, 106
    flash memory, 112–113
    function keys, 107–108
    input devices and LEDs, 106
    internal components, 107
    motherboards, 106–107
    smart card readers, 113
    SODIMM memory, 113–114
    webcams and microphones, 109
    Wi-Fi antenna connectors, 109
  configuring
    Bluetooth, 110–111
    cellular WAN, 111

    power management, 109–110
    Wi-Fi, 111
  preventive maintenance, 126–127
  repairing, 114–115
    battery replacement, 115
    CPU replacement, 117
    DC jack replacement, 116
    internal storage and optical drive replacement, 116
    keyboard replacement, 115
    motherboard replacement, 117
    plastic frame replacement, 117
    screen replacement, 115
    speaker replacement, 117
    wireless card replacement, 116
laser printers
  characteristics, 135
  parts, 136
  preventive maintenance, 144
  printing process, 136
Last Known Good Configuration, 170
LCD (liquid-crystal display), 108
LED (light-emitting diode), 106, 108
legacy ports, 40
legacy systems, 77
legal considerations, 284
  chain of custody, 289
  computer forensics, 287
  cyber law, 287
  documentation, 288
  first response, 288
  licensing, 286
  PCI, 285
  PHI, 285
  PII, 284–285
  types of laws, 286
level one call center technicians, 289–290
level two call center technicians, 290
LGA (Land Grid Array), 6
libraries, 181
licensing, 286
light-emitting diode (LED), 106, 108
line of sight wireless Internet access, 66
link-local addressing, 89
Linux
  administrative commands, 235
  backup and recovery, 232
  best practices, 233–234
  boot managers, 165
  CLI, 232, 234–235
  disk utility tools, 233
  file and directory permissions, 234–235
  file systems, 230–231
  GUI, 231

troubleshooting
  common problems/solutions, 237
  steps in, 236–237
updating, 234
liquid-crystal display (LCD), 108
local passwords, managing, 256
Local Security Policy, 256
  configuring, 257
  exporting, 257
Local Users and Groups Manager, 195, 258–259
locator applications for mobile devices, 228
locks
  screen locks for mobile devices, 227
  types of, 249
log files, 195
logging into routers, 93
login attempts, restrictions, 227
logins (Windows), security, 255
LoJack, 34
loops, scripting, 292

M

M.2 modules, 10
MAC (media access control) addresses, 75, 85–86, 96
macOS
  administrative commands, 235
  backup and recovery, 232–233
  best practices, 233–234
  boot managers, 165
  CLI, 232, 234–235
  disk utility tools, 233
  file and directory permissions, 234–235
  file systems, 230–231
  GUI, 231
  troubleshooting
    common problems/solutions, 237
    steps in, 236–237
  updating, 234
magnetic media storage, 9–10, 253
mail servers, 72
maintenance. *See* preventive maintenance
malware, 241–242
  preventing, 245
    anti-malware programs, 243–244
    signature file updates, 244–245
  remediating infected systems, 245
managed switches, 75
mantraps, 249
mapping drives, 209
Material Safety and Data Sheet (MSDS), 48
MBR (master boot record), 164
md command, 206
mean time between failures (MTBF) for printers, 134

media access control (MAC) addresses. *See* MAC
  (media access control) addresses
media readers
  selecting, 25
  types of, 25
memory, 6–8
  common problems/solutions, 58
  memory modules, 7–8
  printer memory, 140
  RAM (random access memory), 7
  ROM (read-only memory), 7
memory modules, 7–8
Memory Stick, 25
mesh networks, configuring, 93
mice, preventive maintenance, 52
Micro-ATX, 5
microphones, in laptops, 109
MicroSD cards, 25
Microsoft Management Console (MMC), 198
Microsoft OneDrive, 185
MiniSD cards, 25
mini-USB cables, 118
mirroring, 39
MMC (Microsoft Management Console), 198
MMF (multimode fiber), 81
mobile devices, 103–104
  augmented reality (AR), 106
  cell phones, 104–105
    Airplane Mode, 120–121
    communication standards, 120
    components, 117
    hotspots, 121
  connections
    Bluetooth, 121–122
    wired, 118
    wireless, 118–119
  email configuration, 122
    for Androids, 122–123
    Internet email, 123
    for iOS devices, 123
  e-readers, 105
  features
    GPS, 225
    NFC payment, 226
    screen calibration, 225
    screen orientation, 225
    virtual assistants, 226
    VPNs, 226
    Wi-Fi calling, 226
  fitness trackers, 105
  laptops, 104
    backlights and inverters, 108
    battery replacement, 115
    Bluetooth configuration, 110–111

cellular WAN configuration, 111
CPU replacement, 117
DC jack replacement, 116
displays, 108
docking stations versus port replicators, 108
expansion cards, 112
external features, 106
flash memory, 112–113
function keys, 107–108
input devices and LEDs, 106
internal components, 107
internal storage and optical drive replacement, 116
keyboard replacement, 115
motherboard replacement, 117
motherboards, 106–107
plastic frame replacement, 117
power management, 109–110
preventive maintenance, 126–127
repairing, 114–115
screen replacement, 115
smart card readers, 113
SODIMM memory, 113–114
speaker replacement, 117
webcams and microphones, 109
Wi-Fi antenna connectors, 109
Wi-Fi configuration, 111
wireless card replacement, 116
operating systems
apps and content sources, 224
open source versus closed source, 223–224
touch interfaces, 224
troubleshooting, 236–237
preventive maintenance, 126–127
security
anti-malware programs, 228–229
cloud-enabled services, 227–228
locator applications, 228
patches and updates, 230
remote backup, 227
remote lock and remote wipe, 228
rooting and jailbreaking, 229–230
screen locks and biometric authentication, 227
smartwatches, 105
specialty devices, 118
synchronizing
connection types, 125–126
enabling, 124–125
types of data, 124
tablets, 105
troubleshooting
common problems/solutions, 128
steps in, 127–128
virtual reality (VR), 106
wearables, 118

mobile hotspot Internet access, 66, 118, 121
modems, 64
monitor resolution, 41
monitors, 12
characteristics, 41–42
common problems/solutions, 58
display standards, 42
multiple monitors, 42
safe disposal, 47
terminology, 42
motherboards, 4–5
chipsets, 5
common problems/solutions, 58
components, 4, 19
form factors, 5
installing, 19
in laptops, 106–107
replacing in laptops, 117
selecting, 19–20
upgrading, 42–44
mounting drives, 200
mSata modules, 10
MSDS (Material Safety and Data Sheet), 48
MTBF (mean time between failures) for printers, 134
multicore processors, 38
multimode fiber (MMF), 81
multiple monitors, 42, 188
multiprocessing, 160
multitasking, 160
multithreading, 160
multi-user operating systems, 160

N

NAS (network attached storage) devices, 46
NAT (Network Address Translation), 93
native (Type 1) hypervisors, 153–154
native mode, 41
native resolution, 41
near field communication (NFC), 69, 118, 226
Network Address Translation (NAT), 93
Network and Sharing Center, 186
network attached storage (NAS) devices, 46
network attacks, 246–247
network design, 89–90
network devices, 73
bridges, 74
cloud-based network controllers, 78
embedded systems, 77–78
Ethernet over Power, 78
hubs, 74
legacy systems, 77
NICs, 74

patch panels, 78

PoE, 78

repeaters, 74

routers, 75

switches, 74–75

wireless access points, 75

Network File System (NFS), 165

network installations

remote, 168

unattended, 168–169

Network Interface Cards (NICs). *See* NICs
(Network Interface Cards)

network media, 64

network profiles, 211–212

network services, 70

authentication servers, 73

client-server roles, 70–71

DHCP, 71, 88

DNS, 71

file servers, 71–72

mail servers, 72

print servers, 71

dedicated, 142

hardware, 142

purpose, 141–142

software, 142

proxy servers, 73

syslog servers, 73

traditional deployment, virtualization versus, 152

virtualization, 152–153

web servers, 72

network shares, 209

networking

addresses

dynamic addressing, 88

ICMP, 91

IPv4 addresses, 85–87

IPv6 addresses, 85–88

link-local addressing, 89

MAC (media access control) addresses, 85–86

NAT for IPv4, 93

static addressing, 88

viewing, 86

application port numbers, 68

cables

building and testing, 80

coax, 79

fiber optic, 80–81

tools for, 79

twisted pair, 79–80

types of, 79

connections, testing, 91

Control Panel settings, 185–186

firewall configuration, 94

DMZ, 95

MAC address filtering, 96

port forwarding, 95–96

UPnP, 95

whitelisting and blacklisting, 96

homegroups, 186

icons, 63–64

Internet connection types

analog telephone, 65

broadband, 65

cable, 65

cellular, 66

DSL, 65

fiber optic, 65

history of, 64

ISDN, 65

line of sight wireless, 66

mobile hotspot, 66

satellite, 66

IoT device configuration, 97

network design, 89–90

network devices, 73

bridges, 74

cloud-based network controllers, 78

embedded systems, 77–78

Ethernet over Power, 78

hubs, 74

legacy systems, 77

NICs, 74

patch panels, 78

PoE, 78

repeaters, 74

routers, 75

switches, 74–75

wireless access points, 75

network services, 70

authentication servers, 73

client-server roles, 70–71

DHCP, 71, 88

DNS, 71

file servers, 71–72

mail servers, 72

print servers, 71, 141–142

proxy servers, 73

syslog servers, 73

web servers, 72

NICs

configuring, 91

installing, 90–91

selecting, 90

updating, 90–91

physical security, 249–250

security devices, 76
  endpoint management servers, 77
  firewalls, 76, 94
  IPSs and IDSs, 76
  UTMs, 76–77
topologies, 64
transport layer protocols, 67
  TCP, 67
  TCP/IP model, 67
  UDP, 67–68
troubleshooting
  common problems/solutions, 99
  steps in, 98–99
Windows
  administrative shares, 209
  domains and workgroups, 208–209
  homegroups, 208–209
  network shares and mapping drives, 209
  Remote Assistance, 214–215
  Remote Desktop, 214–215
  resource sharing, 210
  SSH (Secure Shell), 214
  Telnet, 214
  VPN configuration, 213–214
  wired network configuration, 211–212
  wireless network configuration, 213
wired network configuration, 92–93, 211–212
  connectivity verification, 212
  ipconfig command, 212
  network profiles, 211–212
  NICs, 211
  nslookup command, 212
  ping command, 212
  tracert command, 212
  in Windows 10, 211
wireless networks
  configuring, 92–93
  logging into router, 93
  NAT for IPv4, 93–94
  QoS, 94
  security best practices, 266–267
wireless protocols
  Bluetooth, 69
  cellular generations, 70
  NFC, 69
  RFID, 69
  smart home standards, 69–70
  WLAN, 69
  Zigbee, 69–70
  Z-Wave, 70
New Technology File System (NTFS), 164
NFC (near field communication), 69, 118, 226
NFS (Network File System), 165

NICs (Network Interface Cards), 8, 23, 74
  configuring, 91, 211
  installing, 90–91
  selecting, 90
  updating, 90–91
noise, 36
Northbridge chipsets, 5
nslookup command, 212
NTFS (New Technology File System), 164
NVMe (Non-Volatile Memory Express) specification, 10

O

Ohm's Law, 35
OLED (organic light-emitting diode), 108
OneDrive, 185
open-ended questions, 55
open source, closed source versus, 223–224
operating systems. *See also* Windows
  compatibility, 162
  data migration, 162
  Disk Management, 165
  installing
    boot managers, 165
    file systems, 164–165
    hard drive partitioning, 163–164
    storage device types, 163
  Linux
    administrative commands, 235
    backup and recovery, 232
    best practices, 233–234
    CLI, 232, 234–235
    disk utility tools, 233
    file and directory permissions, 234–235
    file systems, 230–231
    GUI, 231
    updating, 234
  macOS
    administrative commands, 235
    backup and recovery, 232–233
    best practices, 233–234
    CLI, 232, 234–235
    disk utility tools, 233
    file and directory permissions, 234–235
    file systems, 230–231
    GUI, 231
    updating, 234
  for mobile devices
    apps and content sources, 224
    open source versus closed source, 223–224
    patches and updates, 230
    touch interfaces, 224
  purpose, 160

requirements, 160–161
terminology, 159–160
troubleshooting
  common problems/solutions, 237
  steps in, 236–237
upgrading, 162
optical drives, 11
  installing, 22
  replacing in laptops, 116
  selecting, 21–22
optimizing
  printers
    hardware optimization, 140
    software optimization, 139–140
  storage devices, 200–201
organic light-emitting diode (OLED), 108
output devices, 12–13
  monitors and projectors, 12
  printers, 13
  speakers and headphones, 12
  Virtual Reality (VR) and Augmented Reality (AR)
    headsets, 12–13
overclocking, 38

P

PaaS (Platform as a Service), 156
pairing Bluetooth, 121–122
parity, 39
partitions, 163–164, 169
passwords
  BIOS, 33–34, 255
  Credential Manager, 185
  guidelines, 256
  local password management, 256
patch panels, 78
patches, 230, 265
PCs. *See* personal computers (PCs)
PCI (Payment Card Industry), 285
PCI (Peripheral Component Interconnect), 24
PCIe (PCI Express), 24
Peek, 175
performance enhancement
  of CPU, 37–38
  of Windows, 189
Performance Monitor, 196
Peripheral Component Interconnect (PCI), 24
peripherals, upgrading, 45
permissions, 251–252
  Linux and macOS, 234–235
  Run as Administrator, 180
persistent data, 287
personal computers (PCs)
  assembly
    adapter card installation, 23–25
    adapter card selection, 23–24

case and fan selection, 18
case reassembly and external cable
  installation, 28
CPU selection, 20
external storage selection, 26
front panel cable installation, 26–28
general and fire safety, 17
hard drive installation, 22
hard drive selection, 21
internal data cable installation, 26
internal power cable installation, 26
media reader selection, 25
motherboard component installation, 19
motherboard selection, 19–20
optical drive installation, 22
optical drive selection, 21–22
power supply installation, 17
power supply selection, 18
RAM selection, 20–21
storage device installation, 21
boot process
  BIOS and CMOS, 32
  BIOS/UEFI configuration, 33
  BIOS/UEFI menus, 31
  BIOS/UEFI security, 33–34
  firmware updates, 34–35
  POST (power-on self-test), 31–32
  UEFI, 32–33
components
  adapter cards, 8
  adapters, 11
  case, 2–3
  connectors, 3
  converters, 11
  cooling systems, 6
  CPU (Central Processing Unit), 6
  fans, 3
  input devices, 12
  memory, 6–8
  motherboards, 4–5
  output devices, 12–13
  ports and cables, 11
  power supplies, 3–4
  storage devices, 9–11
device form factors, 3
disassembly, 13
electrical safety, 1–2
explained, 1
hardware upgrades
  CPU, 44
  motherboards, 42–44
  peripherals, 45
  power supplies, 45
  storage devices, 44–45
NAS devices, 46
physical security, 249–250, 254–255

safe disposal, 47–48
thick and thin clients, 46
personal reference tools for troubleshooting, 58–59
personalizing Windows desktop, 176–177
personally identifiable information (PII), 284–285
PGA (Pin Grid Array), 6
PHI (protected health information), 285
physical security, 249
mantraps, 249
personal computers and network hardware, 249–250
types of locks, 249
Windows computers, 254–255
Picture Card (xD), 25
PII (personally identifiable information), 284–285
Pin Grid Array (PGA), 6
ping command, 91, 212
pinned applications, 178
plan of action in troubleshooting, 57
Linux, macOS, mobile operating systems, 236
mobile devices, 128
networking, 98
printers, 146
security, 269
Windows, 219
plastic frames, replacing in laptops, 117
Platform as a Service (PaaS), 156
PoE (Power over Ethernet), 78
POP (Post Office Protocol), 72
pop-up blockers, 263–264
port forwarding, 95–96, 267
port numbers, 68
port replicators, docking stations versus, 108
port triggering, 95–96, 267
ports, 11
legacy ports, 40
video and graphic ports, 40
POST (power-on self-test), 31–32
Post Office Protocol (POP), 72
power button, 26
power fluctuation types, 36
power LED, 27
power management in laptops, 109–110
Power Options (Control Panel), 188–189
Power over Ethernet (PoE), 78
power protection devices, 36–37
disaster recovery, 282–283
preventive maintenance, 52
power supplies, 3–4
common problems/solutions, 58
connectors, 3
form factors, 3
installing, 17
internal power cables, installing, 26
power fluctuation types, 36
power protection devices, 36–37

selecting, 18
upgrading, 45
voltages, 4, 35
wattage, 35
power surges, 36
powerline networking, 78
power-on self-test (POST), 31–32
PowerShell, 204
Preboot eXecution Environment (PXE), 168
preventing
downtime and data loss, 282–283
malware, 245
anti-malware programs, 243–244
signature file updates, 244–245
network attacks, 247
social engineering attacks, 248
preventive maintenance
benefits of, 51
dust, 52
environmental concerns, 53
internal components, 52
laptops, 126–127
Linux and macOS, 233–234
mobile devices, 126–127
printers
3D printers, 145
impact printers, 145
inkjet printers, 143
laser printers, 144
thermal printers, 145
vendor guidelines, 143
security
disabling AutoPlay, 265
restrictive settings, 264–265
service packs and patches, 265
software, 53
Windows
backup tools, 217–218
plan contents, 215–216
restore points, 217
scheduled tasks, 217
Windows Update, 216
primary partitions, 164
Print Management, 197
print servers, 71
dedicated, 142
hardware, 142
purpose, 141–142
software, 142
printers, 13
3D
characteristics, 137–138
component printing, 145
parts, 138
preventive maintenance, 145

cartridge and toner disposal, 47
characteristics, 133
  automatic document feeder, 134
  color process, 134
  quality, 133
  reliability, 134
  speed, 133
  total cost of ownership, 134
configuring, 139
connection types, 135
Devices and Printers (Control Panel), 190–191
impact
  characteristics, 136–137
  preventive maintenance, 145
inkjet
  characteristics, 135
  parts, 135
  preventive maintenance, 143
installing, 138
laser
  characteristics, 135
  parts, 136
  preventive maintenance, 144
  printing process, 136
optimizing
  hardware optimization, 140
  software optimization, 139–140
preventive maintenance
  3D printers, 145
  impact printers, 145
  inkjet printers, 143
  laser printers, 144
  thermal printers, 145
  vendor guidelines, 143
sharing, 210
  configuring, 140–141
  dedicated print servers, 142
  hardware print servers, 142
  print server purpose, 141–142
  software print servers, 142
  wireless printer connections, 141
testing functions, 138–139
thermal
  characteristics, 136
  preventive maintenance, 145
troubleshooting
  common problems/solutions, 147
  steps in, 146
virtual
  characteristics, 137
  cloud printing, 137
problem identification in troubleshooting, 54–56
  Linux, macOS, mobile operating systems, 236
  mobile devices, 127
  networking, 98
  printers, 146
  security, 268
  Windows, 218
problem-solving. *See* **troubleshooting**
professional behavior
  communication skills and, 274
  during customer calls, 277–279
  with customers, 276
Programs (Control Panel), 192
projectors, 12
protected health information (PHI), 285
protection. *See* **security**
proxy servers, 73
public key authentication, 214
PXE (Preboot eXecution Environment), 168

Q

QoS (Quality of Service), 94
quality of printers, 133
question mark (?), in Windows commands, 205
quick format, 165

R

Radio Frequency Identification (RFID), 69
RAID (redundant array of independent disks), 39
RAM (random access memory), 4, 7
  installing, 19
  in laptops, 113–114
  performance enhancement, 189
  preventive maintenance, 52
  selecting, 20–21
read-only memory (ROM), 7
recovery partitions, 169
recycling hard drives, 254
Reduced Instruction Set Computer (RISC), 37
redundant array of independent disks (RAID), 39
refresh rate, 187
Regedit, 198
Region (Control Panel), 191
Registry, 198
regulatory compliance requirements, 280
  PCI, 285
  PHI, 285
  PII, 284–285
reliability of printers, 134
remediating malware-infected systems, 245
Remote Assistance, 214–215
remote backup for mobile devices, 227
Remote Desktop, 214–215
remote lock for mobile devices, 228
remote network installations, 168
remote wipe for mobile devices, 228
repairing laptops, 114–115

battery replacement, 115
CPU replacement, 117
DC jack replacement, 116
internal storage and optical drive replacement, 116
keyboard replacement, 115
motherboard replacement, 117
plastic frame replacement, 117
screen replacement, 115
speaker replacement, 117
wireless card replacement, 116
repeaters, **74**
replacing
  cell phone components, 117
  laptop components
    batteries, 115
    CPU, 117
    DC jacks, 116
    keyboards, 115
    motherboards, 117
    plastic frames, 117
    screens, 115
    speakers, 117
    storage devices, 116
    wireless cards, 116
reset button, **27**
resolution, **41, 187**
resource sharing, **210**
  files and folders, 210
  printers, 210
restore and recovery (Windows), **169**
restore points, **217**
restrictive settings, **264–265**
RFID (Radio Frequency Identification), **69**
Ribbon, **180**
RISC (Reduced Instruction Set Computer), **37**
ROM (read-only memory), **7**
root access, Linux and macOS, **235**
rooting mobile devices, **229–230**
routers, **64, 75, 93**
rude customers, **278**
Run as Administrator, **180**
run line utility, **207–208**

S

SaaS (Software as a Service), **156**
Safe Mode, **170**
Safe Mode with Command Prompt, **170**
Safe Mode with Networking, **170**
safety
  computer assembly, 17
  disposal methods, 47–48
  electrical safety, 1–2
  SDS (Safety Data Sheet), 48
Safety Data Sheet (SDS), **48**

sandboxes, **229**
SAS (Serially Attached SCSI), **9**
SATA (Serial AT Attachment), **9, 40, 162**
satellite Internet access, **66**
scheduled servicing for printers, **134**
scheduled tasks
  Linux and macOS, 233–234
  Windows, 217
SCP (Secure Copy), **72**
screen calibration for mobile devices, **225**
screen locks for mobile devices, **227**
screen orientation, **187, 225**
screen size, **41**
screens, replacing in laptops, **115**
screws, loose, **52**
scripting
  commands, 291
  conditional statements, 292
  examples, 291
  languages, 291
  loops, 292
  variables, 291
SCSI (Small Computer System Interface), **9, 41**
SD (secure digital) cards, **25**
SDS (Safety Data Sheet), **48**
Secure Boot, **34**
Secure Copy (SCP), **72**
secure digital (SD) cards, **25**
secure HTTP (HTTPS), **72**
Secure Shell (SSH), **214**
security
  application installation, 203
  BIOS/UEFI, 33–34
  Credential Manager, 185
  data protection, 250–251
    backups, 251
    BitLocker and BitLocker To Go, 252–253
    encryption, 252
    hard drive recycling, 254
    magnetic media data wiping, 253
    permissions, 251–252
    storage device destruction, 253–254
  malware prevention, 245
    anti-malware programs, 243–244
    signature file updates, 244–245
  malware remediation, 245
  mobile devices
    anti-malware programs, 228–229
    cloud-enabled services, 227–228
    locator applications, 228
    patches and updates, 230
    remote backup, 227
    remote lock and remote wipe, 228
    rooting and jailbreaking, 229–230
    screen locks and biometric authentication, 227

network security devices, 76
  endpoint management servers, 77
  firewalls, 76, 94
  IPSs and IDSs, 76
  UTMs, 76–77
physical, 249
  mantraps, 249
  personal computers and network hardware, 249–250
  types of locks, 249
preventive maintenance, 216
  disabling AutoPlay, 265
  restrictive settings, 264–265
  service packs and patches, 265
security policies, 248
shared printers, 141
System and Security category (Control Panel), 184
threats
  adware, 243
  malware, 241–242
  network attacks, 246–247
  social engineering attacks, 247–248
  Trojan horses, 242
  viruses, 242
troubleshooting
  common problems/solutions, 269
  steps in, 268–269
web browsers
  ActiveX filtering, 264
  authentication, 262–263
  InPrivate Browsing, 263
  pop-up blockers, 263–264
  SmartScreen Filter, 264
Windows
  Account Policies, 257
  Active Directory, 259–260
  BIOS security, 255
  firewall exception configuration, 261–262
  firewalls, 260
  local password management, 256
  Local Security Policy, 256
  Local Security Policy configuration, 257
  Local Security Policy export, 257
  login security, 255
  physical security, 254–255
  software firewalls, 261
  user and group management, 258–260
  username and password guidelines, 256
  Windows Firewall with Advanced Security, 262
wireless
  authentication, 267
  best practices, 266–267
  communication encryption, 266
  firewalls, 267
  firmware updates, 267
  modes, 267

port forwarding and port triggering, 267
  UPnP, 268
security credentials management, Linux and macOS, 234
security policies, 248
  Account Policies, 257
  Local Security Policy, 256
    configuring, 257
    exporting, 257
selecting
  adapter cards, 23–24
  case (for PCs), 18
  CPU, 20
  external storage, 26
  fans, 18
  hard drives, 21
  media readers, 25
  motherboards, 19–20
  NICs, 90
  optical drives, 21–22
  power supplies, 18
  RAM, 20–21
self-grounding, 2
semiconductor storage, 10
Serial AT Attachment (SATA), 9, 40, 162
Serially Attached SCSI (SAS), 9
servers. See network services
service-level agreement (SLA), 284
service packs, 265
Service Set ID (SSID), 266–267
Services console, 196
Settings app, 183
  display settings, 187
  network settings, 185–186
SFTP (SSH File Transfer Protocol), 72
Shake, 175
sharing
  files and folders, 210
  local resources, 210
  printers, 210
    configuring, 140–141
    dedicated print servers, 142
    hardware print servers, 142
    print server purpose, 141–142
    software print servers, 142
    wireless printer connections, 141
shielded twisted-pair (STP) cabling, 80
signature file updates, 244–245
SIM (System Image Manager), 168
Simple Mail Transfer Protocol (SMTP), 72
single-mode fiber (SMF), 81
SLA (service-level agreement), 284
Small Computer System Interface (SCSI), 9, 41
smart card readers in laptops, 113
smart home standards, 69–70

smartphones. *See* cell phones
SmartScreen Filter, 264
smartwatches, 105
SMF (single-mode fiber), 81
SMTP (Simple Mail Transfer Protocol), 72
Snap, 176
social engineering attacks, 247–248
SODIMM memory in laptops, 113–114
software
 firewalls, 261
 licensing, 286
 mobile device security
  anti-malware programs, 228–229
  patches and updates, 230
  rooting and jailbreaking, 229–230
 operating system requirements, 160–161
 preventive maintenance, 53
 print servers, 142
 printer optimization, 139–140
Software as a Service (SaaS), 156
solid-state drives (SSDs), 10
Solid State Hybrid Drives (SSHDs), 10
solution implementation in troubleshooting, 57
 Linux, macOS, mobile operating systems, 236
 mobile devices, 128
 networking, 98
 printers, 146
 security, 269
 Windows, 219
Sound (Control Panel), 191
sound adapters, 8
sound cards, 23
Southbridge chipsets, 5
speakers, 12, 117
specialty devices, 118
speed of printers, 133
spikes, 36
SPS (standby power supply), 37
SRAM (static RAM), 7
SSDs (solid-state drives), 10
SSH (Secure Shell), 214
SSH File Transfer Protocol (SFTP), 72
SSHDs (Solid State Hybrid Drives), 10
SSID (Service Set ID), 266–267
standby power supply (SPS), 37
Start menu
 Windows 7, 178
 Windows 8, 177
 Windows 8.1, 177
 Windows 10, 177
starting Control Panel, 183
startup modes
 Windows 7, 170
 Windows 8 and 10, 171
startup programs, 216

static addressing, 88
static RAM (SRAM), 7
storage controllers, 23
storage devices, 9–11
 common problems/solutions, 58
 destruction, 253–254
 error-checking, 201
 external storage, selecting, 26
 installing, 21
 interfaces, 9
 magnetic media, 9–10
 media readers, selecting, 25
 mounting drives, 200
 optical drives, 11
 optimizing, 200–201
 for OS installation, 163
 preventive maintenance, 52
 RAID, 39
 replacing in laptops, 116
 semiconductor storage, 10
 upgrading, 44–45
Storage Spaces, 200
STP (shielded twisted-pair) cabling, 80
striping, 39
surge protectors, 36
switches, 64, 74–75
Sync Center, 185
synchronizing
 files, 185
 mobile devices
  connection types, 125–126
  enabling, 124–125
  types of data, 124
syslog servers, 73
Sysprep (System Preparation), 167
System (Control Panel), 189
system administration
 Administrative Tools (Control Panel), 194
 Component Services, 196
 Computer Management, 194–195
 Data Sources, 196
 DxDiag, 199
 Event Viewer, 195
 Local Users and Groups Manager, 195
 Microsoft Management Console (MMC), 198
 Performance Monitor, 196
 Print Management, 197
 Regedit, 198
 Registry, 198
 Services, 196
 System Configuration, 197
 System Information, 197
 Windows Memory Diagnostics, 197
System Configuration tool, 197
System Image Manager (SIM), 168

System Information tool, 197
system panel connectors, types of, 26–27
System Preparation (Sysprep), 167
System Properties (Control Panel), 189
System and Security category (Control Panel), 184
system speaker, 27

T

tablets, 48, 105
talkative customers, 277–278
tape drives, 9–10
Task Manager, 178–179
  in troubleshooting, 56
  Windows 7, 179
task and system commands, 207
Taskbar, 178
tasklist command, 207
TCO (total cost of ownership) of printers, 134
TCP (Transmission Control Protocol), 67–68
TCP/IP attacks, 246
TCP/IP model, 67
technician's toolkit, 13
Telnet, 214
testing
  network cables, 80
  network connections, 91
  printer functions, 138–139
  in troubleshooting, 56
    Linux, macOS, mobile operating systems, 236
    mobile devices, 128
    networking, 98
    printers, 146
    security, 268
    Windows, 218
tethering, 66, 118, 121
theory of probable cause in troubleshooting, 56
  Linux, macOS, mobile operating systems, 236
  mobile devices, 128
  networking, 98
  printers, 146
  security, 268
  testing, 56, 98
  Windows, 218
thermal printers
  characteristics, 136
  preventive maintenance, 145
thick clients, 46
thin clients, 46
This PC, 180
threats
  adware, 243
  malware, 241–242

network attacks, 246–247
social engineering attacks, 247–248
Trojan horses, 242
viruses, 242
throttling, 38
thumbnail previews, 178
tiles, 176
time changes, 191
Time Machine, 232–233
topologies, network topologies, 64
total cost of ownership (TCO) of printers, 134
touch interfaces for mobile devices, 224
TPM (Trusted Platform Module), 34, 252
tracert command, 212
Transmission Control Protocol (TCP), 67–68
transport layer protocols, 67
  TCP, 67
  TCP/IP model, 67
  UDP, 67–68
Trojan horses, 242
troubleshooting, 53–54
  common problems/solutions, 58
    for Linux, macOS, mobile operating systems, 237
    for mobile devices, 128
    in networking, 99
    for printers, 147
    for security issues, 269
    for Windows, 219
  communication skills and, 273–274
  data backups, 54
  Internet reference tools, 59
  personal reference tools, 58–59
  steps in
    documentation, 57
    functionality verification, 57
    for Linux, macOS, mobile operating systems, 236–237
    for mobile devices, 127–128
    for network problems, 98–99
    plan of action establishment, 57
    for printers, 146
    problem identification, 54–56
    for security issues, 268–269
    solution implementation, 57
    testing theories, 56
    theory of probable cause, 56
    for Windows, 218–219
  with Windows, 193
Troubleshooting (Control Panel), 193
Trusted Platform Module (TPM), 34, 252
TV tuner cards, 8
twisted pair cables and connectors, 40, 79–80
Type 1 (native) hypervisors, 153–154
Type 2 (hosted) hypervisors, 153–154

U

UAC (User Account Control), 184, 258
UDP (User Datagram Protocol), 67–68
UEFI (Unified Extensible Firmware Interface) chip, 4
  BIOS and, 32–33
  BIOS/UEFI menus, 31
  configuring, 33
  security, 33–34, 255
unattended network installations, 168–169
Unified Threat Management (UTMs), 76–77
uninstalling applications, 203
uninterruptible power supply (UPS), 36
Universal Plug and Play (UPnP), 95, 268
Universal Serial Bus (USB) cables and connectors, 40
Universal Serial Bus (USB) controller cards, 8
Unix. *See* Linux; macOS
unmanaged switches, 75
unshielded twisted-pair (UTP) cables, 79
updating
  firmware
    BIOS, 34–35
    printers, 140
    wireless networks, 267
  Linux and macOS operating systems, 234
  mobile devices, 127, 230
  NICs, 90–91
  signature files, 244–245
  Windows, 216
upgrading
  CPU, 44
  motherboards, 42–44
  operating systems, 162
  peripherals, 45
  power supplies, 45
  storage devices, 44–45
  Windows, 162, 169–170
UPnP (Universal Plug and Play), 95, 268
UPS (uninterruptible power supply), 36
USB (Universal Serial Bus) cables and connectors, 40
USB (Universal Serial Bus) controller cards, 8
User Account Control (UAC), 184, 258
user accounts (Windows), creating, 166, 184
user authentication in shared printers, 141
User Datagram Protocol (UDP), 67–68
user management, 258–260
username/password authentication, 214
usernames, guidelines, 256
Users Folder, 181
UTMs (Unified Threat Management), 76–77
UTP (unshielded twisted-pair) cables, 79

V

variables, scripting, 291
verifying
  connectivity in wired networks, 212
  functionality in troubleshooting, 57
    Linux, macOS, mobile operating systems, 237
    mobile devices, 128
    networking, 98
    printers, 146
    security, 269
    Windows, 219
versions of Windows, 173–174
  Windows 7, 174
    desktop, 175–176
    Start menu, 178
    Task Manager, 179
  Windows 8, 174
    desktop, 176
    Start menu, 177
  Windows 8.1, 174–175
    desktop, 176
    Start menu, 177
  Windows 10, 175
    desktop, 177
    Settings app, 183
    Start menu, 177
video adapters, 8
video ports and cables, 11, 40
viewing network addresses, 86
views, Control Panel, 183
virtual assistants, 226
virtual machines (VMs), requirements, 154–155
virtual memory, 189
virtual printers
  characteristics, 137
  cloud printing, 137
Virtual Private Networks (VPNs)
  for mobile devices, 226
  in Windows, 213–214
virtual reality (VR), 12–13, 106
virtualization, 38
  client-side, 153
  cloud computing and, 151–152
  hypervisors, 153–154
  of servers, 152–153
  traditional server deployment versus, 152
  VM requirements, 154–155
viruses, 242
VMs (virtual machines), requirements, 154–155
volatile data, 287

voltages for power supplies, 4, 35
VPNs (Virtual Private Networks)
  for mobile devices, 226
  in Windows, 213–214
VR (virtual reality), 12–13, 106

W

warranties for printers, 134
wattage, 35
wearables, 118
  augmented reality (AR), 106
  fitness trackers, 105
  smartwatches, 105
  virtual reality (VR), 106
web browser security
  ActiveX filtering, 264
  authentication, 262–263
  InPrivate Browsing, 263
  pop-up blockers, 263–264
  SmartScreen Filter, 264
web servers, 72
webcams in laptops, 109
whitelisting, 96
whoami command, 204
Wi-Fi antenna connectors in laptops, 109
Wi-Fi calling for mobile devices, 226
Wi-Fi configuration in laptops, 111
wildcards, 205
Windows
  32-bit versus 64-bit, 161
  applications
    compatibility mode, 203
    installation methods, 202–203
    security considerations, 203
    system requirements, 202
    uninstalling, 203
  boot process, 170
    Windows 7 startup modes, 170
    Windows 8 and 10 startup modes, 171
  CLI
    cmd command, 204
    disk operations, 206
    file manipulation, 206
    file system navigation, 205–206
    folder manipulation, 206
    gpupdate command, 207
    network commands, 212
    PowerShell, 204
    run line utility, 207–208
    session management, 204–205
    syntax and help, 204–205
    task and system commands, 207
    whoami command, 204
    wildcards, 205

Control Panel
  Administrative Tools, 194
  BitLocker, 193
  categories, 184
  Clock, 191
  computer name, 189
  Credential Manager, 185
  Default Programs, 192–193
  Device Manager, 190
  Devices and Printers, 190–191
  display settings, 187–188
  Folder Options, 193–194
  homegroups, 186
  Internet Options, 186
  Language, 192
  Network and Sharing Center, 186
  network settings, 185–186
  Power Options, 188–189
  Programs, 192
  Region, 191
  Settings app versus, 183
  Sound, 191
  starting, 183
  Sync Center, 185
  System, 189
  System and Security category, 184
  System Properties, 189
  Troubleshooting, 193
  User Account Control (UAC), 184
  user account creation, 184
  views, 183
  virtual memory, 189
  Windows Features and Updates, 192
data migration, 162
desktop
  personalizing, 176–177
  Windows 7, 175–176
  Windows 8, 176
  Windows 8.1, 176
  Windows 10, 177
Disk Management, 165, 199
  array creation, 200
  Disk Error-Checking tool, 201
  disk optimization, 200–201
  drive status indicators, 199–200
  mounting drives, 200
File Explorer, 180
  directory structures, 181
  file attributes, 182
  file extensions, 181–182
  file locations, 181
  libraries, 181
  Run as Administrator, 180
  This PC, 180
  Users Folder, 181

installing
  account creation, 166
  custom installation, 167–168
  disk cloning, 167
  file systems, 164–165
  hard drive partitioning, 163–164
  recovery partition, 169
  remote network installation, 168
  steps in, 166
  storage device types, 163
  unattended network installation, 168–169
networking
  administrative shares, 209
  domains and workgroups, 208–209
  homegroups, 208–209
  network shares and mapping drives, 209
  Remote Assistance, 214–215
  Remote Desktop, 214–215
  resource sharing, 210
  SSH (Secure Shell), 214
  Telnet, 214
  VPN configuration, 213–214
  wired network configuration, 211–212
  wireless network configuration, 213
preventive maintenance
  backup tools, 217–218
  plan contents, 215–216
  restore points, 217
  scheduled tasks, 217
  Windows Update, 216
requirements, 161
restore and recovery, 169
security
  Account Policies, 257
  Active Directory, 259–260
  BIOS security, 255
  firewall exception configuration, 261–262
  firewalls, 260
  local password management, 256
  Local Security Policy, 256
  Local Security Policy configuration, 257
  Local Security Policy export, 257
  login security, 255
  physical security, 254–255
  software firewalls, 261
  user and group management, 258–260
  username and password guidelines, 256
  Windows Firewall with Advanced Security, 262
Start menu
  Windows 7, 178
  Windows 8, 177
  Windows 8.1, 177
  Windows 10, 177

system administration
  Administrative Tools (Control Panel), 194
  Component Services, 196
  Computer Management, 194–195
  Data Sources, 196
  DxDiag, 199
  Event Viewer, 195
  Local Users and Groups Manager, 195
  Microsoft Management Console (MMC), 198
  Performance Monitor, 196
  Print Management, 197
  Regedit, 198
  Registry, 198
  Services, 196
  System Configuration, 197
  System Information, 197
  Windows Memory Diagnostics, 197
Task Manager, 178–179
  Windows 7, 179
Taskbar, 178
troubleshooting
  common problems/solutions, 219
  steps in, 218–219
updating, 216
upgrading, 162, 169–170
versions, 173–174
  Windows 7, 174
  Windows 8, 174
  Windows 8.1, 174–175
  Windows 10, 175
Windows 7, 160, 174
  desktop, 175–176
  Start menu, 178
  startup modes, 170
  Task Manager, 179
Windows 8, 174
  desktop, 176
  Start menu, 177
  startup modes, 171
Windows 8.1, 174–175
  desktop, 176
  Start menu, 177
Windows 10, 175
  desktop, 177
  File Explorer options, 193–194
  Settings app, 183
  Start menu, 177
  startup modes, 171
  wired network configuration, 211
  wireless network configuration, 213
Windows BitLocker, 174, 193, 252–253
Windows Explorer, 180
Windows Features and Updates (Control Panel), 192

Windows Firewall, 261–262
Windows Firewall with Advanced Security, 262
Windows Media Center, 174
Windows Memory Diagnostics, 197
Windows Update, 166, 216
wiping data, 253
wire cutters, 79
wired connectivity for mobile devices, 118
wired networks, configuring, 92–93, 211–212
　connectivity verification, 212
　ipconfig command, 212
　network profiles, 211–212
　NICs, 211
　nslookup command, 212
　ping command, 212
　tracert command, 212
　in Windows 10, 211
wireless access points, 75
wireless cards, replacing in laptops, 116
wireless connectivity for mobile devices, 118–119
　Airplane Mode, 120–121
　cellular generations, 120
　hotspots, 121
wireless LAN (WLAN) protocols, 69
wireless networks
　configuring, 92–93
　　best practices, 266–267
　　in Windows 10, 213
　logging into router, 93
　NAT for IPv4, 93
　QoS, 94
wireless NICs, 8
wireless printer connections, 141

wireless protocols
　Bluetooth, 69
　cellular generations, 70
　NFC, 69
　RFID, 69
　smart home standards, 69–70
　WLAN, 69
　Zigbee, 69–70
　Z-Wave, 70
wireless routers, 64
wireless security
　authentication, 267
　best practices, 266–267
　communication encryption, 266
　firewalls, 267
　firmware updates, 267
　modes, 267
　port forwarding and port triggering, 267
　UPnP, 268
WLAN (wireless LAN) protocols, 69
workgroups, 208–209
WWAN (Wireless Wide Area Network), 186

X

xD (Picture Card), 25

Z

zero-day attacks, 246
zero-hour, 246
Zigbee, 69–70
Z-Wave, 70